MW01049342

The Neoliberal Agenda and the Student Debt Crisis in U.S. Higher Education

Capturing the voices of Americans living with student debt in the United States, this collection critiques the neoliberal interest-driven, debt-based system of U.S. higher education and offers alternatives to neoliberal capitalism and the corporatized university. Grounded in an understanding of the historical and political economic context, this book offers autoethnographic experiences of living in debt and analyzes alternatives to the current system. Chapter authors address real questions such as, *Do collegians overestimate the economic value of going to college?* and *How does the monetary system that student loans are part of operate?* Pinpointing how questionable biases in our political economy are determinative, this book provides an authoritative contribution to research in the fields of educational foundations and higher education policy and finance.

Nicholas D. Hartlep is Assistant Professor of Urban Education at Metropolitan State University, USA.

Lucille L. T. Eckrich is Associate Professor of Educational Foundations at Illinois State University, USA.

Brandon O. Hensley is Basic Course Director and Lecturer in the Department of Communication at Wayne State University, USA.

Routledge Studies in Education, Neoliberalism and Marxism

Series editor: Dave Hill, *Anglia Ruskin University, Chelmsford and Cambridge, England*

For a full list of titles in this series, please visit www.routledge.com

The Neoliberal Agenda and the Student Debt Crisis in U.S. Higher Education

Edited by
Nicholas D. Hartlep,
Lucille L. T. Eckrich, and
Brandon O. Hensley

Routledge
Taylor & Francis Group

NEW YORK AND LONDON

First published 2017
by Routledge
711 Third Avenue, New York, NY 10017

and by Routledge
2 Park Square, Milton Park, Abingdon, Oxon, OX14 4RN

Routledge is an imprint of the Taylor & Francis Group, an informa business

© 2017 Taylor & Francis

The right of Nicholas D. Hartlep, Lucille L. T. Eckrich, and Brandon O. Hensley, and of the authors for their individual chapters, to be identified as the author of this part of the Work has been asserted by them in accordance with sections 77 and 78 of the Copyright, Designs and Patents Act 1988.

Library of Congress Cataloging-in-Publication Data
A catalog record for this book has been requested

ISBN: 978-1-138-19465-6 (hbk)
ISBN: 978-1-315-63876-8 (ebk)

Typeset in Sabon
by Apex CoVantage, LLC

Contents

Figures

Tables

Contributors

T. Jameson Brewer is an Assistant Professor at the University of North Georgia. He completed his Ph.D. in Educational Policy Studies at the University of Illinois at Urbana-Champaign, where the Education Alumni Association named him "Outstanding Doctoral Student." Additionally, he serves as the O'Leary Fellow at the Forum on the Future of Public Education at the University of Illinois. Jameson earned a M.S. in Social Foundations of Education from Georgia State University and a B.S.Ed. in Secondary Education from Valdosta State University. As a former public school teacher, Jameson taught high school history in the Atlanta Public Schools. His research focuses on the impact(s) of privatization/marketization of public schools by way of charters, vouchers, and Teach for America. His work has been published in the peer-reviewed journals of *Education Policy Analysis Archives, Educational Studies, Critical Education,* the *Peabody Journal of Education, Critical Questions in Education,* the *International Journal of Play,* and the *Australian Educational Researcher.* His work has also appeared at the National Education Policy Center, the *Progressive Magazine,* the *Huffington Post,* the *Washington Post,* and *Education Week.* He is co-editor of the book *Teach For America Counter-Narratives: Alumni Speak Up and Speak Out* (edited with Kathleen deMarrais; Peter Lang, 2015).

Linda Elizabeth Coco received her J.D. from the University of Maryland School of Law in 2000 and completed her Ph.D. in Legal Anthropology from the University of California, Berkeley, in 2011. Coco is an Associate Professor of Law at the Barry University School of Law. She also teaches as adjunct faculty at St. John's University School of Law in their Bankruptcy LLM program. Coco clerked in bankruptcy courts in Maryland and California. In addition to her Ph.D. dissertation on bankruptcy and anthropology, she has authored several articles in the area of debt and financial failure, including "Mortgaging Human Potential: Student Indebtedness and the Practices of the Neoliberal State," which appears in *Southwestern Law Review.* Coco provided the research for a book by Ralph Nader, *Children First: A Parent's Guide to Fighting Corporate Predators,* published in 1996.

Daniel A. Collier recently received his Ph.D. in the Education Policy, Organization and Leadership doctoral program at the University of Illinois at Urbana-Champaign. Daniel is currently a post-doctoral research associate for the Center on Research on Instructional Change in Postsecondary Education at Western Michigan University. His scholarship explores higher education politics and examines the political, financial, social, and health related effects associated with student loan debt.

Alan M. Collinge is the founder of Student Loan Justice, an organization whose goal is to reform predatory lending practices in the American student loan industry. He is the author of *The Student Loan Scam: The Most Oppressive Debt in U.S. History—and How We Can Fight Back* (2009, Beacon).

Diane R. Dean is an Associate Professor for Higher Education Administration and Policy at Illinois State University. She earned her Ed.D. and M.A. degrees in Higher Education Administration from Columbia University, and her B.A. in English and American Literature from the University of Maryland, College Park. Dr. Dean's research applies organizational theory, social psychology, and policy analysis to address critical issues in college and university planning, policy, and governance. Her scholarly books include *Generation on a Tightrope: A Portrait of Today's College Student* (2012), *Public Policy and Higher Education* (2nd ed.) (2010), *Women in Academic Leadership: Professional Strategies, Personal Choices* (2009), *Most College Students are Women: Implications for College Faculty and Policymakers* (2008), and *The Balancing Act: Gendered Perspectives in Faculty roles and Work Lives* (2006). You can follow her work on Twitter @DianeRDean.

Melissa A. Del Rio is a Client Experience Coordinator at a small insurance firm in Michigan. She attended Eureka College and Illinois Central College, obtaining an Associate's degree, in addition to studying abroad and volunteering at a hospital in Lesotho, southern Africa.

Lucille L. T. Eckrich is an Associate Professor of Educational Foundations at Illinois State University. She earned a Ph.D. in Philosophy of Education and an M.Ed. in Social Foundations of Education from the State University of New York at Buffalo. Her B.A. in Economics and African Studies is from the College of Wooster, OH. Between her undergraduate and graduate studies she worked in Botswana, southern Africa, doing rural development and adult education work, and in Chicago, Illinois, for a statewide anti-apartheid coalition, a not-for-profit undergraduate urban studies program, and the City Colleges of Chicago. Her scholarship is published in *Teacher Education Quarterly*, *Teachers College Record*, and *Values and Ethics in Educational Administration*, among other journals, and she is past editor of *Planning and Changing: An Educational Leadership and Policy Journal*. Her interest in student debt stems from her 1998 dissertation, which was a study of "Value in Economics, Ethics, and Education" and which led her to critique the private-interest-driven debt-based nature of modern money. Her most recent publication on student debt was the article titled "Ivory Tower Graduates in the Red: The Role of Debt in Higher Education" co-authored with Nicholas D. Hartlep and published online in *Workplace: A Journal for Academic Labor.*

Antonio L. Ellis is an adjunct professor at the College of Charleston School of Education. In 2013 he received an Outstanding Alumni Award from the Howard University School of Education in the category "Leader of Change." Dr. Ellis holds an array of academic degrees, including a Bachelor of Arts in Religion and Philosophy, a Master of Arts in Religious Studies, a Master of Arts in Educational Supervision, a Master of Arts in Special Education and Human Development, and a Doctor of Educational Leadership and Policy Studies. His scholarly work is included in several books and academic journals, including the *Journal of Negro Education, Teachers College Record, Studies on Asia*, and the *Journal of African American Males in Education.* He is the editor of *Ed.D. Programs as Incubators for Social Justice Leadership* (2016, Sense Publishers). Dr. Ellis is currently editing a book entitled *Transitioning Children with Disabilities: From Early Childhood through Adulthood* to be published by Sense Publishers. He is widely known for his advocacy for persons with disabilities, particularly those who are speech and language impaired.

Nicholas D. Hartlep is an award-winning Assistant Professor of Urban Education at Metropolitan State University. Before coming to Metropolitan State University, he taught at Illinois State University for four years and before that he was an Advanced Opportunity Program Fellow at the University of Wisconsin-Milwaukee, an "Urban 13" University, where he earned a Ph.D. in the Social Foundations of Urban Education and was named an "Outstanding Doctoral Student." Dr. Hartlep also has a Master of Science Degree in K–12 Education and Bachelor of Science Degree in Teaching, both conferred from Winona State University. As a former public school teacher, he has taught in Rochester, Minnesota and Milwaukee, Wisconsin, as well as abroad in Quito, Ecuador. Dr. Hartlep's research interests include urban in-service teachers' dispositions, the impact neoliberalism is having on schools and society, the model minority stereotype of Asian/Americans, and transracial adoption. He has received several awards for his scholarship. He received the University Research Initiative (URI) Award in 2015 from Illinois State University in 2015 and a Distinguished Young Alumni Award from Winona State University in 2015, which recognizes graduates who are 45 years old or younger and have distinguished themselves in their work or in their community. In 2015, he also received the Upton Sinclair Award for consistently impacting the field of education. In 2016, the University of Wisconsin-Milwaukee presented him with a Graduate of the Last Decade

(GOLD) Award for his prolific amount of writing. His scholarly books include *Going Public: Critical Race Theory & Issues of Social Justice* (2010), *The Model Minority Stereotype: Demystifying Asian American Success* (2013), *Unhooking from Whiteness: The Key to Dismantling Racism in the United States* (2013), and *The Model Minority Stereotype Reader: Critical and Challenging Readings for the 21st Century* (2014), *Killing the Model Minority Stereotype: Asian American Counterstories and Complicity* (2015), *Modern Societal Impacts of the Model Minority Stereotype* (2015), and *Unhooking from Whiteness: Resisting the Esprit de Corps* (2016). He is currently finishing a co-authored book with Daisy Ball entitled *Asian/Americans: A Critical Analysis of the "Model Minority" as Perpetrators and Victims of Crime* to be published by Rowman and Littlefield. You can follow his work on Twitter @nhartlep or at the "Model Minority Stereotype Project" (www.nicholashartlep.com). He works and writes in St. Paul, MN.

Brandon O. Hensley is Basic Course Director and Lecturer at Wayne State University in the Department of Communication. He earned his Ph.D. in Educational Administration and Foundations from Illinois State University in Spring 2016. Hensley's research interests include critical pedagogy, neoliberalism and its effects on the academic workforce, critical media literacy, autoethnography, impacts of student loan debt, and hegemonic masculinity in U.S. culture. Brandon was an author in and, along with Nicholas D. Hartlep, co-editor of an edited book titled *Critical Storytelling in Uncritical Times: Stories Disclosed in a Cultural Foundations of Education Course* (Hartlep & Hensley, 2015). In addition to contributing a chapter in *Unhooking from Whiteness: Resisting the Esprit de Corps* (Hayes & Hartlep, 2016), Hensley has been invited to author a chapter in a forthcoming volume from Sense Publishers to feature pioneering autoethnographic researchers (to be titled *Doing Autoethnography*). Professionally, Hensley serves on the Associate Council and as a Division Co-Chair for the Mid-Western Educational Research Association (MWERA). Aside from academic endeavors, Brandon likes to spend time cuddling with his wife Melissa and their family of pets, Bobo (cat), Bitsy (cat), and Sugar (dog).

Brian R. Horn is an Associate Professor of Elementary Education at Illinois State University. He earned a Ph.D. in Curriculum, Teaching, and Educational Policy from Michigan State University, an Ed.M. in Administration, Planning, and Social Policy at Harvard Graduate School of Education, and a B.S.E. in Elementary Education/Early Childhood Education at Emporia State University. Prior to coming to Illinois State, Horn taught in elementary and middle-grade classrooms in Kansas and Michigan. Much of his work involves urban teacher preparation and community/school/ university partnerships in Chicago. Dr. Horn's scholarship is published in *Equity & Excellence in Education*, *Voices from the Middle*, *Forum*,

Networks: An On-Line Journal for Teacher Research, Multicultural Perspectives, and *Urban Education*.

Cynthia D. Levy is a principal in the Kankakee School District 111 in Illinois. Previously, she served as Assistant Principal in Champaign Unit 4 School District, Illinois. She has eight years of teaching experience at the high school level. Dr. Levy earned her Ed.D. in Educational Leadership from Chicago State University (CSU). She also has a Master of Art degree in K–12 Education and English and a Bachelor of Art in Teaching degree, all conferred from CSU. Her 2014 dissertation, *Apartheid Education in the 21st Century: Counter-Narratives of the Charter School Movement*, explored how community organizations organize around the charter school movement. Her book chapter in this volume is her first publication.

Pilar Mendoza is an Associate Professor of Higher Education at the University of Missouri, Columbia. Previously, she was Assistant Professor of Higher Education at the University of Florida and Oklahoma State University. She obtained her doctorate at the University of Massachusetts, Amherst. Her research focuses on academic capitalism and its implications for the academic profession, production of knowledge, graduate education as well as for issues of affordability and retention. She is also interested in international perspectives and comparative research in higher education. She is author of 38 publications including journal articles, book chapters, monographs, and one edited book. Her work has been published in *The Journal of Higher Education, Research in Higher Education, Journal of College Student Development*, and *Higher Education: Handbook of Theory and Practice*, among others. Presently, Mendoza serves on the editorial boards of *Community College Review* and *The Journal of Higher Education*. During 2012–2015, Dr. Mendoza participated as PI and Co-PI in two grant projects for the development of higher education in Colombia sponsored by USAID/HED and the Ford Foundation.

P.S. Myers is a Ph.D. student in the Department of Education Policy, Organization and Leadership at the University of Illinois at Urbana-Champaign. As a traditionally trained former teacher in public and charter schools in the Chicagoland area, his research interests include the marketization and privatization of the provision of schooling, as well as the experience of marginalized persons in these schooling arrangements and the edu-semiotics of urban spaces. His interest in marketization and privatization seeks to understand how market solutions proliferate and function in different municipal, regional, and national contexts, with his current focus honing in on specific markets within Sweden and United States. His scholarly publications include "The Rhetoric and Reality of School Reform: Choice, Competition, and Organizational Incentives in Market-Oriented

Education" published in C. Tienken and C. Mullen (Eds.), *Education Policy Perils: Tackling the Tough Issues* (co-authored with Christopher Lubienski, 2015) and "How Neoliberalism Subverts Equality and Perpetuates Poverty in our Nation's Schools" published in S. N. Haymes, R. Miller and M. V. d. Haymes (Eds.), *Handbook of poverty and the United States* (co-authored with T. Jameson Brewer, 2014).

James C. Palmer is a Professor of higher education at Illinois State University (ISU). Prior to joining the ISU faculty in 1992, he served as acting director of the Center for Community College Education at George Mason University, vice president for communications at the American Association for Community and Junior Colleges, staff associate at the Center for the Study of Community Colleges, and assistant director for user services of the ERIC Clearinghouse for Junior Colleges at the University of California, Los Angeles. At ISU, Dr. Palmer teaches courses on the American community college, adult and continuing education, higher education finance, and the history of American higher education. He is past editor of the *Community College Review* and since 2000 has served as editor of the Grapevine compilation of state fiscal support for higher education (http://grapevine.illinoisstate.edu/). His most recent publication, co-authored with Richard M. Romano, is *Financing Community Colleges: Where We Are, Where We're Going* (Rowman & Littlefield. 2015).

Melissa R. Pitcock is a CPA and Ph.D. candidate in the Department of Educational Administration and Foundations at Illinois State University, where her research interests include higher education finance, planning, and policy. She also earned a Bachelor of Science in Accountancy and Master of Business Administration from Illinois State University and spent the first several years of her career in the business and financial sectors. Since 2000, Melissa has served in two roles at Illinois State University: Director of Budgets & Fiscal Management for the Division of Student Affairs and Budget Director for the School of Teaching and Learning in the College of Education. In early 2017, Melissa and her family moved to Texas where she is finalizing her doctoral dissertation, which analyzes the cost to a university to deliver a degree. She remains active in the Mid-Western Educational Research Association, serving as a member of the Association Council and as former Chair for the division of Administration, Organization, and Leadership, and the division of History and Historiography.

Amy E. Swain is an educational activist who currently works as a high school English teacher in Durham, North Carolina. She is a senior research associate for the Center for Policy and Social Justice at Concordia University-Chicago, where her research focuses on alternative schools, the school-to-prison pipeline, and the punitive nature of public schools. Swain has worked as a teacher educator at East Carolina University,

Illinois State University, and Concordia University-Chicago, where she taught courses on social justice and the educational foundations of American schooling. A former elementary school and middle school teacher, Dr. Swain has worked in and with public schools over the last 12 years. She is currently an adjunct professor at Duke University.

Kay Ann Taylor is an Associate Professor of Educational Foundations, Director of Curriculum and Instruction Graduate Programs, Department of Curriculum and Instruction at Kansas State University. She earned a Ph.D. in Historical, Philosophical, and Comparative Studies at Iowa State University, where she received the Research Excellence Award for Outstanding Dissertation Research Accomplishments. Dr. Taylor's Master of Science Degree in Curriculum and Instructional Technology and Bachelor of Science Degree in Elementary Education with a minor in Sociology are from Iowa State University. She taught fifth and sixth grades in Iowa rural public schools. She is the recipient of the prestigious 2012–2013 Commerce Bank Presidential Faculty and Staff Award for Distinguished Service to Historically Under-Represented Students at Kansas State University; 2013 recipient of Woman of Distinction Kansas State University Award; 2013 recipient of the All University Award, Kansas State University; the 2009 recipient of the Commerce Bank Outstanding Undergraduate Teaching Award, Kansas State University, among other university and college recognitions. Her research interests focus on experiences of underrepresented people and intersectionality through lenses of Critical Race Theory, Black Feminist Thought, and postcolonial theory. She presents at national and international conferences and has published in *The Journal of Negro Education, The Journal of Educational Controversy, The Journal of Veterinary Medical Education, Journal of Educational Research, Journal of Latinos and Education*, among others. She has several book chapters.

Celeste M. Walker is an actor, director, and educator, with a B.F.A. in Drawing from Kutztown University, and an M.F.A in Acting from The Actor's Studio Drama School at the New School University in New York. She is a lifetime member of *The Actors Studio* and a member of *Actors Equity*. Her theatre roles include: Melissa in *Love Letters*, Maria Callas in *Masterclass*, and Frankie in *Frankie & Johnny In the Clair de Lune*. Walker serves as a liaison for the Philadelphia Chapter of the New School Alumni Association. She is an Adjunct Professor of Integrated Studies at Arcadia University, Montgomery County Community College, and Community College of Philadelphia. She also develops and directs with Philly Senior Stage creating programs for residents in Senior Living Communities in and around Philadelphia. In 2015, she wrote and directed an original Murder Mystery Production for the Acting Troupe at Shannondell Independent Living Community in King of Prussia, Pennsylvania. In 2003, she was awarded Advisor of the Year at Saint Joseph's University

(Philadelphia, Pennsylvania). In 2012, she was the Organizer and Host of the TEDx ArcadiaUniversity Conference on "Passion and Creativity in the Classroom." In 2014, she organized a second TEDx ArcadiaUniversity Conference, "Feeding America: Body, Mind and Soul."

Allison Witt is the Director of International Programs in the College of Education at the University of Illinois at Urbana-Champaign where she teaches Global Studies in Education and is the Program Leader for the International Education Administration and Leadership program. Allison is a former Assistant Director of Academic Affairs at the Illinois Board of Higher Education where she contributed to state higher education policy in Illinois particularly in the regulation of for-profit institutions, implementation of Dual Credit programs, and policies to increase equity in higher education. She is the author of *Shifting Tides in Global Higher Education* (2011) published by Peter Lang. Allison earned a Ph.D. in Education Policy Studies from the University of Illinois at Urbana-Champaign. She has worked in international education for over 20 years, now dedicating her research and practice to serving the College of Education at the University of Illinois at Urbana-Champaign, with particular interest in internationalizing teacher education.

Enyu Zhou is a Ph.D. candidate of educational leadership and policy analysis at the University of Missouri, Columbia. She received a master's degree in public affairs and a bachelor's degree in public administration. Her research interests include issues of access, affordability, and success in higher education. In addition, she is interested in international and comparative education. Her scholarship is published in *Library and Information Science Research* and *Journal of College Student Retention*.

Foreword

As I write this, federal marshals in Houston, Texas, are planning to arrest 1,500 citizens unable to repay their student loans. These arrests are being executed under the guise of their failure to appear in court. One of the first to be detained under these circumstances, however, says that he never received any summons for this hearing, and the astonishingly high arrest rate (1,500 arrests out of 7,000 cases) suggests strongly that many, if not *most*, of those who have been (or will be) apprehended under federal warrants were never properly notified of these hearings. Whatever the details behind these detentions might turn out to be, the point remains: the federal government is now arresting citizens because of their student loans (The Big Picture RT, 2016).

While mass citizen arrest is the newest disturbing example of the harms being inflicted upon people as a result of student loan debt, it is by no means the only one. In the absence of fundamental protections that exist for all other loans in this country, like bankruptcy protections, statutes of limitations, refinancing rights, Fair Debt Collection Practice laws, Truth-in-Lending Laws, and even state usury laws, citizens are experiencing all manner of injury. In addition to being stripped of astonishing amounts of wealth, far, far above what they originally borrowed, many are being denied professional advancement and even driver's licenses (Kitroeff, 2015). Others are being fired from public employment on the basis of their defaulted loans due to security issues and on other grounds (Farrington, 2014). Senior citizens are seeing their social security and disability income garnished to pay for student debt (Student Loan Borrower Assistance, n.d.). Innocent cosigners are being forced to liquidate their nest eggs to cover loans for their children, grandchildren, and extended family members. People unable to work and live under this debt are forced to leave the country. Tragically, others lose all hope and take their own lives (see the case of Jason Yoder, as reported by Dave Newbart in his September 24, 2007, story published in the *Chicago Sun-Times*).

If, before, the U.S. was facing a student debt *crisis*, now we are looking at something that is better described as a *catastrophe*. In 1996, as a nation, the United States owed less than $50 billion in student loan debt. By 2006, this had risen to almost $500 billion. Today, America owes an astonishing $1.4 trillion, and student loan debt has eclipsed all other categories of non-housing consumer debt. The average undergraduate is now leaving school with an astonishing $35,000 in student loans, more than double what it was a decade ago, and where only one in three students needed to borrow for school two decades ago, today the ratios have been reversed: only one in three don't need to borrow. If the class of 2005 is any example, it is likely that over 60% of loan holders are currently unable to make payments on their student loan debt (Cunningham & Kienzl, 2011).

The American student loan system is an exemplar of unchecked neoliberal policy gone horribly awry. When Richard Nixon created the Student Loan Marketing Association in 1972, the proposition was simple: encourage private banks to make student loans by making it more profitable and risk-free for them to do so. Over time, however, the profit potential was strong enough that, by the 1990s, there was pressure on the government to take back the power to issue federal student loans and issue them directly, as it had done at first (1958–1965). With the writing on the wall, the managing executives of Sallie Mae compelled the board to push through a transition for the company from a quasi-governmental entity to a wholly for-profit enterprise.

As Sallie Mae's transition to being two private corporations[1] was underway, executives at the company wasted no time in leveraging the company's overwhelming clout on Capitol Hill to push through amendments to the Higher Education Act (HEA) that essentially removed standard consumer protections (mentioned above) that exist for every other type of loan. By 1998, these were signed into law, and the now-private Sallie Mae was in an overwhelmingly strong position. Not only was it lending something like 40% of all student loans in the country; the federal government guaranteed these loans while the company was paid 99%—100% of the book value of loans that defaulted.

Even more disturbing, however, is that Sallie Mae went on an acquisitions spree after the 1998 reauthorization of the HEA and acquired most of the nation's largest student loan collection companies, which put the company in prime position to make incredible profits on loans after they defaulted and exploded in size with massive penalties and fees. Sallie Mae also purchased the largest student loan guaranty agency in the country, USA Funds, over strong congressional protest, in an obviously conflicted arrangement. Now, Sallie Mae had gained supreme control of the entire industry, both vertically and horizontally.

The company's stock price shot through the roof. Bonuses were doled out, averaging $680,000 among those who got one. Sallie Mae CEO Albert Lord quickly became the perennial "highest paid CEO" in Washington, D.C. He made a tender offer to purchase a major league baseball team, the Washington Nationals. He even built a private, luxury, 18-hole golf course in Anne Arundel Country, just outside of the Beltway (Collinge, 2009).

The U.S. Department of Education (ED), meanwhile, began behaving like a captured agency. Given that the ED's Office of Federal Student Aid, Office of Financial Partners, and others were run by former executives of Sallie Mae and other lending companies, it frankly became hard to tell where the industry left off and the government began. ED quit calling the entities they were supposed to be overseeing what they were, and instead started an oversight group, called the "Office of Financial Partners." One of the heads of this office, Matteo Fontana (a former Sallie Mae employee who was brought into ED by another former Sallie Mae executive), was found to be holding stock in one of the very lending companies the office was supposed to be overseeing. Also, ED outsourced its Ombudsman office staff, so that people answering the phone, and doing the work of the supposedly neutral office, were actually under subcontract to one of the largest student loan collection companies in the country.

While the ED wasn't making interest from most of its loans, it was, incredibly, profiting on defaults. Years of White House budget data showed that, for every dollar the ED was paying out to Sallie Mae and others for defaults, it was actually recouping $1.23—a tidy profit for the government, to be sure (Collinge, 2015). Only in the absence of fundamental consumer protections like bankruptcy and statutes of limitations could this sort of perverted profit making—a defining hallmark of a predatory lending system—be possible.

When a whistleblower discovered that lenders had been overbilling ED to the tune of billions of dollars (thanks to a generous "dear colleague" letter penned by none other than the aforementioned Matteo Fontana), the whistleblower literally had to sue the lenders in order for the fraudulent billing scheme to be exposed and the money recouped. Left to their own devices, lenders' interests within ED were planning to let the lending companies determine how much, if any, needed to be repaid as a result of this illegal billing!

This corporate, for-profit culture, however, was not confined to ED and the lenders. By the new millennium, it had clearly also found its way into the colleges and universities as well. Colleges had taken to doing deals with the lenders, such as including some on so-called "preferred lending" lists. Every fall and spring semester, the financial aid offices of many institutions of higher education were being staffed by employees from lending companies, who were literally answering the financial aid phones as employees of the universities and using this position to sell students on the lender's proprietary, private loans, to vulnerable and unsuspecting students. The universities, too, had become directly involved in the lending game at this point. By 2005, universities were making loans directly to students, and then selling these loans, at a premium, to Sallie Mae and other lenders in what became known as "School-as-Lender" arrangements.

After a *60 Minutes* piece I was involved with aired in May 2006, detailing these and similar practices, both New York Attorney General (AG) Eliot

Spitzer and the U.S. Senate began investigations. Their efforts hastened the uncovering of the largest and widest scandal that academe in America has ever been through. Financial aid administrators across the country, from schools including the University of Pennsylvania, Columbia, the University of Southern California, and the University of Texas at Austin were summarily fired for taking kickbacks from the lending companies.

These scandals culminated in Senator Edward "Ted" Kennedy's final piece of higher education legislation, a version that was passed into law as a part of a larger bill in August of 2008. The new law prohibited all manner of deceptive practices, disallowed the use of school mascots, emblems, and logos, and so forth. Similarly, the New York AG investigation resulted in penalties leveed against the universities, which paid them with no protest.

Unfortunately, most of the good parts of the Student Loan Sunshine Act—S.486, Kennedy's final piece of higher education legislation—were ultimately undermined and rendered feckless by administrative changes made by the Federal Reserve Bank to Regulation Z, the part of the Truth in Lending Act (TILA) that applies to private student loans. The changes made by the Fed provided safe harbor language that allowed lenders to continue to use university logos, emblems, mascots, etc., and also issued directives to lenders encouraging them to tell student borrowers only about the interest rates for their loans instead of the Annual Percentage Rate (APR). The APR is a much more informative metric for the true cost of a loan because it includes fees, and other costs, that are not part of the interest rate, but that nonetheless increase the cost of the loan over time.

Today, many, if not most, of the deceptive practices still exist at colleges and universities. What is probably most troubling, however, is that currently, just like in the past, students are grossly misinformed about the true risks they are taking when they take out student loans. When prospective students and their parents tour universities, and ask about the default rates for the school, they are universally quoted the school's "cohort" default rate, which is a hugely misleading metric that counts only loans that default in one or two years after the year in which the loans became payable. So a "cohort" default rate of, say, 5% is given to these students and their parents as the default rate, but, in actual fact, the true, lifetime default rate is many multiples of this "cohort rate."

Similarly, students are almost never told explicitly that the fundamental consumer protections that we take for granted for all other loans do not exist for student loans. Indeed ED's own student handbook's discussion of bankruptcy protections for student loans is buried in the middle of the handbook and says only that, in order to discharge student loans in bankruptcy, the borrowers must prove "undue hardship." This sounds reasonable to an 18-year-old entering freshman, who has no idea that "undue hardship" is a test that is impossible to meet for all but a negligibly small fraction of borrowers.

The true default rate across all universities and all students is not published by ED. This very simple number is, in fact, impossible to determine with any accuracy given all publicly available information. My best guess is that the true, lifetime default rate is far greater than 25%. Some estimates put it as high as 50% (Collinge, 2009). I think it is likely somewhere in the middle, but could easily exceed 40%. This is higher than the sub-prime home mortgage default rate. This is higher than the default rate of payday loans, and of credit cards. Indeed, this is a default rate that is higher than any other loan in this country, if not the world. These facts are *never* made clear to students.

While all institutions of higher learning bear much responsibility for the explosion in student loan indebtedness, it is clear that the vilest actors in the Academy are the for-profit colleges. Estimates a decade ago put the lifetime default rate for students attending these colleges at about 60%. This has surely increased since that time, given the proliferation of these kinds of schools, and their increased marketing to lower-income and disadvantaged population groups. This is easily verifiable by simply tuning in to any television channel for a significant length of time and observing the number of advertisements clearly targeting African Americans, Latinx, single mothers, and other economically disadvantaged groups in these ads.

These for-profit schools typically spend more on advertising than they do on their faculty or staff. They have been found to recruit students without high school diplomas from homeless shelters. They also derive most of their revenue through the federal government (from 66% to 94% for the top 15 publicly traded ones in 2010), the vast majority of it from student loans (Mettler, 2014, pp. 168–169). While some well-meaning legislation, such as the Gainful Employment Rule, has been passed to hold these schools accountable for the horrible outcomes that their students typically experience, these fixes have largely been resisted fiercely and successfully by the schools and their lobbyists, and weakened by ED when they were enacted.

It should be noted clearly that colleges and universities in the United States have never before been in a stronger financial position than they are in now. The colleges will claim that they have been raising their prices at double or triple the rate of inflation over the past 30 or more years because of "cuts" in state funding, but the fact of the matter is that, in real, inflation-adjusted dollars, state funding of colleges has kept pace with inflation/the consumer price index over the years. The "cuts" that the colleges are referring to are actually just references to the fact that the relative percentage-share of state funding has decreased in the wake of the dramatic increases in price and in grant-based funding for research.

In fact, since 2008, colleges have essentially been stockpiling cash—over and above their endowments—at an extraordinary rate. When it was reported that the University of Wisconsin had amassed up to $1 billion in so-called "tuition reserves" and the president came under pressure to resign as a result, the university published similar financial information for its peer institutions, and the data were shocking. Nearly every school they reported on had hundreds of millions, or in many cases, billions of dollars in unreserved assets! While the total amount of these stockpiles has yet to be determined, they could very well exceed the total value of all university endowments combined!

While the nation's colleges and universities are doing unprecedentedly well financially, and university administrators are enjoying historically generous compensation, there is no starker illustration of how a for-profit, corporate culture has overtaken academia than what has happened to faculty across the country. The use of low-paid, adjunct professors has exploded. This is very well described and documented in this book. What this book also illustrates clearly, however, is the cruel irony that not only are these low-paid scholars denied participation in the financial boon that the colleges generally are undergoing, but they are in fact among the citizens most hurt by the predatory student lending system. Many, if not most, lead a financially terrifying Dickensian existence, and this will certainly have dire consequences in many unknowable ways going forward.

The Neoliberal Agenda and the Student Debt Crisis in U.S. Higher Education should serve as a clarion call to the Academy, to university stakeholders, ED, and to the general public. Those in the Academy must recognize that they run the great risk of infuriating the public on a scale that this nation has never before seen and that, at long last, they must act (proactively, if that is still possible at this point) both to acknowledge their role in the creation of this problem and to take the responsibility, and make the sacrifices necessary, to earn back the trust that the public has given them to educate—not financially decimate—the citizens of this country. Without those outside the Academy respecting the necessary role of higher education in a vibrant and just political economy and democracy, such education is not possible. The critical perspectives on financing higher education in the United States, the stories of non-dischargeable student debt, and the alternatives to neoliberal financing of higher education that this book shares are invaluable.

Alan M. Collinge
Student Loan Justice

Note

1 There are now (1) Sallie Mae, which issues private loans to students from wealthier families at home and abroad, and (2) Navient, which is a loan servicer for direct government loans and listed with other loan servicers on ED website for financial aid. See (1) www.forbes.com/forbes/welcome/?toURL=www.forbes.com/sites/halahtouryalai/2013/05/29/what-sallie-maes-split-says-about-student-loans/&refURL=&referrer= and (2) http://news.salliemae.com/press-release/corporate-and-financial/sallie-mae-selects-navient-name-new-loan-management-servicing-

References

Big Picture RT. (2016, February 19). *Armed Marshals arrest man on . . . This will shock you!* (Video File). Retrieved from https://www.youtube.com/watch?v=a1 OBJGs2PeE

Collinge, A. (2009). *The student loan scam: The most oppressive debt in U.S. history—and how we can fight back*. Boston: Beacon Press.

Collinge, A. (2015, May 8). Student loans and the presidential race. *The Hill.* Retrieved from http://thehill.com/blogs/congress-blog/education/241348-student-loans-and-the-presidential-race

Cunningham, A. F., & Kienzl, G. S. (2011, March). *Delinquency: The untold story of student borrowing*. Washington, DC: Institute for Higher Education Policy. Retrieved from https://www.bankruptcy-divorce.com/Bankruptcy-Student-Loan/Delinquency-The_Untold_Story_FINAL_March_2011.pdf

Farrington, R. (2014, June 15). 8 freaky ways that student loans can get you fired. *The College Investor.* Retrieved from http://thecollegeinvestor.com/9906/8-freaky-ways-student-loans-can-get-you-fired/

Kitroeff, N. (2015, March 25). Paying student loans: Legislators are fighting such rules in several states. *Bloomberg.* Retrieved from www.bloomberg.com/news/articles/2015–03–25/these-states-will-take-your-license-for-not-paying-student-loans

Mettler, S. (2014). *Degrees of inequality: How the politics of higher education sabotaged the American Dream*. New York: Basic Books.

Newbart, D. (2007, September 24). Crushing debt. *Chicago Sun-Times.* Retrieved from www.ibhe.state.il.us/NewsDigest/NewsWeekly/092807.pdf

Student Loan Borrower Assistance. (n.d.). *Federal benefits offsets*. Retrieved from www.studentloanborrowerassistance.org/collections/government-collection-tools/benefits-offsets/

Preface

Introduction

By the time this volume is published, the U.S. National Debt Clock will likely show that student loan debt has passed $1,500,000,000,000! The Debt Clock—which continuously updates and can be viewed at www.usdebt clock.org—reports the estimated debts on various things such as mortgage debt, credit card debt, and U.S. national debt in real time. The Debt Clock website allows its users to forecast future debt figures, as if it were the same day, but in the year 2020, for instance. One thing is clear; the debt figures that are shown on the debt clock are increasing at a pace that is unsustainable.

When searching for a publisher, Dave Hill's *Routledge Studies in Education and Neoliberalism* book series stood out. We wanted to work with the series because it features books that throw a harsh spotlight on the conditions under which education currently labors and offers analysis, hope, and resistance and civic action in the name of more collective, egalitarian education for social and economic justice.

In lieu of the standard introduction, each of the editors has written a response to "Why this book?" Nicholas shares his reasoning first, followed by Lucille, and then Brandon.

Why This Book?

Nicholas

In 2013, Lucille and I wrote an article entitled "Ivory Tower Graduates in the Red: The Role of Debt in Higher Education," which was published in the Canadian journal *Workplace: A Journal for Academic Labor*. In our co-authored article, I shared personal experiences of incurring a great amount of student debt while earning my B.S., M.S., and Ph.D. As this book goes to press, two recently minted Ph.D. colleagues (Collier and Brewer, this volume) are currently without tenure-track positions. These individuals, just as I did, invested their time, talents, and money into earning a terminal degree.

As a millennial myself, student loan debt is as much a personal research interest as a professional one. It is personal because, in many respects, the economy I have inherited presents prospects worse than those my parents faced; it is professional because I am privileged enough to have a tenure-track position, which affords me the opportunity to pursue and publish research.

I was interested in editing a critical collection of capitalist counter-stories and context pieces due to the fact that many in the millennial generation are NINJAs—they have **N**o **I**ncome and **N**o **J**obs or **A**ssets. As a Christian, I've read in Proverbs 17:16, "It does a fool no good to spend money on an education, because he has no common sense." In times past, pursuit of a college degree was the sensible thing to do, and one could do so without getting into too much debt. This practice is becoming more difficult in the current times. In fact, some—like Melissa Del Rio, this volume—are concluding that it is financially foolish to go to college. I am also reminded of the precarious words of Jim Marrs, who, in his 2011 book *The Trillion-Dollar Conspiracy*, wrote:

> Free people can travel anywhere at any time they like. They can start a business or a new profession, or even take a vacation for as long as they wish. One sure way to create a slave is to ensure a person is indebted. After all, anyone who cannot do any of the things a free person can do because he or she has a mortgage, bills of all sorts, and the need for a monthly paycheck should be considered a slave of sorts—a debt slave.
>
> (p. 21)

This book is needed because student debt slavery is foreclosing freedom from the millennial generation, replacing it with a future of mortgage-size debt payments. The millennial generation has no surplus income because the bulk of whatever they have goes to repaying their student loans. Many don't have jobs—and this doesn't only pertain to those who want to be in the "Ivory Tower." It also includes students who have an undergraduate degree and those who managed to accumulate debt but no college degree to show for it. Finally, the millennial generation doesn't have assets, like homes, because they cannot save enough for a down payment. They live paycheck to paycheck—paying their debts. I have reached the midpoint of the 10-year Public Service Loan Forgiveness Program (PSLFP), and I have hope that all of my student loans will be repaid or discharged. However, as a professor, unless the *status quo* of our political economy and higher education financing changes, I am less optimistic that my students will be free from having a monthly loan payment bill for the rest of their lives (Brown, 2012). Jeffrey Williams (2006) is right:

> "I think we need to talk about student debt more, especially now. We need to talk about it because it affects so many of those in the classroom seats in front of us and because it has increased so precipitously. It is in

fact the new paradigm of college funding. Consequently, it is also, or will soon be, the new paradigm of early to middle adult life. Gone are the days when the state university was as cheap as a laptop, considered a right like secondary education. Now it is, like most social services, a largely privatized venture, and loans are the way that individuals frequently pay for it."

(p. 156)

Although I am now at Metropolitan State University in St. Paul, Minnesota, the bulk of this book was written and edited during my time at Illinois State University, in Normal, Illinois, which is why I am dedicating this book to Jason Lee Yoder of Normal, Illinois.[1] Rest-In-Power Jason; I hope this book honors you and your family and helps others who are indebted to critically examine and ask, "What's up with that?" This volume continues the task that Lucille and I began in 2013 to expose "the role of debt in higher education."

Lucille

For me, this book is important for a number of reasons. First, it addresses an issue that affects an increasing majority of young adults in the United States who have pursued or aspire to post-secondary education—namely, the struggle or inability to finance their schooling while they're in it or their student loan debts once they leave. Second, it situates this issue in its historical, political-economic, and lived contexts. Understanding the historical and political economic contexts (Part I) is necessary for any possibility of effectively addressing the issue, while Part II on its lived context sheds autoethnographic light on what is otherwise a generalized and anonymous or merely personal problem. Finally, this book does not just bemoan the problem. In Part III it offers and analyzes proposals for addressing and even overcoming it. In my view, the latter is possible only if we supersede our existing monetary system, a supersedence that is not only possible but also likely once enough of us understand the money system we have, the money system we need, and what we can and should do to get from the former to the latter. And that points to my last and most important reason for this book: it brings the field of monetary critique and reform—the science of money and exchange relations—to the attention of fellow educators and all who value higher education.

I found my way to monetary critique and reform quite organically through my 1998 dissertation as a student of the social, philosophical, and historical foundations of education. The impetus for my interdisciplinary study of "Value in Economics, Ethics, and Education" was the question why do we use the term "value" in such seemingly disparate ways, as in moral values, economic value, and personal values. I was interested in exploring whether and, if so, how these distinct realms are connected. To make a long study short, I found they connect through our production and exchange relations and through the "interests"—a related and similarly ambiguous concept—that guide us amidst those relations. Two vital insights that I came to through studying medieval, classical, and neo-classical economic literature and the history of secondary education and schooling in the United States were how usury—what we now experience as compound interest on our savings and loans—came to be rationalized and institutionalized at the heart of modern money and how this, in turn, shaped the formation, foci, administration, and funding of, oddly, first tertiary and subsequently secondary public institutions of higher learning in the United States. Six years later, after having a child and getting situated as a tenure-track professor, I discovered a growing body of literature that shared my critique of modern money and taught me—and still is teaching me—much about our unsustainable private-interest-driven largely debt-based money system.

As bad as it is, the looming student debt crisis is but a symptom, one of many, of a disease festering in our body politic that needs to be understood and cured at its source so that people—both individually and collectively, both at home and globally—can survive, heal, and then flourish in the myriad ways we each choose and find others who share. Superseding our existing monetary (dis)order will not, on its own, relieve all the symptoms or solve all the problems that it and its symptoms have triggered, but it *will* establish the conditions of the possibility of our successfully working and learning to do so. We can then finally put to solely good use all the positive by-products of our usurious relations of production and exchange that have accrued over the past 100–500 years, and goods left from even earlier times, and work democratically to put war, sexism, racism, poverty, dehumanization, and ecological degradation behind us as relics of the modern era, living our way humbly but clearly into what some philosophers prematurely dubbed the post-modern age. I am honored and thrilled to accompany the fine co-authors of this text and all its readers into this brave new world that is ours for the making. Only then may we and our descendants realize that our debt to the student debtors of our age has been paid and was worth the struggle.

Brandon

I write to help sound the alarms in the halls of higher education in the United States. Anyone with a stake in postsecondary education, from students to parents to academics to advocates, should not turn off these alarms until the crisis of student loan debt is known and palpable responses commence to combat it. I write (and call) for a rippling, widespread campaign of consciousness-raising, coalition-building, and action on the part of citizens and their lawmakers, policymakers, influential media, and others who want to make common cause of heading off an unmitigated disaster, the likes of which could stunt the American middle class, deter international students from studying at U.S. colleges and universities, and bring about a sea change in the public evaluation of whether college is *really worth it*.

Student loan debt in the United States has reached catastrophic levels (Fossey, 2016) and, unless there are major clarion calls—such as the book before you—and substantial responses, the next generation of college students will graduate with crippling student debt, forming an entire class of the massively indebted. A quick search of "student loan bubble" yields scores of articles by economists warning of dim prospects ahead regarding student loan debt: for social mobility, for investment in a house or retirement account, for family planning, and on (*cf.* El-Erian, 2015). The consequences are many when a student loan system actively buries a body politic under the crushing weight of a debt that, in most cases, follows the former student and her/his family without bankruptcy and despite death or other events that warrant loan forgiveness in other sectors of the economy.

I got involved in this book project because, like many Americans and international students in the United States, I have student loan debt. While mine is below the $35,000 national average for indebted students (Kantrowicz, 2015), it is still an amount large enough to compel my spouse and me to live in austerity: no kids until the debt is paid down, no new(er) cars until we are almost out of debt, and no buying a house until the debt is lower and our credit is improved. I write to problematize the knee-jerk presumption that a baccalaureate degree is *required* of students for personal and professional success. I'm writing to current/prospective students who believe, or have been told or seen through the media, that college (particularly a bachelor's degree) is the *only* option after the high school diploma.

I was robbed of a lot of my childhood because my parents were both working extremely strenuous, 8–10-hour jobs in social work (counseling). Even though they didn't have student debt, they graduated in a field that was becoming saturated with advanced degreed professionals. I believe that they were subscribing to a vision of the American Dream all too similar to prospective and current students in today's colleges and universities. Collegians are still buoyed by that American Dream of mobility, freedom, and independence from constraints. Sadly, a major constraint that hollows out the mythic dream and the college experience is the staggering student loan debt reality in the United States.

Millions of college graduates and current college students are struggling under a tidal wave of debt. As I said, my debt is small compared to the national average, but I am emboldened to contribute to this book because the dreams that have been unethically bolstered by the postsecondary education loan *industry* need to be called out before anyone else suffers unnecessarily while pursuing education, not to mention merely credentials. In my field, Arts and Humanities, there is an enormous glut of unemployed or underemployed people with Ph.Ds. These are people who likely (like me) thought school and degrees would lead to gainful employment, personal/ professional growth, and the means to start families or do other things to enrich life and make it meaningful. How can these be achieved when the debt collector never leaves?

This book is part of the wake-up call to false peddlers of the American Dream that has never happened for millions of Americans. This book is the call to a new college imaginary that centers education as an affordable right for all. Drawing upon T. S. Elliot (1942), I hope you'll join us (the authors and editors of this book) in this critical undertaking of inquiry and action, such that "We shall not cease from exploration, and the end of all our exploring will be to arrive where we started and know the place for the first time" (p. 59).

Conclusion

Connolly (2016) reported that a poll shows that some graduated student loan borrowers would willingly go to extremes to pay off outstanding student debt. Those extremes include experiencing physical pain and suffering and even a reduced lifespan. For instance, 35% of those polled would take one year off life expectancy and 6.5% would willingly cut off their pinky finger if it meant ridding themselves of the student loan debt they currently held.

Neoliberalism's presence in higher education is making matters worse for students and the student debt crisis, not better. In their book *Structure and Agency in the Neoliberal University*, Cannan and Shumar (2008) focus their attention on resisting, transforming, and dismantling the neoliberal paradigm in higher education. They ask how can market-based reform serve as the solution to the problem neoliberal practices and policies have engineered? It is like an individual who loses his keys at night and who decides to look only beneath the street light. This may be convenient because there is light, but it might not be where the keys are located. This metaphorical example could relate to the student debt crisis. What got us to where we are (escalating tuition costs, declining state monies, and increasing neoliberal influence in higher education) cannot get us out of the $1.4 trillion problem. And yet this metaphor may, in fact, be more apropos than most of us on the right, left, or center are as yet seeing because we mistakenly assume the market we have is the only or best one possible. As Lucille (this volume) strives to expose, the systemic cause of our problem is "hidden in plain sight," right there in the street light for all who look carefully enough to see. We only have to realize that the emperor has no clothes and reveal this reality. If and when a critical mass of us do, systemic change in our monetary exchange relations can and, we hope, will become our funnel toward a sustainable and socially, economically, and ecologically just future where public education and democracy can finally become realities rather than merely ideals.

Indeed, the approach our money-dependent and -driven legislators and policymakers have employed has been neoliberal in form and function, and it will continue to be so unless we help them to see the light or get out of the way. This book focuses on the $1.4+ trillion student debt crisis in the United States. It doesn't share hard and fast solutions *per se*. Rather, it addresses real questions (and their real consequences). Are collegians overestimating the economic value of going to college? What are we, they, and our so-called elected leaders failing or refusing to see and why? This critically minded, soul-searching volume shares territory with, yet pushes beyond, that of Akers and Chingos (2016), Baum (2016), Goldrick-Rab (2016), Graeber (2011), and Johannsen (2016) in ways that we trust those critically minded authors—and others concerned with our mess of debts, public and private, and unfulfilled human potential—will find enlightening and even ground-breaking.

Note

1 Johannsen, C. C. (2012). The ones we've lost: The student loan debt suicides. *The Huffington Post*. Retrieved from www.huffingtonpost.com/c-cryn-johannsen/student-loan-debt-suicides_b_1638972.html

References

Akers, B., & Chingos, M. M. (2016). *Game of loans: The rhetoric and reality of student debt*. Princeton, NJ: Princeton University Press.

Baum, S. (2016). *Student debt: Rhetoric and realities of higher education financing*. New York: Palgrave Macmillan.

Brown, H. E. (2012). *Web of debt: The shocking truth about our money system—the sleight of hand that has trapped us in debt and how we can break free* (5th ed.). New York: Third Millennium Press.

Cannan, J. E., & Shumar, W. (Eds.). (2008). *Structure and agency in the neoliberal university*. New York: Routledge.

Connolly, A. R. (2016). Poll: Some borrowers would cut off pinkies, take punch to dump student loans. *UPI Quirks in the News*. Retrieved from www.upi.com/Odd_News/2016/02/12/Poll-Some-borrowers-would-cut-off-pinkies-take-punch-to-dump-student-loans/8041455295095/

El-Erian, M. A. (2015, November 9). The U.S. education bubble is now upon us. *Market Watch*. Retrieved from www.marketwatch.com/story/the-us-education-bubble-is-now-upon-us-2015-11-09

Elliot, T. S. (1942). *The complete poems and plays*. London, UK: Faber & Faber, Inc.

Fossey, R. (2016, March 1). The $tudent loan crisis. *Condemned to DEBT*. Retrieved from http://www.condemnedtodebt.org

Goldrick-Rab, S. (2016). *Paying the price: College costs, financial aid, and the betrayal of the American dream*. Chicago: University of Chicago Press.

Graeber, D. (2011). *Debt: The first 5,000 years*. New York: Melville Press.

Hartlep, N. D., & Eckrich, L. L. T. (2013). Ivory tower graduates in the red: The role of debt in higher education. *Workplace: A Journal for Academic Labor, 22*,

82–97. Retrieved from http://ices.library.ubc.ca/index.php/workplace/article/view/184428/184114

Johannsen, C. (2016). *Solving the student loan crisis: Dreams, diplomas, & a lifetime of debt*. New York: New Insights Press.

Kantrowicz, M. (2015). *Who graduates with excessive student loan debt?* Washington, DC: MK Consulting, Inc. Retrieved from http://studentaidpolicy.com/excessive-debt/Excessive-Debt-at-Graduation.pdf

Marrs, J. (2011). *The trillion-dollar conspiracy: How the new world order, manmade diseases, and zombie banks are destroying America*. New York: Harper.

Williams, J. (2006). The pedagogy of debt. *College Literature, 33*(4), 155–169.

Acknowledgments

Our individual and collective editorial and authorial work was a labor of love; it also proved to be highly educative for us. We appreciate each contributed chapter, and we know the project would not have come to fruition without the guidance of Dave Hill and the talented team at Routledge: Karen Adler (Education Editor), Katherine Tsamparlis (Editorial Assistant), and Christina Chronister (Education Editor). We also would like to thank Kevin Kelsey (Project Manager at Apex CoVantage) for his assistance getting the book formatted. Thank you all.

Part I

Critical Perspectives on Financing Higher Education in the United States

1 Financing Higher Education in the United States

A Historical Overview of Loans in Federal Financial Aid Policy

Enyu Zhou and Pilar Mendoza

Introduction

This chapter provides an overview of how American higher education has historically been partially financed through student loans, signaling a neoliberal approach since the beginning of the 20th century whereby students have been carrying a sizable burden of the financing of higher education for their own private good. In particular, we illustrate the evolution of financial aid policies from the GI Bill to the massification of higher education in the 1960s, followed by rapid growth in the 1970s, marketization and endowment in the 1980s, and intensification of neoliberalism in the 1990s into the present.

The 1940s to 1960s: Initiation of Student Loan Programs

Before World War II, college was regarded as an option only for higher-income students due to its up-front expense and the delay in workforce entry caused by college attendance. However, college access and affordability became open to a wider segment of society with the first federal grant program, known as the GI Bill, which was established by the passage of the Servicemen's Readjustment Act of 1944. To support the postwar economy and recovery, the 1944 GI Bill provided federal grants for all returning veterans who wanted to enroll in postsecondary institutions (public or private for-profit and not-for-profit) (Thelin, 2007).

The GI Bill paid up to $500 a year ($6,765 in 2016 dollars) directly to any accredited 2–4 year public or private accredited postsecondary institution to cover tuition, fees, and supplies for each veteran, as well as a monthly living allowance (Thelin, 2007). The development of the GI Bill had a significant impact on college access and success. Nearly 3.9 million veterans received some education benefits from the GI Bill to attend postsecondary institutions, and college graduates increased from four to ten percent (Best & Best, 2014). Moreover, the GI Bill offered benefits regardless of race, although minority veterans faced more difficulties accessing those benefits (Frydl, 2009). Overall, the GI Bill created social mobility opportunities for many veterans and fostered economic growth after World War II (Mumper, Gladieux, King, & Corrigan, 2011; Thelin, 2011).

One prominent contribution of the GI Bill was its pioneering of the notion of federal grants for college students. However, for-profit schools had unexpectedly cashed in on the GI Bill, and so, when it was renewed after the Korean War, lawmakers passed the 85/15 rule, whereby at least 15% of the students—and revenue—at any school receiving education benefits had to be from non-veterans in order to prevent schools from surviving by virtue of heavy influx of federal payments (Mettler, 2014).

The GI Bill's contribution to college access was limited to veterans. However, later in the 1950s, federal financial aid programs became available to all college students (Hearn, 1998) as a national strategy to regain U.S. leadership in science and technology during the Cold War and the Space Race. To that end, Congress passed the National Defense Education Act (NDEA) in 1958 to increase federal support for higher education and to encourage college enrollment, especially in fields of national interest, such as science, technology, mathematics, and foreign languages (National Defense Education Act, 1958). One important feature of the NDEA was its Title II, which created the National Defense Student Loan program, later renamed as the Perkins Loans in 1986, as a mechanism to increase college access (Best & Best, 2014; Thelin, 2007). The NDEA's loan program was the first of its kind targeting low-income college students (Hearn, 1998).

Before the NDEA's loan program, most college student loans were provided by private, institutional, or state lending agencies. Although some states offered guaranty funds to support private student loans, the interest of these loans was not subsidized. There were no federally supported loans for college students before the 1950s (Hearn, 1998). Federal NDEA's loan funds went directly from the government to postsecondary institutions, which had to match $1 for every $9 of federal funds they received. The government subsidized these loans in that no interest accrued and no payments had to be made as long as borrowers were enrolled. In addition, students who went into full-time public school teaching were further subsidized by having up to half their loan forgiven. The federal NDEA's loan program provided low interest (3%) loans of $1,000 per year, up to a maximum of $5,000 ($41,199 in 2016 dollars), to students with financial need (Best & Best, 2014; Hearn, 1998). The NDEA's loan program provided an initiation of federal involvement in student loans. As the NDEA's loan program expanded its eligibility and increased its funds in the late 1950s, the number of students using loans to pay for college dramatically increased. Federally supported loans became a new alternative for students to finance their higher education (Best & Best, 2014).

Despite its significance, the NDEA's loan program remained narrowly focused until the passage of the Higher Education Act (HEA) of 1965. As part of the Great Society Program established by President Lyndon Johnson, the HEA of 1965 promoted equal opportunities of college access for all

Americans by providing financial aid for low, middle, and even high income students (all but the top 10%) to support their higher education (Hearn, 1998; Higher Education Act, 1965; Mumper et al., 2011).

The Title IV of the 1965 HEA created three types of federal financial aid programs: the Educational Opportunity Grant, the Federal Work Study, and the Guaranteed Student Loans. The Educational Opportunity Grant (EOG), later renamed the Basic Educational Opportunity Grant and later the Pell Grant, was the largest need-based program providing federal grants to undergraduate students based on their financial need. The purpose of the EOG was to provide college access to low-income students who otherwise could not go to college (Federal Student Aid, 2016b; Mumper et al., 2011; Thelin, 2011).

The eligibility of the Pell Grant was based on a calculation of a student's expected family contribution (EFC) and the cost of attendance (COA). The rationale behind the EOG was the belief that broad access to higher education could serve national economic interests and contribute to a better society (Curs, Singell, & Waddell, 2007). The need-based Federal Work Study (FWS) program provided part-time employment for low-income students to work on or off campus while they were enrolled in college. Both EOG and FWS were administered and delivered by on-campus financial aid offices (Avery & Turner, 2012; Hearn, 1998; Mumper et al., 2011).

For those students who did not qualify for the EOG but who still needed additional financial support, the HEA of 1965 created the Guaranteed Student Loan (GSL) program, also called the Stafford Loan program. The GSL program offered student loans from private lenders with lower interest rates than regular private loans. It provided interest subsidies and a deferral of repayment while students were enrolled in college; and most importantly for financial institutions, GSL was underwritten by the federal government with a guarantee (Avery & Turner, 2012; Mumper et al., 2011). Compared to the NDEA's loan program, the GSL expanded the loan eligibility to students whose family income was less than $15,000 ($113,396 in 2016 dollars). In addition, GSL shifted the government's role from providing the loans themselves to only subsidizing and guaranteeing them. In order to attract private financing, it raised the interest rate to 6%, all of which the government paid for low-income students while they were in school and half of it thereafter in order to protect the 3% low interest rate for low-income students. This approach to loans is essentially neoliberal in that the private sector earns interest from the ransomed future earning power of indebted collegians who for years pay that interest and eventually the principal too. These neoliberal changes opened the floodgates of student loans (Best & Best, 2014). At the same time, higher education became more and more a private good worthy of investment for personal gain.

Eligibility for these federal guarantee loans and direct loans was expanded to students who enrolled in postsecondary business, trade, vocational, and technical schools by the passage of the National Vocational Student

Loan Insurance Act (NVSLI) of 1965. The features of the NVSLI's loan program were similar to the GSL program. In fact, the NVSLI's loan program was merged with the GSL through the HEA reauthorization of 1968 (Coomes, 1998).

In sum, a neoliberal approach to financing higher education started during the decades of the 1940s and 1950s through two main strategies: giving funds to students and allowing private institutions to enroll students with federal monies. The policy of financing students directly assumes higher education as a private good and fosters competition among institutions for students who bring federal funds and who have the freedom to choose what institution to attend in a market of private and public institutions. A non-neoliberal approach would have been to give public funding directly to public institutions and provide free tuition for all admitted, as it is the case in many countries, or all under a certain income bracket. What's more, allowing private schools to receive federal funds through students, including state-guaranteed loans, fostered growth of private industry around higher education services, including loan intermediaries and for-profit institutions.

The 1970s: Expansion of Student Loan Programs

The passage of the Education Amendments of 1972 initiated a period of expansion of federal higher education financial aid policy. It created the Basic Educational Opportunity Grant (BEOG) program designed to distribute federal grants (as opposed to loans as they already happened with the GSL) and so students now had more choices for their higher education because grants could also go to any public or private institution. The logic behind this measure was to increase competition among institutions by allowing students to choose where to enroll, pushing institutions to find their niche in an emergent market of higher education institutions (Curs et al., 2007).

This publicly subsidized market fostered the proliferation of different types of institutions, programs, and amenities, each designed to attract specific students. Another program created from the 1972 Education Amendments was the State Student Incentive Grants (SSIG), also called the LEAP program. This program aimed to provide funds, mostly matching, to states to establish state need-based aid and work study programs (Zumeta, Breneman, Callan, & Finney, 2012).

To increase the availability of student loans, the Higher Education Reauthorization of 1972 also established the Student Loan Marketing Association (SLMA), known as Sallie Mae. This was a government-sponsored enterprise (GSE), which aimed to support the GSL program through commercial and institutional lending to college students. Sallie Mae was created to work similarly to how Fannie Mae works with mortgage loans. Banks would lend money to students (the primary market) but then sell their loans to Sallie Mae, enabling banks to offload the risk and get cash back rather than having to wait years for those loans to be repaid. In turn, Sallie Mae would issue its own government-guaranteed debt in the capital markets, creating a secondary market where investors (probably some of whom had just sold the original loans to Sallie Mae) could purchase bundles of student loans as long-term investments (Best & Best, 2014).

Another significant impact of the Education Amendments of 1972 was the expansion of the eligibility criteria for federal aid. The income ceiling on GSL eligibility increased to $25,000 ($142,423 in 2016 dollars). The new criteria allowed students enrolled in accredited postsecondary institutions, including for-profit and vocational institutions, to receive federal aid. The federal aid expansion, particularly of student loans, to for-profit institutions sowed the seeds of the high student loan defaults in the future (Deming, Goldin, & Katz, 2012; Hearn, 1998; Thelin, 2011).

During the economic downturn of the 1970s, many students, especially middle-income students, could not afford to go to college. Therefore, in 1978, the Middle Income Student Assistance Act (MISAA) was passed to support more middle-income families by increasing the income ceiling for the Guaranteed Student Loans. The $25,000 ($142,423 in 2016 dollars) income ceiling of GSL eligibility was removed, and any student who enrolled in a postsecondary institution could participate in the GSL program (Hearn, 1998; Zumeta et al., 2012).

Student participation in the federal loan program dramatically increased after the passage of MISAA. In 1980, the number of GSL borrowers was 2.9 million (Hearn, 1998). From 1978 to 1981, the amount of student loans increased from $2.2 billion to $6.2 billion (Zumeta et al., 2012). Over time, with continual growth of higher education through the GSL program, student loan default rates also grew. In 1978, Congress passed legislation to limit bankruptcy protection for GSL borrowers in order to prevent students discharging debts and filing for bankruptcy after graduation. Under this ruling, the GSL could not be discharged in bankruptcy for five years after graduation unless borrowers could show "undue hardship." This non-dischargeability of student loans would be tightened in the future (Fossey, 1998).

The Education Amendments of the 1970s clarified the post World War II role of the federal government in financing American higher education and laid the foundation for future expansion of federal support. However, the cost of attending college continued to increase over the years. Through the passage of HEA Reauthorization of 1972 and the MISAA of 1978, American higher education finance policy continued to emphasize student loans and higher education as a private good.

The 1980s and 1990s: The Rise of Private Lenders and Student Debt

In the 1980s, the number of students who were eligible for federal financial aid grew significantly. Government officials were under pressure to provide more financial aid to low-income students to offset raising college costs. There was a heated debate over whether federal aid programs harmed students and helped drive up college costs. At the end of the decade, as college costs continued to rise, more and more students had to obtain loans to support their higher education (Mumper et al., 2011).

Coincidentally, during the 1980s the country went through a significant economic recession and, as a result, employment opportunities for college graduates declined. Unlike his predecessors, President Ronald Reagan believed that market-based economies, in which private rather than public interests drive the economy, were the best alternative. Under these ideas of a free-market economy, justification for public support of higher education began to weaken (Kotz, 2015; Zumeta et al., 2012). In this climate, liberal advocates' views of cost-sharing—a shift of higher education cost from government to students—rested on two rationales: (1) there is a need to increase other-than-governmental resources to meet the growing demand of higher education, and (2) cost-sharing generates greater equity and efficiency (Johnstone, 2011).

Cost-sharing imposed full costs on students who were capable of paying for college and provided public support only to students in need. Therefore, under this model, the high tuition-high aid model was viewed as more equitable than the low tuition-low aid model. The efficiency argument of cost-sharing claimed that high tuition had little influence on the college consumption of upper-class students; therefore, it was inefficient to use public funds to support higher education for students who would purchase it anyway (Johnstone, 2011). Moreover, this view supported individualistic theory, in which higher education is viewed as a private good. The debate about who pays and who should pay for higher education is still current. At the heart of such a debate is the question of whether higher education is a public or private good (Best & Best, 2014).

During the 1970s, about 50% of public institutions' revenue came from states; however, the amount of state appropriations did not keep pace with growing university budgets in the 1980s. Since then, public universities and colleges have been forced to seek new ways to generate revenue and support their operations. This intense competition between institutions for students and other resources solidified the need for the marketization of higher education. As a result, evidence shows that public universities and colleges have changed revenue patterns from mainly relying on state appropriations to reliance on alternative resources such as tuition and fees, research grants, patents, donations and endowments (Weisbrod, Ballou, & Asch, 2008).

The passage of the 1980 HEA Reauthorization established the Parent Loans for Undergraduate Students (PLUS) programs. The PLUS programs were federal loans provided to parents of dependent undergraduate college students. These programs did not require students to demonstrate financial need. However, they were unsubsidized loans, which meant that borrowers were responsible to pay for all interest (Hearn, 1998).

In the 1986 Reauthorization of the HEA, the Supplemental Loan to Students (SLS) was established to provide unsubsidized loans for independent, graduate, and professional students. This reauthorization, also renamed as the Perkins Loan Program, required a need analysis for GSL eligibility consolidation of federal student loans options. The loan consolidation program aimed to help students pay back loans by combining their various federal loans into one loan (Hearn, 1998). There were both advantages and disadvantages associated with this loan consolidation. On one hand, it could simplify loan repayments into one bill and had lower monthly payments and longer repayment time. Borrowers could also have more repayment options and change the loan interest rates to a fixed interest rate.

On the other hand, consolidation loans would lose the benefits of the original loans, such as the interest rate discounts, principal rebates, or loan cancellations for working in public sector human service jobs. Most federal loans could be consolidated, such as subsidized loans, unsubsidized loans, and the PLUS Loans. However, PLUS Loans that were borrowed by a parent of a dependent student were not eligible for consolidation to the child's loan (Federal Student Aid, 2016c).

The Clinton administration believed that private lenders were generating too much profit through federally guaranteed loans to students and parents. In fact, by 1990, Sallie Mae was a member of the New York Stock Exchange with assets of $41.4 billion (Mettler, 2014). In 1996, Sallie Mae was privatized and it started making loans directly to students. Sallie Mae made significant profits through interest rates resulting in loan holdings of $45 billion in 1997 (Collinge, 2009; Soederberg, 2014).

To address this issue, a similar 85/15 rule for loans was passed where only 85% of a postsecondary institution's revenue could come from loans in 1992, but lawmakers diluted this rule to 90/10 in 1998 under pressure from the sizable profit-school sector (Best & Best, 2014). Moreover, President Clinton proposed a direct government loan program to replace the bank-based federal guaranteed loan program (Hearn, 1998; Mumper et al., 2011). Despite the efforts of the Clinton administration, there was a heated debate on the most efficient way to deliver federal loans. Opponents claimed that private lenders were better than the federal government in managing risks, student loans, and serving students (Holtz-Eakin & Hsiao, 2011).

Finally, in 1993, Congress adopted a compromise plan by creating a voluntary direct loan program while maintaining the bank-based non-direct loan program. The bank-based loan programs including GSL, PLUS and SLS were folded into the Federal Family Education Loan Program (FFELP). Universities were allowed to choose either the direct lending program or the government-guaranteed private student loans—whichever they believed best fit their needs. The institutions that participated in the direct loan program could provide student loans directly from the federal government (Hearn, 1998; Mumper et al., 2011).

In addition to the direct loan program, the Clinton administration also promoted tax benefits to finance higher education in 1997 through the Taxpayer Relief Act, which created the Hope Scholarship Credit and the Lifetime Learning Credit programs to address financial problems of the middle-upper-income students. The Hope Scholarship Credit program provided tax credits to support the first two-years of college expenses for taxpayers, their spouse, or dependents (Zumeta et al., 2012). The Lifetime Learning Credit program provided 20% of the first $10,000 ($14,836 in 2016 dollars) of educational expenses for taxpayers who enrolled in postsecondary education, or up to one credit under $2,000 ($2,967 in 2016 dollars). In addition, the Taxpayer Relief Act created several new programs for families to save for college, such as the Education Individual Retirement Accounts (IRA), the College Saving Plans, and the State Prepaid Tuition Plans. However, only students from families with enough income to have tax liability could claim these credits; thus, many low-income students did not benefit from this policy. The other savings plans of the IRA were beneficial for those who had money to save as well as access to knowledge on how to do so (Mumper et al., 2011).

The 21st Century: Student Debt Crisis

Student federal grant and loan programs continued to increase in the 2000s. Figure 1.1 shows the trends in federal grants and loans in millions (in 2014 dollars) from 1970–1971 to 2014–2015. In 1970–1971, the

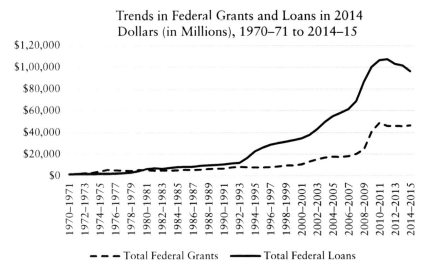

Figure 1.1 Trends in Federal Grants and Loans in 2014 Dollars (in Millions), 1970–1971 to 2014–2015

Source: College Board. (2015c). Total student aid and nonfederal loans in current dollars over time.

federal grants expenditure was $1,250 million, and this amount increased to $5,282 million in 1979–1980, then boosted upward to $10,472 million in 2000–2001. The total amounts of student loans continued to grow over these years since 1970. In 1970–1971, the amount of federal loans awarded to students was $1,129 million (in 2014 dollars), and this amount increased to $4,088 million in 1979–1980, and $34,326 million in 2000–2001 (College Board, 2015c).

In 1981, federal loans ($6,124 million) became a greater share than grants ($4,944 million) in federal spending on higher education for the first time (College Board, 2015c). During the 2014–2015 academic year, the total federal funding of all aid was $161.3 billion (in 2014 dollars). In particular, $46.2 billion of it was for grants, $95.9 billion was for loans, $0.9 billion was for federal work-study, and $18.2 billion were education tax benefits (College Board, 2015a). The trend of federal spending in grants and loans overtime shows how dependent higher education in the United States steadily came to be on student loans and, thus, on students' ransomed futures. And from 1972–2014 this was at the benefit of all the private lenders who got to issue government-guaranteed loans more or less at market rates.

The number of the Pell Grant recipients has continued to increase from 2.5 million in the 1979–1980 to 8.2 million in 2014–2015. In 1979–1980, the total expenditure of the Pell Grant program was $7.7 billion, which was boosted to $30.3 billion (in 2014 dollars) in 2014–2015. However, the maximum amount of Pell Grant a student can receive has not changed much over the same fifty-year period. The average amount of Pell Grant was $5,867 (in 2014 dollars) in 1979–1980 and $5,730 (in 2014 dollars) in 2014–2015 (College Board, 2015a).

In the meantime, college costs have significantly increased over the past fifty years. The average cost of tuition and fees (excluding room and board) for public four-year institutions for a full year has increased from $2,387 (in 2015 dollars) for the 1975–1976 academic year, to $9,410 for 2015–2016. The tuition for public two-year colleges averaged $1,079 in 1975–1976 (in 2015 dollars) and increased to $3,435 for 2015–2016. At private non-profit four-year institutions, the average 1975–1976 cost of tuition and fees (excluding room and board) was $10,088 (in 2015 dollars), which increased to $32,405 for 2015–2016 (College Board, 2015b). The purchasing power of Pell Grants has decreased. In fact, the maximum Pell Grants coverage of public four-year tuition and fees decreased from 83% in 1995–1996 to 61% in 2015–2016. The maximum Pell Grants coverage of private non-profit four-year tuition and fees decreased from 19% in 1995–1996 to 18% in 2015–2016 (College Board, 2015a).

As a result of these trends, increasing numbers of students have relied on loans to pay for their higher education. Accordingly, loan programs have continued to grow and so has the number of students in debt. In 2010, student debt rose to $830 billion, which surpassed credit-card debt for the first time (Avery & Turner, 2012; Soederberg, 2014). Federal student loans exceeded $1 trillion in 2013 and grew to $1.22 trillion in 2016 (Federal Student Aid, 2016a). In 2013–2014, 61% of bachelor's degree recipients from public and private non-profit four-year institutions graduated with an average debt of $16,300 per graduate. In 2011–2012, 50% of bachelor's degree recipients from for-profit institutions borrowed more than $40,000 and about 28% of associate degree recipients from for-profit institutions borrowed more than $30,000 (College Board, 2015a).

Rising student debt has become a key issue of higher education finance among many policymakers and researchers. Recently, the government has implemented a series of measures to address student debt. In 2005, the Bankruptcy Abuse Prevention and Consumer Protection Act (2005) was passed, which barred the discharge of all student loans through bankruptcy for most borrowers (Collinge, 2009). This was the final nail in the bankruptcy coffin, which had begun in 1976 with a five-year ban on student loan debt (SLD) bankruptcy and was extended to seven years in 1990. Then in 1998, it became a permanent ban for all who could not clear a relatively high bar of undue hardship (Best & Best, 2014).

By 2006, Sallie Mae had become the nation's largest private student loan lender, reporting loan holdings of $123 billion. Its fee income collected from defaulted loans grew from $280 million in 2000 to $920 million in 2005 (Collinge, 2009). In 2007, in response to growing student default rates, the College Cost Reduction Act was passed to provide loan forgiveness for student loan borrowers who work full-time in a public service job. The Federal Direct Loan will be forgiven after 120 payments were made. This Act also provided other benefits for students to pay for their postsecondary education, such as lowering interest rates of GSL, increasing the maximum amount of Pell Grant (though, as noted above, not sufficiently to meet rising tuition rates), as well as reducing guarantor collection fees (Collinge, 2009).

In 2008, the Higher Education Opportunity Act (2008) was passed to increase transparency and accountability. This Act required institutions that are participating in federal financial aid programs to post a college price calculator on their websites in order to provide better college cost information for students and families (U.S. Department of Education [U.S. DoE], 2015a). Due to the recession of 2008, the American Opportunity Tax Credit of 2009 (AOTC) was passed to expand the Hope Tax Credit program, in which the amount of tax credit increased to 100% for the first $2,000 of qualified educational expenses and was reduced to 25% of the second $2,000 in college expenses. The total credit cap increased from $1,500 to $2,500 per student. As a result, the federal spending on education tax benefits had a large increase since then (Crandall-Hollick, 2014), benefits that, again, are reaped only by those who file income taxes.

The same year, Congress passed the American Recovery and Reinvestment Act of 2009 (ARRA), also called the Recovery Act, as part of their response to the "Great Recession" of 2008. The ARRA provided economic stimulus packages to help the recovery of education, energy, health, infrastructure, and job opportunities (The Recovery Board, 2015). To support higher education, the ARRA provided an additional $17 billion to support the Pell Grant program and boosted the maximum amount of Pell Grant from $4,850 to $5,350. Moreover, $13.8 billion was spent to increase the tax credit programs. In addition, the ARRA also provided $40 billion direct funding for states to stabilize government support of public higher education and to prevent the state appropriation cuts during the economic downturn (U.S. DoE, 2015b).

Finally, to eliminate subsidies to private lenders and increase funds for need-based aids, the Obama administration proposed replacing the Federal Family Education Loan Program (FFELP) with the Direct Loan programs. In 2010, the passage of the Health Care and Education Reconciliation Act (2010) eliminated the FFELP and all new federal loans were made under the Direct Loan Programs. This is a crucial change, finally moving the federal approach in student loans back to where it had been at first in 1958. Moreover, to increase the Pell Grant budget, the Federal government ended the direct subsidized loans for graduate and professional students in 2011 (Federal Student Aid, 2016c; The White House, 2015). At the same time, the LEAP program was terminated, which had significant effects on states' grant programs (College Board, 2015a).

In 2013, Sallie Mae split into two publicly traded companies. One, since named Navient, houses Sallie Mae's legacy of federally guaranteed and now-underperforming private sector loans, which are no longer issued; it also services a portion of the U.S. Department of Education's new "direct" student loans. The other, called Sallie Mae, houses its newer, better-performing, and multiplying private loans for students, increasingly including international students who banks as well as colleges and universities are now trying to capitalize on (Best & Best, 2014, p. 154).

Over the last decade, policymakers have advocated boosting college information and increasing transparency and accountability related to college choices, college costs, and financial aid. Since 2013, the Department of Education has provided the Financial Aid Shopping Sheet, a form with data from postsecondary institutions meant to deliver better information and tools for students who are making a selection regarding which institution to attend. The Department of Education has also established online tools such as the College Affordability and Transparency Center, the College Scorecard, and the College Navigator to assist students with their college selection process (The White House, 2015).

Starting in 2015, the higher education community began actively preparing proposals for Congress to assist with the reauthorization of the Higher Education Act. Several bills related to higher education funding, student loan regulations, and indebtedness have been proposed. For example, the Empowering Students through the Enhanced Financial Counseling Act (2015) proposed to provide counseling for students and parents to increase knowledge about higher education finance. The Financial Aid Simplification and Transparency Act (2015) proposed providing more public college information, consumer tools, and grant and loan counseling. These proposed changes aim to provide better information and tools for students to choose among institutions and to ensure that students have adequate information regarding college cost and financing higher education.

In this period, financial aid was not considered as the only way to reduce college cost. To make college more affordable, researchers and policymakers started to seek alternatives to financial aid, for example, a Free Two-Year College Option (F2CO) (Goldrick-Rab & Kendall, 2014). For example, in 2013, Tennessee started to provide free community college education to students. States such as Mississippi and Oregon also started to push legislations to offer free tuition at community colleges (Goldrick-Rab & Kendall, 2014). In 2015, President Obama proposed making community college free for students, and, after that, it was a major issue in the 2016 presidential campaign (The White House, 2015).

Conclusion

We conclude with several issues that will continue to influence the finance policy of American higher education over the next decade of the 21st century. First, with the support of government financial aid programs, college enrollment has increased significantly over the past fifty years. However, college access is stratified by socioeconomic status. Low-income students are more sensitive to tuition and financial aid change and the increasing net price of college tuition has been shown to lead to unequal access of students from low-income families (Heller, 2008). Moreover, compared to students from upper-income families, lower-income students are less likely to be well prepared for college, more likely to enroll in two-year colleges, and less likely to attain a Bachelor degree and less likely to be able to take advantage of tax credits (Price, 2004). Many continue to raise concerns about college access and affordability. In a nutshell, the critical question is *who has access to what?*

A second concern has to do with unequal access to credit markets and imperfect information. Although government financial aid has increased, many aid-eligible students still fail to go to college because of the complicated nature of aid application, lack of assistance, and lack of information about financial aid programs (Long, 2004; Perna, 2006; Tierney & Venegas, 2009). As the purchasing power of student aid decreases, many students have to turn to loans to support their higher education and/or take on employment that gets in the way of full-time studies. Lacking understanding of student loans, private lenders, and the consequences of debt makes disadvantaged students more vulnerable.

Third, the question on whether higher education should be viewed as a public or private good has been debated throughout the history of higher education finance. Some policymakers and scholars argue that higher education is a private good because of its business features, entrepreneur behaviors, and its private benefits for students (Geske & Cohn, 1998; Slaughter & Leslie, 1997). The emphasis on private benefits supports the view that students and their families should bear most of the cost of higher education, which in turn enables the emphasis on loans rather than grant aid. The perspective of academic commercialism has become popular in American higher education in the past few decades, in which students play the role of consumers with universities as service providers.

In short, postsecondary education has become a factory of knowledge and a growing industry aggressively competing for students (Slaughter & Rhoades, 2004). Critics believe that higher education should, rather, be viewed as a public good due to its many benefits to society (Goldrick-Rab & Kendall, 2014; Winston, 1999). In addition, St. John and Asker (2003) provide three justifications for the government to finance more broadly higher education: (1) access for the majority, (2) equal opportunity to enroll, and (3) justice for taxpayers (St. John & Asker, 2003). While the business model of higher education becomes more and more prevalent, questions about who benefits, who pays, and who should pay for the cost of higher education will continue to be the central debate in higher education finance.

References

Avery, C., & Turner, S. (2012). Student loans: Do college students borrow too much—or not enough? *The Journal of Economic Perspectives*, 26, 165–192.

Bankruptcy Abuse Prevention and Consumer Protection Act of 2005, S.256, 109th Cong. (2005). Retrieved from https://www.congress.gov/bill/109th-congress/senate-bill/256

Best, J., & Best, E. (2014). *The student loan mess: How good intentions created a trillion-dollar problem*. Berkeley, CA: University of California Press.

College Board. (2015a). *Trends in student aid 2015*. Retrieved from http://trends.collegeboard.org/student-aid

College Board. (2015b). *Trends in college pricing 2015*. Retrieved from http://trends.collegeboard.org/college-pricing

College Board. (2015c). *Total student aid and nonfederal loans in current dollars over time*. Retrieved from http://trends.collegeboard.org/student-aid/figures-tables/student-aid-nonfederal-loans-current-dollars-over-time

Collinge, A. (2009). *The student loan scam: The most oppressive debt in US history, and how we can fight back*. Boston: Beacon Press.

Coomes, M. D. (1998). Trade school defaults: Proprietary schools and the federal family educational loan program. In R. Fossey & M. Bateman (Eds.), *Condemning students to debt: College loans and public policy* (pp. 126–160). New York: Teachers College Press.

Crandall-Hollick, M. L. (2014). *The American opportunity tax credit: Overview, analysis, and policy options*. Retrieved from http://fas.org/sgp/crs/misc/R42561.pdf

Curs, B. R., Singell, L. D. J., & Waddell, G. R. (2007). The Pell program at thirty years. In J. C. Smart (Ed.), *Higher education: Handbook of theory and research* (Vol. XXII, pp. 281–334). New York: Springer.

Deming, D. J., Goldin, C., & Katz, L. F. (2012). The for-profit postsecondary school sector: Nimble critters or agile predators? *The Journal of Economic Perspectives*, 26(1), 139–164.

Empowering Students through Enhanced Financial Counseling Act, H.R. 3179, 114th Cong. (2015–2016). Retrieved from https://www.congress.gov/bill/114th-congress/house-bill/3179?q=%7B%22search%22%3A%5B%22Empowering+Students+Through+Enhanced+Financial+Counseling+Act%22%5D%7D&resultIndex=1

Federal Student Aid. (2016a). *Federal student loan portfolio.* Washington, DC: U.S. Department of Education. Retrieved from https://studentaid.ed.gov/about/data-center/student/portfolio

Federal Student Aid. (2016b). *Grants and scholarships.* Washington, DC: U.S. Department of Education. Retrieved from https://studentaid.ed.gov/sa/types//grants-scholarships

Federal Student Aid. (2016c). *Loans.* Washington, DC: U.S. Department of Education. Retrieved from https://studentaid.ed.gov/sa/types/loans

Financial Aid Simplification and Transparency Act, S. 108, 113th Cong. (2015–2016). Retrieved from https://www.congress.gov/bill/114th-congress/senate-bill/108?q=%7B%22search%22%3A%5B%22Financial+Aid+Simplification+and+Transparency+Act%22%5D%7D&resultIndex=1

Fossey, R. (1998). Are bankruptcy courts creating "the certainty of hopelessness" for student loan debtors? Examining the "undue hardship" rule. In R. Fossey & N. Badway (Eds.), *Condemning students to debt: College loans and public policy* (pp. 161–178). New York: Teachers College Press.

Frydl, K. J. (2009). *The GI Bill.* New York: Cambridge University Press.

Geske, T. G., & Cohn, E. (1998). Why is a high school diploma no longer enough? The economic and social benefits of higher educaiton. In R. Fossey & N. Badway (Eds.), *Condemning students to debt: College loans and public policy* (pp. 19–33). New York: Teachers College Press.

Goldrick-Rab, S., & Kendall, N. (2014, April). *F2CO: Redefining college affordability: Securing America's future with a free two-year college option.* Madison, WI: The Education Optimists.

Health Care and Education Reconciliation Act of 2010. H.R. 4872. (P.L. 111–152). 111th Cong. (2010). Retrieved from www.gpo.gov/fdsys/pkg/PLAW-111publ152/pdf/PLAW-111publ152.pdf

Hearn, J. C. (1998). The growing loan orientation in federal financial aid policy: A historical perspective. In R. Fossey & N. Badway (Eds.), *Condemning students to debt: College loans and public policy* (pp. 47–75). New York: Teachers College Press.

Heller, D. E. (2008). The impact of student loans on college access. In S. Baum, M. McPherson, & P. Steele (Eds.), *The effectiveness of student aid policies: What the research tells us* (pp. 39–68). New York: The College Board.

Higher Education Act of 1965, H.R. 567, 89th Cong. (1965). Retrieved from www.gpo.gov/fdsys/pkg/STATUTE-79/pdf/STATUTE-79-Pg1219.pdf

Higher Education Opportunity Act. (P.L. 110–315), H.R. 4137. 101st Cong. (2008). Retrieved from www.gpo.gov/fdsys/pkg/PLAW-110publ315/pdf/PLA110publ315.pdf

Holtz-Eakin, D., & Hsiao, A. (2011). *Federal student loan programs: Risks to students and taxpayers.* Retrieved from http://americanactionforum.org/uploads/files/research/Student_Loans_AAF.pdf

Johnstone, D. B. (2011). Financing higher education: Who should pay? In P. G. Altbach, P. J. Gumport, & R. O. Berdahl (Eds.), *American higher education in the twenty-first century: Social, political, and economic challenges* (3rd ed., pp. 315–341). Baltimore: Johns Hopkins University Press.

Kotz, D. M. (2015). *The rise and fall of neoliberal capitalism.* Cambridge, MA: Harvard University Press.

Long, B. T. (2004). *The role of perceptions and information in college access: An exploratory review of the literature and possible data sources.* Boston: The Education Resources Institute.

Mettler, S. (2014). *Degrees of inequality: How the politics of higher education sabotaged the American dream.* New York: Basic Books.

Middle Income Student Assistance Act, S. 2539, 95th Cong. (1978). Retrieved from www.gpo.gov/fdsys/pkg/STATUTE-92/pdf/STATUTE-92-Pg2402.pdf

Mumper, M., Gladieux, L., King, J. E., & Corrigan, M. E. (2011). The federal government and higher education. In P. G. Altbach, P. J. Gumport, & R. O. Berdahl (Eds.), *American higher education in the twenty-first century: Social, political, and economic challenges* (3rd ed., pp. 113–138). Baltimore: Johns Hopkins University Press.

National Defense Education Act of 1958, H.R.13247, 84th Cong. (1958). Retrieved from www.gpo.gov/fdsys/pkg/STATUTE-72/pdf/STATUTE-72-Pg1580.pdf

National Vocational Student Loan Insurance Act of 1965, Cong. (1965). Retrieved from https://www.gpo.gov/fdsys/pkg/STATUTE-82/pdf/STATUTE-82-Pg1014.pdf

Perna, L. W. (2006). Understanding the relationship between information about college prices and financial aid and students' college-related behaviors. *American Behavioral Scientist, 42*(12), 1620–1635.

Price, D. V. (2004). *Borrowing inequality: Race, class, and student loans.* Boulder, CO: Lynne Rienner Publishers.

Recovery Act Board. (2015). *The Recovery Act.* Retrieved from www.recovery.gov/arra/About/Pages/The Act.aspx#act.

Slaughter, S., & Leslie, L. L. (1997). *Academic capitalism: Politics, policies, and the entrepreneurial university.* Baltimore: Johns Hopkins University Press.

Slaughter, S., & Rhoades, G. (2004). *Academic capitalism and the new economy: Markets, state, and higher education.* Baltimore: Johns Hopkins University Press.

Soederberg, S. (2014). *Debtfare states and the poverty industry: Money, discipline and the surplus population.* New York: Routledge.

St. John, E. P., & Asker, E. H. (2003). *Refinancing the college dream: Access, equal opportunity, and justice for taxpayers.* Baltimore: Johns Hopkins University Press.

Thelin, J. (2007). Higher education's student financial aid enterprise in historical perspective. In F. M. Hess (Ed.), *Footing the tuition bill: The new student loan sector* (pp. 19–40). Washington, DC: American Enterprise Institute Press.

Thelin, J. (2011). *A history of American higher education* (2nd ed.). Baltimore: Johns Hopkins University Press.

Tierney, W. G., & Venegas, K. M. (2009). Finding money on the table: Information, financial aid, and access to college. *Journal of Higher Education, 80*(4), 363–388.

United States Department of Education (U.S. DoE). (2015a). *Higher Education Opportunity Act—2008.* Retrieved from http://www2.ed.gov/policy/highered/leg/hea08/index.html

United States Department of Education (U.S. DoE). (2015b). *Recovery Act.* Retrieved from www.ed.gov/recovery

Weisbrod, B. A., Ballou, J. P., & Asch, E. D. (2008). *Mission and money: Understanding the university.* New York: Cambridge University Press.

The White House. (2015). *Higher education.* Retrieved from https://www.white house.gov/issues/education/higher-education

Winston, G. C. (1999). Subsidies, hierarchy and peers: The awkward economics of higher education. *The Journal of Economic Perspectives, 13*(1), 13–36.

Zumeta, W., Breneman, D. W., Callan, P. M., & Finney, J. E. (2012). *Financing American higher education in the era of globalization.* Cambridge, MA: Harvard Education Press.

2 Bankruptcy Means-Testing, Austerity Measures, and Student Loan Debt

Linda Elizabeth Coco

Introduction

In 2013, Senator Elizabeth Warren introduced a bill to prevent the doubling of the interest rates of federal subsidized student loans for the 2013–2014 academic year for loans provided through the U.S. Department of Education.[1] The bill sought to ensure that students receive the same interest rate for loans from the Federal Government as banks. In a letter to the director of the Federal Housing Finance Agency, Senator Warren wrote that the largest student loan lender, Sallie Mae, received an $8.5 billion line of credit from the congressionally-created Federal Home Loan Bank at a rate of $0.23%.[2] The difference between Senator Warren's proposed 3.4% interest rate and the set 6.8% interest rate is $6 billion, based on the outstanding loans in 2013. Keeping the interest at 6.8% as proposed by the several members of Congress would help the U.S. balance the budget in ten years.[3] This proposal was voted down before it could gather too much momentum. Nevertheless, Americans who seek education must still pay a significantly higher rate than large banks; in 2015–2016 the rate was even higher at 4.29%, though it dropped to 3.76% for 2016–2017. These higher interest payments generate a steady stream of revenue for the federal government, after all, and for the large banks from whom the government must borrow whenever its tax receipts and revenues don't cover its bills.

Between 2008 and 2013, the United States Department of Education (ED) earned a profit of over $101 billion from a steady stream of monthly student loan payments (Nasiripour, 2013). While educational debts comprise about 15% of the national debt, hovering a little over $1.4 trillion (U.S. Debt Clock, 2016), the stream of payments from middle- and low-income students generates about $41.3 billion in income for the federal government annually (Jesse, 2013). Forgiveness of these student loan obligations for middle- and low-income individuals, according to some, is impossible because the stream of payments goes toward paying the national deficit. This argument is proffered at the same time as tax cuts to the upper 1%[4] eliminated $3 trillion of income for the federal government from 2010 to 2014 (Bell, 2012), contrasting to the 1950s and 1960s, when the rate was over 90%.[5] It is important to note that without those tax cuts for the top 1%, the national deficit would be $600-$900 billion less than it is currently (Goldfarb, 2013).

During a visit to the University of Southern Indiana for its Innovative Speaker Series, former U.S. Federal Reserve Chairman Ben Bernanke reportedly "urged the college students in the crowd to focus on their studies."

> Find a field you enjoy, he said, but make sure it's something you can make a living at—especially if you take out student loans. For the past 30 years or so, America's middle class has been experiencing a "hollowing out" because good-paying but low-skilled jobs are disappearing. As the world becomes more technologically advanced, it's workers who learn those skills who will land good jobs. If you're in college, you need to finish. You need to get those skills.
>
> (Orr, 2015, para. 24–28)

The Federal Reserve Chairman, like many others, endorses education as the answer to the elimination of the blue collar working class employment in the United States and a path to the middle class. The importance of education amplifies the existing educational debt issue. However, as middle-class individuals seek education, they are cast into a new form of indentured servitude.

As social theorist Pierre Bourdieu (2000) explains, the political, social, and economic structure of a society imposes a particular arrangement and ordering of conditions for individuals and groups.[6] This develops and grows, becoming entrenched in daily practice. Such arrangements endure through time, resulting in particular arbitrary legal structures. The legal structures that order access to education appear neutral and natural. And yet they are extremely significant in terms of social, political, and economic power in the United States. Educational attainment is recognized as the manner in which our society determines an individual's access to collective resources and influence. Limited or conditional access to education is, therefore, detrimental to individuals.

This chapter starts by discussing the steady development of a "user-pay" approach to funding higher education for individuals as neoliberal policy became dominant in the United States. The second section describes how the Bankruptcy Code protects educational lenders, making them into a form of "super-creditor" in the process of an individual case. The third section discusses the 2005 amendments to the U.S. Bankruptcy Code, the means test and disposable income test, and educational loan monthly payment obligations. Finally, the fourth section proposes an educational loan modification mediation program that could be implemented in the bankruptcy courts to address the growing educational loan debt. The chapter concludes by linking the structure of the means test and disposable income to the neoliberal turn.

Neoliberalism and Privatization of Education

As the view of education drifts toward models of marketization, financing education becomes part of the foundation of our credit-based financial structure. As discussed in another law review by this author (Coco, 2012), since the mid-1980s, the population of the United States has experienced an increase in the price of higher education (Archibald & Feldman, 2011, p. 29) as neoliberal discourses of privatization and individualism encouraged a shift away from education as a public good and toward education as an individual investment (Levin, 2007, pp. 3–5; St. John, Daun-Barnett, & Moronski-Chapman, 2013; Tobin, 1983). Neoliberal discourse persuades state and federal legislative bodies to abandon the view that educating individuals benefits the social collective by encouraging the expansion of knowledge, protection of equality, and supporting democratic structures. The benefits of education are increasingly calculated on individual economic terms (Price, 2004). This *user-pay* vision of education emerged as normal over decades, and the resulting educational policies have led to tuition hikes (Quinterno, 2012), reductions in scholarships and grant funding for students (Mumper, 1996, pp. 80–105), and an increase in students drawing on loans to pay tuition costs (Mumper, 1996, pp. 104–106; NCES, 2008; Price, 2004, pp. 48–53). This neoliberal shift began with President Johnson and was accelerated under the Reagan Administration.

By the 1980s, the possibility to attend college for low- and middle-income students was more available than it had ever been in U.S. history (Hearn & Holdsworth, 2004, p. 40; Mumper, 1996, p. 89). The prior decade, viewed as the "golden age" in federal student aid policy, emphasized need-based grants rather than loans (Hearn & Holdsworth, 2004, p. 40; Mumper, 1996, p. 89). But with the 1980 election year commenced the incremental revision of the existing structure that continued over the following three decades (Mumper, 1996, p. 92). The 1980 amendments to HEA increased interest rates from 7 to 9% charged to student borrowers under the Guaranteed Student Loan (GSL) program, shortened the post-graduation grace period on start of repayment, and limited the federal subsidy of student loans, transferring the responsibility to parents. When President Reagan took office in 1981, his administration waged a full-scale effort against middle- and low-income student educational aid (Mumper, 1996, p. 93; St. John & Parsons, 2004, pp. 2–3). His administration, employing neoliberal approaches, dismantled the newly created social safety nets and generously decreased taxes for the rich (Tobin, 1983). The Reagan Administration championed significant cuts in federal student educational grant programs. The administration successfully replaced ever-decreasing educational grants with access to loans for students (Mumper, 1996, p. 94). By 1985, the scales tipped in favor of providing future college students with educational loans rather than federal grants. Loan financial aid surpassed federal grant aid by over $3 billion in 1985 (Cervantes et al., 2005, p. 47).

Reagan Administration approaches spread to the reauthorization in 1986 of the Higher Education Act, and Congress adopted mandates therein that made it more difficult for low- and middle-income students to qualify for and obtain Pell grants (Higher Educational Amendments of 1986, Pub. L. 99–498, Section 401–407; Mumper, 1996, p. 98). In the gap caused by the deep educational grant cuts, Congress provided liberal loan provisions allowing middle- and low-income students to borrow more per year than ever before to fund their college educations (Higher Educational Amendments of 1986, Pub. L. 99–498, Section 401–407; Mumper, 1996, p. 98). As Congress cut grant aid to students, college tuition and other educational costs grew (Cervantes et al., 2005, pp. 39–42; Higher Education Amendments of 1992, Pub. L. 102–325, Section 422; Higher Education Act of 1998, Pub. L. 105–244). Instead of addressing the pressing need for grants, the 1992 HEA reauthorization established the unsubsidized Stafford loan program, which provided federally guaranteed loans on which borrowers paid all the interest, though payment could be deferred until after graduation (Cervantes et al., 2005, pp. 39–42).

Loans have always been geared toward those who did not have the means to pay for their education, whether in one fell swoop or through monthly payments. With the development of the Stafford loan program, low- and middle-income students could now borrow unsubsidized funds to pay for their educations in addition to any grants or subsidized loans for which they qualified. Continuing the user-pay approach, the 1998 HEA reauthorization maintained the loan-to-grant-ratio in student financial aid (Cervantes et al., 2005, p. 41). At the close of the 1990s, loan aid increased 125% in comparison with only a 55% increase in grant aid over the decade (Hearn & Holdsworth, 2004, p. 42).

From 2003 to 2005, the reauthorization of HEA faced $13 billion in cuts due to budget deficits from two foreign wars. Increasing the burden on low- and middle-income students, in 2003 the Department of Education (DOE), without Congressional approval, altered the financial aid formula governing student eligibility for federal grant aid (Winter, 2003). In effect, the DOE "shaved off" hundreds of millions of dollars in Pell grants to low-income students (Winter, 2003). By 2007, federal loans accounted for 70% of the federal funding provided to students (Archibald & Feldman, 2011, p. 179). Notably, the reauthorizations of HEA in 2007 (Higher Education Act Amendments of 2007) and 2008 (Higher Education Act Amendments of 2008, Pub. L. 110–315. 122 Stat. 3078) focused primarily on loan repayment plans, interest rates, and limited loan forgiveness.

Over the last decade, Congress has declined numerous opportunities to redesign and overhaul student financial aid statutes (Burd, 2001). As a result of these approaches, the federal government has "been responsible for shifting a larger portion of the cost of higher education on to middle- and low-income students and their families" (Mumper, 1996, p. 109). This shift is explained through neoliberal narrative and the ideological shift toward neoliberalism that has occurred globally for the last forty years. This shift began to take root in the United States in the 1980s. The result is limited access to higher education. A requirement that education meet market imperatives of capitalism and competition increases as the user-pay theory dominates (Mumper, 1996, p. 109). Education as a purely individual responsibility is further ensured by the U.S. Bankruptcy Code's adoption of the Higher Education Act's non-dischargeability provisions for student loan debt.

History of Educational Lenders' "Super-Creditor"[7] Status Under the United States Bankruptcy Code

Student loan lenders from 1958–1965, private bankers from 1965–2010, and the United States Government since 2010 had or have limitless legal powers and unlimited time (i.e., no statute of limitations) to collect on student loan debts (National Consumer Law Center, 2012, p. 8). The federal government as educational loan creditor has the ability to garnish wages without a state court judgment. It can seize federal tax refunds of the student borrower, and it can limit social security payments in order to obtain repayment of student loans. Under the Bankruptcy Code, the U.S. Congress incrementally curtailed the ability to discharge educational debts (Pardo & Lacey, 2009, pp. 179, 181). The Bankruptcy Code casts the federal government and any federally sponsored student loan lender as "super-creditors" with greater powers than any other non-priority, unsecured creditor.

Under the U.S. Bankruptcy Code, the federal government lender enjoys a special carve-out (Pardo & Lacey, 2009). This power runs counter to a fundamental purpose of the bankruptcy code that individuals receive forgiveness and a fresh start free from debts in the form of the bankruptcy discharge,[8] making educational debts an exception to the general bankruptcy discharge provisions (see 11 U.S.C. §523 (a)(8)). The educational debtor is allowed only a conditional discharge of student loan debts.[9]

Before the enactment of the 1978 Bankruptcy Code, educational debts were treated as any other unsecured debt and were dischargeable. The original Bankruptcy Act of 1898 did not address student loans as a separate category of unsecured debt, and, as a result, if they existed, they were simply discharged with other similarly situated debts. In 1970, Congress created the Commission on the Bankruptcy Laws of the United States to study and recommend changes to the 1898 Act.[10] Due to the emphasis on loans rather than grants as the primary source of federal financial aid for higher education in the U.S, educational debt began to demand legislative attention. In the legislative process, a protected category of unsecured debt emerged. The federal government sought ways to protect educational lenders from borrowers who could not repay loans. As a result, educational lenders—both public and private federally sponsored—became super-creditors substantially immune from the powerful consumer protections found under the U.S. Bankruptcy Code.

The super-creditor status for educational lenders was first introduced in the 1976 Educational Amendments (Pub. L. No. 94–482, § 439A, 90 Stat 2081, 204), which was repealed and replaced by the Bankruptcy Reform Act of 1978 (Pub. L. No. 95–598, §317.) to the Higher Education Act of 1965. The amendments gave educational debts for federally insured loans a special debt status under the law. These amendments legislatively categorized student loan debt as different from all other forms of non-punitive consumer debts (H.R. Rep. No. 95–595 at 150; Ryman, 1993, p. 219). It provided that under the federal bankruptcy laws student loans would not be treated like any other unsecured debt; instead, specific requirements had to be met before an educational debt could be discharged. The "conditional discharge" was thus created.

Responding to the 1976 Educational Amendments, the Bankruptcy Review Commission reported that the discharge of student loans was "an abuse of the discharge."[11] The Commission recognized that increasing numbers of students financed their educations through loans, and that this financing may cause defaults.[12] In an attempt to protect all educational lenders, the Commission drafted a new non-dischargeability provision in the proposed Bankruptcy Reform Act for educational loans.[13] This proposed provision prevented educational debts from the general discharge, allowing only a conditional discharge tested by undue hardship (namely, "extenuating circumstances, such as illness") and a five year bar.[14] Congress then enacted this as Section 523(a)(8) of the Bankruptcy Reform Act of 1978.[15]

In 1990, Congress further restricted the conditional discharge by increasing the five-year waiting period to a seven-year waiting period for the educational debtor. Congress amended Section 523(a)(8) to read that a discharge under the bankruptcy code does not discharge an individual debtor from any educational debt unless "such loan . . . became due more than seven years before the date of filing of the petition."[16] This was the first step in limiting the conditional discharge given to student loan debtors.

Four years later, Congress passed the Bankruptcy Reform Act of 1994[17] establishing the National Bankruptcy Review Commission. One of the commission's charges was to investigate and study the principles behind declaring student loans non-dischargeable.[18] The Commission found the existing non-dischargeability provisions ineffective in solving the problem and recommended that "Congress eliminate Section 523(a)(8) so that most student loans are treated like all other unsecured debts."[19] Notwithstanding the recommendation by the Commission, Congress eliminated the seven-year requirement in 1998, as part of a Health Professions Education Act.[20] Therefore, all government-insured student loans became presumptively non-dischargeable in the absence of undue hardship.

The Bankruptcy Abuse Prevention and Consumer Protection Act of 2005 ("BAPCPA") further reduced the minimal consumer protections under the bankruptcy code for student debtors.[21] Under Section 220 of BAPCPA, the protections afforded the government and non-profit lenders are extended to private student loan lenders. Satisfying the system's neoliberal nature, private lenders now enjoy the same "super-creditor" status as the federal government in the bankruptcy system because private loans are non-dischargeable pursuant to Section 523(a)(8).[22]

Educational debtors are no longer able to discharge private educational loans that have higher interest rates and less flexibility in repayment.[23] This provision marks a change from the 1978 Bankruptcy Code, which allowed debtors to discharge a portion of their educational debts as long as a private lender held the debt.[24] Under 523(a)(8), debtors with significant student loan debt can obtain bankruptcy relief vis-à-vis those student loans only by establishing undue hardship in repaying both public and private student loans (11 U.S.C. § 523(a)(8)).

The "conditional discharge" of Section 523(a)(8) requiring a showing of "undue hardship" for the debtor and the debtor's dependents remains the only possibility for relief of student loan indebtedness (11 U.S.C. § 523(a)(8)). Considering this standard, it is important to reconsider its history and nature. First included in the Bankruptcy Code in 1978, the undue hardship language addressed a situation in which a debtor did not want to wait the five-year statutory period under the Code to have student loans discharged. Initially under the 1978 Code, a debtor with student loan debt could obtain a discharge of those obligations if the debtor allowed the statutory period to run. If a debtor chose not to wait the statutory period, the debtor was required to show that continuing to pay on the obligation posed an undue hardship on the debtor and the debtor's dependents.

A discharge under Section 523(a)(8) is further complicated because the phrase "undue hardship" is undefined in the Bankruptcy Code. The interpretation of the standard is left to bankruptcy and circuit court judges (Pardo & Lacey, 2005, pp. 405, 411). Failure to create a coherent standard has resulted in significant inconsistency and subjectivity in the standards for finding the requisite undue hardship (11 U.S.C. § 523(a)(8); Hancock, 2009, pp. 153–154). Further, the vague and indeterminate standard is inherently subjective, and results in varied treatment of debtors (11 U.S.C. § 523(a)(8)). The meaning and the decision of whether to grant a discharge rests with a particular judge, and, unfortunately, research has shown that the outcomes vary depending on the identity of the judge, the identity of the creditor, and the experience of debtor's attorney (Pardo & Lacey, 2009, pp. 233–234).

Further, the burden on the debtor to prove that his or her educational debts pose an "undue hardship" is substantial and perhaps prohibitive (Pardo & Lacey, 2009, p. 183). The debtor is expected to initiate and pay for a full-blown trial in the bankruptcy court, called an adversary proceeding, against the educational loan creditor (11 U.S.C. § 523(a)(8)). The debtor is expected to come forward with considerable evidence and expert testimony to establish illness, disability, and inability to pay. Finally, even if the educational debtor proceeds under 523(a)(8) and provides sufficient evidence, the rate of amount discharged hovers around 57% (Pardo & Lacey, 2009, p. 213). On average, debtors obtain a discharge of a little over 60% of their indebtedness (Pardo & Lacey, 2009, p. 213). Thus, the bankruptcy discharge remains a limited option for student debtors.

The inevitable result of the lack of protection under the U.S. Bankruptcy Code for student debtors is that a large portion of the population has enduring educational indebtedness with slim chance for relief. With about two-thirds (69%) of bachelor's degree recipients at public and non-profit colleges and universities graduating with significant indebtedness (an average of $28,950 per borrower) in 2014 (TICAS, 2016), up from 34% of graduates leaving college with debt in 1995–1996 (NCES, 2008), it is a significant and growing number of Americans who are going into debt to obtain an education. Thus, the shift in state and federal government educational financial aid policies away from need-based grants and Pell grants toward loans with public and private lenders who have super-creditor powers is deeply troublesome and deserves further investigation (Quinterno, 2012, p. 25).

The U.S. Bankruptcy Code's protection of student loan lenders as "super-creditors" means that a significant portion of the adult population lives under a 10–25 year (or longer) contract to pay the federal government and investors a percentage of their income, which is nothing less than 21st-century debt peonage (Galenson, 1984). Unlike the typical consumer debtor in bankruptcy, the student loan debtor is denied a fresh start through relief from his or her unsecured debts under the U.S. Bankruptcy Code. The student loan debtor is denied legal protections, freedoms, and rights given to the typical debtor in bankruptcy who is unencumbered by student loan debts. As if that's not bad enough, the 2005 amendments to the Bankruptcy Code hurt the student loan debtor in other ways too.

Student Loans under Bankruptcy Abuse Prevention and Consumer Protection Act of 2005[25]

Although long debated, a means test[26] was implemented only through the Bankruptcy Abuse Prevention and Consumer Protection Act of 2005 ("BAPCPA"). The idea of a means test, or income test for individual consumers entering into the bankruptcy process, originated in the 1930s, but was ultimately abandoned in the amending process that resulted in the 1938 Chandler Acts, the first significant revision of the 1898 Bankruptcy Act (Skeel, 2001, pp. 89–100). The means test was revived, debated, and again rejected during the overhaul of the 1898 Bankruptcy Act with the adoption of the 1978 Bankruptcy Code (Skeel, 2001, p. 154). The concept again emerged in discussions surrounding the 1984 amendments to the Code, but resulted only in the creation of nebulous and undefined Section 707(b) substantial abuse test (Skeel, 2001, pp. 194–196). Finally, in 2005 with the adoption of BAPCPA, the means test was integrated into the Bankruptcy Code. Its purpose was to identify those individual human debtors with primarily consumer debts who could pay a portion of their unsecured debts[27] with "disposable income" (Skeel, 2001, pp. 204–205).

Stated differently, BAPCPA was enacted to ensure that unsecured obligations of a consumer debtor are not discharged in a Chapter 7 bankruptcy unless a debtor's annual income and disposable monthly income fall below statutory thresholds (11 U.S.C. Section 707(b)). If an individual debtor's annual income does not fall below the median income for his/her particular state and his/her disposable monthly income exceeds the amounts allowed under the Code, a debtor cannot remain in Chapter 7 bankruptcy and receive a discharge of unsecured debts under Section 727 of the Bankruptcy Code. Rather, an individual's bankruptcy case can be dismissed from Chapter 7. As a result, Chapter 13, with its three to five-year repayment plan, would be the only remaining option for an individual debtor who fails the means test calculations.

Monthly student loan payments are excluded from means test calculations for determining Chapter 7 eligibility for an individual seeking bankruptcy relief under Chapter 7.[28] The debtor's disposable monthly income for payment of unsecured debts does not include a deduction for required monthly payments for student loans. Further, for debtors seeking to create a repayment plan to pay unsecured creditors in a Chapter 13 case, student loan payments are not included in the allowable expense deductions to determine a debtor's projected monthly disposable income for payment of such creditors. Unsecured debts under the bankruptcy code are typically dischargeable debt in all chapters at the completion of the bankruptcy case.

For example, in Chapter 7 bankruptcy, an individual debtor is no longer required to pay unsecured debts when those debts are discharged at the conclusion of the Chapter 7 bankruptcy case. Unsecured debts, it is reasoned, are therefore not included in the means test calculation for a monthly expense to determine Chapter 7 eligibility. In a Chapter 13 bankruptcy case, monthly student loan payments are excluded from the calculation that determines what a debtor must pay monthly into a Chapter 13 plan. The calculation accounts for a debtor's monthly income reduced by a debtor's allowable monthly expenses. The remaining balance generates the debtor's "projected disposable income" (11 U.S.C. Section 1325(b)). That excess income must be contributed to a Chapter 13 plan for payment to the unsecured creditors. Monthly student loan payments are not identified as an expense allowed for deduction from a debtor's income to reduce the amount of a debtor's projected disposable income. Debtors must pay this projected disposable income into a Chapter 13 plan over a period of three to five years (11 U.S.C. Section 1325(b)(4)).

As discussed above, educational debts are classified as unsecured debts under the bankruptcy code. As such, they are paid under a Chapter 13 plan through a pro-rata share similar to any other general unsecured debts if the

Chapter 13 trustee allows it during the pendency of the plan. During the plan period of repayment, the interest capitalization on an educational debt is frozen by the automatic stay under the Code (11 U.S.C. Section 362(a)). Once the Chapter 13 plan is completed, the debtor is discharged and the case closed. At this point, the automatic stay is lifted and the interest once again accrues, plus all the missed interest owed is added for the period when the debtor was protected by the automatic stay. This leaves the debtor farther behind on his or her loan payments and debt obligation than when the petition was filed. In fact, individual debtors who file a Chapter 13 and pay into a Chapter 13 plan for three to five years often emerge from those payments with a greater student debt load.

Educational debts are ultimately not discharged in a Chapter 7 plan or after the completion of a Chapter 13 plan. The practical application of the means test and disposable income test in bankruptcy cases involving individuals with large student debt loads compounds an already difficult situation. BAPCPA's mandated austerity reduces the overall benefits gained from the bankruptcy process for those individuals with significant educational debt burdens. As a result, an individual with significant educational debts is denied a fresh start.

Proposing an Educational Loan Modification Mediation Program

A potentially effective approach to addressing the student loan crisis in the United States is the creation of a student loan modification program similar to the mortgage modification mediation programs established in the U.S. Bankruptcy Courts to address debtors' mortgage defaults and foreclosures. Similar to homeowners seeking the protection of the bankruptcy courts, debtors with significant student loan debt could use the bankruptcy courts' power to restructure the terms of their educational debts: adjusting interest rates and repayment periods, reducing principle, curing defaulted accounts, addressing arrearages, and considering hardship.

A student loan modification program could be crafted similar to the Mortgage Modification Mediation program created by the U.S. Bankruptcy Court and local bankruptcy practitioners in Florida. Similar to this Mortgage Modification Mediation program, a student loan debt program could be administered as part of an existing bankruptcy case either under Chapter 7 or under Chapter 13. The debtor would petition the court for a modification of the automatic stay, allowing the student loan lender to communicate with the debtor. Once a modification mediation order is entered, the debtor and the lender would participate in a mediation to determine the debtor's ability to pay, current and projected income, expenses and liabilities, property holdings, and other circumstances of the debtor.

During the mediation, the debtor can propose potential payment plans as part of his or her Chapter 13 bankruptcy or as a result of a Chapter 7 discharge. The lender could also propose payment, interest, and term options based on the debtor's ability to pay. The bankruptcy court order could require that a resolution be reached on all issues. The mediator would be required to report mediation processes to the bankruptcy judge.

A student loan modification order would be generated by the bankruptcy court providing the monthly payment, the interest rate, debt load, and the length of time for payment. The payments and amounts not included in the modification order would be discharged as an unsecured debt either in a Chapter 7 or a Chapter 13. Once the order is entered, it would bind both parties by the legal effect of a federal judge's order. This order with payment amounts, interest, and remaining balance would survive a discharge order for the debtor. The outstanding amount not accounted for in the student loan modification order would no longer exist, because the Chapter 13 plan, by court order, establishes a new contract. It is not a discharge of debt; rather, it is a new contract for payment of the existing educational debt.

The student loan modification process could function similarly to the manner in which the mortgage modification mediation process is conducted in the Middle District of Florida, Bankruptcy Court (Coco, 2015). After a debtor files a bankruptcy petition, he or she could file a motion requesting student loan mediation. The court would enter an order granting it and lifting the automatic stay for the limited interaction between an individual debtor and a lender. The mediation process could occur under the guidance of a trained mediator. An income analysis and expense consideration would be determined based on documentation. From this interaction and based on the documents provided by a debtor, a monthly payment amount can be reached, an interest rate, a total amount of indebtedness, and a term of payments. Once agreed, a debtor could integrate the proposed agreement into a Chapter 13 plan. The judge would then be able to confirm or deny confirmation of the Chapter 13 plan by court order.

Once an order confirming a Chapter 13 plan is entered, it carries the weight of law and would be binding on the parties. If a debtor successfully completes the monthly payments under the Chapter 13 plan, the debtor will receive a discharge of the remainder of the debt. The payment plan for the student loans would survive and bind the parties beyond the conclusion of a bankruptcy case.

Conclusion

Since the enactment of the Bankruptcy Abuse Prevention and Consumer Protection Act of 2005, the means test and the disposable income test have limited individuals' access to a fresh start under the 1978 Bankruptcy Code. They have diverted consumer debtors into monthly repayment plans for five years. The new provisions found in BAPCPA, as this author argues elsewhere (Coco, 2012), shift the risk and responsibility of the lending relationship onto debtors, thus furthering neoliberal policies and practices. The exclusion of student loan monthly payments from either the means test or disposable income test puts those individuals with such debt at a significant disadvantage. They are not allowed to deduct them in the Chapter 7 eligibility test, nor are they allowed to include the payment as required when calculating a Chapter 13 repayment plan. A student loan modification program could be developed that would go a long way to help college students and graduates in finding paths toward productive and responsible adult citizenship. That will better enable them to contribute to the more significant systematic monetary reform needed to supersede neoliberalism.

Acknowledgments

The author thanks G. Ray Warner, Laura Nader, Dean Leticia Diaz, Anthony G. Matricciani, M.K. Matricciani, Thomas Edens, Louis Rosen, and Bryana Dye. The idea for this chapter resulted from volunteering in the *pro se* clinic for the U.S. Bankruptcy Court for the Middle District of Florida, and the author thanks other attorneys who volunteered in the clinic and with whom the author discussed approaches to student indebtedness.

Notes

1 This Act, brought to the floor by the Senate in the 113th Congress, may be titled the "Bank on Students Loan Fairness Act." Section 3. Adjustment of Federal Direct Stafford Loan Interest Rates. (a) In general, Section 455(b)(7) of the Higher Education Act of 1965 (20 U.S.C. 1087e (b)(7)) is amended by adding at the end of the following: (E) Reduced rates for FDSL loans disbursed on or after July 1, 2013, and before July 1, 2014.
2 Senator Elizabeth Warren. Letter dated June 24, 2013. Addressed to Acting Director DeMarco of the Federal Housing Finance Agency. "According to its corporate filings, Sallie Mae was initially able to borrow on that line of credit for $0.23%. It was able to borrow at less than one-quarter of one percent interest because the government's sponsorship of the Federal Home Loan Banks allows them extraordinarily cheap access to capital. That government sponsorship was intended to bolster the banks' support for the housing market—not to be a backdoor way to subsidize highly-profitable private student lenders."
3 Elliott, Philip. Associated Press. "Student Loan Interest Rates to Double July 1." March 23, 2013. "House Republicans' budget would double the interest rates on newly issued subsidized loans to help balance the federal budget in a decade."
4 In 2014, the upper 1% paid an average income tax rate of 24.7% (*cf.* http://ctj.org/ctjreports/)
5 Urban Institute & Brookings Institution (www.taxpolicycenter.org/statistics/historical-highest-marginal-income-tax-rates).
6 See Pierre Bourdieu's *Pascalian Meditations* (2000, pp. 168–205) where he observes "Pascal himself also notes that 'custom makes authority' and constantly reminds us that the social order is merely the order of bodies" (p. 168). Bourdieu adds, "In modern society, the State makes a decisive contribution towards the production and reproduction of the instruments of construction of social reality" (p. 175).
7 A phrase generally used in bankruptcy practice to describe creditors who fall outside the mandates of the U.S. Bankruptcy Code. The author employs it to

describe the special protections given to educational lenders when the debtor is in bankruptcy. It will be discussed further below. See Shanker (1987).

8 Kesler v. Department of Public Safety, 368 U.S. 153, 184–185 (1962). Justice Black dissenting (Addressing the Court's decision to uphold a Utah state law imposing the reaffirmation of a pre-petition debt, Justice Black explains the power and purpose of the Bankruptcy Act of 1898 stating: "The Bankruptcy Act serves a highly important purpose in American life. Without the privileges it bestows on helplessly insolvent debtors to make a new start in life, many individuals would find themselves permanently crushed by the weight of obligations from which they could never hope to remove themselves and the country might, therefore, be deprived of the value of the endeavors of many otherwise useful citizens who simply would have lost their incentive for constructive work. I cannot agree with a decision which leaves the States free—subject only to this Court's veto power—to impair such an important and historic policy of this Nation as is embodied in its bankruptcy laws. I therefore respectfully dissent.") See also Robert F. Salvin. (1996). Student Loans, Bankruptcy and the Fresh Start Policy: Must Debts Be Impoverished to Discharge Educational Loans? 71 Tul.L.Rev 139, 175–176, ("With these thoughts in mind, an essential principle for interpreting undue hardship becomes evident. Student loan debtors, following bankruptcy, should be afforded a lifestyle that enables them to live with dignity to the extent possible. They should have a clear ability to afford the essentials and necessities of life at a degree of quality and quantity in line with the values and expectations of mainstream American culture. The ability to live at such a level ensures debtors' rehabilitation by providing them with a stake in their position in society. It is consistent, therefore, with the fresh start policy for student loan debtors to be permitted to have a lifestyle within the boundaries of the middle class.")

9 Testimony of Rafael I. Pardo before the House Judiciary Committee's Subcommittee on Commercial and Administrative Law held a hearing on "Undue Hardship? Discharging Educational Debt in Bankruptcy." ("Debts for student loans are exceptional insofar as they are the only type of debt that is conditionally discharged in bankruptcy—that is, the debt is not automatically discharged but can be upon the satisfaction of a certain condition.") Amer Bankr. Inst. J. 28, 8 (November 2009): 10, 66–67.

10 Pub. L. 91–354, Act of July 24, 1970, 84 Stat. 468. The Commission consisted of nine members. Three, including the chairman, were appointed by the President. Two were appointed by the speaker of the House, and two were appointed by the president of the Senate. Two were appointed by the Chief Justice. The Commission began operation in June 1971, and filed it final report with Congress on July 30, 1973 (H.R. Doc. No. 93–137 (1973) entitled "The Report of the Commission on the Bankruptcy Laws of the United States.")

11 The Report of the Commission on the Bankruptcy Laws of the United States. H.R. Doc. No. 93–137 (1973) Collier Edition reprint.

12 H.R. Rep. No. 95–595 at 148–149, Statements of Rep. James O'Hara ("the bankruptcy provision of this bill is, in my opinion, a discriminatory remedy for a "scandal" which exists primarily in the imagination. The proponents of this amendment assert that a large and growing number of students are cheating the government by utilizing a loophole in the law, which enables them to simply, easily, and harmlessly evade paying their debts. Each of the components of that argument has to examined in the cold light of fact. First, 'a large and growing number of students.' There have been nearly 8 million loans made under this program involving about 8 billion dollars. Of those, according to the office of education's own testimony before the judicial committee, there have been a total of 15,270 loans discharged in bankruptcy involving a total of $20.9 million

dollars. In other words, two-tenths of one percent of the loans made have been discharged in bankruptcy, involving less than three-tenths of one percent of the dollars. . . . [T]he second implication alleged to be supported by the statistical evidence brought before the committee is that this phenomenon is particularly pronounced among students. The facts are that it is not. Students are, indeed, going bankrupt in larger numbers than they used to but so are college presidents, garage owners, federal and state civil servants.")

13 The Report of the Commission on the Bankruptcy Laws of the United States. H.R. Doc. No. 93–137 (1973) Collier Edition reprint. App. Pt. 4(c) 4–710. (Proposed Section 4–506. Exceptions to Discharge. Subsection (a)(8). Notes: "It responds to the rising incidence of consumer bankruptcies of former students motivated primarily to avoid payment of educational loan debts. It can be anticipated that the incidents will continue to increase as greater numbers of high [sic.] educational loans become payable.")

14 The Report of the Commission on the Bankruptcy Laws of the United States. H.R. Doc. No. 93–137 (1973) Collier Edition reprint. App. Pt. 4(c) 4–432 ("Some individuals have financed their education and upon graduation have filed petitions under the Bankruptcy Act and obtained a discharge without any attempt to repay the educational loan and without the presence of any extenuating circumstances, such as illness. The Commission is of the opinion that not only is this reprehensible but that it poses a threat to the continuance of educational loan programs. The Commission, therefore, recommends that, in the absence of hardship, educational loans be non-dischargeable unless the first payment falls due more than five years prior to the petition.")

15 Bankruptcy Reform Act of 1978, Pub. L. No. 95–598, §317. (The section initially read: "A discharge . . . does not discharge an individual debtor from any debt (g) for an educational loan made, insured or guaranteed by a governmental unit, or made under any program funded in whole or in part by a governmental unit . . ., unless (A) Such loan first became due before five year . . . before the date of the filing of the petition; or (B) excepting such debt from discharge under this paragraph will impose an undue hardship on the debtor and the debtor's dependents."

16 Crime Control Act of 1990. Pub. L. No. 101–647, §3621(1), effective November 29, 1990.

17 Pub. L. No. 10–394, §603, effective October 1994.

18 Report of the National Bankruptcy Review Commission, Volume I, October 20, 1997 p. 207. The commissions findings are discussed in the next section.

19 Report of the National Bankruptcy Review Commission, p. 216.

20 The Health Professions Education Partnership Act of 1998. Pub. L. No. 105–392, November 13, 1998.

21 Bankruptcy Abuse Prevention and Consumer Protection Act (BAPCPA) of 2005, Pub. L. No. 109–8, 119 Stat. 23 (codified as amended in scattered sections of 11 U.S.C.). Most provisions of the Act became effective October 17, 2005.

22 11 U.S.C. § 523(a)(8)(B) (2012) (stating that any other educational loan that is a qualified educational loan, as defined in section 221(d)(1) of the Internal Revenue Code of 1986, incurred by a debtor who is an individual).

23 11 U.S.C. § 523(a)(8)(B) (2012).

24 See 11 U.S.C. § 523(a)(8)(i) (2012) (stating that private educational loans are not exempt). See H.R. REP. NO. 95–595 at 132–152 (1977). (discussing the dischargeability of student loans focused exclusively on the class of student loans guaranteed under the Higher Education Act of 1965. Extensive concern was expressed about potential abuse by lenders if educational loans are entirely non-dischargeable. Particularly, this view is expressed by former House Representative

James O'Hara). This is precisely what BAPCPA does: it protects the private lender.

25 Bankruptcy Abuse Prevention and Consumer Protection Act (BAPCPA) of 2005, Pub. L. No. 109–8, 119 Stat. 23 (codified as amended in scattered sections of 11 U.S.C.). Most provisions of the Act became effective October 17, 2005.

26 Initially a test of a debtor's ability to pay was proposed in the 1930s. It was rejected. In the 1970s during the drafting of the 1978 Code, a test of a debtor's ability to pay unsecured creditors was again proposed and rejected. It was not accepted until the 2005 Amendments. (Skeel, Tabb and others)

27 Unsecured debt is an obligation to pay money that is unattached to any form of collateral (e.g., medical bill, most credit cards, phone bills, personal loans, etc.).

28 Secured debt payments and priority unsecured debt monthly payments are allowed to be deducted as expenses in the means test calculations. See B122A-1 Official Bankruptcy Form, and B122A-2 Official Bankruptcy Form.

References

Archibald, R. B., & Feldman, D. H. (2011). *Why does education cost so much?* New York: Oxford University Press.

Bell, K. (2012, March 13). Eight tax breaks that cost Uncle Sam big bucks. *Bankrate*. Retrieved from www.foxbusiness.com/features/2011/08/31/eight-tax-breaks-that-cost-uncle-sam-big-money.html

Bourdieu, P. (2000). *Pascalian meditations* (R. Nice, Trans.). Stanford, CA: Stanford University Press.

Burd, S. (2001, February 2). Bringing market forces to the loan program. *The Chronicle of Higher Education*. Retrieved from http://chronicle.com/article/Bringing-Market-Forces-to-the/20801

Cervantes, A., Creusere, M., McMillion, R., McQueen, C., Short, M., Steiner, M., & Webster, J. (2005). *Opening the doors to higher education: Perspectives on the Higher Education Act 40 years later*. Round Rock, TX: Texas Guaranteed Student Loan Corporation. Retrieved from https://www.tgslc.org/pdf/HEA_History.pdf

Coco, L. E. (2012). Debtor's prison in the neoliberal state: 'Debtfare' and the cultural logics of the Bankruptcy Abuse Prevention and Consumer Protection Act of 2005. *California Western Law Review*, 49(1), 1–50. Retrieved from http://scholarlycommons.law.cwsl.edu/cgi/viewcontent.cgi?article=1002&context=cwlr

Coco, L. E. (2015). "Foaming the runway" for homeowners: U.S. bankruptcy courts "preserving homeownership" in the wake of the home affordable modification program. *American Bankruptcy Institute Law Review*, 23, 421–455.

Galenson, D. W. (1984). The rise and fall of indentured servitude in the Americas: An economic analysis. *The Journal of Economic History*, 44(1), 1–26. Retrieved from www.colorado.edu/ibs/es/alston/econ8534/SectionIII/Galenson,_The_Rise_and_Fall_of_Indentured_Servitude_in_the_Americas.pdf

Goldfarb, Z. (2013, January 2). The legacy of the Bush tax cuts, in four charts. *Washington Post*. Retrieved from https://www.washingtonpost.com/news/wonk/wp/2013/01/02/the-legacy-of-the-bush-tax-cuts-in-four-charts/

Hancock, K. E. (2009). A certainty of hopelessness: Debt, depression, and the discharge of student loans under the bankruptcy code. *Law & Psychology Review*, 33, 151–166.

Hearn, J. C., & Holdsworth, J. M. (2004). Federal student aid and the shift from grants to loans. In E. P. St. Johns & M. Parsons (Eds.), *Public funding of higher education: Changing contexts and new rationales* (pp. 40–59). Baltimore: Johns Hopkins University Press.

Higher Education Act of 1998, Pub. L. 105–244.

Higher Education Act Amendments of 2007, Pub. L. 110–315 (August 14, 2008).

Higher Education Act Amendments of 2008, "Higher Education Opportunity Act," Pub. L. 110–315. 122 Stat. 3078.

Higher Educational Amendments of 1986, Pub. L. 99–498 (March 12, 1987).

Higher Educational Amendments of 1986, Pub. L. 99–498, Section 401–407.

Higher Educational Amendments of 1992, Pub. L. 102–325, Section 422.

H.R. Rep. No. 95–595 at 150.

The Institute for College Access & Success (TICAS). (2012, October). *Student debt and the class of 2011*. Retrieved from http://ticas.org/sites/default/files/pub_files/classof2011.pdf

The Institute for College Access & Success (TICAS). (2016, October). *Student debt and the class of 2015*. Retrieved from http://ticas.org/sites/default/files/pub_files/classof2015.pdf

Jesse, D. (2013, November 25). Government books $41.3 billion in student loan profits. *Detroit Free Press*. Retrieved from www.usatoday.com/story/news/nation/2013/11/25/federal-student-loan-profit/3696009/

Levin, J. S. (2007). *Nontraditional students and community colleges: The conflict of justice and neoliberalism*. New York: Palgrave Macmillan.

Mumper, M. (1996). *Removing college price barriers: What government has done and why it hasn't worked*. Albany, NY: State University of New York Press.

Nasiripour, S. (2013, April 17). Student loan rates boost government profit as debt damps economy. *Huffington Post*. Retrieved from www.huffingtonpost.com/2013/04/09/student-loan-rates-debt-economy_n_3048216.html

National Center for Education Statistics (NCES). (2008, February). *National trends in undergraduate borrowing II: Federal student loans in 1995–96, 1999–2000, and 2003–04: Postsecondary education descriptive analysis report*. Retrieved from http://nces.ed.gov/pubs2008/2008179rev.pdf

National Consumer Law Center. (2012, July). *The student loan default trap: Why borrowers default and what can be done*. Retrieved from www.studentloanborrowerassistance.org/wp-content/uploads/2013/05/student-loan-default-trap-report.pdf

Orr, S. (2015, March 23). Former Fed chair Ben Bernanke speaks at USI. *Evansville Courier & Press*. Retrieved from http://archive.courierpress.com/news/local/former-fed-chair-ben-bernanke-speaks-at-usi-ep-1005591569-324601841.html

Pardo, R. I., & Lacey, M. R. (2005). Undue hardship in the bankruptcy courts: An empirical assessment of the discharge of educational debt. *University of Cincinnati Law Review*, 74(2), 405–530.

Pardo, R. I., & Lacey, M. R. (2009). The real student-loan scandal: Undue hardship discharge litigation. *American Bankruptcy Law Journal*, 83(1), 179–235.

Price, D. V. (2004). *Borrowing inequality: Race, class, and student loans*. Boulder, CO: Rienner Publishers.

Quinterno, J. (2012). *The great cost shift: How higher education costs undermine the future middle class*. New York: Demos. Retrieved from www.demos.org/sites/default/files/publications/TheGreatCostShift_Demos_0.pdf

Ryman, A. (1993). Contract obligation: A discussion of morality, bankruptcy, and student debt. *Drake Law Review*, 42(1), 205–224.

Shanker, M. G. (1987). A bankruptcy superfund for some super creditor from Ohio to midtlantic and beyond. *The American Bankruptcy Law Journal*, 61(2), 185–194.

Skeel, D. A. (2001). *Debt's dominion: A history of bankruptcy law in America.* Princeton, NJ: Princeton University Press.

St. John, E. P., Daun-Barnett, N., & Moronski-Chapman, K. M. (2013). *Public policy and higher education: Reframing strategies for preparation, access and college success.* New York: Routledge.

St. John, E. P., & Parsons, M. D. (Eds.). (2004). *Public funding of higher education: Changing contexts and new rationales.* Baltimore: Johns Hopkins University Press.

Tobin, J. (1983). The conservative counter-revolution in economic policy. *The Journal of Economic Education*, 14(1), 30–39.

U.S. Debt Clock. (2016). Retrieved from www.usdebtclock.org

Winter, G. (2003, June 13). Change in aid rule means larger bills for college students. *New York Times*. Retrieved from www.nytimes.com/2003/06/13/us/change-in-aid-rule-means-larger-bills-for-college-students.html

3 African American Student Loan Debt
Deferring the Dream of Higher Education

Cynthia D. Levy

Deferred Dreams

When Langston Hughes (1951) penned his famous poem about Harlem, New York, and asked, "What happens to a dream deferred?" he probably never could have guessed that obtaining a college education would lead to deferring the American Dream. African Americans, Hispanics, and other racial and economic minority groups have viewed a college degree as a ladder for upward socioeconomic mobility and an opportunity for achieving the American Dream. Today, many African American and Hispanic college graduates experience what Langston Hughes deemed to be "A Dream Deferred." These graduates leave college with massive amounts of student loan debt. Even more challenging for them, when they transition into the work force, they are confronted with a poor job market that is reluctant to hire them (Weissmann, 2013). Approximately 12% of African Americans with post-secondary degrees are unemployed, compared to 5.6% of other races combined (Ross, 2014). At the time of writing this chapter—fall of 2016— the overall unemployment rate for African Americans in the United States is 22.9% (Bureau of Labor Statistics, 2016).

Ironically, African American and Hispanic college graduates are worse off than their parents and grandparents; in fact, many experience the "last-hired-but-first-fired" phenomenon, which in many ways excludes them from higher-paying positions that would afford them the ability to repay their student loan debt. College graduates of color—both African American and Hispanic—are not experiencing the upward mobility their college degrees theoretically would have provided them; rather, they quickly are becoming, and remaining, a part of the "working poor" (read: part of a permanent underclass). Approximately 81% of African American college undergraduates and 67% of Hispanic undergraduates leave college with student loan debt, compared to 63% of White undergraduates who leave college with debt (Flores, 2016; Huelsman, 2015a). These college graduates were far more likely to use federally funded student loans to pay for their education and are more likely to default on their loans (Deming, Goldin, & Katz, 2012).

I am a part of the 81%, having incurred a total college debt of nearly $80,000 to pay for one undergraduate degree (B.A. in English Secondary Education), two intermediate degrees (M.A. in English and M.A. in Educational Leadership), and one terminal degree (Ed.D. in Educational Leadership). I know from personal experience how unaffordable student loan debt can cripple one's life financially, and how it has caused many to join the "working poor." This inequitable amount of student loan debt, coupled with fewer job opportunities, has driven many African Americans into the ranks of a permanent underclass. To illustrate, in 2014, the average income of African Americans nationwide was $35,398. That same year, Whites earned nearly 58% more, making on average $60,256 (DaNavas-Walt & Proctor, 2015). African Americans make up less than 15% of the American population, but they receive far less from their higher education (Huelsman, 2015a). America's neoliberal higher education system results in raced and classed outcomes for its citizens: African Americans have higher student loan debt than their Asian/American and White counterparts, and the poor are disproportionate carriers of student loan debt. Additionally, nearly 40% of African American undergraduates leave college without a degree but with student loan debt compared to 29% of their White counterparts (Huelsman, 2015a).

This chapter focuses specifically on neoliberalism and African American student loan debt for several reasons: (1) African Americans are more likely to be unemployed or underemployed than Asians, Hispanics, and Whites; (2) African Americans are targeted by for-profit postsecondary learning institutions and are more likely to incur higher student loans from these institutions than other races; and (3) more African Americans leave both for-profit and traditional colleges and universities with student loan debt and without a degree than other races. These three factors lead to unique economic hardships for African Americans.

Neoliberalism: The Chicago Context

The desire to attend college with the intention of becoming a contributing member of society as a public school teacher has been financially costly for many students. In fact, the high amount of student loan debt has forced many of these aspiring young educators to live in poverty. Currently, student loan debt in the United States is a $1.4 trillion problem, and it continues to grow. Students of the class of 2015 graduated with an average of $35,051 in student loan debt (Grinstein-Weiss, Perantie, Taylor, Guo, & Raghavan, 2016; Kantrowicz, 2016). And, according to Picchi (2016), "Members of the class of 2016 who borrowed to finance their degrees will leave college with a record level of debt: $37,173 per student on average . . ." (para. 2). Student loan debt has grown nearly 300% in the last decade (Coy, 2012). Given the increasing costs of college education, these debts are not optional for most students who take them on, as I know from personal experience.

Throughout my nine-and-a-half years at the now-threatened Chicago State University (CSU)—where I earned four degrees—I had to take out federal student loans to pay for tuition, books, and materials, and to make up for lost income that resulted from switching from full-time to part-time work in order to concentrate on my studies.

It is also important to note that, while the cost of obtaining a college degree has steadily increased over the past two decades, federal and state aid has remained stagnant for college students, especially for African Americans (Austin, 2010; Deming, Goldin, & Katz, 2012; Grinstein-Weiss, Perantie, Taylor, Guo, & Raghavan, 2016). As noted earlier, the average student loan debt is nearly $40,000 for students who attend for-profit colleges (Snider, 2014), and relatively few college students graduate without any student loan debt. Collegians in Illinois are no exception. The average amount of student loan debt in Illinois grew 51% from 2004 to 2014, according to Flores (2016).

How does neoliberalism play a role in this debt crisis? Cassell and Nelson (2013) describe neoliberalism as an "invisible hand" in free-market, private-interest-driven economics. The overarching narrative of neoliberalism, and of the student loan debt crisis, is that of "pay to play." African Americans acquire student loans to pay for education at postsecondary public or private learning institutions. This means that, while many college students will personally have to bear a large financial cost to obtain a postsecondary education, this cost is even greater for African American students. In their study, Addo, Houle, and Simon (2016) found that "racial differences in student loan debt are not solely a product of differences in family economic and social resources, and that wealth—a key family resource—is not as protective from debt accumulation among blacks as it is for whites" (p. 74). Huelsman (2015b) contends that for-profit postsecondary learning institutions target African Americans because, as highly oppressed people, they are easy prey. Neoliberal higher education encourages competition within the financial aid "free market," which, in turn, leads students to finance their education mostly through loans because of a reduction in grant-based aid. Neoliberal higher education policy and practice play a central role in the ever-increasing interest rates student loan borrowers are commanded to pay.

This supposed "free market" approach for establishing the "cost" of formal higher education has allowed both non-profit and for-profit colleges/ universities to increase their tuition costs and to shift from being a public educational system to a privatized one. The entrenchment of a neoliberal higher education financing mindset has also allowed the Department of Education to become a quasi-lender that profits from student indebtedness (Grinstein-Weiss, Pernatie, Taylor, Guo, & Raghavan, 2016; Nasiripour, 2014).

In Illinois, these problems were and still are further compounded by the state budget impasse. State colleges and universities found themselves in dire straits when the state failed to pass a 2015–16 state budget and appropriate funds for higher education. This budget deadlock threatened to force the closure of CSU and to adversely affect many other state schools. On April 25, 2016, Illinois Governor Bruce Rauner signed Senate Bill 2059 into law, which provided the necessary short-term funding for Illinois colleges and universities, including CSU. It also provided funds for Monetary Assistance Plan (MAP) grants (Hinz, 2016), for low-income college students, and for the Illinois Math and Science Academy, a state-wide magnet school for 10th–12th graders founded in 1985. Thus, colleges and universities throughout the state of Illinois were able to meet their obligations and continue to serve students enrolled in postsecondary programs. Although this budget impasse was temporarily resolved, the disinvestment in postsecondary education is still painfully obvious. With no state budget for 2016–2017 either, stop-gap funding for colleges and universities for half of 2016–2017 was signed into law July 1, 2016, but only at 85–90% of what was appropriated in 2014–2015. As of March 2017, no funds for the second half of the fiscal year (January–June) had been appropriated.

State disinvestment, under the guise of austerity measures in higher education, by the Illinois state legislature and governor has had a profound effect on many of the state's colleges and universities. For instance, CSU has been adversely affected by Governor Rauner's "turn around agenda" effort allegedly to balance the state budget by withholding state funding for colleges and universities. Peck (2015) discusses how neoliberalism's adoration of austerity causes constituent citizens to become disinvested from, and eventually dumped from, government protection. The fact that CSU was forced to cancel its spring break and to hold its commencement ceremony a month earlier is a concrete example of how college students are being disinvested of higher education by the state of Illinois. Moreover, in March 2016, CSU sent out 900 layoff notices in preparation for possible closure (Douglas-Gabriel, 2016). Because it had not received state appropriations, CSU did not have enough money to pay its expenditures.

As an alumnus of CSU, I know firsthand the benefits that this postsecondary institution offers to lower-income students and their families. Neffer Kerr (2016), a CSU alumnus, explains how CSU helped her to shred the stereotype of "African American single parent" and instead to be, and be perceived as, a successful, productive member of society. In her article "How Chicago State University Saved My Life and Helped Me Shed the Single Mother Stereotype," published in *Chicago Now*, Kerr writes the following:

> As a science major, Chicago State University is where I truly learned how to write and present my ideas in an eloquent manner. During my tenure at CSU, I worked as a research assistant in the Chemical Sciences and Engineering division at Argonne National Laboratory as well as in the Pulmonology lab at the University of Chicago. These are the types

of opportunities this particular institution provides to students from under resourced communities. I would have never been able to accomplish the things that I've done if it were not for being a student of CSU.

(Kerr, 2016, para. 1)

Kerr's experiences at CSU are not unique. CSU has helped many students in similar situations to obtain college degrees and enter into the world as productive, contributing citizens. Because Governor Rauner and the state legislature took more than 10 months to appropriate funds for higher education and didn't pass a state budget in FY2016 (CTBA, 2016) or, so far, for FY2017, CSU and the nearly 5,000 students it serves are still being potentially displaced as a result. CSU has announced the layoff of nearly 300 employees, with more potential layoffs in the future. Because of the neoliberal free-market approach embraced by Rauner, the survival of CSU and other Illinois higher-education institutions remains in limbo. CSU has traditionally served a lower-income, predominantly African American student population, and its possible closure could be devastating, displacing nearly 5,000 deserving students and leaving them to scramble to find other ways to complete their programs. Additionally, the possible closure of CSU would leave some 900 employees without jobs and would have a profound effect on their economic welfare. In fact, Rauner's neoliberal agenda has far-reaching effects across the educational spectrum; austerity and lack of annual budgets are destabilizing the current system of public K–12 as well as higher education. Rauner blocked the passage of a $36 billion state budget in an effort to reconstruct the collective bargaining rights of educators and other public employee groups.

These types of extreme measures pass the burden of funding higher education on to college students. Rauner's obstruction also opens the door for more privatization of the Illinois higher educational system in the future (Douglas-Gabriel, 2016). As we have seen, the increasing privatization of higher education has already had adverse effects on college students— especially poor, first-generation, and students of color—who rely heavily upon state and federal financial assistance to fund their college education. For example, college students who qualify for state aid in Illinois, such as the Pell and Monetary Award Program (MAP) grants, will be forced to pay a larger portion of their tuition out-of-pocket if these grants are not funded. The lack of MAP funding impacts Illinois colleges and universities because they cannot enroll and register MAP-eligible students.

How do these state budget fights impact students like Kerr (2016) who are trying to improve themselves, become more productive members of society, and achieve some form of the American Dream? According to the Illinois Student Assistance Commission's (ISAC, 2016) "2015 Data Book," 75% of Illinois college students receive some form of state or federal financial aid for college. Between 2001 and 2015, the number of applications for college state aid in Illinois grew by more than 50%. ISAC received 400,000 applications for state aid in 2001. In 2015, ISAC reported receiving over 800,000 requests for state aid. In light of the current Illinois budget crisis, a large number of students receiving state aid to attend these universities may be forced to either leave college without a degree or take out more student loans to cover the cost of their education.

"Montage of a Dream Deferred"

When President Lyndon Johnson signed the Higher Education Act in 1965, he declared that "a high school senior anywhere in this great land of ours can apply to any college or any university in any of the 50 States and not be turned away because his family is poor" (as cited in Huelsman, 2015a, p. 4). He probably never imagined that lower- and middle-class students would be leaving college with such high debt burdens coupled with such dismal job prospects that higher education might not be worth their time and investment (Huelsman, 2015b). Illinois Governor Rauner, a business-man through-and-through, has firmly rooted his governing policies within a neoliberal capitalist ideology. With cuts to state financial aid for Illinois residents, Rauner has begun the process of shifting the responsibility of the government to Illinois constituents. Making matters far worse, in recent months, Rauner has announced cuts to Temporary Assistance for Needy Families (TANF) and other social welfare programs. Many of those affected by the cut to TANF also qualify for state and federal financial assistance to attend college (Peck, 2015). Cuts in state and federal financial aid as-sistance increase the likelihood that poor, African American, and Hispanic students will acquire astronomical student loan debt out of financial neces-sity, not personal choice. According to Huelsman (2015a), "Given racial wealth disparities, black students are far more likely to be low-income and thus be eligible for Pell Grants, and are also far more likely to need to bor-row, and thus be eligible for student loans" (p. 11). But what happens when these students receive monthly student loan bills once they graduate, paying perhaps $1,500 per month for what seems like a lifetime, like me? I raise a question many of the contributors in this book ask in one form or another: Was college worth it?

Many college students are taking out student loans to fund associate degrees as well, and 57% of Blacks leave community colleges and two-year institu-tions with student loan debt. Nearly 30% of undergraduates leave school without earning a degree and face student loan default (Cunningham & Kienzl, 2011). Pinto and Mansfield (2005) found that lower-income students were more likely to carry higher student loan balances and more likely to have difficulties paying or to default on student loans. As was previously mentioned, African American undergraduates are more likely to need finan-cial assistance in the form of student loans than their White counterparts.

In 2014, Chicago Mayor Rahm Emanuel introduced the Star Chicago Scholarship, which pays for tuition, fees, and books at any City College of Chicago. While the Star Scholarship provides opportunity to some students—"qualified" students possessing a 3.0 or higher G.P.A. can access this scholarship—it is neoliberal and merit-based. The Star Chicago Scholarship fails to serve the communities that the City Colleges have historically served: lower-income students; older and non-traditional students; students of color; and students who have had G.P.A.s below 3.0. With cuts to state financial aid for college, traditionally struggling students from lower socioeconomic statuses will be forced into the corner: either acquire student loan debt to supplement the cost of community college or to pay for the cost of a stronger four-year college, or give up the dream of college. CSU represents one of very few affordable four-year colleges geared toward preparing underserved populations of African American and other minority students in Chicago (Bosman, 2016). These students might not have been accepted to a four-year postsecondary learning institution if CSU did not exist.

Giroux and Evans (2015) argue that certain groups and individuals are "consigned to zones of abandonment"; they write that the "expansive politics of disposability can be seen in the rising numbers of homeless, the growing army of debt-ridden students whose existing and future prospects remain bleak . . ., and widespread destruction of the middle class by new forms of debt servitude" (Giroux & Evans, 2015, p. 4). With the shrinking middle class and cuts in funding to schools that serve high populations of minorities, it is not difficult to identify those who fall into the "disposable" zones of our society. These are the types of communities especially targeted by for-profit postsecondary learning institutions. For many, the allure of obtaining a fast-tracked education from a for-profit higher learning institution is the gateway into financial (in)security.

For-Profit Institutions and Student Loan Debt

Over the past two decades, for-profit postsecondary learning institutions have rapidly increased in number. These postsecondary schools tend to appeal to minority non-traditional students, specifically African American and Hispanic students. Most students who attend for-profit postsecondary school receive some form of state and/or federal financial assistance, such as state MAP and Federal Pell grants and subsidized and unsubsidized student loans (Deming, Goldin, & Katz, 2012; Huelsman, 2015a). For-profit higher education institutions exist to generate a profit for their investors and top executives. The largest for-profit institution of higher education in 2015 was the Apollo Group. At its height in 2009, the Apollo Group made $580 million (Deming, Goldin, & Katz, 2012, p. 16). The more students who enroll in their programs, the more money the for-profit college will receive.

Deming, Goldin, and Katz (2012) offer the following definition of for-profit colleges and universities: "[A]t its simplest level, [it] is a group of institutions that give post-secondary degrees or credentials . . ." (p. 5). From a neoliberal perspective, for-profit institutions have fewer constraints or salary limits on how much top managers can be paid (Deming, Goldin, & Katz, 2012). As private-sector, for-profit institutions have increased in number, so too have the salaries of their owners, chief executive officers (CEOs), and other executive level managers. For example, Andrew Clark, the CEO of Bridgepoint Education, Inc., and Charles Edelstein, the co-CEO of the Apollo Group, Inc., made $20 million and $11 million respectively in 2009. Many of these private for-profit institutions are considered Title IV institutions and meet the state and federal guidelines to receive financial aid for their students, and in large part they attract lower income African American and Hispanic students who qualify for state and federal aid (Deming, Goldin, & Katz, 2012; Huelsman, 2015a).

To be considered a Title IV institution, colleges and universities—including private for-profit institutions—must be accredited by one of the accrediting agencies approved by the United States Department of Education. One of the requirements to get and maintain accreditation is that for-profit colleges and universities must enroll students who have earned either a secondary diploma from a high school or earned a general education diploma (GED) (Deming, Goldin, & Katz, 2012). Fitting into neoliberalism's model, for-profit colleges and universities have tailored their focus to attract nontraditional students. Their rationale for offering accelerated curricula and programs is mutually beneficial for generating profit: (1) it allows a student to finish a program in a shortened period, and (2) it increases the number of students that the institution can enroll. This, in turn, increases the profit for the college or university. Deming, Goldin, and Katz (2012) found that students leave (graduate from or drop out of) for-profit colleges/universities with larger student loan burdens: "For-profit students end up with higher unemployment and 'idleness' rates and lower earnings from employment six years after entering programs than do comparable students from other schools" (p. 4).

For-profit colleges and universities hold the gravest implications for African American and Hispanic students. Not only are their students saddled with high amounts of student loan debt, but the cost of attendance is comparatively higher than that of traditional two-year colleges and community colleges. Sixty-five percent of African American and 67% of Hispanic students who attend for-profit learning institutions are likely to drop out with higher student loans (Huelsman, 2015a; Grinstein-Weiss, Perantie, Taylor, Guo, & Raghavan, 2016). Because these students leave for-profit colleges and universities without a certificate or degree, they are less likely to find a job that pays a living wage. In fact, nearly 70% of African American students who drop out of college default on their student loan debt, compared to less than 50% of Whites (see Huelsman, 2015a). Dropping out of college not only results in lower income for African Americans and Hispanics, but carrying higher student loan debt while working in significantly lower-paying jobs makes becoming financially independent nearly impossible. Huelsman (2015a) points out that "low-income, Black and Latino students almost universally must borrow to attain a degree, while white, middle- and upper-class students are far less likely to need to borrow" (p. 5). African American and Hispanic college-bound students, thus, face more limited choices in where they can afford to attend post-secondary school. For-profit colleges/universities also have a higher population of older students and women (Deming, Goldin, & Katz, 2012).

Cassell and Nelson (2013) contend that the "dismantling of the public sector is a natural accompaniment" of the neoliberal assault on public higher education (p. 248). Fly-by-night for-profit higher education institutions are increasingly competing with traditional public educational institutions with promises of accelerated courses and quicker routes into the job market. Cassell and Nelson (2013) point out that the "impact of the neoliberal agenda and policy suite runs in line with the general proposition upon which they are based. At the most basic level, this means that the ethos of education is being steadily refocused away from the idea of education as public good by the state as a right of citizenship" (pp. 250–251). For-profit schools are composed of nearly 45% African American and Hispanic students (Bennett, Lucchessi, & Vedder, 2010; Huelsman, 2015b). At the same time, traditional colleges and universities are being shaped into privatized institutions where the profit outweighs the public good (Letizia, 2015).

Traditional colleges and universities are becoming training grounds for workers, rather than cultivators of democratic citizens. This trend is the primary motivation of neoliberalism (Cassell & Nelson, 2013). According to McCafferty (2010), "Overall, the increasingly pervasive 'enterprising education' agenda amounts to an officially sanctioned blunting of potential critique of a market-driven, neoliberal economy from within and beyond education" (p. 543). Much like private sector businesses, a large number of for-profit colleges/universities are corporations that are publicly traded on the stock market (Bennett, Lucchesi, & Vedder, 2010). For-profits thrive on increasing their student enrollment numbers. Because the majority of students enrolling in for-profits are lower-income and/or first-generation African American and Hispanic students, many for-profits receive funding from state and federal financial aid. Deming, Goldin, and Katz (2012) found that audits of many of these for-profit colleges/universities revealed "highly aggressive and even borderline fraudulent recruiting techniques" (p. 4).

Implications

African American, Hispanic, and low-income first-generation students are more likely to obtain and bear higher student loan burdens than White students. When states such as Illinois face budget crises, the withholding of state funding has a profound effect on these students. Inaction on the part of legislators jeopardizes the futures of students who might not otherwise have access to an affordable education. For instance, inaction on the part of the Illinois legislature threatened the very future of CSU, a university that serves historically and contemporarily underserved student populations and relies heavily upon state and federal funding. This is of particular concern to me not only because it is my alma mater but also because I want CSU to be there when the public school students I currently serve are ready for college. The recontextualization of neoliberalism in terms of race and economic power causes traditional higher-education institutions to move further and further out of reach for many poor and non-White students.

A second concern of mine relates to adequately addressing the lack of accessible, affordable postsecondary education for lower-income students. As public colleges and universities move beyond the reach of African American students, private for-profit colleges/universities attract more non-traditional minority students, especially African Americans. Huelsman (2015a) posits that African American students are more likely to attend for-profit higher-learning institutions and are also most likely to borrow more and less likely to graduate than their counterparts (p. 6). The neo-liberal ideology of market-driven education has created more workers and fewer viable opportunities for gainful employment. In fact, Austin (2010) argues, "[a]mong recent college graduates, once again African Americans are the worst off. In the first half of 2007, the unemployment rate for black recent college graduates was 8.4%", whereas the unemployment rate during the same period for Hispanic recent grads was 4.1% and for White recent grads 4%, though it increased thereafter for Hispanics more rapidly than for Whites (p. 5). Austin concludes that "Black college graduates have the misfortune of having the highest unemployment rates and the largest share of graduates with high education loan debt" (p. 8).

The third concern I have is about the student population that finds itself overrepresented at for-profit colleges and universities. Huelsman's (2015b) study found that 90% of African Americans use student loans to pay for tuition at for-profit schools and leave with about $40,000 in student loan debt. Because African American college graduates have a higher rate of unemployment than their White counterparts, they are the most vulnerable. As neoliberalism advocates for the privatization of education, the economic outlook for minority graduates—and African American graduates in particular—remains bleak. Since higher education has become a "pay to play" enterprise, opportunities are becoming costlier and further out of the reach of those who could most benefit from a college education.

Conclusion

> *What happens to a dream deferred?*

When the dream of becoming a doctor was deferred for Dennis Brown, as noted in Jamal Watson's (2013) article "Drowning in Debt," it remained deferred. Brown states, "I have so many loans from my undergraduate years, and the cost of medical school is simply too much" (Watson, 2013, p. 9). Addo, Houle, and Simon (2016) found that the average cost of tuition for postsecondary public and private education has increased 57% and 93% respectively. While tuition costs have continued to rise, state and federal financial aid for postsecondary education has not kept up with the increased cost. African American collegians rely more heavily on student loans to pay for college than their White counterparts: "Black debtors owe $5,000 to $10,000 more that white debtors on average" (Addo et al., 2016, p. 65).

> *Does it dry up like a raisin in the sun?*
> *Or fester like a sore—*
> *and then run?*

In a free market that emphasizes competition, for-profit colleges and universities serve as predators that are allowed to prey upon lower-income minorities, especially African Americans. Rosalyn Harris, a single mother described in *Harvard Law Review* (2015), found that her search for opportunities for a better life became more of a struggle as she sought gainful employment in her field after completing a two-year criminal justice program at Everest College (p. 2018).

Free-market competition has afforded for-profits the ability to expand at a much faster rate than traditional colleges and universities; their enrollments have increased more than 200% over the past 20 years (Huelsman, 2015b). Yet for-profits have a poor record of success. Large for-profits have recently come under scrutiny for their predatory recruiting practices, including inflated data on post-education employment and graduation rates (Huelsman, 2015a, 2015b). As reported in *Harvard Law Review* (2015), students who obtain degrees and certificates from for-profit colleges are not as readily accepted by employers (p. 2018).

> *Does it stink like rotten meat?*
> *Or crust and sugar over—*
> *like a syrupy sweet?*

In the build up to and in the wake of the housing market crash, the neoliberal project has ushered in an era of free-market overload. Deming, Goldin, and Katz (2012) found that for-profit college/university enrollment tripled over the past decade. While for-profit postsecondary institutions account for approximately 11% of college students, they account for more than 40% of student loan debt (*Harvard Law Review*, 2015, p. 2019). More than 60% of African Americans who do not complete their higher education cite student loan debt as the catalyst for not completing their programs (Addo et al., 2016, p. 65). Because African Americans are more likely to default on their student loan debt than their Asian, Hispanic, and White counterparts,

African Americans will continue to lag academically and economically if the opportunities to access high-quality higher education dry up (Addo et al., 2016; Deming et al., 2012). This surely will result in their dreams being deferred or mobilized into black lives mattering for monetary reform.

> *Maybe it just sags*
> *like a heavy load.*
> *Or does it explode?*
> ~ *Langston Hughes,*
> "Harlem"
> (1994/1951)[1]

Note

1 Ober grants the right to use the poem in the world in countries not subject to Random House Contract 14706 in print on paper form. Ober grants the electronic display right in the world in English for a period of ten years. Additional rights by permission of Harold Ober Associates Incorporated.

References

Addo, F. R., Houle, J. N., & Simon, D. (2016). Young, black, and (still) in the red: Parental wealth, race and student loan debt. *Race Social Problems, 8,* 64–76.

Austin, A. (2010, October 28). *Graduate employment gap: Students of color losing ground* (Briefing Paper #282). Economic Policy Institute. Retrieved from www.epi.org/publication/graduate_employment_gap_students_of_color_losing_ground/

Bennett, D. L., Lucchesi, A., & Vedder, R. R. (2010). For-profit higher education: Growth, innovation and regulations. *Center for College Affordability and Productivity.* Retrieved from http://files.eric.ed.gov/fulltext/ED536282.pdf

Bosman, J. (2016, April 9). Chicago state, a lifeline for poor blacks, is under threat itself. *New York Times.* Retrieved from www.nytimes.com/2016/04/10/us/chicago-state-a-lifeline-for-poor-blacks-is-under-threat-itself.html

Bureau of Labor Statistics. (2016). Retrieved from www.bls.gov/news.release/empsit.t02.htm

Cassell, J. A., & Nelson, T. (2013). Exposing the effects of the "invisible hand" of the neoliberal agenda on institutional education and the process of sociocultural reproduction. *Interchange: A Quarterly Review of Education, 43*(3), 245–264.

Coy, P. (2012, September 18). Student loans: Debt for life. *Bloomberg.* Retrieved from www.bloomberg.com/news/articles/2012–09–18/student-loans-debt-for-life

CTBA. (2016, October 27). Illinois General Fund spending in FY2016: How elected officials cut billions in core service expenditures while worsening the deficit—all without casting a vote. *Center for Tax and Budget Accountability: Reports.* Retrieved from www.ctbaonline.org/reports/illinois-general-fund-spending-fy2016-how-elected-officials-cut-billions-core-service

Cunningham, A. F., & Kienzl, G. S. (2011). Delinquency: The untold story of student loan borrowing. *Institute for Higher Education Policy.* Retrieved from www.ihep.org/sites/default/files/uploads/docs/pubs/delinquency-the_untold_story_final_march_2011.pdf

DaNavas-Walt, C., & Proctor, B. D. (2015, September). *Income and poverty in the United States: 2014.* Washington, DC: U.S. Department of Commerce. Retrieved from

48   Cynthia D. Levy

https://www.census.gov/content/dam/Census/library/publications/2015/demo/
p60–252.pdf

Deming, D. J., Goldin, C., & Katz, L. F. (2012). The for-profit postsecondary school
sector: Nimble critters or agile predators? *Journal of Economic Perspectives*, 26(1),
139–164. doi:10.1257/jep.26.1.139. Retrieved from https://www.aeaweb.org/
articles?id=10.1257/jep.26.1.139

Douglas-Gabriel, D. (2016, February 26). Chicago State University sends layoff notices
to all employees amid Illinois budget battle. *Washington Post*. Retrieved from
https://www.washingtonpost.com/news/grade-point/wp/2016/02/26/chicago-
state-university-sends-layoff-notices-to-all-employees-amid-illinois-budget-battle/

Flores, A. (2016, March, 17). Illinois budget battle jeopardizes college access
and affordability. *Center for American Progress*. Retrieved from https://www.
americanprogress.org/issues/education/news/2016/03/17/133638/illinois-
budget-battle-jeopardizes-college-access-and-affordability/

Giroux, H., & Evans, B. (2015). *Disposable futures: The seduction of violence in the
age of spectacle*. San Francisco: City Lights Books.

Grinstein-Weiss, M., Perantie, D. C., Taylor, S. H., Guo, S., & Raghavan, R. (2016).
Racial disparities in education debt burden among low- and moderate-income
households. *Children and Youth Services Review*, 65, 166–174.

Harvard Law Review. (2015, May 9). Forgive and forget: Bankruptcy reform in the
context of for-profit colleges. *Harvard Law Review*, 128(7), 2018–2039. Retrieved
from http://harvardlawreview.org/2015/05/forgive-and-forget-bankruptcy-reform-
in-the-context-of-for-profit-colleges/

Hinz, G. (2016, April 25). Rauner signs $600 million emergency education aid bill.
Crain's Chicago Business. Retrieved from www.chicagobusiness.com/article/
20160425/BLOGS02/160429903/rauner-signs-600-million-emergency-educa
tion-aid-bill

Huelsman, M. (2015a). Betrayers of the dream: How sleazy for-profit colleges disproportionately targeted black students. *The American Prospect*, 26(3), 9–11, 13.

Huelsman, M. (2015b, May 19). The debt divide: The racial and class bias behind
the "new normal" of student borrowing. *Demos*. Retrieved from www.demos.
org/publication/debt-divide-racial-and-class-bias-behind-new-normal-student-
borrowing

Hughes, L. (1951). *Montage of a dream deferred*. New York: Holt.

Hughes, L. (1994). Harlem. In A. Rampersad & D. Roessel (Eds.), *The collected poems of
Langston Hughes* (p. 426). New York: Knopf. (First published in 1951). Retrieved from
http://library.globalchalet.net/Authors/Poetry%20Books%20Collection/The%20
Collected%20Poems%20of%20Langston%20Hughes.pdf. Also retrieved from
https://www.poetryfoundation.org/poems-and-poets/poems/detail/46548

Illinois Senate Bill 2059. (2016, April 25). *99th Illinois general assembly*. Retrieved
from www.ilga.gov/legislation/billstatus.asp?DocNum=2059&GAID=13&GA=9
9&DocTypeID=SB&LegID=90603&SessionID=88&SpecSess=

Illinois Student Assistance Commission (ISAC). (2016). *2015 Data book*. Retrieved
from https://www.isac.org/e-library/research-policy-analysis/data-book/

Kantrowicz, M. (2016, January 11). Why the student loan crisis is even worse than
people think. *Time Money*. Retrieved from http://time.com/money/4168510/why-
student-loan-crisis-is-worse-than-people-think/

Kerr, N. (2016, January 31). *How Chicago State University saved my life and helped
me shed the single mother stereotype*. Retrieved from www.chicagonow.com/

boom-show/2016/01/how-chicago-state-university-saved-my-life-and-helped-me-shed-the-single-mother-stereotype/

Letizia, A. (2015). Revitalizing higher education and the commitment to the public good: A literature review. *InterActions: UCLA Journal of Education and Information Studies, 11*(2), 1–20.

McCafferty, P. (2010). Forging a 'neoliberal pedagogy': The 'enterprising education' agenda in schools. *Critical Social Policy, 30*(4), 541–563.

Nasiripour, S. (2014, April 14). Student loan borrowers' costs to jump as education department reaps huge profit. *Huffington Post*. Retrieved from http://huffingtonpost. com/2014/04/14/student-loan-profits_n_5149653.html

Peck, J. (2015). *Austerity urbanism: The neoliberal crisis of American cities*. New York: Rosa Luxemburg Stiftung. Retrieved from www.rosalux-nyc.org/austerity-urbanism/

Picchi, A. (2016, May 4). Congrats, class of 2016: You're the most indebted yet. *CBS Money Watch*. Retrieved from www.cbsnews.com/news/congrats-class-of-2016-youre-the-most-indebted-yet/

Pinto, M. B., & Mansfield, P. M. (2005). Financially at-risk college students: An exploratory investigation of student loan debt and prioritization of debt repayment. *NASFAA Journal of Student Financial Aid, 35*(2), 22–32.

Ross, J. (2014, May 27). African Americans with college degrees are twice as likely to be unemployed as other graduates. *The Atlantic*. Retrieved from www.theatlantic.com/politics/archive/2014/05/african-americans-with-college-degrees-are-twice-as-likely-to-be-unemployed-as-other-graduates/430971/

Snider, S. (2014, October 1). 3 must know facts for students to know about for-profit colleges, student loan debt. *U.S. News & World Report*. Retrieved from www.usnews.com/education/best-colleges/paying-for-college/articles/2014/10/01/3-facts-for-students-to-know-about-for-profit-colleges-and-student-debt

Watson, J. (2013). Drowning in debt. *Diverse: Issues in Higher Education, 30*(19), 9–10.

Weissmann, J. (2013, April 4). How bad is the job market for college grads? *The Atlantic*. Retrieved from www.theatlantic.com/business/archive/2013/04/how-bad-is-the-job-market-for-college-grads-your-definitive-guide/274580/

4 Monetary Critique and Student Debt

Lucille L. T. Eckrich

Introduction

Student loan debt derives from the *systemic* source that drives capitalism, which is private power to create money. Bring that money creation power back into the government, where it constitutionally (in both senses of the word) belongs, and we eliminate the *systematic imperative* for student debt (and many other liabilities, inefficiencies, inequities, and irrationalities of our current system) and properly ground our commerce. Then, in due time yet relatively short order, it will be possible for existing debtors to pay down their debt, perhaps at a publicly approved discount for goods like higher education, and for our diverse polity to decide how best to pay for the cost of goods that we collectively and personally value, such as education, health care, clean air and water, and fertile soil, to name just a few.

This chapter develops the above thesis in four steps. The first section articulates, as succinctly as I could, the nature of money and the monetary system that follows from it. I encourage readers to read this short section carefully, as it attempts to communicate an understanding that has been millennia in the making and yet is also cutting edge. It describes money and its system as they should and can be, which differs somewhat from how they currently are. The second section shares how I and others have come to this understanding. While money is one of the wisest, most progressive, and inherently equitable of human inventions, people's efforts to make sense of money and put it into practice have also suffered some false starts and misunderstandings along the way and often been misled, so much so that the modern monetary system is antithetical to the nature of money. For that reason and for efficiency's sake, I delimit the resources I recommend to those that most help one to understand the nature of money and the monetary system that follows from it compared to the money system we currently have. The chapter's final sections describe the latter, how we got it, and how it not only led to escalating student debt but will continue to do so as long as we leave it in force. The chapter concludes by foreshadowing how it, in the context of the rest of this book, lays the ground work for Chapter 15, which details how we can achieve monetary reform and transformation and the critical role that education plays therein.

The Nature of Money and the Monetary System That Follows From It

To the best of my knowledge, money is an agreement between and among people to use it as a means of exchange. It emerges within customary or lawfully constituted communities and becomes whatever the custom or law makes receivable (i.e., legal tender) for taxes, payments, and debts within its territorial jurisdiction. It doesn't much matter what is used to signify it—cowries (mollusk shells), stones, tally sticks, other useful or useless objects, metal coins, paper notes, and numbers in accounts and via debit or credit cards have all been used—*as long as* its oneness and quantity can be and are assured and managed by its sovereign authority (lawful government) so as to maintain its purchasing power, which is to say the stability or easing of prices over time, within the community whose name it bears and commerce it lubricates. Put another way, money's essence is abstract, whereas its existence is concrete. Its *essence* is to measure value, which, as a social phenomenon that appears through production and in exchange, is a dynamic arithmetic relation between and among all goods and services traded within that community whose well-being the government exists to promote and protect. Its *existence* is established by fiat or governmental decree—hence the term "fiat money" or, in Greek, *nomisma*, which derives from the word for law (*nomos*).[1] In sum, money, in and of itself or *sui generis*, exists by law as an informational unit of account to circulate goods and services commensurably among the people who create them so as to promote their general welfare—their survival and diverse ways of flourishing together—and that of the polities they and their lawmakers/guardians comprise.

If that, in a nutshell, describes the nature of money, it follows that it is—or should be—the constitutional right and responsibility of each lawful sovereign government to create and spend its nation's money into circulation through its federal and provincial (i.e., state, county, and municipal) bodies and/or constituents in amounts sufficient for their commerce (their production and trade of goods and services) and taxation. "Sufficient" means no more and no less than is collectively needed for all members therein to survive and flourish within the ecosystem of which we humans are but a part and for which we are stewards for future generations. The role of banks in this monetary system is secondary but pivotal, namely, to provide accounting services associated with checking (demand deposits/current transactions), saving, loaning, and borrowing existing money for members—personal and corporate—of this body politic who choose to take advantage of and, thus, pay for such liquidity and investment services. The price of such services, like that of every other service or good in the economy, revolves around their average cost of production. Finally, although the primary purpose of taxes is to pay for the government's work of ensuring the common good and public infrastructure both now and for posterity, taxation also has a useful, albeit secondary, role to play in monetary policy. That is, whenever it is clear there is too much money in circulation for the common good—because there is way more money in long-term savings accounts than bankers can find producers or consumers to borrow, even at low or zero interest rates, and/or because prices are inflating—that excess money can and should be taxed out of circulation and either used to pay off any public debt or simply extinguished. If and when, sometime in the future, the money supply proves no longer sufficient, government can and should then reduce taxes and/or issue and spend new money into circulation so commerce flows anew.

How We Know This

How do we—or I—know that this is the nature of money and the monetary system that follows from it? There are a number of answers to this, all of which are preceded with the caveat that, as with all knowledge, what we know is not certain and is always subject to inquiry, revision, verification, correction, even "paradigm shifts" (Kuhn, 1970) in relation to the phenomena we are trying to make sense of, understand, and know. Were this not so, we would have no need for education on those matters—indoctrination or mere socialization into what's known to be true would suffice and be more efficient. But what if we are wrong or have overlooked something? Indoctrination and socialization are presumptuous and potentially misleading because our current knowledge may be partially or seriously mistaken or shortsighted. They also fail to prepare the next generation with the tools of inquiry they need to resolve problems that arise or make sense of matters still unknown or not deemed curriculum-worthy at present. To neglect education is to impede the enterprises of art and science through which humanity has learned so much and still has much more to learn. Furthermore, to think that we've figured anything or anyone out once and for all is to dominate it, to violate its very being, to forget "the preponderance of the object" (Adorno, 1973, pp. 183–186) and that it or others can teach us something more about it. Thus, ethically and epistemologically, we must stay critically open while striving to know something or someone as best we can. Those are values internal to science and education (Jackson, 2012; Phillips & Burbules, 2000).[2]

My own path to making sense of money has been long and sometimes circuitous but always heuristic, interdisciplinary, and analytical. These also characterize the approaches of the eclectic authors from whom I have learned the most about money and humanity's varied experiences with it over time and place, though the most common approach among them is historical. While it took until 1996 for my focus to be drawn specifically to that which mediates our trade relations and another eight years until I started to connect its micro, meso, macro, and mundo dots (Scharmer,

2009), it was my upbringing and subsequent self-conscious experiences from adolescence on—both in the United States and abroad; in suburban, small town, subsistence farming, and urban communities; in school and at work; and through community-based educational engagement and political action—that provided both the fertile territory and the compelling questions that led, and still lead, me to focus on money.[3] These questions are about the nature of value in economics, ethics, and education and what, if anything, connects the three, and about the conditions of the possibility not only of public education but also social, economic, and environmental justice and what impedes us from achieving those conditions. In what follows, I provide resources for an efficient route toward understanding not only the nature of money and the monetary system that follows from it, as described above, but also how the system legally sanctioned and institutionalized in the United States just over 100 years ago is similar to yet differs fundamentally from that and how it necessarily issues in escalating debt, student and otherwise, which are the foci of the final section of this chapter.

While money is surely relevant for us as individuals at the micro level (what the subfield of microeconomics focuses on while taking the monetary system for granted as given) and modern money is having increasingly devastating effects on our global ecosystem (the mundo level, which includes but is not limited to humans), the science of money resides primarily at the macro level, which involves large-scale or state institutions or systems within a global context of sovereign nation-states, and arguably, but secondarily, at meso levels, which lie somewhere between the micro and the macro.[4] Thus, the resources that follow focus mainly on the macro level. Viewing money from macro and meso vantage points manifests in sometimes opposing approaches to monetary reform that are succinctly presented by John Rogers (2004) in a two-page piece called "Two Sides of the Money Coin." It is a good place to start an efficient journey into monetary issues because, while macro-level transformation is, in my view, absolutely necessary first and foremost, I don't think its eventuality precludes the possibility and even economic desirability of meso-level initiatives such as local and regional complementary currencies (Kennedy, 1995, 2012). The best, most concise articulation of my both/and-but-macro-transformation-first point-of-view is the mission statement of Monetative, a monetary reform movement that began in Berlin in 2009.[5] If nothing else, give that a good read.

The next best piece for the reader strapped for time, a common plight given our existing "time-is-money" system, is a 2016 journal article by Stephen Zarlenga and Robert Poteat entitled "The Nature of Money in Modern Economy: Implications and Consequences." This is a distillation and update of Zarlenga's over 700-page 2002 book called *The Lost Science of Money*, which, though long, is best read cover to cover over a few weeks' time, rather than piecemeal, in order for its historical sweep to sink in. While not an academic by training and after working for 35 years in finance, Zarlenga (2002) spent 12 years gathering and digesting a vast amount of historical economic literature that enabled him to write "a monetary interpretation of history" (p. 8). It ranges from money in ancient times (Chapters 1–3) to an enlightened analysis of the then-forming European Monetary Union (Chapter 23, prescient in light of the 2016 Brexit decision) and, in the final Chapter (24), to a new formulation of a monetary reform proposal for the United States that was already largely conceived and introduced as a bill in the late 1930s and forms of which had already played crucial roles in U.S. history: that is, both the Continental Currency (referred to as "Continentals") with which the colonies waged the Revolutionary War (Chapter 14) and the Greenbacks that the North spent into circulation to wage the Civil War and to unify the nation with afterwards (Chapter 17) were real money in a way that most of our money today is not and hasn't been since our Federal Reserve System was instituted in 1913 (Chapters 19 and 20). But both times, the combination of elite private bankers, who understood but hid the nature of money so that it would continue to serve primarily their own interests, and the insufficient understanding of the nature of money among most people and elected leaders, despite keen interest in it among many sectors of the population from colonial days through WWI, combined to lead us astray from those right-minded attempts at real money (Chapters 14–20). Earlier parts of the book also cover the role of money as economic power shifted from the Mediterranean and Middle East northward between 800 and 1600 (Chapters 4–6, 8), the role of religion and religious powers in monetary history (Chapters 7, 13, and elsewhere), the rise of capitalism and modern money and banking first in Amsterdam and then London in the late 1500s–1700s with the global exploitation and slavery that helped to fuel them (Chapters 9–11), and the role of dominant economists and political economists in rationalizing or overlooking the significance of private control over money creation (Chapter 12 and elsewhere). This book, along with working papers and conference presentations posted on the website of the American Monetary Institute (AMI), which Zarlenga and a few others founded in 1996 and whose annual conferences I have mostly attended since the first in 2005, is an invaluable resource for anyone who wants to understand the nature, history, and possible future of money, while the co-authored article named at the start of this paragraph is a timely and time-saving resource with which to start.

A key source among many for Zarlenga was Alexander Del Mar (1836–1926), a civil and mining engineer who, starting in 1866, served as the first director of the U.S. Treasury Department's Bureau of Statistics and was a prolific historian and analyst of money whose work was largely disregarded by mainstream economics until recently. His 1895 *History of Monetary Systems*, 1896 *The Science of Money*, 1899 *The History of Money in America*, and 1899 *A History of Monetary Crimes* are only four of the over 30 books or monographs and 100 articles he wrote that I have worked with. However, two contemporary scholars—Joseph Aschheim, emeritus faculty member of the Department of Economics at the George Washington University, and George S. Tavlas, researcher and member of the Monetary Policy Council at the Bank of Greece—have done extensive work with Del Mar's *oeuvre*. Their 1985 article uncovers his influence on Irving Fisher, a Yale University economist who was one of the six authors of the 1930s program for monetary reform featured in Chapter 24 of Zarlenga's book and from which current monetary reform legislation, which I present in Chapter 15, hails. Their 2004 article summarizes Del Mar's "prescient and profound" contributions to monetary economics and discusses the possible reasons for his "academic exclusion." Finally, their 2006 article discusses the contributions of Del Mar, Knapp ([1924] a German economic historian who lived at the same time as Del Mar, who also influenced Zarlenga, and who coined the term *chartal*, from the Latin word for 'paper,' to describe a state-proclaimed unit of account called money and that, seemingly unbeknownst to Knapp, Del Mar had also theorized), and J. M. Keynes (who himself was influenced not only by Knapp but by Silvio Gesell [1958], another early 20th-century keen observer of money and banking) on our understanding of "money as numeraire," meaning as a unit of account. These three articles not only confirm the validity of Zarlenga's reading of Del Mar but are excellent, succinct sources in their own right for understanding the nature of money as articulated above and the monetary system that follows from it.

Finally, perhaps the most cutting-edge work on monetary critique and reform is that of Joseph Huber, a German emeritus professor of economic and environmental sociology, creator of "Sovereign Money," a website for new currency theory and monetary reform,[6] and member of Monetative, mentioned above. There are many valuable and more recent resources available on the Sovereign Money website, but I highly recommend *Creating New Money: A Monetary Reform for the Information Age*, a book Huber co-authored with James Robertson, co-founder of the London-based New Economics Foundation. In fewer than 70 understandable pages plus an appendix, it lays out the reasons for and facility of achieving a reform that would transform our existing monetary system into the monetary system that follows from the nature of money as articulated above. Basically, any sovereign nation that chooses to can transition from our existing private-interest-driven debt-based money system, as I describe below, to a sovereign money system, as I described above, by extending the prerogative of its government to originate all that country's money, not merely the percentage (about 3–5% today) that's issued in notes or coins, while leaving checking account and savings-and-loan services to commercial banks, where financial services properly belong. Other scholars of money and banking are contributing to this work, which is even reaching up into the highest levels of central bank research and correcting misunderstandings and clarifying processes that most bankers and even some central bankers don't fully understand or acknowledge.[7] There are authors and organizations focused on meso-level monetary reform that have also influenced my understanding,[8] but I think the resources named above (along with a 2017 book by Huber) provide a sound and efficient path toward understanding the nature of money and the monetary system we need versus the one we have.

That said, I must conclude this section with a word of caution and advice, the latter first: do not take my word for it. Yes, use my studied recommendations as points of entry into the literature and organizations involved, and stay open and attentive to what others have to teach you. But read, learn, listen, think critically, and search deeply for yourself, following the questions and leads that make most sense to you and your experience with money. For monetary reform to have any chance of success this time around, we need a critical mass of people from all walks of life who have made sense of the nature of money and its systematization instead of too easily and superficially accepting what others tell us or, worse, not thinking about it because we were schooled or socialized not to. But be forewarned: There are many partial truths and falsehoods out there and have been nearly as many missteps and false starts as firm footings and right roads along the way. Whatever else they are, the science and history of money are dialectical—always have been and probably always will be, unless we drive ourselves into a dead end.

The Money We Have and How We Got It

The key difference between the nature of money and the monetary system that follows from it, on the one hand, and our money and monetary system today, on the other, is that the former entail a public unit of account called money created and spent into circulation by each lawful government as needed to facilitate the commerce and well-being of its people, including but not limited to those who offer banking services, whereas the latter entail bank-created money lent into circulation in a system that primarily and mostly serves the interests of those who already have the vast majority of money and wealth at the expense of everyone else, human and otherwise, and does so at an exponentially escalating rate, interrupted only by the inevitable "market corrections" that allow both its beneficiaries to regroup and the system to continue yet another day. My objectives for the remainder of this chapter are three: first, to shed light on how this, our current money and monetary system, came to be; second, to explain how it, for lack of a better word, works; and third, to illustrate how it led to increasing student debt and will continue to do so as long as we leave it in place or until the system it is symptomatic of collapses in chaos or worse.

The monetary system the United States has today was institutionalized through the Federal Reserve Act, which was signed into law by President Woodrow Wilson an hour after Congress passed it on December 23, 1913, a day many people are typically otherwise focused. The Federal Reserve Act institutionalized (legally, whether or not constitutionally) for all 50 U.S. states private money-creation practices that had gradually crept into otherwise sovereign money systems here and abroad for centuries already. Del

Mar (1895/1969)[9] suggests that such practices took root in India with the advent of global conquest, at first perhaps for the common good, after occupying Arabian powers over the ninth to fifteenth centuries failed to preserve Indian money from degradation and instability, but increasingly for private gain in contention with or cooptation of sovereign authorities, whether they were sacerdotal, imperial, pontifical, royal, dynastic, princely, republic, democratic, or what have you. These private money-creation practices were first legalized with Holland's 1575 enactment of its "free coinage" law, which paved the way for the Bank of Amsterdam's secret overdrafts to the Dutch East Indies Company and was precursor to England's Free Coinage Act of 1666 spearheaded by the British East India Company, an early bastion of British imperialism and colonialism, and adopted later for the United States by the actions of Alexander Hamilton and his Federalist party—despite strong opposition from anti-Federalists Martin Van Buren, Thomas Jefferson, James Madison, and Andrew Jackson—as the United States was founded (Del Mar, 1895/1969, 1899b; Zarlenga, 2002).[10]

At least that is my reading, nascent as it is so far, of monetary history, standing confidently on the shoulders of Zarlenga, whose 2002 *Lost Science of Money* I fully read, and less securely on those of Del Mar (1867, 1885, 1895/1969, 1896, 1899a, 1899b, 1902), whose works I have hungrily but only spottily read thus far. That the challenge we face has been long in the making and that there is rich resource in our human heritage to help us through it to a more secure, sustainable, humanizing (Freire, 2000), ecological future are, I think, communicated in the first paragraph of the final chapter—called "Private Coinage"—of Del Mar's 1895/1969 *History of Monetary Systems*. Though long, it is worth quoting in its entirety:

> If we survey the entire history of money (not merely, as in Chap. V, with reference to the Ratio), it divides itself into five distinct periods. First, the Pontifico-royal period, which lasted from the earliest times to the epoch of the Greek republics. In the pontifico-royal period money was coined exclusively in the temples, and stamped with the sacred emblems of religion. Second, the Republican period, when money was controlled by the senates of Sparta, Clazomenæ, Byzantium, Athens, and Rome. Third, the Pontifico-imperial period, when the coinage was assumed by the Cæsars, and so regulated by them that for thirteen centuries its essential features remained substantially unaltered. Fourth, the Kingly period, when the princes of the West, having freed themselves from the dominion of Rome, seized the coinage prerogative and exercised it independently. Fifth, the period of Private Coinage, when the goldsmiths and merchant adventurers chartered to trade with and despoil or conquer the Orient, obtained control of the royal prerogative of coinage, and thus opened the door to that last of degradations, Private Coinage. This period has not yet ended.
>
> (pp. 463–464)

One hundred and twenty plus years later, it still hasn't. But I agree with James Robertson, who, in thanking the publisher for the opportunity to write with Joseph Huber, says he believes Huber's approach of "sovereign money" and "to restoring the prerogative of seigniorage as a source of public revenue marks the start of a new phase in the long history of money, and that in the coming years many other people will be inspired by it" (Huber & Robertson, 2000, p. ii). That inspiration and superseding the flaws of modern money so as to end the "period of Private Coinage" and usher in the post-modern period for which critical theorists and philosophers have been pining for decades are my motivations in writing this chapter and its sequel in Part III.

So, how does the modern monetary system—which includes but is not limited to the U.S. Federal Reserve System, which constitutes our central bank—actually work? This is difficult to understand let alone explain, not to mention succinctly, because much of it is counterintuitive, complex, and unknown to most people. Stimulated by monetary reformers and, presumably, by their own scientific commitments, central bank researchers themselves have only recently realized or acknowledged that modern "money creation in practice differs from some popular misconceptions" (McLeay, Radia, & Thomas, 2014, p. 1). Specifically, although it is commonly thought that they do—and in the sovereign money system described above and advocated in Chapter 15 (this volume) they would—banks in our *existing* monetary system "do not act simply as intermediaries, lending out the deposits that savers place with them. . . . [R]ather . . . the act of lending creates deposits—the reverse of the sequence typically described in textbooks" (Mcleay et al., 2014, pp. 1, 2). Noting late in their paper (p. 12) that reserves "are an IOU from the central bank to commercial banks" and only traded between and among banks, McLeay et al. further explain:

> In reality, neither are reserves a binding constraint on lending, nor does the central bank fix the amount of reserves that are available. As with the relationship between deposits and loans, the relationship between reserves and loans typically operates in the reverse way to that described in some economics textbooks. Banks first decide how much to lend depending on the profitable lending opportunities available to them—which will, crucially, depend on the interest rate set by the Bank of England [or the central bank of any nation]. It is these lending decisions that determine how many bank deposits are created by the banking system. The amount of bank deposits in turn influences how much central bank money banks want to hold in reserve (to meet withdrawals by the public, make payments to other banks, or meet regulatory liquidity requirements), which is then, in normal times, supplied on demand by the Bank of England [or any central bank].
>
> (Mcleay et al., 2014, p. 2, bracketed parts added; see also p. 8)

In other words, what we use as money in our now-global "fractional reserve" modern monetary system is mostly (95–97%) interest-driven debt-based "deposits" (i.e., monetary units in accounts) literally created and lent into circulation first by commercial banks and, if need be, later by their respective central banks. Jakab and Kumhof (2015) further explain:

> The fact that banks *technically* face no limits to increasing the stocks of loans and deposits instantaneously and discontinuously does not, of course, mean that they do not face other limits to doing so. But the most important limit, especially during the boom periods of financial cycles when all banks simultaneously decide to lend more, is their own assessment of the implications of new lending for their profitability and solvency, rather than external constraints such as loanable funds, or the availability of central bank reserves.
> (pp. iii, emphasis original; see also p. 5 and pp. 6–15, 38–39)

Combined with the prior McLeay et al. (2014) quote, this means that there is nothing controlling the quantity of what functions as money in the modern economy except individual bankers' decisions about whether loans they could make will net their bank the interest payments it desires (and each banker the quotas or commissions s/he needs or covets). If so, they literally create this debt-based money "out of thin air," as many describe the process, by writing that amount into the borrower's account in order to gain those interest payments (and any fees) from the borrower who eventually must also pay down the principal, which extinguishes it from the money supply. It is only when a bank reconciles all its accounts that it sees whether it has the fraction of reserves (i.e., central bank money or IOUs) it needs to be able to meet typical withdrawals by its customers, make payments to other banks, or meet regulatory liquidity requirements. If not, it borrows reserves short-term from other banks or, if that's not possible, from the central bank, which itself, as banks' lender of last resort, creates any needed reserves "out of thin air." The central bank ensures some positive rate of interest by itself charging the banks at least a minimal level of interest on the central bank reserves held by commercial banks, which in-turn affects short-term interbank rates (what banks charge or pay each other when they need or have extra central bank reserves) and, eventually, commercial interest rates (McLeay et al., 2014, p. 8), at least theoretically. In actuality, "there is no hard empirical evidence that there is any cause-and-effect relationship between the monetary policy rate and bank lending. . . . This has been called a 'decoupling' of monetary policy from the money supply (and economy), rendering such monetary policy useless" (Jamie Walton, AMI researcher, personal communication, 8/1/2016).

Why are these points about the quantity or supply of money important? Recall from this chapter's first section that it is the amount of money in circulation that matters for its relative value and purchasing power. Our modern monetary system is impotent and reckless (not to mention undemocratic) in this regard, with the supply of money and debt growing in increasingly high disproportion to GDP, and the prior paragraph is not even the whole of it. While banks making loans and borrowers repaying them are "the most significant ways" in which bank deposits (i.e., what we use as money) are created and destroyed in the modern economy, they are not the only ways; "[d]eposit creation or destruction will also occur any time the banking sector (including the central bank) buys or sells existing assets from or to consumers, or, more often, from companies or the government" (McLeay et al., 2014, p. 4). These so-called "assets" are often debt instruments, namely government or corporate bonds and, more recently, "securitized" risky loans (which means aggregated and repackaged debt) resold as low-risk investments such as the asset-backed securities (ABS) and collateralized debt obligations (CDOs) that triggered the 2008 economic collapse and, amazingly, are on the rebound today (Barr, 2013). But banks in the modern monetary system can also create money out of thin air to buy real assets like land, gold, real estate, whole companies or stock in them, labor, equipment, supplies, buildings, technology, intellectual property—all a free lunch. While their purchases of their own labor (bank tellers, loan officers, managers, custodians, etc.) and enterprise (bank buildings and furnishings, ATM machines, computers, supplies, etc.) are usually paid out of their own income, which comes mainly from the interest they charge on money they created out of thin air, their purchase of other tangible assets (land, gold, real estate, stock, or whole companies) is . . .

> . . . straight-out money creation to obtain someone else's property or product for no cost. Economists would argue that banks forgo the interest they could get on making a loan or buying a bond or stock instead, but, as we've seen, banks are not constrained by the amount of loans they can make, because the central bank is there to create as many reserves and as much currency as the banks need, effectively for free, so it's not really an opportunity-cost situation.
>
> (Jamie Walton, AMI researcher, personal communication, 8/1/2016)

Finally, central banks' so-called Quantitative Easing (QE) practices—which followed in the wake of the 2008 collapse after government bailouts did the initial dirty work, necessarily with borrowed money at taxpayers' expense and to serve bankers' interests, precisely because government ceded its money creation power to those very bankers when it passed the Federal Reserve Act—also entail buying already existing government bonds mainly from non-bank financial companies, such as pension funds or insurance companies, with money the central bank creates out of thin air by crediting the bond sellers' accounts.

Last but not least, there is one more historical and, though to a lesser extent, still present feature of humanity's modern monetary system that reveals its origins and still has major implications for all nations and peoples even if it implicates fewer today than it did 100 years ago. This feature is the ownership of central banks. Bernard Lietaer (2001) explains:

> Until 1936, almost all central banks were directly owned by the main private banks in each country. To this day, nine of the central banks are still private corporations owned by private banks, including the US Federal Reserve, the Swiss National Bank, the Bank of Italy and the South African Reserve Bank. By the 1950s, there were 56 countries with central banks. Now there are 170[11], with most of the newcomers being government controlled. But there are also central banks whose ownership situations involve both government and banks (e.g., Belgium or Japan).
>
> (pp. 323–324)

Lietaer goes on to say, "[c]ontrary to expectations, there has been no evidence that the various ownership arrangements have made any significant difference to either central banks' actions or effectiveness," but I only partially agree and wonder if he still would say this today. At the very least, in these nine countries—most centrally the United States—private interests drive the creation of what is used as money from top to bottom of the banking system. But, no matter their ownership structure now, central banks everywhere were and, along with their supranational overseers in the World Bank, International Monetary Fund (IMF), and Bank of International Settlements (BIS), still are the linchpins in a global monetary system of private banking systems that create national money out of thin air by lending it into circulation when, and only when, it serves private interests to do so and at the expense of both their governments, which now must borrow everything they need and don't get in taxes, and the people who produce the goods and services in the first and final analysis. This is arguably unconstitutional in most if not all modern democracies (Suhr, 1989, 1990), though Zarlenga (2002, Chapter 15) explains that and how the U.S. Constitution (Article 1, section 8) came to be much less clear and more ambiguous on money than the Articles of the Confederation before it were, thanks to Alexander Hamilton, now of Broadway fame, and insufficiently developed understandings of money among most so-called founding fathers.

That, in a nutshell or two, is how modern money "works"—and, quite frankly, how it makes the vast majority of us work to produce much more than what we earn in order to serve the private interests of a tiny minority who come to own an ever increasing amount and percentage of the real estate and wealth in the world largely by extracting surplus value *systemically* and, in that way, effortlessly via modern money. We do this not merely or even necessarily because we don't own our own means of production (some of us

do) or have to borrow (some of us don't) but *systematically* because, as part
of the price of everything we buy, we pay the private interest that modern
money bears. While all of us—well, all who have a bank savings account,
which excludes at least the 8% of Americans (FDIC, 2013) and 38% of
people world-wide (Gallup, 2015) who don't even have a checking/transac-
tion account—were cut in on the deal a long time ago, as signified by the few
dollars or cents we earn in interest on our savings, which is what the system
pays for our consent, Helmut Creutz produced some telling graphs for his
(2001/2010, pp. 328–336) and Kennedy's (1995, p. 26) and (2012, p. 25)
books, which show how income and assets are redistributed up via interest.
Based on figures in Germany in 1982, 2000, and again in 2007, 80% of
us pay over our lifetimes far more in interest than we ever earn in interest,
10% more or less break even, and 10% earn far, far more in interest than
they pay in interest. Furthermore, the extreme skewedness of interest earnings within the top 20%, 10%, and even 1% bears witness to the validity
of the Occupy Movement's critique of the 1% and call for solidarity among
the 99%, though 90% is more reasonable while less than 80% is ignorant
or stupefied. Finally, the plight of the middle class and the legitimacy of the
Black Lives Matter movement both gain credence and gravity when Creutz
details the positionality of ten numerically equal sections of the population:

> If the situation in the individual groups is compared, then it is clear that,
> in absolute figures, the household groups 4–6 had to accept the largest
> negative balances. Regarded relatively, that is, measured as a ratio to
> earnings, the poorest household groups 1 and 2, however, turn out to
> be the biggest losers, because the interest burdens are opposed to almost
> no corresponding interest revenues.
>
> (pp. 335–336)

How Our Modern Monetary System Leads to Student Debt

At long last, this chapter arrives at its reason for being in this book. How
does our private-interest-driven debt-based monetary system lead inevitably
to student debt? While it may already be obvious, the answer lies in what
this system does to government, which of course was responsible for insti-
tutionalizing these monetary relations in our Federal Reserve System and
still is accountable for allowing it to continue, and what it does to normal
people, namely the 80% who have nothing or very little and who consent—
by our political inaction—not only to getting next to nothing but also to
paying for a monetary system that lubricates commerce for the net gain of
the tiny minority. I conclude this chapter by taking up both effects in order.

In founding the Federal Reserve System, the U.S. government ceded its
sovereign power and constitutional right and responsibility to create the
public's money and regulate the value thereof, relinquishing that power and
right, if not responsibility, to an oligarchy of private bankers. Having given

away its power to create money, the government was and still is left with only two means of survival: tax the people (or charge them for services) and/or borrow from the bankers whose power to create what passes for money the government had just legalized and institutionalized as the new norm. Since the political will for taxes has waned over the last century, tax rates, especially for the wealthy (Scranton, 2016), have come down and, thus, unless spending was going to decrease too, government borrowing has had to go up. Of course, government borrowing also benefits the oligarchy that operates like Oz behind the curtain (Baum, 1900) because its members and beneficiaries earn the interest from public debt on money banks largely create out of thin air. Who pays that interest? If current tax receipts don't cover it, new money must be borrowed—inevitably requiring the so-called "debt ceiling" to be raised—and future taxpayers are on the hook for even more. One might say the U.S. government was hoisted with its own petard, and still is, but at the expense or indebtedness of its taxpaying people and their descendants.

In any case, all this explains why the federal government's entry into higher education funding, which began in 1958 with the National Defense Education Act (NDEA), entailed student loans rather than grants (except for veterans who, starting in 1944 after a small two-year federal student loan program for veterans in science and medicine, could get GI Bill grants for education and loans for houses, farms, or businesses; Frydl, 2009). Even with the country's victorious status and subsequent economic boom after WWII, the U.S. government, through its own 1913 undoing, did not have the means to issue grants for the increasing number of so-called baby boomers who by 1965 were clamoring for more than secondary schooling in a political economy ripe with potential and newly won civil rights. In fact, the government didn't even have the means to sustain the NDEA loan program long enough for it to become the revolving fund its creators intended (Best & Best, 2014, p. 44). Thus, while the Higher Education Act (HEA) of 1965 did inaugurate some scholarship and work-study opportunities for low-income students, it was the change in the way federal dollars would be used in its loan program that was HEA's real significance:

> Under the NDEA, federal funds had been allocated to colleges, which then loaned that money to students (after matching one dollar for each nine dollars received); in other words, when a student received an NDEA loan, 90 percent of the money came from federal coffers [whether from tax receipts or interest-bearing loans the Bests don't say]. As the NDEA grew each year, its annual cost to the federal government rose (it reached $108 million in 1964). The HEA sought to provide federal support for student borrowing at a lower cost by establishing *guaranteed student loans* (GSL), in which the money for the actual loans would come from banks [who by law could create most of it out of thin air] and other lenders, not the federal government. Instead of lending

all the money students borrowed, the government would use its funds to make lending money attractive to bankers. As *Time* explained, "This program requires students to find their own private lender. The Government then pays the lender 6% interest while the student is in school and, except for high-income families, splits the 6% with the student when he repays the loan after graduation."

(Best & Best, pp. 32–33, emphasis original; bracketed parts added)

That the government was hamstrung and extorted by having surrendered its money-creation power to the bankers 50 years prior seems apparent enough in 6% interest on guaranteed loans, but even that was not enough. "Whenever interest rates rose," a result of acts originating in the Federal Reserve System, "Congress was under pressure to quickly pass legislation authorizing higher payments" (Best & Best, 2014, p. 38). Furthermore, within seven years, and just a year after President Nixon unilaterally ended the international convertibility of the U.S. dollar to gold, rendering the post-war Bretton Woods monetary system inoperative, he signed the 1972 HEA reauthorization which created the Student Loan Marketing Association, or "Sallie Mae"—a government-sponsored enterprise (GSE) or financial services corporation empowered by the government to borrow at U.S. Treasury rates in order to buy already-created GSLs from banks, bundle them, and "issue its own government-guaranteed debt in the capital markets, creating a secondary market where investors could purchase bundles of student loans as long-term investments" (Best & Best, 2014, p. 39). Between 1979 and 1988 Sallie Mae's assets grew from $1.6 billion to $28.6 billion (Loonin, 2014, p. 3). Five years later, when the government started to revert back to issuing student loans directly rather than guaranteeing private sector loans, so as to cut out the middleman, Sallie Mae somehow won Congressional approval to privatize and had completely done so by 2004, well before GSLs finally came to end in 2010 through the Health Care and Education Reconciliation Act (Pub. L. 111–152). While Sallie Mae's story has been told elsewhere (Loonin, 2014; Steele & Williams, 2016), I have yet to ascertain whether its "privatization" entailed paying the government the market value, amassed over its over 30 years as a quasi-governmental entity, not to mention for all the expenses that the government paid during all those years. Lobbying is just part of its privatization story (at least $44 million since 1997 according to Steele & Williams, 2016), evidence of our country becoming a plutocracy. Understanding and rooting out the systemic source of plutocracy in our modern monetary system is the only way, in my humble estimation, to transform the "monstrous moral hybrid" (Eckrich, 1998, pp. 154–179; Jacobs, 1992, Chapters 6 and 9) that our nation has become and enforces others to follow. Only then will the conditions of the possibility of public education and flourishing exist on this planet.

The other way that our private-interest-driven debt-based monetary system has led and, as long as we leave it in place, will continue to lead to escalating student debt is through what this system does to normal people, the 80% of us who must make a living for ourselves and our loved ones in order to survive and possibly flourish. Nobody forced students or their families to take out loans once the government made them available, but borrow they did in ever increasing numbers, as evinced by the "milestones" in new student loans that Best and Best (2014, pp. 30, 36, 49, & 80) provide for 1962, 1971, 1986, and 2011 as they detail, unfortunately without realizing or disclosing the *systemic* source of the problem, "how good intentions created a trillion-dollar problem" by 2012 (p. 106). By March 2017, this number was almost $1.44 trillion and rising (FinAid, 2017). While some students may not live as frugally as they could and should, given that they are borrowing from their own expected but uncertain future earnings to live now and paying private interests for the privilege of doing so, no students go into debt of their own free will. Those who have—or whose parents have (as mine did 1970–1985, though as I don't for my own children post-9/11)—the money to pay for school do so. But all of us are subject to the system imperative that this chapter has laid bare that forces the majority, who don't have the money, to go into debt for higher education, except perhaps at DIY U (Kamenetz, 2010). Although, unfortunately, he too has not yet grasped the key source of the systemic problem, Maurizio Lazzarato (2015/2013) does an excellent job describing how debt in the modern economy constitutes a "technique of power. The power to control and constrain debtors does not come from outside, as in disciplinary societies, but from debtors themselves" (p. 69). He is exemplifying what Freire (2000/1970) calls "internalized oppression" or housing the oppressor within ourselves (pp. 47–49, 61–62). Though lengthy, it is worth concluding this section with Lazzarato's words because they unmask and expose the reality we are enduring, even if at the expense of others even worse off than ourselves:

> Students contract their debts by their own volition; they then quite literally become accountable for their lives and, to put it in the terms of contemporary capitalism, they become their own managers. Factory workers, like primary school students, are controlled within an enclosed space (the factory walls) for a limited time and by people who and apparatuses which remain exterior to them and are easily recognizable. To resist, they might rely on their own resources, on those of other workers, or on the solidarity between them. Control through debt, however, is exercised within an open space and an unlimited time, that is the space and time of life itself. The period of repayment runs to twenty, sometimes thirty, years, during which the debtor is supposed to manage his [or her] life, freely and autonomously, in view of reimbursement.
>
> The question of time, of duration, is at the heart of debt. Not only labor time or "life time," but also time as possibility, as future. Debt bridges the present and the future, it anticipates and pre-empts the

future. Students' debt mortgages at once their behavior, wages, and future income. This is the paradigm of liberal freedom, which is, as we have seen, freedom in name only. Credit produces a specific form of subjectivation. Debtors are alone, individually responsible to the banking system; they can count on no solidarity except, on occasion, on that of their families, which in turn risk going into debt. Debtors interiorize power relations instead of externalizing and combatting them. They feel ashamed and guilty. The only time that American students began to free themselves from the guilt and responsibility that afflicts them was perhaps, fleetingly, during the Occupy Wall Street movement: three months of revolt and thirty years of payback.

Debt is the technique most adequate to the production of neoliberalism's *homo economicus*. Students not only consider themselves human capital, which they must valorize through their own investments (the university loans they take out), but they also feel compelled to act, think, and behave as if they were individual businesses. Debt requires an apprenticeship in certain behavior, accounting rules, and organizational principles traditionally implemented within a corporation on people who have not yet gone on the job market.

(Lazzarato, 2013/2015, pp. 69–71)

Conclusion

This is how our monetary and exchange relations presently are, but they do not have to stay this way. Part III of this book will propose alternatives not only to higher education funding and student debt but also, in Chapter 15, to modern money itself. Transforming the monetary system we have into the monetary system we can and should have will enable us to resolve not only the student debt problem but many other social, economic, environmental, and ethical problems that inhibit the vast majority of people in our global village from realizing their potential as diverse individuals, communities, and societies in an interconnected world.

Before we explore those alternatives and how to achieve them, Part II of this book dives deep into the lives of seven well-schooled adults who are struggling to survive with the noose of student debt around their necks but not their minds. Their autoethnographic accounts bring to life the bare bones of our monetary system and constitute seven drops in the bucket of 43 million Americans bearing student loan debt (Josuweit, 2016), a bucket that will *systematically* grow as long as we leave our modern monetary system in place or until the vital physical constraints of Gaia (Lovelock, 2000/1979) give way. Virtually every religious or philosophical tradition has an edict against usury, and when enough of us grasp that usury is "the structural misuse of society's money system" (Zarlenga, 2002, p. 186),[12] a critical mass will exist to supersede it. In this there is hope.

Notes

1 Most simply put, Aristotle said of money: "this is why it has the name nomisma—because it exists not by nature, but by law (nomos)" (*Ethics* 1133, cited in Zarlenga, 2002, pp. 34, 56, 656). The quote comes from Book 5, which is on justice and injustice, of Aristotle's *Ethics* (often called *Nicomachean Ethics*). Here are two English translations of the passage: (1) "its name is derived from the word signifying law, which indicates it is founded, not on nature, but on convention; and that human laws, which have thought fit to employ it as a measure of value, may, at pleasure, set this use of it aside, and employ some other measure in its stead." That is from p. 376 of Volume 1 of *Aristotle's Ethics and Politics* (J. Gillies, transl. 3rd ed.) published in 1813 in London by T. Cadell and W. Davies and available online at https://www.hathitrust.org/. (2) "This is why money is so called, because it exists not by nature but by custom [translator's footnote explains, "the word *nomisma* 'money' has the same root as *nomos* 'law' or 'custom'"], and it is in our power to change its value or render it useless." That is from the 1976 Penguin Classics edition first translated by J. A. K. Thompson and published in 1953 and 1955, and reprinted 13 more times before it was revised by Hugh Tredennick for the 1976 edition. This passage is part of a few pages (from the end of 1132 through the beginning of 1134) on proportional reciprocation and the role of money therein. Another enlightening statement therein is "So money acts as a measure which, by making things commensurable, enables us to equate them. Without exchange there would be no association, without equality there would be no exchange, without commensurability there would be no equality" (from the Thompson/Tredennick translation).

2 See Phillips & Burbules, 2000, pp. 50–61, most succinctly stated on p. 54: "The values that do, and must, play a role within research are restricted to the category of epistemically relevant, internal values—values like dedication to the pursuit of truth, openness to counter evidence, receptiveness to criticism, accuracy of measurements and observations, honesty and openness in reporting results, and the like. These values foster the epistemic concerns of science as an enterprise that produces competent warrants for knowledge claims. In short, these relevant values are constitutive of scientific inquiry; that is, without them scientific inquiry loses its point." While Jackson's entire 2012 book contributes to defining education and making and contextualizing the following point, near the end he suggests that "these forms of attachment reduce the separation between subject and object. They bring the two closer together, which is the principal goal of education" (p. 91).

3 The following summarizes major experiences in my journey toward monetary critique and reform: (1) Being raised in a large family by a small-business man (thermometer maker) and full-time mom who later became a Teachers' Assistant for elementary science education, both of whom lived frugally and put all six kids through liberal arts colleges or universities between 1971 and 1989; (2) adolescent activities related to recycling, the so-called "world food crisis," and migrant farm workers; (3) a self-designed undergraduate major in economics and African studies; (4) a summer in west Africa and a senior thesis on adult education in Tanzania during college and a month-long seminar with Paulo Freire (whose *Pedagogy of the Oppressed* provided the theoretical framework for that thesis) the summer after college (Teichert, 1981); (5) three years of adult education and community development work in a subsistence-farming community in Botswana, followed by overland travel north to east Africa and then two months of study at INODEP, a critical education institute that Freire helped to found in Paris, and a few weeks in Germany, from where my own ancestors had

emigrated to the U.S. two and three generations before me; (6) a year of re-entry back home that included travel to visit family and friends, a factory job, and half-a-year's study at a Mennonite seminary; (7) six years of anti-apartheid and undergraduate urban education work in Chicago, followed by a year of adult GED and ESL teaching there; (8) four years of master's and doctoral course work in the social, philosophical, and historical foundations of education, followed by four more years of researching for and writing my dissertation (Eckrich, 1998), which used Jacobs's 1992 *Systems of Survival: A Dialogue on the Moral Foundations of Commerce and Politics* as its philosophical framework and through which I came to a critique of institutionalized interest (i.e., usury) as an instance of what Jacobs calls a "monstrous moral hybrid" and "systemic moral corruption" (Chapters 6 & 9); (9) co-parenting two step-children and one birth-child; (10) a tenure-track job at a public university teaching social and philosophical foundations of education to preservice and inservice teachers, all of whom I try to inspire and prepare for work in urban or other low-income contexts; and (11) finding my way since 2004 to a much larger and more diverse group of authors, people, and organizations doing monetary critique and reform work at macro or meso levels than I had encountered while working on my dissertation. Through all this I came to monetary critique and transformation as a necessary response to my questions about value in economics, ethics, and education and about social, economic, and environmental justice, questions that have compelled and guided me throughout my life and still do.

4 My delineation of micro, meso, macro, and mundo levels of experience and analysis was inspired by, although may be slightly different from, that of Scharmer, 2009, pp. 20, 239–241.

5 Monetative "Mission Statement" in English at www.sovereignmoney.eu/ monetative-mission-statement-engl/?rq=Monetative. Monetative's German website is at www.monetative.de/

6 Huber, Joseph. *Sovereign money: Website for new currency theory and monetary reform*. Retrieved from www.sovereignmoney.eu/

7 See Huber, 2014, 2015, and www.sovereignmoney.eu/. For papers related to monetary critique issues written by central bank researchers, see: Benes & Kumhof, 2012; Coibion, Gorodnichenko, Kueng, & Silvia, 2012; Jakab & Kumhof, 2015; Martin, McAndrews, & Skeie, 2011; and McLeay, Radia, & Thomas, 2014. For Iceland's current monetary reform efforts, see Sigurjónsson, 2015. For other work on macro-level monetary critique and reform, see: DeFremery, 1994; Japanese economist Kaoru Yamaguguchi, 2011, and at www.muratopia. org/index.html and his 2011 paper; Jackson & Dyson, 2013, and the website of Positive Money, a monetary reform group Dyson started in 2010, http://positivemoney.org/; Robertson, 2012, and his www.jamesrobertson.com/index.htm; Chris Martenson's "The Crash Course" at www.peakprosperity.com/crashcourse

8 Helpful authors and organizations focused in part on monetary reform at meso levels include Greco, 2001, 2009; Kennedy, 1995, 2012; Solomon, 1996; Qoin at www.qoin.com/; London-based New Economics Foundation (NEF, founded 1986) at www.neweconomics.org/ and its U.S.-based sister organizations New Economy Coalition (NEC) at http://neweconomy.net/ and Schumacher Center for a New Economics (SCNE) at www.centerforneweconomics.org/ (history of latter two at http://neweconomy.net/about/history); Monetary Network Alliance (MONNETA) at http://monneta.org/en/; Transition US at www.transitionus.org/, part of the worldwide Transition Towns movement at https://transitionnetwork. org/; Community Exchange System at https://www.community-exchange.org

9 See the introduction and Chapters I, IX, and XX of Delmar (1895/1969), but take care that Chapter I is on India, as some extent copies of the book, including

an ebook on https://www.hathitrust.org/, omit the first four chapters (on monetary systems of ancient Indian, Persian, Hebrew, and Greek origins) and make the fifth, on Rome, the first.
10 In particular, see Del Mar, 1895/1969, pp. 14–22, 463–469, 479–484, and 1899b, pp. 7, 27–30, 41–44; Zarlenga, 2002, pp. 231–233, 255, 269–274, 277, 352, 393–408.
11 As of 2016 and according to my count of a list on Wikipedia, 201 sovereign countries have central banks, 175 each having their own (including Hong Kong and Palestine) and another 26 sharing one of four central banks. Nineteen European countries are also part of the European Central Bank in addition to each having their own national central bank. In addition, the Vatican City has its own central bank and four partially recognized countries also each have their own central bank, making for a total of 185 central banks in the world today. Only eight sovereign countries at present do not have a central bank for their monetary affairs.
12 See also Zarlenga, 2002, pp. 181, 202, 230, 278, 335–360, and 508.

References

Adorno, T. W. (1973/1983). *Negative dialectics* (E. B. Ashton, Trans.). New York: Continuum.
Aschheim, J., & Tavlas, G. S. (1985, May). Alexander Del Mar, Irving Fisher, and monetary economics. *Canadian Journal of Economics*, 18(2), 294–313.
Aschheim, J., & Tavlas, G. S. (2004, March). Academic exclusion: The case of Alexander Del Mar. *European Journal of Political Economy*, 20(1), 31–60.
Aschheim, J., & Tavlas, G. S. (2006, December). Money as numeraire: Doctrinal aspects and contemporary relevance. *Banca Nazionale del Lavoro Quarterly Review*, 59(239), 333–362.
Barr, A. (2013, September 9). Beware: Wall St. debt re-packaging machine is back. *USA Today*. Retrieved from www.usatoday.com/story/money/markets/2013/09/08/investing-risk-2008-financial-crisis-lehman/2766835/
Baum, L. F. (1900). *The wonderful wizard of Oz*. Chicago: George M. Hill Company.
Benes, J., & Kumhof, M. (2012, August). *The Chicago plan revisited* (IMF Working Paper 12/202). International Monetary Fund.
Best, J., & Best, E. (2014). *The student loan mess: How good intentions created a trillion-dollar problem*. Berkeley, CA: University of California Press.
Coibion, O., Gorodnichenko, Y., Kueng, L., & Silvia, J. (2012). *Innocent bystanders? Monetary policy and inequality in the U.S.* (Working Paper 18170). Cambridge, MA: National Bureau of Economic Research. Retrieved from www.nber.org/papers/w18170
Creutz, H. (2001/2010). *The money syndrome: Towards a market economy free from crises* (5th ed., R. Aruna, Trans.). Northampton, UK: Adeolu Alao. Retrieved from www.themoneysyndrome.org/
De Fremery, R. (1994). *Rights vs. privileges: An analysis of two powerful privileged interests that have deprived us of fundamental rights*. San Anselmo, CA: Provocative Press.
Del Mar, A. (1867). *Money and civilization*. New York: Burt Franklin.* [*Del Mar's books are available in the public domain from https://www.hathitrust.org/]

Del Mar, A. (1885). *A history of money in ancient countries.* New York: Burt Franklin.*

Del Mar, A. (1895/1969). *History of monetary systems.* London, UK: Effingham Wilson, Royal Exchange. (Reprinted 1969, New York: Augustus M. Kelley Publishers).*

Del Mar, A. (1896). *The science of money* (2nd ed.). New York: Burt Franklin.*

Del Mar, A. (1899a). *The history of money in America: From the earliest times to the establishment of the constitution.* New York: Burt Franklin.*

Del Mar, A. (1899b). *A history of monetary crimes.* Washington, DC: Cleaners' Press [republished for the Del Mar Society in 1975].*

Del Mar, A. (1902). *History of precious metals* (2nd ed., revised). New York: Burt Franklin.*

Eckrich, L. L. T. (1998). *Value in economics, ethics, and education.* Unpublished doctoral dissertation, State University of New York, Buffalo.

FDIC. (2013). *2013 National survey of unbanked and underbanked households.* Retrieved from https://www.fdic.gov/householdsurvey/

FinAid. (2017). Student loan debt clock. *FinAid! The SmartStudent Guide to Financial Aid.* Retrieved from www.finaid.org/loans/studentloandebtclock.phtml

Freire, P. (2000). *Pedagogy of the oppressed* (30th Anniversary ed., M. B. Ramos, Trans.). New York: Continuum. (Originally published in English in 1970)

Frydl, K. J. (2009). *The GI Bill.* New York: Cambridge University Press.

Gesell, S. (1958). *The natural economic order* (P. Pye, Trans.). London: Peter Owen. Retrieved from http://userpage.fu-berlin.de/~roehrigw/ (Originally published in two volumes, 1906 & 1911, and as one volume, 1916)

Greco, T. H. (2001). *Money: Understanding and creating alternatives to legal tender.* White River Junction, VT: Chelsea Green.

Greco, T. H. (2009). *The end of money and the future of civilization.* White River Junction, VT: Chelsea Green.

Health Care and Education Reconciliation Act of 2010, Pub. L. No. 111–152, Title II, Subtitle A, Part II. Retrieved from https://www.gpo.gov/fdsys/pkg/PLAW-111publ152/content-detail.html

Huber, J. (2014, October). *Sovereign money in critical context.* Berlin, Germany: Sovereign Money. Retrieved from www.sovereignmoney.eu/sovereign-money-in-critical-context

Huber, J. (2015, January). *The Chicago plan (100% reserve) and plain sovereign money.* Berlin, Germany: Sovereign Money. Retrieved from www.sovereignmoney.eu/

Huber, J. (2017). *Sovereign money: Beyond reserve banking.* London: Palgrave Macmillan.

Huber, J., & Robertson, J. (2000). *Creating new money: A monetary reform for the information age.* London: New Economics Foundation. Retrieved from www.sovereignmoney.eu/books-and-sites/ and www.neweconomics.org/publications/entry/creating-new-money

Jackson, A., & Dyson, B. (2013). *Modernizing money: Why our monetary system is broken and how it can be fixed.* London, UK: Positive Money. Retrieved from http://positivemoney.org/publications/

Jackson, P. W. (2012). *What is education?* Chicago: University of Chicago Press.

Jacobs, J. (1992). *Systems of survival: A dialogue on the moral foundations of commerce and politics.* New York: Random House.

Jakab, Z., & Kumhof, M. (2015, May). *Banks are not intermediaries of loanable funds—and why this matters* (Working Paper No. 529). Bank of England.

Josuweit, A. (2016). A look at the shocking student loan statistics for 2016. *Student Loan Hero*. Retrieved from https://studentloanhero.com/student-loan-debt-statistics-2016/

Kamenetz, A. (2010). *DIY U: Edupunks, edupreneurs, and the coming transformation of higher education*. White River Junction, VT: Chelsea Green.

Kennedy, M. (1995). *Interest and inflation free money: Creating an exchange medium that works for everybody and protects the earth* (new revised & expanded ed.). Okemos, MI: Seva International. Retrieved from http://userpage.fu-berlin.de/~roehrigw/Welcome.html#english

Kennedy, M. (2012). *Occupy money: Creating an economy where* everybody *wins*. Gabriola Island, BC: New Society Publishers.

Knapp, G. F. (1924/1973). *The state theory of money*. Clifton, NJ: Augustus M. Kelley. (Reprint of the first English translation, which was an abridged version of the 1905 original)

Kuhn, T. S. (1970). *The structure of scientific revolutions* (2nd ed.). Chicago: University of Chicago Press.

Lazzarato, M. (2013/2015). *Governing by debt* (J. D. Jordan, Trans.). South Pasadena, CA: Semiotext(e).

Lietaer, B. (2001). *The future of money: Creating new wealth, work and a wiser world*. London, UK: Century.

Loonin, D. (2014, January). The Sallie Mae saga: A government-created, student debt fueled profit machine. *National Consumer Law Center*. Retrieved from www.studentloanborrowerassistance.org/wp-content/uploads/File/report-sallie-mae-saga.pdf

Lovelock, J. (2000/1979). *Gaia: A new look at life on earth* (3rd ed.). Oxford: Oxford University Press.

Martin, A., McAndrews, J., & Skeie, D. (2011, May). *A note on bank lending in times of large bank reserves* (Federal Reserve Bank of New York Staff Reports, no. 497). New York: Federal Reserve Bank of New York.

McLeay, M., Radia, A., & Thomas, R. (2014, Q1). Money creation in the modern economy. *Quarterly Bulletin*, Bank of England. Retrieved from www.bankofengland.co.uk/publications/Pages/quarterlybulletin/2014/qb14q1.aspx

Oudheusden, P., & Sonnenschein, J. (2015, April 17). Number of bank account owners worldwide grows by 700 million. *Gallup*. Retrieved from www.gallup.com/poll/182420/number-bank-account-owners-worldwide-grows-700-million.aspx (for the full Policy Research Working Paper, conducted with Gallup for the World Bank and funded by the Bill & Melinda Gates Foundation, see http://documents.worldbank.org/curated/en/187761468179367706/pdf/WPS7255.pdf#page=3)

Phillips, D. C., & Burbules, N. C. (2000). *Postpositivism and educational research*. Lanham, MD: Rowman & Littlefield.

Robertson, J. (2012). *Future money: Breakdown or breakthrough*. Devon, UK: Green Books.

Rogers, J. (2004, August). Two sides of the money coin. *Prosperity*. Retrieved from www.ccmj.org/old/two-sides-of-the-money-coin.htm

Scharmer, C. O. (2009). *Theory U: Leading from the future at it emerges*. San Francisco: Berrett-Koehler.

Scranton, P. (2016). *Tax rates of the mid-20th century*. Retrieved from http://teachinghistory.org/history-content/ask-a-historian/24489

Sigurjónsson, F. (2015, March). *Monetary reform: A better monetary system for Iceland*. Reykjavik, Iceland: Author, commissioned by the Prime Minister of Iceland. Retrieved from https://www.forsaetisraduneyti.is/media/Skyrslur/monetary-reform.pdf

Solomon, L. D. (1996). *Rethinking our centralized monetary system: The case for a system of local currencies*. Westport, CN: Praeger.

Steele, J. B., & Williams, L. (2016, June 28). Who got rich off the student debt crisis. *Reveal/Center for Investigative Reporting*. Retrieved from https://www.revealnews.org/article/who-got-rich-off-the-student-debt-crisis/

Suhr, D. (1989). *The capitalist cost-benefit structure of money: An analysis of money's structural nonneutrality and its effects on the economy*. Berlin: Springer Verlag.

Suhr, D. (1990, April 30). *The neutral money network: A critical analysis of traditional money and the financial innovation 'neutral money.'* Paper presented in Brussels. Retrieved from http://userpage.fu-berlin.de/~roehrigw/Welcome.html#english

Teichert, L. (1981). Class/cultural suicide: Preparing for Botswana. In V. Suransky, A. Wood, & M. Day (Eds.), *Paulo Freire in Ann Arbor* (Vol. 2, pp. 75–79). Ann Arbor, MI: School of Education, University of Michigan.

Thoroddsen, S., & Sigurjónsson, S. B. (2016, September). *Money issuance: Alternative money systems*. A report commissioned by the Icelandic Prime Minister's Office, KPMG. Retrieved from http://internationalmoneyreform.org/blog/2016/09/kpmg-iceland-report-sovereign-money/

Yamaguchi, K. (2011, September 30). *Workings of a public money system of open macroeconomics: Modeling the American Monetary Act completed*. Paper first presented at the 29th International Conference of the System Dynamics Society, Washington, DC on July 25; next at the US Congressional Briefing, Cannon 402, on July 26; and last at the 7th annual conference of the American Monetary Institute, Chicago, IL.

Zarlenga, S. (2002). *The lost science of money: The mythology of money—the story of power*. Valatie, NY: American Monetary Institute.

Zarlenga, S., & Poteat, R. (2016, July). The nature of money in modern economy—implications and consequences. *JKAU Islamic Economics, 29*(2), 57–73. Retrieved from http://iei.kau.edu.sa/Pages-VOL-29–02.aspx

Part II

The Debt That Won't Go Away

Stories of Non-Dischargeable Student Debt

5 The Rise of the Adjuncts

Neoliberalism Invades the Professoriate

Amy E. Swain

Enter Debt: Stage Right

My student loan debt (SLD) currently sits somewhere around $250,000. That's how much five years of undergraduate study, one year of certification, and seven years of graduate school cost me in North Carolina. When I tell people the total, their eyes widen in bafflement and I usually make some lame joke about my brain being "kinda pricey." I figure it this way: the everyday, run-of-the-mill thoughts in my head cost me $432 each month, the equivalent of a car payment—but a really nice car, much nicer than the eight-year-old Toyota hatchback I currently drive around town. And that SLD payment is the reduced, income-based repayment (IBR) plan that I still can't really afford—because it is based on the joint tax return that my ex-husband and I filed the year before. Turns out that separating your finances is way more complicated than separating your family.

As a high school English teacher in non-unionized North Carolina, I make just under $40,000 annually—even with a Ph.D. in education. My state ended incentive pay for advanced degrees several years ago, which is one reason among many that North Carolina is ranked 49th nationally in teacher pay (Bernardo, 2016). FedLoan Servicing estimates that, by the time I finish paying my loans on the Income-Based Repayment (IBR) plan, I will have paid the Federal Government over $450,000 in school loan payments. Four-hundred-and-fifty-thousand-dollars for an original loan amount of $210,000. Four hundred and fifty thousand dollars for an education I couldn't afford in the first place. I cannot even conceive of that amount of money.

At the University of North Carolina (UNC) at Chapel Hill, the flagship university where I attended graduate school, the current chancellor makes $520,000 annually. She recently was awarded a $50,000 pay raise, bringing her total annual salary to over $570,000 (Hyland, 2015). Full-time lecturers on the non-tenure track clear a little over $53,000 (Bolduc, 2015). Those who work as part-time adjunct professors receive on average, $3,000 a course, meaning an individual working a 5–5 load (10 courses per year) earns just $30,000. The normal load for full-time tenure-track professors is 3–3.

Excessive pay for higher education administrators is not the exception in the neoliberal structured university; it's the rule. Consider for a moment that UNC Chapel Hill Chancellor Folt's annual salary is equivalent to nearly 20 adjunct professors teaching a 5–5 course load. In reality, though, Folt receives more than $570,000 each year she serves as chancellor. In addition to her salary, Folt receives valuable fringe benefits: living in the 6,000-square-foot university-owned Quail Hill residence, health insurance coverage, and retirement benefits (Bazzaz, 2015; Binker, 2015). I don't know how to calculate the monetary value of her fringe benefits, but I am confident that they amount to more than the salary of the non-tenure-track faculty members who teach at UNC Chapel Hill. A hallmark of UNC Chapel Hill, like other neoliberal universities, is the incredible compensation differentials pointed out above, as well as the influence of corporate ideology. Higher education administrators and managers are paid royally, but when instructional staff is remunerated less, they are encouraged to secure their own grant funding to sustain their scholarship (Saul, 2015). According to data analyzed by *The Chronicle of Higher Education* (2015), executive compensation at public and private colleges continues to rise. Related to the neoliberal belief that corporate-like compensation packages are warranted because it allows institutions of higher learning to retain effective and innovative leaders, Giroux (2002) warns his readers about the impact of corporate culture and ideology on higher education: "As universities become increasingly strapped for money, corporations are more than willing to provide the needed resources, but the costs are troubling and come with strings attached" (p. 433).

At UNC Chapel Hill, non-tenure track faculty members comprise almost 60% of the teaching staff, up from 12% in 2003. Part-time and full-time adjunct teaching positions are a growing trend at many colleges and universities across the United States, and this was the playing field I entered in August of 2013. Before I graduated, I worked as a part-time adjunct teaching 2–3 courses a semester to help supplement my "income" (read: student loans). The work was spotty and inconsistent. Frantic department chairs e-mailed me a week or two before the semester began and asked me to pick up an "extra" class. It was work, and I figured that the added teaching experience would make me a more desirable candidate for the tenure-track job market I was attempting to enter.

Unfortunately, the job market was competitive and difficult to enter. Many of the positions that were advertised were for non-tenure track positions with yearly renewals, short-term post-docs, or positions at for-profit colleges and universities, such as the University of Phoenix. When I didn't land a legitimate position for the fall semester following my dissertation defense, I didn't worry about it too much—I decided I'd continue working part-time adjunct gigs. My advisor told me this was the "new" normal. "A lot of people aren't finding jobs," he said. "Us old folk aren't retiring."

Staying put and continuing as an adjunct made perfect sense (at least at that time): my husband and I wouldn't have to move our two kids somewhere for a rotten job I'd leave within a year or two; my mom could continue watching my kids; I could write and get my publication numbers up in the interim. I'd get my dream job the next year. Everything would work out. *Right?*

Job application #98505
Dear Dr. Chair and Search Committee Members . . .

Trajectory

When I entered college as an undergrad, I didn't know anything about anything. My mom had done a semester at a community college, but we'd never talked about college or school or even education—I just knew that it was what was expected of students after high school. All of my friends were attending, so I should, too.

During my very first (and only) campus visit for orientation, I remember having a vicious argument with my mom about whether or not I would have a car when I went away to school that fall. We were walking up some steps behind the main gaggle of parents and kids led by the over-eager blonde orientation adviser. Summers are sticky-hot in North Carolina and absolutely the worst time to trek across a giant university campus in the middle of the day. Sidewalks smolder and even the strongest of breezes barely cut the humidity.

The answer to the car question was, of course, no. My mom couldn't afford it. As a single mother, she worked two jobs seven days a week to barely scrape by with her own car. It wasn't like we could ask anyone else for money; everyone we knew was as broke as we were. Thus, a second car was a forgone luxury.

Student loans were an inevitable part of college, and the associated debt just as suffocating as summers in North Carolina. Freshman year and every year thereafter, loans provided me with tuition and housing and a meal plan and a little extra to buy books and have some spending money. Debt clouds gathered and grew exponentially every year. In undergrad, my mom helped when and where she could—a twenty here, a twenty there, but I knew better than to treat my mother like an ATM. I can remember the villainous envy I would feel every time my dorm-mate called her parents and demanded an extra $200 to help her "get through" the month.

At the end of my freshman year of college, my grandmother gifted me with a twelve-year-old rust-laden car purchased from a family friend. I only cared that it had four tires and a steering wheel. My sophomore year, I worked 20 hours a week to supplement my "needs": clothes, an apartment off campus, gas, alcohol, and the type of rocketing credit card bills that came with a free t-shirt. By my senior year, I was working 40 hours a week to make ends meet, and still I struggled to fill my gas tank at the end of each month. But I looked forward to getting a "real job" after graduation, of being able to live like an adult with my own house and a nice car. Of being able to plant roots and grow up. Because that's what people do after college. And everything would work out. *Right?*

Adjunct Life

Only things didn't work out so well for me after college. There isn't much that one can do with degrees in creative writing and philosophy, even if you did graduate with honors. I'd chosen those majors because that was what I was "good at" in school—there was no foresight to what I'd actually do with degrees in those fields. I had no idea how to manage the job market or even what kind of career I was suited to hold. Following graduation, I worked for Sears as a store-manager-in-training until I could no longer stomach the daily examination of reports and sales and parity and goals. Somewhat haphazardly, I entered the field of Education and began teaching in elementary school, and then transferred to middle school.

It was hard to make ends meet on a new teacher's salary—much harder than I ever imagined it would be in the adult world. The bills were overwhelming: rent, utilities, debt, and more debt. My freshman year, leaving the dining hall, I had signed up for the free t-shirt from Visa and racked up $6,000 in debt as a result. My student loan payments started six months after graduation. My eighth graders used to tease me for not having cable and for driving my old beater, especially once the muffler went and my car howled down the road.

And then, more of a struggle: I needed a teaching certification to continue teaching in North Carolina. That required more school and more loans. My mom used to joke that I'd stay in school forever if I could, and I suppose some part of that is true—if it meant my loan payments would continue to be deferred.

While working on my licensure, a professor encouraged me to apply to graduate school. So I did. Somewhere during graduate school, I decided it was a great idea to get married and have kids. Of course, my husband and I couldn't afford a ring or a wedding or even the kids, but that's what school loans were for during graduate school: living life. Only, childcare in the yuppie college town where I attended graduate school was expensive, like cost-of-a-mortgage-expensive. A good daycare cost over $1,000 a month, and even the daycare centers where parents would be scared to leave their child(ren) were not far off that mark. Luckily, over the years my husband's salary continually increased and so we managed. I took out the maximum allocation every year to help supplement our income as well as to feel that I was contributing to the marriage partnership. But our spending was complicated by the fact that both my husband and I were brought up as working-class kids with absolutely no financial literacy. We lived with a fistful of cash and no money in the bank. As my grandmomma would say, we got by on a wing and a prayer.

While pregnant with our second child, the funding for my research assistantship folded. My assistantship was funded through a grant-based evaluation of the state of North Carolina's post-secondary educational opportunities for incarcerated individuals. When the state hit hard times, the decision was made to move the evaluation of the educational program in-house, run by Department of Corrections, and thus I lost my healthcare coverage, itty-bitty stipend, and what little tuition reimbursement I received. I also lost a year and a half of dissertation research and data—but that's another story for another day.

I gave birth to my second son in a hospital with no health care coverage while we waited on COBRA.[1] Once the nearly $500 COBRA bill was added to our over-stretched budget, and my husband and I found ourselves looking at the impending added daycare costs of our second child, we realized we couldn't afford to live in Chapel Hill anymore, or anywhere in a 75-mile radius of Chapel Hill. It occurs to me to wonder, aloud, if the folks who work in Chancellor Folt's Quail Hill residence can afford to live in Chapel Hill themselves.

So our family moved to rural, eastern North Carolina where our parents lived. It was one of those tiny cities where it takes only about 15 minutes to drive from end to end, even in heavy traffic. I was through with doctoral coursework and only needed to finish writing my dissertation. With the cost of living dramatically reduced, all of sudden we felt "rich"—but what we traded in financial fortitude we lost in cultural and academic stimulation.

In small-town Elizabeth City, North Carolina, there are three small local institutions of higher education: a community college, a private Christian university, and a historically black university established in 1898. All three of these institutions of higher learning were under hiring freezes, and/or had no use for a Sociologist of Education. I needed a job, and I checked every semester for three years.

I taught a combined total of 275 students over 11 courses during the 2013–2014 academic year; six courses in the fall and five courses in the spring. I was also driving two hours to a "local" university campus two days a week, clocking 8 hours and 400 miles on the road and listening to an untold number of audiobooks. In my "spare" time I volunteered 20-plus hours a week at the local alternative school, which was also the site of my dissertation on last-chance education. Volunteering at the school provided me with a much-needed connection to kids and education and allowed me to stay involved. I did my best to continue my scholarship and keep to a writing schedule, but it was next to impossible to publish articles. Instead of writing new stuff, I polished off some old work and managed to get a few publications accepted. Then I graduated. And my student loan payments were estimated at over $2,000 a month. I really, really, really needed a job. Like *really*.

I worked online as an adjunct professor for two universities in the Midwest during the 2014–2015 academic year. The schools were some 1,000 miles away from where we lived in North Carolina. And for the record, these schools were not those pseudo-intellectual-for-profit-get-your-bachelors-in-two-weeks colleges. They were legit universities. The kind with a campus and a mascot, and everything else brick-and-mortar schools have.

But I always felt like I had to validate my job(s). I was a "real" professor—*kind of*. I didn't have my name on the door, or an office on which to put a door, but my students called me Dr. Swain in their e-mails, so that sort of counted. I couldn't afford my student loan payments, or my health insurance through the Affordable Care Act, because I wasn't making more than $30,000 a year; but I was still Dr. Swain!

My husband and I bought a house that year, at his insistence, for a financial investment, but I found myself thinking of our home as temporary and at times, actively resisted making temporal investments in our house. Should I plant annuals or perennials in the yard? Would we be here to see the bulbs bloom? What's the point of planting a dogwood tree if we won't see it grow? This place will turn into a rental, anyway, once I get a job, and once we move away. . . .

At times, despite owning our own home and having a doctorate, I felt like I was still in graduate school—that liminal space of waiting for life to begin. Waiting for the next semester to start. Waiting for the job offer I felt would have to come. I was waiting for roots and I was hoping for wings; my "prayers" echoed without response.

Teaching online created in me a deeply rooted sense of failure and subordination compared to my peers. From across the screen on Facebook, I watched as friends and colleagues entered new positions at universities all over the United States. With every new contract that was signed, I felt my own self-value plummet. Why were others being hired and I wasn't? What were they doing that I wasn't? Then, these newly hired friends without teaching experience would contact me for advice on a new syllabus or class design: "What do you use in your classes?" Somehow, teaching and having experience teaching worked against me in actually getting a job, because working as an adjunct is considered "less than" or subordinate to a faculty position—even when you are working for a university with an actual campus and mascot.

Initially, I tried to tell myself all the things that Stuart Smiley would have advised me: Your work is valid; you are a real professor; you should be proud to work with both graduate and undergraduate students; your students are learning and growing because of you; look at it this way, you don't have to drive anywhere; you can work in your pajamas and nap whenever you want and your family can live near your mom and she can spend time with the grandbabies; and . . . and . . .

At the end of the day, I felt as though my job as an adjunct professor was similar to winning a small consolation prize; it was like I had received a trophy for participating. "Thanks for playing. We really enjoyed having you on the team."

The inconvenient truth was that my work as an adjunct didn't pay my bills. After working for two years and having no health insurance, the only thing I did have was my growing loan interest. Two years I had spent scanning *HigherEdJobs*, *Chronicle Vitae*, and *Academic Keys* for my golden ticket out, my dream job, my next chapter in the next semester.

Two years of "no job yet" and "I'm still looking."
Two years of "waiting on a call back" or "I got an interview—cross your fingers."
Two years of cover letters.
But I had to get a job that paid my bills, eventually.
Right?

. . . I am writing to happily submit my candidacy for the position of Assistant Professor of Education in the School of Education at Four Year University. I have a great degree from a great college and I'm qualified because . . .

Rise of the Adjuncts

When university departments cannot staff their course enrollments, they look to burgeoning lists of "substitute teachers," otherwise known as adjunct professors, or part-time faculty. The list of adjuncts grows every year because it's more economical and feasible for a university to keep two part-time people on staff than to hire a full-time faculty member who requires an actual salary and benefits—a living wage. I was told once that I could teach three courses a semester, but not four, oh no—never four, because four would make me eligible for benefits. Four would mean a contract, benefits, some possible say in the departmental decisions, some semblance of permanence, some responsibility on the part of the university to ensure my job satisfaction.

During the time I spent wasting away on Adjunct Island, I witnessed a few full professorship positions at the very universities where I was employed become reconfigured as non-tenure track faculty lines. The calculus makes sense from the neoliberal university's perspective: if a full professor was making $135,000 plus benefits (I'm being generous in some cases, though I know this salary figure can be higher!) and left their position, the university could recoup up to $80,000 by hiring a non-tenure track faculty (NTTF) member. By replacing a full professor position with a non-tenure track position, the university also relinquishes any obligation or contractual commitments to the new hire. NTTF have no status within the neoliberal austere university. Without tenure, there is no power, no academic freedom, and no security for contingent faculty.

Without the very tenets that created the professoriate, NTTF are reduced to atomized individuals who are silenced on a variety of levels, divested of having a voice and/or personhood. NTTF members often do not have a vote within and regarding the governance of a department, and thus lose their voice. But also, due to the yearly, renewable contractual nature of their employment by the university, NTTF are also discouraged from speaking out or being gadflies regarding their subordinated position. Silence is the rolling fog of neoliberalism that creeps in during the night and chokes out any hope of voice or collective organizing. But, despite their subordination, even NTTF members recognize that below them exists an underclass of workers: part-time faculty. Part-time faculty aren't even privy to the limited boons granted to NTTF: a yearly contract, health benefits, a laptop, a meager conference budget, and a name on the door to an office.

So let's return to the scenario above, the vacancy created by a full professor's absence. Instead of filling the vacancy with a NTTF, the university could ostensibly save another $10,000—$15,000 by hiring two adjuncts, part-time faculty members—and they could increase course enrollments by more than two sections. These part-time faculty members are even more divested of status and ownership of their labor.

The critical theoretician in me has to acknowledge the brilliance of such a strategy. It really comes as no surprise that K–12 education, and especially higher education, has submitted to the "McDonaldization"[2] of its workforce and Wal-Martization of its public schools.[3] Within the private sector, companies such as McDonald's and Walmart are leading the charge to subvert and divest their workers of power and status. Across the United States, unions are being busted, while workers are discouraged from collective organizing. Workers are pitted against one another within the neoliberal cult of individualism, which is accelerated by "right-to-work" policies and dictates.

Unlike my friends who held full-time and tenure-track positions in the academy, I felt exploited and alienated. As a part-time instructor, I often had more classes—sometimes double—than other professors. Some of my friends complain about needing time to write, or having to sit in on too many meetings at the university. And although in some ways I was happy that I didn't have to attend faculty meetings, the working conditions in which I worked at home were less than ideal. Working on a broken laptop and having to pay exorbitant sums of personal money to attend conferences to share the research and work I was carrying out were realities my friends did not face.

The following quote is taken from an article posted on *Vitae*:

> New PhDs are expected to move around the country in temporary postdocs or visiting professor jobs until finding tenure-track

positions—financially impossible for me as a mother of two—or stay where they are and work as adjuncts with no job security and an average wage of $2,700 per course. While making an income below the poverty line, a new PHD is expected to spend thousands of dollars on job interviews at conferences in expensive cities and write paywalled papers for free.

(Kendzior, 2014, para. 2)

The writer, Sarah Kendzior (2014), advocates for everyone within the academy—everyone from administrators to faculty members—to help support the struggles of adjunct professors and other contingent laborers. Situating the existence of adjunct professors within a climate of labor exploitation, Kendzior argues for the (re)allocation of students' tuition away from "administrative salaries and lavish infrastructure" and into job security and higher wages for part-time faculty.

Certainly, Kendzior's suggestion fits within the neoliberal University of North Carolina model in which Chancellor Folt continues to make an obscene amount of money, while the "workers" within the university, from part-time faculty to cafeteria staff, operate within a climate of insecurity and precariousness.

Direct Action

In 2015, there was a National Adjunct Walkout Day on February 25. In a news blog entry on the *Insider Higher Ed* website, the comment section following the intended walkout's announcement was telling. I know you aren't supposed to read the *Dreaded Comment Section*; I know trolls hide under the bridge there, and I'm no Billy Goat. But the trolls on *Inside Higher Ed* are, presumably, my academic peers, who take up the debate regarding an adjunct professor's worth and quality as a teacher, and thus their opinions mattered to me.

In the comment section, self-identified adjuncts claimed to hold their positions for a love of teaching and not the money—the old "I-teach-because-I-love-it" mantra. Other commenters (job unknown) described adjuncts as having marginal competencies comparable to their tenured colleagues; because otherwise, why wouldn't they have a full-time or a tenure-track position?

And still, other commenters seemed to be of the mind that adjuncts must themselves be held accountable for their low-wage positions and increasing workloads—after all, it was the adjunct who signed the contract and accepted the terms provided therein. Along these lines, one commenter wrote, "Adjuncts don't have a value problem, but rather a supply problem. Clearly they are valuable. Colleges can't run without them. However, there are too many people willing to work as adjuncts relative to the need. As long as there are 'scabs' willing to work for lower wages, then all adjunct wages will remain low."

This last comment gave me great pause. Is that who I am to my colleagues? An educational martyr? A lackluster educator? A *scab*? Was it my own fault that I was unable to land a job? Should I have done more to make myself "marketable"? Should I have published more? Was my teaching subpar?

What proved really interesting from the comment section were the two main narratives that came out regarding non-tenure track faculty, both full-time, and part-time: either you are a martyr doing work you love for low pay; or you are getting what you deserve for taking a low-level position. Martyrs are somewhat revered, their positions ignoble. But scabs are not revered; they are just that, scabs. Deadened skin intended to be flaked off.

It is ironic to me that these were the exact same narratives leveled against K–12 teachers—either that schoolteachers deserve their low pay because they are teachers and cannot "do better" in the "real world," or they get the sparsely modest salary owed to martyrs. Because surely we as a society don't undervalue education, especially given that higher education is required to qualify teachers to educate our children.

> *Dear Dr. Swain,*
> *Thank you for your interest in our university. With such a talented and diverse pool of applicants from which to choose, it was a challenge to determine the final list of candidates. We have, at this time, finalized the hiring of the selected candidate.*
> *Please keep us in mind for possible future employment, as new positions may become available with time.*

Opting Out

Ultimately, I couldn't sustain life and living on subpar subsistence. Especially once my marriage failed at the end of 2014 and I realized that I couldn't allow failure—or waiting—to determine my life. I realized that I was waiting for my degree, my education, my teaching, and my qualifications to be recognized by the professoriate and validated by the academy, and I realized that I didn't need the professoriate or the academy for validation of the good work I'm capable of doing. So I made a decision and called a press conference: "*This Fall . . . this is very tough . . . this Fall I'm going to take my talents to the public school sector and join the last remaining bastions of non-neoliberalism. I feel like it's going to give me the best opportunity to pay my college loans and to pay on my loans for multiple years, and not only just to pay my loans when and if I can or just as I'm able; I want to be able to make a decent living and feel good about my life. And I feel like I can do that outside of the academy.*"

I still have student loan debt. I still have bills. Currently I pay $432, but I've asked for a deferment while FedLoans processes my request for a lower monthly payment. In some ways, I'm right back where I started after under-grad—teaching and barely making ends meet on an educator's salary. But in a sad ironic twist, I'm right back where I was as an undergraduate, except this time, like my mother, I too am the single mother who will be unlikely to buy a car for my kids before sending them off to college.

Only now, my loan debt is crippling, and I have no hope of ever paying it off. My student loan debt, like the hot, stifling summers in North Carolina, is inevitable. I hold the highest possible degree in a state educational system that doesn't value my educational achievements—and yet we in the business of education encourage high-school students every day to go to college, whether or not they can afford it. We say that college is necessary and that education is about possibility—and for the poor and working class, possibility is necessary to continue in a world determined by neoliberal constraints.

> I've come to view my enormous student loan debt as a tax on possibility. But everything will work out.
> *Right?*

Notes

1 The Consolidated Omnibus Budget Reconciliation Act (COBRA) gives workers and their families who lose their health benefits the right to choose to continue group health benefits provided by their group health plan for limited periods of time under certain circumstances such as voluntary or involuntary job loss, reduction in the hours worked, transition between jobs, death, divorce, and other life events.
2 McDonaldization is a term used by sociologist George Ritzer in his book *The McDonaldization of Society* (1993). I am drawing on Ritzer here in that McDonaldization becomes manifested when a higher education adopts the characteristics of a fast-food restaurant.
3 Wal-Martization is a term used by sociologist Lori Martin in her book *Big Box Schools: Race, Education, and the Danger of the Wal-Martization of Public Schools in America* (2015).

References

Bazzaz, M. (2015, February 2). *Chancellor's house shaped in 20 years*. Retrieved from www.dailytarheel.com/article/2015/02/chancellors-house-shaped-in-20-years

Bernardo, R. (2016, April 4). *2015's best and worst states for teachers*. Retrieved from https://wallethub.com/edu/best-and-worst-states-for-teachers/7159/

Binker, M. (2015, November 2). *UNC Board of Governors raised salaries of 12 chancellors in closed meeting*. Retrieved from www.wral.com/unc-board-of-governors-raised- salaries-for-12-chancellors-in-closed-meeting/15054474/

Bolduc, J. (2015). Adjunct faculty, supporters demonstrate at UNC. *News & Observer*. Retrieved from www.newsobserver.com/news/local/education/article 11313128.html

The Chronicle of Higher Education. (2015, December 6). Executive compensation at private and public colleges. Retrieved from http://chronicle.com/interactives/executive-compensation#id=table_private_2013

Giroux, H. A. (2002). Neoliberalism, corporate culture, and the promise of higher education: The university as a democratic public space. *Harvard Educational Review*, 72(4), 425–463.

Hyland, M. (2015, November 19). *UNC chancellor Folt sidesteps questions on raise.* Retrieved from http://wncn.com/2015/11/19/unc-chancellor-folt-sidesteps-questions-on-raise/

Kendzior, S. (2014, October 17). The adjunct crisis is everyone's problem. *Vitae.* Retrieved from https://chroniclevitae.com/news/762-the-adjunct-crisis-is-everyone-s-problem

Martin, L. L. (2015). *Big box schools: Race, education, and the danger of the walmartization of public schools in America.* Lanham, MD: Lexington Books.

Ritzer, G. (1993). *The McDonaldization of society.* Thousand Oaks, CA: Sage Publications.

Saul, S. (2015, December 6). Salaries of private college presidents continue to rise. *Chronicle Survey Finds.* Retrieved from www.nytimes.com/2015/12/07/us/salaries-of-private-college-presidents-continue-to-rise-survey-finds.html?_r=0

6 "BFAMFAPhD"

An Adjunct Professor's Personal Experience With Student Debt Long After Leaving Graduate School

Celeste M. Walker

In 1992, fourteen years after completing my Bachelor of Fine Arts (B.F.A.) from Kutztown University in Pennsylvania, I returned to school to begin working on my Master of Theatre (M.A). In the years between 1978 and 1992, I had a career as a graphic designer. I was able to find employment but was never truly satisfied with the work and pursued other artistic areas of discovery including photography, dance, and, finally, acting. After being laid off at a Medical Marketing Agency in 1988, I earned a living as a free-lance designer, board ("paste-up") artist, and assistant art director, and was eventually offered a full-time position at an ad agency. While I could do the work, it wasn't fulfilling to me.

When I took my first acting class and appeared on stage for the first time, I understood where my passion lay. In the mid-1980s, after several classes and many acting jobs in the area where I lived, three friends and I began our own theatre company. The "Theatre Outlet" was a place where we could create the kind of theatre that we were interested in without having to answer to any other directors, producers, or managers. We became adept at every aspect of theatre production, including dramaturgy, acting, directing, stage management, theatre production and design, marketing, grant writing, and facilities maintenance. We did everything from cleaning the bathrooms in our make-shift performance space to traveling to New York City to read and preview new plays for consideration on our small stage. Eventually we applied for non-profit status. Even though no one was getting paid and we had to survive on our day jobs, due to great reviews, positive press, and word of mouth, we became the darlings of the theatre community in Allentown, Pennsylvania.

In 1991, I was invited to become a member of the Educational Outreach Acting Ensemble at the Pennsylvania Stage Company (PSC), a professional theatre in Allentown. I was hired for the ensemble without an audition, and I spent a year at PSC honing my craft by serving as a reader for actors auditioning for main stage productions, performing in "second stage" pro-ductions and readings at the theatre, touring in educational theatre produc-tions to local schools, and teaching community acting classes. At the end of that year, I was promoted to Director of Outreach and Assistant to the

Artistic Director at PSC. At the same time, I knew that my own acting and theatre training needed to be developed. I wanted a career in the theatre arts as an actor; however, I also wanted to direct others and teach.

I applied and was accepted into the Master of Theatre Program at Villanova University in the fall of 1992. At this time, tuition at Villanova was $2,000 for one course, per semester. Not having that amount of money, I auditioned for an acting scholarship (only one was offered per year). Because I was not awarded the scholarship, I applied for a student loan of $4,000 for the first academic year.

In order to qualify for a loan, I had to attend full-time or take four graduate courses per academic year. Since I lived far from Villanova, I had to commute an hour each way for my night classes, while also being on call for any issues that needed my attention at the theatre; this was a 24/7 job. My annual income at this time was $15,000, which I supplemented by working part-time as a teaching artist at a Performing Arts Program for children and teens called Stage Door Workshop.

After my first year at Villanova, I decided to take two courses per year instead of the eight. Reducing the number of credits I was enrolled in took a toll on me financially since it meant I had to pay for my tuition out of pocket. I also grew restless with the graduate program itself. I wanted to act, teach, and direct. I realized, after doing research, that the degree I really needed was a Master of Fine Arts (M.F.A) in Acting, a terminal degree (rather than an M.A.).

As a result, I began applying to M.F.A. programs in early 1994. I knew that my age (at that time I was 42) and not having an undergraduate degree in theatre might hurt my chances at being admitted, but I still hoped against hope that I would find the right program for my professional goals. I found an excellent program for my situation: I was accepted to the first graduating class of the Actors Studio Drama School at The New School for Social Research (later, The New School University). This was a brand new M.F.A. program for actors, directors, and playwrights. Despite not having an established track record, the association with the Actors Studio[1] legitimized the graduate program in my eyes because the Actors Studio and its membership represented the most well-respected trained actors since its inception in the 1940s. From my perspective, training with the faculty associated with this organization represented a golden opportunity.

In September of 1994, I began three years of study with some of the best theatre artists in the business. Unfortunately, I had no way to pay for graduate school, and, since the program was brand new, there weren't scholarships or grants available for incoming students in the "cohort." Complicating matters, my acceptance came so late that I was enrolled in Villanova's M.A. Program and barely had time to withdraw from Villanova and cancel my student loan from that school in order to apply for the maximum school loans to pay for The New School tuition. My tuition for one semester at The New School in 1994 was $8,020, and it increased every semester afterwards until May of 1997, when the amount was $8,595 for the final semester. However, I took out the maximum in student aid every semester of graduate school because I could work only part-time and I had no money to pay for food and other living expenses. I should also mention that I used credit cards to pay for my books and travel. The campus was very close to the Foundation Center, a facility where I could research available grants and scholarships; however, the only grants and scholarships I was able to secure—two scholarships until the third year, when I received a third scholarship from the university—were through The New School, and those were far from sufficient.

In retrospect, The New School may have been a poor choice, given that totally financing my graduate school experience with student loans was a recipe for disaster unless I was guaranteed secure, lucrative employment at the end of the three years. Other M.F.A. programs had funds available for financing graduate school without the need for student loans. Personally, I felt lucky to have been accepted at the Actors Studio Drama School at The New School. I believed that I received first-class training in my craft, and I truly thought that the credentials would give me a competitive edge when I would later audition for jobs.

During my first year of graduate school in New York I commuted five days a week. I took a 6:15 a.m. bus (which meant leaving at 5:55 a.m. to drive to the bus station) to New York for my 9:00 a.m. dance class on Monday, Wednesday, and Friday. On Tuesdays and Thursdays I got to sleep in; I took an 8:15 a.m. bus for my 11:00 a.m. Theatre History course. I usually got home around 7:30 p.m. every night. I slept on the way to school and read theatre texts or scripts on the way home. That was a positive. By the second year, I had to have an apartment in New York because rehearsals and other events with the school made the daily commute next to impossible. I still maintained my home in Pennsylvania and took the bus on Monday at 6:15 a.m. and returned Friday evening. By the third year, I came home less often due to weekend rehearsals and thesis obligations. I shared a one-bedroom apartment in New York with two other classmates and paid rent there and in Pennsylvania.

When I graduated in 1997, my total student loan debt for both Villanova and the Actors Studio Drama School at The New School (including for living expenses during those years) totaled $59,500. As of today, August 1, 2016, I owe (approximately) $121,254. That amounts to an increase of $61,754 in capitalized interest since I borrowed 20 years ago. At the time of writing this chapter, I pay $400/month, which does not touch the principal of my debts (see Table 6.1). I will be paying on my student loans well into my nineties.

Following graduation in May 1997, I secured my first acting job. I performed in a Prudential Securities Industrial Video filmed across from the

Table 6.1 School Loan Summary as of August 2016

Type of loan	Loan amount	Loan date	Disbursed amount	Canceled amount	Outstanding principal	Outstanding interest
DIRECT CONSOLIDATED UNSUBSIDIZED	$73,998	8/26/13	$73,998	$0	$75,128	$168
DIRECT CONSOLIDATED SUBSIDIZED	$45,530	8/26/13	$45,530	$0	$46,126	$102
FFEL CONSOLIDATED	$40,929	7/27/05	$40,929	$0	$0	$0
FFEL CONSOLIDATED	$56,080	7/27/05	$56,080	$0	$0	$0
STAFFORD UNSUBSIDIZED	$10,000	8/21/96	$10,000	$0	$0	$0
STAFFORD SUBSIDIZED	$8,500	8/21/96	$8,500	$0	$0	$0
STAFFORD UNSUBSIDIZED	$10,000	7/13/95	$10,000	$0	$0	$0
STAFFORD SUBSIDIZED	$8,500	7/12/95	$8,500	$0	$0	$0
STAFFORD UNSUBSIDIZED	$10,000	10/18/94	$10,000	$0	$0	$0
STAFFORD SUBSIDIZED	$8,500	10/17/94	$8,500	$0	$0	$0
STAFFORD SUBSIDIZED	$4,000	7/20/94	$0	$4,000	$0	$0
STAFFORD SUBSIDIZED	$4,000	8/12/92	$4,000	$0	$0	$0
STAFFORD SUBSIDIZED	$2,000	4/27/77	$2,000	$0	$0	$0
Total DIRECT CONSOLIDATED UNSUBSIDIZED					$75,128	$168
Total DIRECT CONSOLIDATED SUBSIDIZED					$46,126	$102
Total FFEL CONSOLIDATED					$0	$0
Total STAFFORD UNSUBSIDIZED					$0	$0
Total STAFFORD SUBSIDIZED					$0	$0
Total all loans					$121,254	$270

Note. SUBSIDIZED means that I didn't have to pay interest on the loan while I was a student or in deferment. Every time I refinanced, however, the interest on unsubsidized loans (or all loans if I was in forbearance) was capitalized, which is why I owe more than I borrowed. FFEL stands for Federal Family Education Loan (FFEL) Program.

World Trade Center. My second job was for a cigarette patch commercial; I was also cast in an independent film shot in New York. My next two jobs were as a part-time bartender and a theatre arts teacher at the same theatre program for children and teens—Stage Door Workshop—that I had worked at in 1992 near my home in Pennsylvania. For the next year, I maintained two residences, one with my graduate-school roommates in the East Village and the second with my significant other in Whitehall, Pennsylvania. I would travel back and forth going on auditions and working part-time as a personal assistant for the late Kitty Carlisle,[2] as a receptionist in a doctor's office on the Upper West Side in Manhattan, and as a teaching artist in schools in Queens and the Bronx for a theatre program called Theatre for a New Audience. I maintained my residence part-time in New York to access theatre jobs and auditions and in order to have my answering service and mailing address for my New York agent.

Simultaneously, I was applying for adjunct and tenure-track teaching positions at institutions of higher education. I was recommended for, and accepted, my first adjunct teaching position at the University of Scranton and began teaching there in the spring semester of 1998. This was followed by an adjunct position at Northampton County Community College in Bethlehem, Pennsylvania, and another adjunct position at Muhlenberg College in Allentown, Pennsylvania. All of these were adjunct, teaching-only gigs; none came with benefits.

My life changed significantly when my relationship with the man I'd been living with ended suddenly in September of 1998. At this point, I was auditioning in New York several days a week and working no less than six part-time jobs—between Scranton, New York, and the Lehigh Valley bordering Pennsylvania and New Jersey—and still not making enough money to pay for the security deposit, rent, and other expenses. Instead, I put most of my furniture and possessions into storage and moved in with a dear friend and employer. I had a small room with private bath off the garage in her home for the next year and a half. During this time, I continued to apply for faculty positions all over the country. In 1999, a full-time tenure-track position became available at the University of Scranton. I was interviewed and made the shortlist, but I did not get the job due to my lack of academic teaching experience.

Eventually, I let go of all of my adjunct positions in Manhattan, with the exception of the teaching artist position. I was still managing several part-time teaching positions and serving as a guest artist and master teacher at the Theatre Outlet. In 2000, I moved to Philadelphia to live with my new partner, now fiancé, and to plan our 2001 wedding. I continued to work as an adjunct in the Lehigh Valley, but after one semester of commuting to Scranton from Philadelphia to teach one course, I resigned. I was able to get two more adjunct teaching jobs in Philadelphia, and by the spring of 2002, I was teaching seven courses at five colleges and two summer theatre programs with an annual income hovering around $30,000. Hoeller

(2014) argues that for many adjunct faculty—particularly part-time faculty on semester-to-semester contracts—working at several schools is sometimes not enough "to eke out the financial existence offered to fast-food workers" (pp. 2–3).

Adjunct professors are paid per teaching hour, permitted to teach a limited number of courses at any individual institution, and their pay differs from that of tenure-track faculty and from college to college. For instance, I could earn $1,300 for one three-credit course at one private university and earn nearly twice as much at another university. In my experience, state universities that were unionized paid adjunct professors the most. As an adjunct, health insurance was never included in my compensation, and only one university provided me matching funds for a required retirement account. My combined income was still not enough to make the $800/month student loan payments. I was no longer able to defer my loan payments (which had allowed me to postpone payment on my loans without interest accruing on the subsidized ones), so I took the "forbearance" option, which meant that I could still postpone loan repayment but interest would now accrue on all of them.[3]

I thought that my financial problems were going to be a thing of the past when I was hired as a Visiting Assistant Theatre Professor at Saint Joseph's University in Philadelphia for the 2002–2003 academic year. The teaching contract was $35,000, plus another $5,000 stipend for directing. It also included a retirement fund and healthcare for me and my family. During that year I was finally able to begin making payments on my school loan.

For the next year, two new tenure track positions were becoming available at the university. One was in the Fine Arts Department and the second, which required a Ph.D. in Theatre Studies, was in the English Department. The first position, for which I applied, required a terminal degree (a Ph.D. or M.F.A.) and experience in teaching, acting, and directing. During my visiting professorship at Saint Joseph's University I served as Artistic Director/Producer of Cap and Bells Theatre Arts Society.

As Artistic Director, I produced and directed productions of *Anything Goes* and *A Doll's House*, hired directors, musicians, technical, and design personnel as needed, and supervised all play production elements as well as the marketing, community outreach, production, and printing of promotional materials. I mounted a successful advertising campaign for the programs, advised theatre organization members (in group development, community service, alumni involvement, fundraising, membership expansion and development), initiated and expanded theatre-related trips and activities with the Student Activity Organization and the entire university community, organized and facilitated the 2003–2004 Cap and Bells scholarship application and audition process, was responsible for distribution of scholarship awards, managed organizational budget, oversaw fundraising activities, initiated a successful proposal to double the production budget for the 2003–2004 year, oversaw rewriting of the organization's constitution, reorganized officer elections, and served as advisor to the newly formed dance component of Cap and Bells. My teaching load during this academic year was two courses each semester and included the following: (a) Drama in Performance I and II, (b) Actor into Director, (c) Theatre Medium, and (d) an Independent Study student in Theatre Production and Directing.

At the end of the year, I was awarded the Advisor of the Year award. However, I was refused an interview for the tenure track position. The only reason I was given was that all of my references were professional, not from former professors. I later discovered that there were "politics" involved in why I was not granted an interview and that, no matter how successful I was as a visiting professor, I was never going to be considered for the tenure-track position. I learned, following the end of my contract, that the Fine Arts Department had someone in mind for the full-time position at the university prior to my one-year contract. They were *required* to do a search, and I was encouraged to apply. I was told early on that the full-time, tenure position would be "mine to lose" if I was successful after my first year. However, in April of 2003, the Fine Arts Department Chair informed me that I wouldn't be interviewed for the position because I had not provided the committee with letters of recommendation from graduate school faculty at The New School. It should be noted that I provided the committee with four letters of recommendation, one more than the required three, and that providing letters from former graduate school faculty was not listed as a part of the application requirements. Immediately following the conversation with the Chair, I had two faculty members from The New School send letters; however, by then it was a moot point. The decision had already been made.

Since I left all of my adjunct positions to take the Visiting Professorship, I was jobless. Even though it was late in the hiring season for adjunct and other faculty assignments for the 2003–2004 year, I sent out letters of inquiry to all of the colleges and universities in the Philadelphia area and went on unemployment while teaching part-time as a teaching artist at the Wilma Theatre in Philadelphia. While on the teaching staff at the Wilma Theatre, I continued to audition and also designed and taught a Continuing Legal Education Course called Acting for Attorneys. I taught the course for several years, which lead to my role as a Presenter at the New York State Bar Association Annual Conference at Lincoln Center in New York in 2005 and as a Workshop Leader at the 2015 Conference for the Department of the Navy.

By the fall of 2004, I was back to teaching as an adjunct at two colleges in the Philadelphia area. The number of adjunct positions increased to five, until 2010, when I was able to reduce the number of schools to Arcadia University and Montgomery County Community College.

I taught at La Salle University for seven years, beginning in the fall of 2003. Just prior to the beginning of the fall 2010 semester, I received a phone call from Mike Lemon Casting in Philadelphia and was offered a role in an upcoming re-enactment for *The Learning Channel*. This was an unsolicited acting assignment, as I was cast by my professional headshot (read: photograph) alone due to my resemblance to the woman whose reenactment I was being cast to play. The employment would involve a one-and-a-half day commitment and the first day of shooting was on the very first day of the fall semester. It should be noted that I would be paid approximately $1,000 a day for this acting job. This is a significant amount of money for an adjunct. I contacted a fellow adjunct professor who served as a liaison to the department and coordinator of the adjuncts in the Communication Department. I informed her of the offer and asked if I would need to have coverage for not attending the first day of the semester for my two sections of Public Speaking courses or would this be something that I could communicate electronically with my class over our Blackboard course page, reminding the class to read over the published syllabus and assigning them their reading for the second day of class. My liaison said that I must have coverage for both sections and provided me with the list of faculty e-mail addresses from the department. I was able to secure coverage within minutes.

However, I also received an e-mail from the Chair of the Communication Department. In the e-mail, I was congratulated on the role and then reprimanded for my lack of commitment to my students and La Salle University. I immediately telephoned the chair and further explained that I didn't audition for the work on *The Learning Channel*, that commitment to my students was indeed present and that as an adjunct professor, this extra employment was in my area of study and that it was a significant amount of money. She thanked me for talking with her directly. I then contacted my liaison and asked if she thought that this "extra" employment would place my teaching appointment at La Salle University in jeopardy. She said that I had followed procedure and that there didn't seem to be any reason why it would be a problem. In mid-December, following the last day of finals, I still had not heard about my class schedule for the spring. After several attempts to contact my liaison, I was able to get through to her by telephone. I was then told that my contract at La Salle University was not going to be renewed.

According to Clausen and Swidler (2013), "Part-time or adjunct faculty are by far the largest subset of all higher education faculty and constitute a strong majority (70%) of contingent faculty, forming roughly half of college and university faculty and 40 percent of all teachers (the category that includes teaching assistants) employed in higher education" (p. 3). As Yaffe (2011) writes in *The Chronicle of Higher Education*,

> The university system is rife with inequities that need to be publicly exposed. Most egregious is the exploitation of part-time, adjunct faculty members, who are often dedicated, passionate professionals who work for low wages, with no stability. But I also encourage you to take

your cameras outside the campus gates. Remember the middle-class people you saw disappear in Flint? Their descendants who strive to get a college degree—and a shot at the middle class—might face student-loan debt in six figures.

(para. 7)

In 2014, my annual income reached $62,000. During that academic year, I taught a total of 15 college courses, and directed theatre programs at two senior citizen facilities.[4] I have a small retirement account at one school and, although the school doesn't contribute to my retirement, it does pay half of my health insurance premium—$3,804 annually. In my experience at these institutions, adjunct professors cannot earn more than a 50% discount on health insurance premiums. Part-time and full-time staff at the same institution can earn up to 75% discount after a specific number of years. According to BFAMFAPHD (2015), an organization for artist academics who are struggling to find work while under enormous student loan debt pressure from attaining their degrees:

The 2000 United States Census revealed that there are more people who identify their primary occupation as "artist" than as lawyer, doctor, or police officer combined. And each year, our schools graduate another 100,000 students with arts-oriented BFAs, MFAs, and PhDs. Since 7 of the 10 most expensive schools in the country are art schools, artist-graduates live with unprecedented debt burdens. Looking at the Census Bureau's 2010–2012 American Community Survey, BFAMFAPhD Census Report shows that most artists (85%) in New York City have non-arts-related day jobs. Only 15% of people with arts degrees in New York City make a living from their work. Artists who are lucky enough to make a living in New York City (and these are mostly people without arts degrees) have median earnings of $25,000 a year. This is one-half of the annual median earnings of other professionals. With elite art schools charging $120,000 for an art degree, and with tuition rising at public universities, both artists and culture are under threat.

(para. 3)

While I still act occasionally, my professional acting career has taken a back seat. Because of the teaching load that comes with being an adjunct professor, I have little time for my own professional research or academic writing, although I am in the process of developing a new solo show aimed at baby boomer audiences that I plan to produce in 2017 with my own theatre company.

I am fortunate to have a good relationship with Arcadia University. At Arcadia I am able to design and develop my own courses, which provides me with a bit of job security. At Montgomery County Community College, I am the only faculty member who teaches one of the courses on my teaching roster, and my supervisor is very accommodating as far a scheduling is concerned. It has taken me more than 10 years to develop a kind of employment security with both institutions. But my job as an adjunct professor is based on student enrollment and can change at any time. If enrollment falls below 10 students, I will not be paid my contracted amount, but a lesser tutorial rate per student. In addition, if a course is canceled due to low enrollment, I may not find out about it until just prior to the beginning of the semester. While I am able to design and develop new courses, I am not compensated nearly enough (perhaps $800—$1,000) for the time it takes to research, develop, and organize each course. In contrast, tenured or tenure-track faculty members are afforded funds for course development, technology, research, and travel.

Over the past 12 years, at one university, I have developed no less than a dozen courses and seminars. The neoliberal university—an enterprise of profit over people (Chomsky, 1999)—has benefited not only from my desire to introduce new and interesting curriculum to students, where I combine my theatre and actor training in an interdisciplinary approach to subject matter, but also from my *precariat* labor.[5] Morris (2015) writes of the precariat academic workforce, suggesting adjunct employment trends are a "bellwether" of higher education: "[Many people] know about the 'proletariat,' but what about the 'precariat?' It's a pun of sorts, designating the class of people who labor in academia in a permanently precarious state of employment—the adjuncts and contingent faculty who increasingly make up the majority of faculty at many institutions" (para. 1.).

There are also academic changes that take place regarding procedure and course allotment that I am not privy to as an adjunct. For example, even though my courses may fill enrollment and even have wait lists, I am not permitted to offer an additional section. There is a new policy for adjuncts at the university where I teach a very popular seminar—and I found it out accidently when a student wanted to sign up for the course—that I can no longer offer University Seminars every semester, but only once an academic year. Not being able to teach multiple sections of courses cuts into my personal income significantly. Luckily, I have an alternative University Seminar I can offer, but I was never made aware of the policy change because I do not belong to any one department and adjuncts are not invited or welcomed to attend department meetings and therefore depend on "word of mouth" from friends on the full-time faculty and students for information. My realities, the realities I have shared heretofore, are similar to those documented in the literature (see Chell, 1982; Coalition on the Academic Workforce, 2012; Gappa & Leslie, 1993; Hoeller, 2014; Kezar, 2012; McGee, 2002) and artist communities like BFAMFAPhD (online @ http://bfamfaphd.com/).

Each time I had to "consolidate my loans" in order to continue to use low-income forbearance status—which would give me a certain amount of time to place my payments on hold (during the summer months when I could not count on full-time teaching assignments)—my balance capitalized. This is partially why my original school loan debt, which was around $60,000, has ballooned to more than $121,000.

To clarify, the difference between subsidized and unsubsidized is that subsidized loans are interest free while one is in school or in deferment, whereas unsubsidized loans always have interest attached. When the deferment weeks expire, the only thing a borrower can do is start paying, try to obtain forbearance and refinance, or default on the loan. During forbearance, and when a loan is re-financed, all interest is capitalized. So, even though my original loans were just under $60,000, I now owe more than twice the original amount. As an adjunct professor, I am responsible for educating my students while I live under constant pressure and anxiety regarding my ability to make a living wage and (re)pay my student debt.

Since my employment is so variable, I still must apply for forbearance during months when I am not getting paid or am teaching a smaller number of courses and have not been able to find other income over shorter time periods. It should also be noted that I am not eligible for any unemployment during the summer months because, even though I am technically laid off, I do anticipate being re-hired for the fall.

Notes

1 The Actors Studio is a non-profit organization for professional actors, directors, and playwrights founded in 1947 in New York City by Elia Kazan, Cheryl Crawford, and Robert Lewis. The Actors Studio was formed to provide a place where professional actors could work together between jobs or during long runs to continue to develop their craft and to experiment with new forms in creative theatre work. Many known and renowned actors have benefited from their membership with the Actors Studio. Membership is a commitment that affords a place for its members to work on their craft and techniques in private and in concert with master moderators and close colleagues. This commitment is free to our membership. The Actors Studio in New York serves as the administrative headquarters for both the New York Actors Studio and its only branch, located in West Hollywood, California. The Actors Studio, which is not a school but an active studio for its members, has also created a completely separate, unique, fully accredited, degree granting three year Masters of Fine Arts Program located at Pace University in New York City. Work is constantly being developed and when it is deemed ready for public viewing, audiences are invited in for free. Ellen Burstyn, Harvey Keitel, and Al Pacino serve as co-Presidents. Mark Rydell and Martin Landau serve as co-Artistic Directors in West Hollywood. The Actors Studio Drama School at The New School moved from The New School to Pace University roughly eight years after I received my Master's Degree. There was a power struggle between the Program Directors and the President of the University. The President did not want the focus of the program be the connection with the Actors Studio.

2 Kitty Carlisle Hart wore a cloak of many professional and elegant colors—actress, opera singer, Broadway performer, TV celebrity, game show panelist, and patron of the arts. At age 95, this vital woman continued her six-decade musical odyssey with songs and reminisces in her one-woman show, "Kitty Carlisle Hart: An American Icon," which toured from her beloved New York to Los Angeles. She developed pneumonia soon after her tour folded toward the end of 2006 and passed away of congestive heart failure in April of 2007. In 1946, she had

married Pulitzer Prize-winning playwright Moss Hart and later appeared in a number of his works, including his classic "The Man Who Came to Dinner" (1949) and the witty Broadway comedy "Anniversary Waltz" (1954). The couple had two children. He died in 1961 and she never remarried, spending much of her remaining 45 years keeping his name alive for future generations. For a quick Kitty Carlisle biography, see her webpage on the International Movie Database (IMDB). I worked for Mrs. Hart for two-and-a-half years.

3 For more on "forbearance," see https://studentaid.ed.gov/sa/repay-loans/deferment-forbearance.

4 According to their website: www.phillyseniorstage.com/landing/about/mission/ Philly Senior Stage is dedicated to providing the thrill of the performing arts to senior adults in their own communities.

5 The term "precariat" is a portmanteau obtained by merging "precarious" with "proletariat." I acknowledge that lacking job security and/or intermittent employment or underemployment and the resultant precarious existence is not only limited to those who work in academe. Nonetheless, the precariat class has been ascribed to the entrenchment of neoliberal capitalism. Noam Chomsky (2012) writes in *The Huffington Post* about what the precariat means for society.

References

BFAMFAPhD. (2015). *About*. Retrieved from http://bfamfaphd.com/#artists-report-back

Chell, C. (1982). Memoirs and confessions of a part-time lecturer. *College English*, 44(1), 35–40. Retrieved from http://dx.doi.org/10.2307/377194

Chomsky, N. (1999). *Profit over people: Neoliberalism and global order*. New York: Seven Stories Press.

Chomsky, N. (2012). *Plutonomy and the precariat*. Retrieved from www.huffington post.com/noam-chomsky/plutonomy-and-the-precari_b_1499246.html

Clausen, J., & Swidler, E. (2013). Academic freedom from below: Toward an adjunct-centered struggle. *Journal of Academic Freedom, 4*, 1–26. Retrieved from www.aaup.org/sites/default/files/files/JAF/2013%20JAF/ClausenSwidler.pdf

Coalition on the Academic Workforce (CAW). (2012). *A portrait of part-time faculty members*. Retrieved from www.academicworkforce.org/CAW_portrait_2012.pdf

Gappa, J. M., & Leslie, D. W. (1993). *The invisible faculty: Improving the status of part-timers in higher education*. San Francisco: Jossey-Bass.

Hoeller, K. (2014). *Equality for contingent faculty: Overcoming the two-tier system*. Nashville, TN: Vanderbilt University Press.

Kezar, A. (2012). *Embracing non-tenure track faculty: Changing campuses for the new faculty majority*. New York: Routledge.

McGee, M. (2002). Hooked on higher education and other tales from adjunct faculty organizing. *Social Text, 20*(1), 61–81. Retrieved from http://dx.doi.org/10.1215/01642472–20–1_70–61

Morris, C. (2015, January 14). State of adjunct, contingent faculty may be higher ed bellwether. *Diverse: Issues in Higher Education*. Retrieved from http://diverseedu cation.com/article/68849/

Yaffe, D. (2011, January 9). An open letter to Michael Moore. *The Chronicle of Higher Education*. Retrieved from http://chronicle.com/article/An-Open-Letter-to-Michael/125825/

7   Debt(s) We Can't Walk Out On

National Adjunct Walkout Day, Complicity, and the Neoliberal Threat to Social Movements in the Academy

Brandon O. Hensley

Waking Up and Walking Out: Selling Out or Business as Usual?

Wednesday, February 25, 2015, is going to be like any other teaching day for me; at least that's what I want to think when I wake up before my alarm, the radiator in my bedroom clanging me to consciousness. I want to think it will be like any other day despite having made a decision that will change my trajectory as an academic and activist. I've decided I won't be participating in National Adjunct Walkout Day.

I take a slow shower, embracing the cold water's chill through my hair and down my body. Keeping the water on cold, I hope to freeze a recurring question out of my mind. *Am I selling out?* I didn't sleep well the night before, but the chill of the water does the trick to wake me up.

While shaving, I think of the tasks awaiting me today—*just another day*, I remind myself—and end up cutting my upper lip. "Damn it." Out comes the styptic pen, and I apply it to the small cut while looking in my cramped closet for an outfit. I select black dress pants, a light blue dress shirt, red paisley tie, and black dress shoes. Taking one more look in the mirror, I pluck a stray gray hair out of my 28-year-old head. *Just another day.*

Frost coats the kitchen window, sun peeking into the kitchen. I check my university e-mail while waiting for the coffeemaker to percolate. No e-mails from students who can't make it to class today (yet). I gather the essentials—banana, granola bar, coffee, and multivitamin. This is my breakfast and lunch for the day. I don my well-worn gray houndstooth coat and grab my trusty tote bag, one of the better ones I've received from a conference I paid full freight to attend. The tote bag is durable; it can easily hold 30–40 pounds of books and papers. I also grab my attaché bag, a large hole visible in the faux black leather. I can't afford a new one, not yet. The question keeps echoing in my mind: *Am I selling out?*

I walk out the door of the apartment building, hustling across a busy street to a side street where my car is parked. There's ice on my car windshield, so I grab a plastic ice-scraper—chipped and split in the middle from overuse—out of my car to quickly hack some clear spots through the frost, just enough to see. *Just another day.* I blast the car defrost, turn on *NPR Morning Edition*, and make the short drive to the small, private university where I teach.

* * *

A couple of weeks before, I'd been summoned to my department chair's office and offered a promotion from my semester-to-semester adjunct appointment to a year-long Visiting Instructor position. Just like that. Full-time employment offered out of nowhere, seemingly out of the blue.

This unexpected news came after I'd taught five years at the university as an at-will, semester-to-semester adjunct. I never took on additional teaching jobs because I was able to *just* make (both) ends meet after combining my menial income from the university, a graduate research assistantship at the university where I was finishing my Ph.D., assistance from my wife's salary ($30,000 a year at a local hospital), and occasional financial help from my family. These are privileges I'm aware not all adjuncts have, but I accepted them because, more than money, I needed time to complete my degree and get the most education out of it. Nevertheless, after over five years of demeaning work conditions, I kept hoping that someday I'd be compensated fairly, both as an adjunct and eventually as a tenure-track faculty member for my teaching, research, and service in higher education.

At this university, I taught as many as four courses per semester and as few as two, always making below the poverty line ($15,930 for an individual, according to the U.S. Department of Health and Human Services "2015 Poverty Guidelines"). Nevertheless, one summer when I was offered no classes I applied for unemployment and food stamps out of necessity, but I was denied. The reason was because I had "reasonable assurance of employment" with the university, meaning there was a preponderance of evidence—consecutive semesters of employment—to "reasonably" expect I'd have another contract the next semester. This was an institution where I was provided a small stipend for my work as Assessment Coordinator of the department *at first*, but within a couple years this stipend evaporated entirely. An administrator told me that I didn't have to write the assessment report. I ended up writing it anyway, for free. In my five years of working at this institution, my debt situation—both in terms of credit card debt and student loan debt—worsened significantly.

Needless to say, I was surprised when my department chair called me into her office to offer me the Visiting Instructor position. She stressed that it was an interim position; I'd be taking the place of a recently hired junior faculty member who had accepted a job at the state flagship university. She mentioned what my salary would be, which was a substantial increase from even my heaviest semester teaching at the university. I was taken aback, not just for the sudden pay raise and inclusion into the faculty experience that I'd gain, but because I was expecting more of a "talking to," given that

I'd recently published several pieces storying my experience as an adjunct (Hensley, 2013, 2015) that were critical of the institution. Maybe I was paranoid, but I figured that because I was an at-will employee I didn't have much academic freedom to work with, especially in calling out exploitative practices at my place of work. Besides, publishing was not particularly expected of tenured or tenure-track faculty members at this school, much less adjuncts. The university benefited from my compliance to teach for poverty wages and not "rock" the proverbial "boat."

Perhaps it was good luck, a nod toward my five years of excellent teaching ratings at the university, or the fact that the Assistant Professor we just hired from a Big Ten school accepted a more prestigious job and gave late notice to the department. In any case, my chair didn't bring up anything I'd been publishing. She just made me this offer and asked what classes I'd like to teach for my 4/4 load.

Suddenly, I'd have medical insurance, a paycheck that would allow me to pay down my significant credit card debt and student loan debt (detailed later in this chapter), the option to pay into a 401(k) retirement plan, and other benefits previously unavailable to me as an adjunct professor. In a blink of an eye I'd be making roughly five times what I was before, and I'd have a voice in faculty governance for the first time. Yet, in the back of my mind the question arose: *Am I selling out?*

The day I was offered the interim position, my department chair also informed me that a tenure-track faculty search would begin for my replacement in the fall, when my new one-year appointment was slated to begin. "You should certainly apply, we would give you full consideration," my chair said reassuringly. I told her I would, and that I was extremely grateful for this opportunity. I emphasized how big of a difference this position would make for me, telling my chair about the amount of student debt I had that, although at the time in deferment, would soon come due because my dissertator status was ending. "When the repayment phase kicks in, I'll be in a *much* better place to handle it," I gushed to her.

Walking out of the chair's office to the adjunct office, I let out a relieved sigh, but I felt conflicted. My new position would be steeped in tenuousness, just with a higher salary and with health and retirement benefits. I felt, after the offer, that I wasn't granted this opportunity for the 20-plus conference presentations I paid for entirely on my own during my five years of adjunct-hood, or the 10 journal publications, or the evidence of teaching effectiveness, or the campus service, all of which I had. Rather, I was simply in the "right place" at the "right time."

The uncertainty of full-time employment beyond my *visiting* appointment was not lost on me. All of this was swirling through my head during the days leading up to February 25, 2015. I felt like I was walking out on my adjunct colleagues with no guarantee that I'd actually remain full-time. I felt like a sellout, but I managed to minimize and avoid my feelings of guilt.

* * *

On that late February morning, I arrived on campus (where at that point I still worked as an adjunct) around 8:00 in the morning for my 9:00 a.m. class. The sun emblazoned the cold red bricks of the stately Elizabethan building, Main Hall, with an iridescent glow, some of the bricks spangled with frost and bright as gold bars. *This campus has always been a beautiful one. I hope I'm doing the right thing.*

I haul my tired body, worn attaché, and tote bag of graded papers up four winding flights of stairs to the floor where my department is housed. Somewhat out of breath, I mumble "Good morning" to a mostly asleep student sitting at the front desk of the department office suite. He's holding down the fort until the administrative assistant arrives. *Today is just another day.*

I unlock the adjunct office, put my bags down and sit down at the desk where we—the adjunct faculty in the department—share an old Dell desktop computer. I had hoped to print off Peer Evaluation sheets (I teach Public Speaking and it's a speech day) using a Word document I'd saved on the Dell, but alas, when I turn on the computer it immediately begins installing dozens of updates that have been put off by all of us, a game of "hot potato" that finally ends with me.

Luckily, I have my laptop with me today (I use a speech recording program so the students can watch and reflect on their speeches), so I quickly draft the peer evaluation slips, send them to my university e-mail, and rush to the Psychology Lab down the hall where I know I can print quickly and for free. While I'm in the lab, I check my e-mail and see that new e-mails have arrived: two students are extremely ill and will not be able to give their speeches today. *It's just another day, indeed.*

Once my sheets are printed and I've responded to the e-mails, I trek back to the adjunct office, get from the administrative assistant the key to the closet where the department "technology" is stored, and collect the webcam for recording student speeches. I then go to the classroom where my two classes will be today—luckily in the same building this semester—and begin preparing the classroom for a speech day, which entails writing the speakers' names on the board, setting up the computer and projector for visual aids (again completing the necessary computer updates), arranging my computer and webcam in a good spot for recording the speeches, and cutting the peer evaluation sheets into slips for the students to pass around. Today, there are 10 speeches scheduled in my first class (eight after the e-mails), and students who aren't speaking fill out the slips for their peers, noting strengths and suggestions.

On my laptop, I click on a web browser icon to load the speech recording website. A previously loaded window pops up on the screen. This is one of many windows I keep open with various tabs I'm reading or that I've read but can't bring myself to close. The most recently opened tab greets my eyes. It's one that's been open for weeks and that I've re-read many times by now. It is "A Day Without Adjuncts," an *Inside Higher Ed* article in which Flaherty (2015) writes:

Adjuncts sometimes say they make up higher education's invisible class. So an idea pitched on social media a few months ago struck a chord. What would happen if adjuncts across the country turned that invisibility on its head by all walking out on the same day? National Adjunct Walkout Day, proposed for Feb. 25, immediately gained support, and *adjuncts continue to use social media and other means of communication to plan what the protests will look like on their campuses.*

(para. 1, emphasis added)

I minimize the window, move my cursor purposefully and click to open a new window, a blank window, a white window, a blank slate for my choosing what to view. I am aware that I'm making a choice of what *not* to *view.* A choice to turn away, to ignore an issue my heart is in but my body is not. Not today. Yet my mind remains conflicted.

The job offer for "Visiting Professor" is the beginning of my ascent out of adjuncthood, and at the same time it's the end of my adjunct activism from the standpoint of an adjunct, my minimization of the computer window, a conscious turning away from a cause I vociferously supported. Not today, though. I have students to teach, a paycheck to collect in a few days, and a promise of a bigger paycheck in the fall. I minimize and turn my back on the adjunct cause because I'm a coward and I need(ed) the money. I sent no e-mails about National Adjunct Walkout Day to adjunct colleagues I know struggle to make ends meet. All I did was keep the window with "A Day Without Adjuncts" open, but minimized, on my computer.

I smile at my students as they filter into the classroom, tired as usual. I pass around a bucket of candy, leftovers from Valentine's Day (I always try to bring candy once each fall and spring, around Halloween and Valentine's Day, respectively). The candy perks them up, and conversation starts as wrappers open.

"Anything going on to announce? Any campus events we need to know about?" I ask this often because it gets people talking, and reminds me of events to attend to support my students. Nothing is volunteered today. Back on the task at hand, I load the speech recording software, a slow and clunky program that frequently drops connections in the retrofitted classroom I'm in. Wi-Fi in this room is not always a guarantee, and there is nowhere for me to plug in an Ethernet cord.

I robotically continue the rest of my speech day routine, asking for a volunteer to keep time and count sources. I pass the peer evaluation slips to a student to pass on, and I take my place at the strategically positioned desk where I can get good video and audio. The desk is somewhat comical because it is missing one of the leg tips, so I put an eraser under the leg so it doesn't wobble. This is the only desk in the classroom that has enough room for my laptop and Speech Evaluation Grading forms. I feel a pang of dismay for the physical classroom environments my students are paying dearly for. The rest of the desks are roughly the size of what you might see in an elementary school. This isn't a classroom a campus tour guide would show parents and prospective students. The desks have enough room for an 8 ½" x 11" spiral notebook.

I prop my coffee cup precariously on a desk in front of me, slanted slightly as all the other warped wooden desks in the room are. I've mused many times about the money being spent on superficial window dressing to the detriment of the students in terms of the learning environment: a new football field and track, an "arrival court" with a burbling fountain, and plans for a new union building that will force the temporary movement of the campus library to a dormitory. At what cost? Research finds this is common on today's college campuses: "Intoxicated by magazine and college guide rankings, most colleges and universities have lost track of learning as the only educational outcome that really matters" (Keeling & Hersh, 2012, p. 13).

I often feel bad for my students. I feel bad about the amount they are paying to be here, many of them working 15-plus hours a week and taking out substantial student loans. They are paying to be at a university that looks pretty on the outside but is crumbling on the inside. They are paying exorbitant amounts of money to be taught by someone who doesn't make half that amount in a year. They are paying to be taught by adjunct faculty members who do not hold a Ph.D., have health insurance, job security, or hope of securing a tenure-track position, given the intensifying neoliberal conditions of work for professors and workers in many other fields.

We manage to *just* get the last speech in as time runs out. *Just another day.* I gather the peer evaluation forms as my students head to their next class, another 50-minute interval that counts toward their progress on degrees that cost nearly $29,000 a year in tuition to attain.

In my second class—I'm contracted for only two courses this semester— we have eight speeches scheduled and only get through six (due to technology issues and people going over their time limit). After class, I go to my apartment to grade, rather than the adjunct office where I must share a computer and space. I paperclip the students' evaluation forms, peer evaluation slips, and outlines together, organizing their speech materials strewn about my floor. A poem forms in my mind's eye, finding a rhyme: *National Adjunct Walkout Day came and went, and I did nothing. Nothing to participate, nothing to demonstrate, nothing to commemorate.*

Why/Why not? I try to rationalize my (in)action: I did nothing because I *need* the paycheck and because I don't want to "make trouble" for my university, where I love my work. I tell myself that it's okay to avoid "rocking the boat" and walking out today, because *maybe* there's a future for me here where I'm now valued as a full-time employee by the administration.

To my knowledge, when I was an adjunct, my students didn't know I made very little, received no health or retirement benefits, and had no access to faculty channels of award, promotion, or governance. Students treated me as a respected educator, addressing me as "Professor Hensley."

I often wonder how surprised they'd be if they knew how I and about half the faculty teaching them were given piecemeal contracts for fast-food wages.[1]

Discussion: Critical Reflection, Neoliberalism, and Social Movements in the Academy

The day my department chair called me into her office, I was very nervous because, as I have written previously (Hensley, 2015), there'd been talk (and worry) among my adjunct colleagues that Public Speaking—the main course of the department, predominantly taught by adjuncts—was being reduced to a couple of sections so that other departments could teach forms of the class that aligned with the *professional expectations* of those majors. In other words, Public Speaking wasn't neoliberal enough; it was a liberal arts class where students were encouraged to find their voices and think critically, and this didn't translate neatly into a linear scheme to produce commoditized "assets" (read: graduates) for the market (Keeling & Hersh, 2012). More pragmatically, a fight for survival was brewing at the school, which is hurting financially, and other departments, whose enrollments are declining, saw Public Speaking as something they could colonize as their own.

In any case, I'd been writing publicly about maltreatment of adjunct faculty the past few years, penning a piece called "The Absent Adjunct" (Hensley, 2013), which appeared in *The Chronicle of Higher Education's* ongoing *Adjunct Project*. I was worried that either I may have "rocked the boat" for the last time or there wasn't a job for a Public Speaking adjunct anymore. But, as I stated earlier in this chapter, my chair didn't call me into her office to fire me. Quite the opposite. She called me in to offer me a job. I wonder, as I write this chapter, whether I would have done differently on National Adjunct Walkout Day if, say, I'd been fired that day in her office. If I had been fired, I think I would have had the courage to walk out, make a sign, and spend the rest of the day picketing in front of the main campus building. Instead of the complicit silence I demonstrated on February 25, 2015, I might have done something to make some noise, to make a difference, somehow. Complicity won out this time, in a way that makes me feel like I might have minimized the window to the issue in a substantial way. I feel like I sold out as a passionate scholar activist for adjuncts. I chose to work, instead of walk out, because I needed the money to pay down my student loan and credit card debt. I sold out.

Neoliberalism, as defined by Chomsky (1999), Clawson and Page (2011), Giroux (2005, 2014), Reich (1992), and others, is a force that impacts my story and the experience of many adjunct professors and graduate students in higher education who—like other workers or professionals who aspire to move up in their respective fields—toil and are exploited because they aspire to admission into the academy. Silence, complicity, and acquiescence are (or feel like) necessary moves in "playing the game" and being rewarded in higher education, just like workers in other neoliberal corporate arenas. In his discussion of the neoliberal turn in higher education, Giroux (2014) notes that

> [a]s universities turn toward corporate management models, they increasingly use and exploit cheap faculty labor. Many colleges and universities are drawing more and more upon adjunct and nontenured faculty, many of whom occupy the status of indentured servants who are overworked, lack benefits, receive little to no administrative support, and are paid salaries that qualify them for food stamps.
>
> (p. 20)

Thirty-plus years of neoliberal policies have brought a barbaric form of vulture capitalism into higher education which preys upon vulnerable communities, such as college students and adjunct faculty who need the degree and work, all while raising tuition and operating on a model that depends on student debt and privileges commodification, privatization, deregulation, and unchecked selfishness, among other "free market" ideals (Crouch, 2011; Harvey, 2005, 2010). According to Giroux (2014), free-market fundamentalism, another phrase for neoliberalism, "has become not only a much vaunted ideology that now shapes all aspects of life in the United States but also a predatory global phenomenon" (p. 1).

Bauman (2010) suggests that inequality has a lived experience in which there is "a fatal attraction between poverty and vulnerability, corruption and the accumulation of dangers, as well as humiliation and the denial of dignity" (p. 68). My Faustian bargain to turn my back on the adjunct social movement came in the form of a guarantee of a bigger paycheck down the road. It was in my best interest economically not to offend my employer who paid me. It was only a one-year "visiting" glimpse into the full-time faculty life—10 months' pay during the academic year with an option to distribute part of the salary in the summer—but this was more money and job security than I'd ever been offered at the university. After accounting for taxes, I'd make only a small dent in my $23,000 student loan debt that was accruing interest at an alarming rate. On my four student loans the interest rate varies from 5% to 7.5%, with all of the loans accumulating interest that I have to pay off before I am able to pay down the principal loan amount (although, if I pay beyond the $294 monthly payment, I can have the extra payment go to the principal). In addition, I have four credit cards that are all but maxed out (as of spring 2016, my credit card debt stood at $14,860), with interest rates in the high teens and low twenties. The Visiting Instructor job I was offered would be the first year since I was a freshman undergraduate (11 years prior) that I'd be able to stop adding to my debt.

On February 25, 2015, the contract hadn't yet been sent to me for my signature. I'd accepted the offer from my chair, but the paperwork still wasn't executed. This may be the best explanation for why I remained quiet and went about my teaching without uttering a word about National Adjunct Walkout Day.

I went so far as to avoid posting articles dealing with adjunct exploitation on my Facebook page. Actually, I did more than that: I went through the multiple clicks necessary to hide a post from a colleague, an article about the day I was avoiding. The article I hid from my Facebook wall, making it invisible to everyone but me, was a *Chronicle* article titled "Today Is 'National Adjunct Walkout Day': Will It Make a Difference?" (Schmidt, 2015). I did everything in my power to make sure that National Adjunct Walkout Day *didn't* make a difference, not on my campus or through my social media presence. My deliberate absence from the movement, manifested in my actions of docile compliance and avoidance, is something I still feel torn about today.

Although my prospects had improved drastically by February 25, 2015, the same day many adjunct professors were walking out of their respective universities in protest, I didn't feel any better walking out of my chair's office. I felt relieved that I wasn't being let go for my critique of the neoliberal university, but I was not happy. I wasn't happy because, while I had bided my time until receiving a promotion that bettered my individual well-being, I was enacting a performance of complicity within the larger neoliberal system of hierarchy—the two-tier system of faculty inequality (Hoeller, 2014)—keeping the system of inequity in place with my actions of accepting the offer and not participating in the National Adjunct Walkout Day.

Van Arsdale (1978) saw the current plight of precarious adjunct employment coming four decades ago when he noted that "the diminishing opportunity for full-time employment is but one of the grim problems part-time faculty face. . . . [T]he broadest implications of their situation signal a de-professionalizing of university teaching itself" (p. 195). Today, the higher education landscape is one filled with specialized faculty professionals who are, indeed, "knowledge workers" (Lee, Cheslock, Maldonado, & Rhoades, 2005), but the "new majority" (Kezar, 2012) of faculty are non-tenure track and treated as sub-professionals, devalued, de-professionalized (Giroux, 2014) and continuously uncertain about future employment.

With current U.S. Department of Labor statistics indicating that 75% of the U.S. professoriate is part-time (Edmonds, 2015; U.S. House Committee on Education and the Workforce, 2014), adjuncts who are individually offered a full-time job—a lift up out of the lower, subordinate tier of the faculty workforce (Hoeller, 2014)—are rare exceptions in a faculty system where the longer one toils as an adjunct, the more one will remain stuck, separated from the tenure track and branded as contingent, a label that becomes a self-fulfilling prophecy for too many of today's professors. Aside from the occasional section of Public Speaking taught by the department chair, adjuncts teach all offered sections of the course at the university where I teach.

Neoliberalism is a culture "marked by fear, surveillance, and economic deprivation" (Giroux, 2014, p. 12). Fear, surveillance, and economic deprivation are present when working as an adjunct. In my case, anxiety over having accepted a short-term offer that allowed me to better my financial situation for a year despite my publications on adjunct exploitation made me fearful and governed my conduct of avoidance, acquiescence, and silence on National Adjunct Walkout Day. I'm still amazed at the proficiency, even normalcy, with which I performed that day. I graded my students' speeches after class, going through my same ritual of sorting through peer comments, grading the outlines, watching the speeches again on the recording program, and writing comments on their grading form and in the End Notes section of the speech recording website.

Reflecting back, I am ashamed at how I detachedly minimized the story about National Adjunct Walkout Day on my computer before going back to business as usual, how I actively removed a Facebook post on my wall about adjunct social movements, and how I sealed my acceptance of the Visiting Professor position with active complicity, going about my job, going through the motions, and not making any noise. I feel, at least in part, like I've sold out, like I'm not doing enough/anything to stand in solidarity with the more than one million adjuncts working at U.S. colleges and universities (Coalition on the Academic Workforce [CAW], 2012; Fredrickson, 2015).

Instead of standing up and speaking out, I drove home from the university on February 25, 2015, and graded my students' papers. Quietly. Laying my soul bare as I write this, I feel that I committed a deplorable act of treason against my fellow adjunct colleagues, an act of turning away, for the money. That day in my chair's office, after I "signed" with my verbal agreement, I walked out, sighed and was surprised that *this didn't feel like I thought it would, being offered the gig I so desperately need.* But that initial thought was replaced with self-centered thoughts drowning out the cognitive dissonance of my decisions:

> *Maybe I can pay down my debts,*
> *increase my job security,*
> *increase my abysmal credit score,*
> *enjoy the benefits of medical insurance for a year,*
> *have that voice at the full-time faculty meetings I always wanted to have,*
> *be able to teach courses I have always wanted to teach, (and other me-related self-interests).*

As a neoliberal subject, I am "disciplined" (Foucault, 1977) to keep quiet, make nice, and keep up appearances . . . that is, if I ever want to "make it" as a tenure-track professor. Neoliberalism minimizes collective good by glorifying individual gain; and it glorifies "profit over people" at all costs (Chomsky, 1999). After all, if the individual has "made it," then clearly she or he deserved it. This myth of meritocracy persists in higher education, and I must admit that it has blinded me at times since being offered a full-time position at my university. Thoughts such as *I've put in the time and work, maybe I have a right to realize my dream to have gainful employment in the academy* and *Don't I deserve this promotion?* may have some truth in them, but they also reify the myth of meritocracy and effectively silenced my voice in the collective adjunct struggle, a tradeoff for job security, benefits, and other *individual* gains.

Conclusion

Investigating my personal reality of poverty wages and ever-increasing debt, and the precarious promise of (re)employment in a neoliberal system that privileges a shrinking slice of haves over a wide swath of have-nots and have-too-littles, I made the choice of attending to the debts I can't walk out on. I made the choice to join the circle of "haves" for a year, with an inter-view looming for the tenure track spot my chair would be doing an external search for soon after my position began. I also made a choice to ignore what I feel in my heart and what I've written about adjunct exploitation, shun-ning signs of National Adjunct Walkout Day. I intentionally ignored the day to the extent that I don't even know whether any faculty demonstrated on our campus. Instead of taking a stand on a day when thousands of other adjunct faculty were likely putting their jobs on the line, I did my job and kept quiet. I was a neoliberal "machine . . . an automaton" (Frankl, 1959, p. 155) on February 25, 2015. A cowardly cog.

But all is not lost. Reflexively examining my thoughts, actions, and mem-ory of National Adjunct Walkout Day, I can trace the veering away from my justice-oriented voice to a silenced simulacrum of myself and write about it. Even if writing doesn't make it right, it helps me and, when published, others to make sense of our conditioned if not socially constructed actions. I may have accepted a *visiting* offer, but the lesson I learned in the process gives me reason to believe that I can interrupt our stay with neoliberalism and fight through my future words and actions, in ways large and small, to resist and transform the neoliberal cult of individualism and meritoc-racy, returning as an ally to help adjuncts and other exploited laborers to achieve fair working conditions and gainful employment. As adjunct profes-sors or tenure-track faculty members, we can use our courses to dismantle the master's neoliberal project, something I am doing through my teaching and scholarly activity (see Hartlep & Hensley, 2015; Hartlep, Hensley, Bra-niger, & Jennings, 2017). After investigating my performance on National Adjunct Walkout Day 2015, I won't walk out on the adjunct movement in the future.

Note

1 See https://www.youtube.com/watch?v=kbWFcqbefMs for a video that offers an insightful look into the lives of professors who live on poverty wages.

References

Bauman, Z. (2010). *Living on borrowed time: Conversations with Citlati Rovirosa-Madrazo*. Cambridge, MA: Polity Press.

Chomsky, N. (1999). *Profit over people: Neoliberalism and global order*. New York: Seven Stories Press.

Clawson, D., & Page, M. (2011). *The future of higher education*. New York: Routledge.

Coalition on the Academic Workforce (CAW). (2012). *A portrait of part-time faculty members*. Retrieved from www.academicworkforce.org/CAW_portrait_2012.pdf

Crouch, C. (2011). *The strange non-death of neoliberalism*. Cambridge, UK: Polity Press.

Edmonds, D. (2015, May 28). More than half of college faculty are adjuncts: Should you care? *Forbes*. Retrieved from www.forbes.com/sites/noodleeducation/2015/05/28/more-than-half-of-college-faculty-are-adjuncts-should-you-care/#7156814b1d9b

Flaherty, C. (2015, January 27). A day without adjuncts. *Inside Higher Ed*. Retrieved from https://www.insidehighered.com/news/2015/01/27/national-adjunct-walkout-day-approaches-attracting-both-enthusiasm-and-questions

Foucault, M. (1977). *Discipline and punish: The birth of the prison*. New York: Vintage Books.

Frankl, V. (1959). *Man's search for meaning*. Boston: Beacon Press.

Fredrickson, C. (2015, September 15). There is no excuse for how universities treat adjuncts. *The Atlantic*. Retrieved from www.theatlantic.com/business/archive/2015/09/higher-education-college-adjunct-professor-salary/404461/

Giroux, H. A. (2005). The terror of neoliberalism: Rethinking the significance of cultural politics. *College Literature, 32*(1), 1–19. Retrieved from http://dx.doi.org/10.1353/lit.2005.0006

Giroux, H. A. (2014). *Neoliberalism's war on higher education*. Chicago: Haymarket Books.

Hartlep, N. D., & Hensley, B. O. (Eds.). (2015). *Critical storytelling in uncritical times: Stories disclosed in a cultural foundations of education course*. Rotterdam, The Netherlands: Sense Publishers.

Hartlep, N. D., Hensley, B. O., Braniger, C., & Jennings, M. (Eds.). (2017). *Critical storytelling in uncritical times: Undergraduates share their stories in higher education*. Rotterdam, The Netherlands: Sense Publishers.

Harvey, D. (2005). *A brief history of neoliberalism*. New York: Oxford University Press.

Harvey, D. (2010). *The enigma of capitalism*. New York: Oxford University Press.

Hensley, B. O. (2013). The absent adjunct. *The Adjunct Project*. Retrieved from http://adjunct.chronicle.com/the-absent-adjunct/

Hensley, B. O. (2015). We are not "cordwood": Critical stories and the two-tier system in U.S. higher education. In N. D. Hartlep & B. O. Hensley (Eds.), *Critical storytelling in uncritical times: Stories disclosed in a cultural foundations of education course* (pp. 75–92). Rotterdam, The Netherlands: Sense Publishers.

Hoeller, K. (Ed.). (2014). *Equality for contingent faculty: Overcoming the two-tier system.* Nashville, TN: Vanderbilt University Press.

Keeling, R. P., & Hersh, R. H. (2012). *We're losing our minds: Rethinking American higher education.* New York: Palgrave Macmillan.

Kezar, A. (2012). *Embracing non-tenure track faculty: Changing campuses for the new faculty majority.* New York: Routledge.

Lee, J., Cheslock, J., Maldonado, A., & Rhoades, G. (2005). Professors as knowledge workers in the new, global economy. In J. Smart (Ed.), *Higher education: Handbook of theory and research* (pp. 55–132). London: Springer. Retrieved from http://dx.doi.org/10.1007/1-4020-3279-x_2

Reich, R. B. (1992). *The work of nations: Preparing ourselves for 21st-century capitalism.* New York: Vintage Books.

Schmidt, P. (2015, February 25). Today Is 'National Adjunct Walkout Day.' Will It Make a Difference? *The Chronicle of Higher Education.* Retrieved from http://chronicle.com/article/Today-Is-National-Adjunct/190339?cid=megamenu

U.S. Department of Health and Human Services. (2015, September 3). *2015 Poverty guidelines.* Retrieved from http://aspe.hhs.gov/2015-poverty-guidelines

U.S. House Committee on Education and the Workforce Democratic Staff. (2014, January). *The just-in-time professor: A staff report summarizing eForum responses on the working conditions of contingent faculty in higher education.* Washington, DC: House Committee on Education and the Workforce.

Van Arsdale, G. (1978). De-professionalizing a part-time teaching faculty: How many, feeling small, seeming few, getting less, dream of more. *The American Sociologist, 13*(4), 195–201.

8 Misplaced Faith in the American Dream

Buried in Debt in the Catacombs of the Ivory Tower

Brian R. Horn

Introduction

During graduate school at Michigan State University (MSU) in the early 2000s, I taught a Social Foundations of Education course for one of my two graduate assistantships. An essential component of the course was to engage pre-service teachers in analysis of power, privilege, and how schools impact people based on their race, socioeconomic class, sexuality, gender, language, (dis)ability, religion, and other sociocultural constructs. A second aspect of the course was to have students confront the *achievement ideology*. This was accomplished by having students read Jay MacLeod's (1995) *Ain't No Makin' It: Aspirations and Attainment in a Low-Income Neighborhood*. In his book, MacLeod described the *achievement ideology* as the belief that if a person works hard s/he will be successful. Presenting this critique at an elite public research university to groups of college students who generally believed that their lot in life was almost exclusively due to their hard work and wise choices was a large and exciting task each semester.

During class discussions I would often share personal experiences from my own youth in order to push back against a student's assertion, reveling in the fact that I felt I had the intellectual upper hand. By the end of the course I would feel accomplished if I saw that my students were articulating ideas such as "hard work is essential, but it is no guarantee," and "people can make choices, but they can't choose the consequences of their choices." I seemingly was having my students question the *achievement ideology* and, in turn, question their faith in the middle-class American Dream of prosperity, social mobility, and success via hard work. The entire reasoning behind pushing the students in this way was so that they would have a deeper sociological and systemic understanding of themselves and the students who would soon fill their classrooms. Would they encourage their students to "pull themselves up by their bootstraps," or would they help develop curricula that would allow their students to better understand, critique, and challenge the social structures that shape their lives?

Looking back, I wonder what effect these discussions had on them personally, especially in the face of a collapsing Michigan economy and narrowing job market that awaited them post-graduation. Moreover, in retrospect, how has my own relationship with the American Dream changed since I completed graduate school and entered the academy as a professor? It is this latter question that I take up in this chapter.

College and the American Dream

In 1944, Congress passed the controversial and somewhat radical Serviceman's Readjustment Act, commonly known as the GI Bill. Under the bill, veterans would receive home loan benefits, a weekly $20 stipend, and financial support for a college education (U.S. Department of Veterans Affairs, 2016). Detractors thought the stipend would diminish veterans' incentive to work, and that combat-experienced veterans had no place on college campuses alongside the privileged and economically rich (U.S. Department of Veterans Affairs, 2016). At the time of the bill's passing, about 2 million Americans were enrolled in U.S. colleges and universities, roughly an even split between private and public institutions. However, by the mid-1960s private college and university enrollment had almost doubled to just less than 2 million while public college and university enrollment hit around 5 million. This overall increase of college and university enrollment, particularly in public institutions, continued in the coming decades—by 2009, around 5 million Americans were enrolled in private colleges and universities and almost 15 million Americans were enrolled in two- or four-year public institutions of higher education (Bennett, 2011).

Prior to World War II, college and homeownership were, for the most part, unreachable dreams for the average American. However, in the wake of the GI Bill, millions of veterans who would have otherwise entered the job market instead chose to further their education. In the peak year of 1947, veterans accounted for 49% of college admissions. The authors of the GI Bill had anticipated that about 800,000 veterans would take advantage of the education and training provisions, but by the time the original GI Bill ended on July 25, 1956, 7.8 million of 16 million WWII veterans had participated in an education or training program (U.S. Department of Veterans Affairs, 2016). In the second half of the 20th century, the function of colleges and universities had dramatically changed; a college education was more available to the proletariat and could be directly parlayed into the American Dream of prosperity, social mobility, and success. Unfortunately, the benefits of the GI Bill were not justly available to all veterans. The GI Bill became a deliberate and *de facto* extension of *de jure* Jim Crow laws. For example, of the first 67,000 mortgages insured by the GI Bill, fewer than 100 were taken out by veterans of color (Katznelson, 2005). While the Bill had become a huge success for white veterans in achieving the American Dream, it became another roadblock for veterans of color to do the same.

As demand for college and university education increased across the country, particularly among public institutions, states embraced this change.

Rather than take advantage of the flood of new "customers" by becoming more selective and/or increasing tuition, states rushed to keep up by expanding current institutions and building new ones. The federal government became more involved by creating a series of loan programs, which made college more accessible for middle-class civilians as the GI Bill had done for white veterans (Sanchez, 2014). And in the midst of the civil rights movement, the Higher Education Act of 1965 encouraged greater college access for women and people of color. Two decades after the GI Bill was passed, states and the federal government were investing in their citizens by making college more accessible and affordable than ever before.

In the early 1970s, college enrollment continued to steadily increase and the national average for a school year of tuition and fees at a four-year public college or university in 1975 was $542, or $2,387 in 2015 dollars (College Board, 2015). However, the three-decade-long era of college access and affordability began to change. During the late 1970s, the national economy weakened, federal and state budgets tightened, the backlash to the civil rights movement strengthened, and the public investment in college and university enrollment was in stark contrast to the rising neo-conservative movement. Public colleges and universities started to get less funding from their states, so tuition began to increase across the country to fill the void. Prior to the 1970s, tuition rates increased around 2–3% per year, on par with the national rate of inflation. But since the mid-1970s, tuition at public institutions has increased 5–6% above the national rate of inflation per year. In 2003 alone, average college costs went up 14% (Ferguson, 2012).

Today the average annual cost of tuition and fees at a public four-year college or university is $9,410—an almost 400% increase from 40 years ago (College Board, 2015). Roughly during this same time period, by comparison, the real median household income has only increased by 144% (Committee for Economic Development, 2012). More students are going to college, college is becoming more expensive, household incomes are not keeping pace, and college debt is exploding. In 1993, the average college debt of a recent graduate was $9,450, while the real median household income that year was $50,421. Compare these figures to 2012, when the average college debt of a recent graduate was $29,400, while the real median household income that year was $52,605 (Federal Reserve Bank of St. Louis, 2014; The Institute for College Access and Success, 2014). A college education, the cornerstone of the American Dream, has become increasingly burdensome on graduates long after their last class on campus, to the point that many young people are wondering whether college is worth it.

Experiencing the American Dream

I grew up always knowing I would go to college. At the time of my birth, my mother, who was a teacher, and my father, who was a graduate student, rented a small duplex in Wichita, Kansas, that was home to my parents, my older sister, and me. Going to college was always a given growing up, even though I did poorly in school and generally felt disengaged from kindergarten through high school graduation. When my father graduated with his master's degree in 1980, my parents bought a modest house in a working class neighborhood in our large city. Even as a young child I got to see the "natural" progression of the middle-class American Dream. My parents went to college, even graduate school, got good jobs, and were able to buy a house in a good neighborhood while accruing very little debt. Yet as I got older I saw the inconsistency and fragility of the American Dream.

Right as I started school, my parents divorced and my father moved out. The ideal stability and economic momentum of a two-income household was no longer a reality. As a single, working mother, my mom was fiercely frugal. I remember going out to eat only on special occasions, and when we did, we went to Hardee's. While there, we'd gather ketchup and jelly packets that we would take home for our daily use. Instead of driving 500 miles to visit my grandparents, we would take the Greyhound bus. Instead of buying new shorts for summer, my mom would make them herself. As I grew older and developed friendships with the five boys in the neighborhood, I learned that we had a lot in common. My friends hated school like I did, and we never felt like school had anything important to offer us. My friends' mothers were single moms, like mine. They, too had penny-pinching stories about their moms similar to mine. But my mom was the only one who had gone to college. She was the only one who drew a salary, instead of an hourly wage. And as we entered middle school, I was the only one who knew he was going to college. When the subject was brought up with my friends, they scoffed at the idea, said they hated school, they couldn't afford it, and that college wasn't for them. I really didn't think it was necessarily for me either, or that I could afford it, but I knew that it was expected of me.

By the time of high school graduation, I was the only one who was headed to college. I hadn't graduated with honors, or done anything remarkably better or different than my five childhood friends. In fact, I had the worse academic reputation of the lot, having been academically ineligible to compete in athletics the second half of my senior year. Nonetheless, I was the only one of the six of us going to college. In retrospect, it looked as if the schools in our working-class neighborhood had done their jobs. Regardless of our effort, or engagement, or success, we had been socially reproduced and were set to follow in our mothers' footsteps (Bourdieu, 1992).

I had only a few options when it came to colleges, and I certainly wasn't offered any scholarships. Luckily, I lived in a state that (at the time) had a guaranteed admission policy at all state universities for all high school graduates. I chose to go to a small state university close to home, and, surprisingly, I eventually studied to be an elementary school teacher. While going through the application process, I remember being shocked at the cost of tuition. I don't remember the exact figure, but tuition in the early 1990s per semester at my university was around $980. This meant that

I could work during the summer and school year and write a check out of my own bank account at the beginning of each semester and pay for college. It wasn't something that I appreciated or even realized at the time, but I was on course to graduate from college certified to have a high-demand, modestly compensated career with zero debt.

I returned to my hometown to teach in city public schools similar to the ones I attended. Early in my career I saw more and more examples of parents, community members, and students who disproved the mythic American Dream. I saw people who worked hard, made rational decisions, and yet still butt against systemic obstacles in school, banking, housing, and the criminal justice system, and who didn't experience the prosperity and social mobility embodied in the "American Dream." Notwithstanding, I felt immune to their challenges. Subconsciously, I believed that I was, and would be, working hard, making rational decisions, and facing no obstacles that would interrupt my pursuit of the American Dream. In retrospect, I suspect that I assumed that as a white, middleclass, male, I wouldn't have to worry.

After three years of teaching second grade, I decided to attend graduate school. Just like college, this seemed like a natural progression for me. In preparation for graduate school, I wanted to have the options that I didn't have coming out of high school. I was developing into a strong beginning teacher. I researched programs of study, studied for the Graduate Record Examination (GRE) for over a year, and looked into grants and loans, given that my teacher base salary of around $26,000 in 2001 ($34,800 in 2015 dollars) would disallow me from paying as I went this time around. I was married, and my wife worked full-time, but I knew I'd work part-time and the cost of living at the universities we were considering was so high that we knew we would take out loans to cover tuition as well as living expenses. I applied to education programs at Harvard University, the University of Michigan, the University of Wisconsin-Madison, the University of California-Los Angeles, and the University of California-Berkeley. I was accepted and decided to attend the Harvard University Graduate School of Education (HGSE) for a Master's degree in Education. Attending the HGSE epitomized the American Dream for me; an Ivy League education—a Harvard education—for the kid who was kicked off his high school basketball and baseball teams for not passing five classes. It didn't matter what tuition cost me, or how much I would owe after I graduated, or how I was ever going to pay off my loans. All that mattered to me was my abiding faith that my American Dream was going to come to pass in an ivory tower adorned with ivy.

What came after my master's degree was a doctorate. My wife had a decent job in Boston, and I worked part-time at a coffee shop, yet I had accumulated over $40,000 of debt for one year of schooling at Harvard. I looked for more affordable options for my Ph.D. program. I decided to attend MSU. I turned down two other highly regarded public Research 1 institutions because MSU offered me paid assistantships. At MSU, I could take my doctoral courses without charge and work two quarter-time assistantships that allowed me to earn a modest monthly stipend, which amounted to almost half of my previous teaching salary. Cost of living in East Lansing was lower than in Boston, and my wife's employment in accounts at a grocery store corporate office, with my stipend income, kept us from having to take out any more student loans. I was on track to graduate, working hard, making wise financial decisions, and becoming a more educated professional so I could better prepare the next generation of urban public school teachers. I had faith things were working out as I'd initially planned.

My first three years at MSU went as smoothly as I trusted they would. I was progressing in my coursework, challenging my students in my Social Foundations of Education courses, and supervising yearlong student teachers. But at the same time the Michigan economy was in sharp decline. Lansing was a General Motors (GM) town. While I was at MSU, three GM plants were shuttered. My student teachers were graduating, but they weren't landing teaching positions. I was approaching the age of 30 and was interested in owning a home, the culminating step to achieving the American Dream. In retrospect, this was the worst possible decision my wife and I could have made: to buy a house in 2005, when the housing market took a hit. Earlier that year, I finished my coursework at MSU and prepared for the dissertation phase of my doctoral program. I wanted to return to the K–12 classroom full time and dissertate as a current—not former—teacher. I knew that my teaching salary would be noticeably larger than my graduate assistant stipend, and I knew my wife and I would be able to find a good home in a buyer's market. Surrendering my assistantships meant that I had to begin paying tuition at MSU and my student loans that I had taken while a student at Harvard. I didn't think this would be a problem. It would take me only two years to finish my dissertation, so it would not be that challenging financially to make payments on the two years of student loans I had taken out. Unfortunately, life took a different turn.

During the summer of 2005, the Lansing School District offered a retirement bonus to over 100 of their most experienced teachers in an attempt to cut costs and downsize their teaching force in order to keep pace with their declining student enrollment. Later that summer, roughly 50 new teachers were hired, including myself. I taught a 4th/5th grade split classroom at a newly developed magnet school and was excited to be a teacher again. Returning to the classroom to teach provided me with a larger annual salary than what MSU was giving through my assistantships, but because I relinquished my assistantships I had to start taking out loans to cover in-state tuition. Not long after, my wife and I bought our first house for our growing family (by then our daughter was born). Rather than jumping right into a dissertation proposal, I decided to spend my first year back in the K–12 classroom honing my rusty teaching skills, getting to know the school community, and finding the best dissertation project to pursue. However, this seemingly well-conceived plan was abruptly interrupted during the spring of 2006 when, at the end of the school year, I was laid off.

Despite their massive downsizing the previous summer, the school district had more teachers than they needed based on the district's enrollment, and most of the previous summer's new hires were pink-slipped. I was a 31-year-old all-but-dissertation (ABD) doctoral student, an Ivy League graduate, a homeowner, a husband, a father, and unemployed. I quickly learned that all of these accomplishments did not grant me immunity from an economy in recession.

There were no teaching jobs in the surrounding area of Lansing, so I started receiving unemployment benefits. My wife and I put our house on the real-estate market, where it stayed for the next four years until we were finally able to complete a short-sale. Our family of three moved back to Wichita, Kansas. There, I easily found a teaching job, but because I had moved 922 miles away from my dissertation committee, I had to begin my dissertation process over again. Also, because I had moved out of state, I started taking out additional loans to pay for out-of-state tuition, as well as loans to cover housing expenses in Michigan and Kansas. My initial plan of being able to teach full-time and complete my dissertation in two years had been pushed back another year due to moving from Michigan to Kansas. My two-year dissertation plan was further delayed after my son was born in 2007. He was born with a heart defect and my mother-in-law was diagnosed with Lou Gehrig's Disease. This was a very difficult time for my family and me. In May of 2010, I defended my dissertation and graduated from MSU—five long and difficult years after I finished my doctoral coursework (and after one year of taking out loans to pay for graduate tuition while I was a student at Harvard). My faith in the American Dream had taken a hit. Like my mom, familial events outside of our control—in her case, my father divorcing her—had derailed our upward mobility. Despite our best work and intentions, like the parents of many of the middle-school students I taught in Michigan and Kansas, systems of labor and housing were creating seemingly impassible obstacles to my family's America Dream. During the fall of 2010, I accepted a tenure-track assistant professorship at Illinois State University (ISU). My base salary at ISU was $57,000. Not long after I began working at ISU, the notices from all of my student loan lenders came rushing in. All told, I owed an excess of $250,000 in graduate school and graduate school-related debt, over 400% of my base salary.

In retrospect, I'm comfortable with my decisions to attend Harvard and then Michigan State. Attending both universities offered unique and instrumental experiences that shaped me as a person, as well as an educator. Yet I'm still left with persisting questions regarding paying back the debt I've incurred. Despite making regular payments and pursuing loan forgiveness programs, the debt persists, and there is no definite payoff date in sight. When I set out to pursue graduate education and work in higher education, I had faith that if I could earn my spot in top universities, I would be able to parlay that academic success into financial success. Extenuating familial circumstances and a misunderstanding of the new neoliberal economics of higher education proved that my faith was egregiously misplaced.

Based on my personal experiences—growing up in a working-class environment and working as an urban teacher, parenting three children, becoming heavily indebted through higher education, and now working as an urban teacher educator—I see the importance of teachers and youth actively resisting the *achievement ideology*. I work with my students to critique American schooling models that frame curricula, instruction, assessment, and discipline in the shadow of the achievement ideology, whereas individualism, blind effort, obedience, and conformity are presented as antecedents of success. We also look beyond school and examine what structures in American media, politics, history, and culture influence acceptance of the achievement ideology.

Buried in Debt in the Catacombs of the Ivory Tower

Paris is famously known as the "City of Lights." For over 2,000 years, the city of Paris has grown to be a centerpiece of Western culture, art, food, revolution, and scholarship. Paris is home to the iconic Eifel Tower, the beautiful Louvre, the Notre Dame Cathedral, and the Arc de Triomphe. Additionally, Paris is home to the remains of over 6 million former Parisians who are buried far below the famous city's streets. The Catacombs—famous in their own right—were developed in the late 1700s to address cave-ins and overflowing cemeteries in Paris. Known as the world's largest cemetery, the Catacombs are a place of history, reverence, starkness, and finality that stands in clear contrast to the often-extravagant city above.

Figure 8.1 The Paris Catacombs
Joe deSousa (The Paris Catacombs) [CC0], via Wikimedia Commons

Like Paris, the academy in the United States is seen as the centerpiece of our society's culture. Art, scholarship, medicine, science, research, and law are all perfected there, potentially for the greater good. Colloquially, the academy is often described as the "Ivory Tower," a gilded place where much is thought about, but with little connection to the practicalities of the real world. When I left teaching the first time to begin my pursuit of a doctoral degree, my reason was twofold: (1) I believed that doing so would be financially advantageous (even wise) because I would earn much more as a university professor over my lifetime than I would as a K–12 classroom teacher, and (2) I wanted to be a part of the university community that contributed to cultural (r)evolution. My two goals seemed attainable, mostly because I had faith in my ability to control conditions surrounding achieving the American Dream. But, as I've noted already, my journey to the professoriate has been filled with familial and financial difficulties. I've achieved my goal of employment at a university, but, in doing so, my family and I am buried beneath it: in debt.

Just as there are millions of Parisians buried (with)in the Catacombs, there are countless university adjunct and tenure-line professors buried in debt. Just over half (50%) of all university faculty members are adjuncts, up from 30% in 1975. These faculty members teach, research, and often have the same responsibilities as their tenure-lined peers, while more than half of them make less than $35,000 per year (Edmonds, 2015). Furthermore, 22% of adjuncts live below the federal poverty line, and an incredible 14% of all university faculty (adjunct or tenure-track) live at or below the poverty line (see SEIU, 2016). Many recent Ph.D. graduates who are teaching in higher education are coming to terms with the difficult math of having borrowed tens or hundreds of thousands of dollars to complete their terminal degrees, while simultaneously working in a field that won't allow them to pay off their debt anytime soon. In June 2014, Audrey Williams June interviewed academics about their debt and prospects of paying it off while having a tenure-line position. One respondent who possessed $209,000 of graduate-school debt noted the following: "I make a payment every month, bigger than my rent, but I'll likely die with this debt unpaid, despite a TT job" (June, 2014, para. 17). Another recently graduated academic who had $96,000 in graduate-school debt wrote, "I have no plan but some hope for the 10-year forgiveness program for teaching at a public institution. I currently make so little money that I am not even making monthly payments. This entire endeavor was a big mistake" (para. 19).

What happens when many of society's experts, innovators, researchers, and teachers are consigned to a lifetime of debt? What happens when many of the most educated professionals in society are obstructed from gaining prosperity and social mobility? What happens when people's faith in the promise of a better life through advanced education is proven false for the educated and the educators? The current trend of rising college and post-graduate tuition alongside stagnant wages is debilitating for American society. In 1944, and again in 1965, the federal government and states made bold and concerted efforts to expand access to college for veteran, low-, and, especially, middle-income groups to aid social mobility so as to make the American Dream a reality. Now is the time for a renewed investment in higher education to make college more affordable, easing the noose to make loans more manageable, to make university faculty more supported, to rekindle faith in the American Dream.

Much of the shift toward the proletariats' increased dependence on a college education can be linked to the rise of neoliberalism; most notably the ubiquity of markets, privatization, and elimination of the public good. The movement to open college access and affordability to poor people and people of color coincided with the economic shift from a manufacturing economy to a service economy (Hess, 2007). This change meant that "good jobs" would require a college education. Neoliberals would use the market to exploit a new block of "consumers" eager to be the first in their family to attend college and get a "good job." College would continue to be established as a necessity, and, with greater demand, the neoliberal markets obliged with higher tuition costs. With greater demands and higher costs came a greater dependence on loans. Along with moving from "direct" to "guaranteed" loans in 1965, Sallie Mae was the tool created by neoliberal government to enable the finance sector to benefit from federal student loan programs. Sallie Mae itself is not a loan program. It's the Fannie Mae of education. Not only was there money to be made by colleges with greater access to and demand for higher education, but there was big money to be made by big private banks and finance corporations. Finally, neoliberalism's reach into higher education is seen in public sentiment regarding college graduates and their loans. Instead of seeing the people being college-educated as a social asset that requires collective investment, the rhetoric of "individual responsibility," "deadbeats," and "why didn't you go somewhere else then?" permeates the larger conversation. With the increased need for a college education in modern American society, the role of a college professor is of increasing importance. But for the overwhelming majority of college professors, annual salaries (by today's dollars) will likely stay under $100,000 for the entirety of their career. Thus, with the necessity of going to college as well as graduate school, many college professors are caught in the trap of borrowing more to fill a role society needs, only to be paid a salary that doesn't allow them to readily repay their debt.

References

Bennett, D. L. (2011, January 5). Chart of the week: College enrollment growth. *Center for College Affordability and Productivity*. Retrieved from http://collegeaffordability.blogspot.com/2011/01/charts-of-week-college-enrollment.html
Bourdieu, P. (1992). *The logic of practice*. Stanford, CA: Stanford University Press.

College Board. (2016). Tuition and fees and room and board over time, 1975–76 to 2015–16, selected years. *Trends in Higher Education*. Retrieved from http://trends.collegeboard.org/college-pricing/figures-tables/tuition-and-fees-and-room-and-board-over-time-1975-76-2015-16-selected-years

Committee for Economic Development. (2012, April 3). *Boosting secondary education performance*. Retrieved from https://www.ced.org/reports/single/boosting-postsecondary-education-performance

Edmonds, D. (2015, May 28). More than half of college faculty are adjunct: Should you care? *Forbes Magazine*. Retrieved from www.forbes.com/sites/noodleeducation/2015/05/28/more-than-half-of-college- faculty-are-adjuncts-should-you-care/#569853391d9b

Federal Reserve Bank of St. Louis. (2014). *Real median household income in the United States*. Retrieved from https://research.stlouisfed.org/fred2/series/MEHOINUSA672N

Ferguson, A. (2012). *Crazy U: One dad's crash course in getting his kid into college*. New York: Simon & Shuster.

Hess, F. M. (2007). *Footing the tuition bill: The new student loan sector*. Washington, DC: AEI Press.

The Institute of College Access & Success. (2014, March). *Quick facts about student debt*. Retrieved from http://ticas.org/sites/default/files/pub_files/Debt_Facts_and_Sources.pdf

June, A. W. (2014, January 16). The cost of a Ph.D.: Students report hefty debt across many fields. *The Chronicle of Higher Education*. Retrieved from http://chronicle.com/article/The-Cost-of-a-PhD-Students/144049/

Katznelson, I. (2005). *When affirmative action was white: An untold history of racial inequality in twentieth-century America*. New York: W.W. Norton.

MacLeod, J. (1995). *Ain't no makin' it: Aspirations and attainment in a low-income neighborhood*. Boulder, CO: Westview Press.

Sanchez, C. (March 18, 2014). How the cost of college went from affordable to sky-high. *National Public Radio*. Retrieved from www.npr.org/2014/03/18/290868013/how-the-cost-of-college-went-from-affordable-to-sky-high

SEIU. (2016). Professors in poverty. *Faculty Forward*. Retrieved from http://seiufacultyforward.org/professors-in-poverty/

U.S. Department of Veterans Affairs. (2016). *History and timeline, education and training*. Retrieved from www.benefits.va.gov/gibill/history.asp

9 An Adjunct Professor's Communication Barriers With Neoliberal Student Debt Collectors

Antonio L. Ellis

A Brief Overview

For all of 2015, the challenges I faced while trying to communicate with debt collectors were insurmountable. As a person with a speech impediment, I desired to communicate with my student debt collectors online; however, they insisted that I communicate with them verbally over the telephone, claiming "this is our only method of communication." Due to the fact that my speech impediment prohibits me from effectively communicating by phone, my student loans went into default. Thereafter, I was forced to ask other people to call my student loan debt collectors for me. Asking others to call for me meant giving them my personal information such as my social security number, debt amount, and other personal information. While I asked people whom I trusted, I still was uncomfortable. To add insult to injury, the debt collectors told my advocates that they could speak on my behalf only if I verbally grant them permission, which caused me to have to strain words to them over those phone calls so that others could speak on my behalf.

In my opinion, it's absurd that in the age of progressive technology, someone with a verbal disability is forced to talk to federal government employees over the phone. This chapter will draw upon similar daunting experiences to situate neoliberalism as terrorizing those it pathologizes as "different," with student loan collection being but one example of this dehumanizing treatment.

Introduction

In this chapter, I aim to raise more awareness regarding the plight and life experiences of people who are speech impaired and who have student loan debt. My research (dissertation and otherwise) has focused on the experiences of people who stutter. Here, I write about my own experiences with student loan debt and student debt collectors, sharing how my verbal communicative disorder caused my student loans to default with FedLoan Servicing, the loan servicer for my United States Department of Education (ED) federal student loan. In addition, I will offer suggestions for how government agencies and student loan collection companies can accommodate people with verbal communicative disorders, particularly those who stutter. My perspective of neoliberalism is rooted in the critical literature of Henry Giroux (2014) and David Harvey (2005). In his book *A Brief History of Neoliberalism*, Harvey (2005) offers a somewhat lengthy definition of neoliberalism, which alludes to education debt:

> Neoliberalism is in the first instance a theory of political economic practices that proposes that human well-being can best be advanced by liberating individual entrepreneurial freedoms and skills within an institutional framework characterized by strong private property rights, free markets, and free trade. The role of the state is to create and preserve an institutional framework appropriate to such practices. The state has to guarantee, for example, the quality and integrity of money. It must also set up those military, defense, police, and legal structures and functions required to secure private property rights and to guarantee, by force if need be, the proper functioning of markets. Furthermore, if markets do not exist (in areas such as land, water, education, health care, social security, or environmental pollution) then they must be created, by state action if necessary. But beyond these tasks the state should not venture. State interventions in markets (once created) must be kept to a bare minimum because, according to the theory, the state cannot possibly possess enough information to second-guess market signals (prices) and because powerful interest groups will inevitably distort and bias state interventions (particularly in democracies) for their own benefit.
>
> (p. 2)

In light of Harvey's working definition of neoliberalism, I encourage readers of this chapter to think critically about educational debt agencies as incubators of neoliberalism. Therefore, I raise the question, "What is neoliberalism doing within educational spaces, and how does it impact people with stuttering disabilities?"

Student Loans and People Who Stutter

People who stutter represent a small portion of our total population in the United States. According to the National Institute of Deafness and Other Communication Disorders (2016), roughly three million Americans stutter and the majority of these are male. A meta-analysis by Yairi and Ambrose (2013) suggests there is considerable confusion on the incidence of stuttering in the population, but they conclude it may be almost 5%. Furthermore, the National Stuttering Foundation (2012) reports that the number of males who stutter is about four times that of females. Out of the entire population of persons who stutter, one might suggest that African American men who stutter represent an even smaller portion and often face both racial and communicative challenges. As an African American man who stutters,

I am a representative of this "small" population, and I have a critical story to share.

Although people who stutter may have stories to share, researchers typically study the physical actions of speech, instead conducting studies on their overall life experiences (Corcoran & Stewart, 1998; Prud'homme & Hensley, 2013). Most of the literature written about stuttering reveals physical dimensions of speech. Not much attention is given to the multiple ways a communicative disorder negatively impacts the quality of life for this population. People who stutter have life experiences—constituting marginalized standpoints—that differ from those of people who do not stutter. For me, the problem of stuttering became amplified with student loan providers and led to my loan default designation. Meanwhile, there is a dearth of literature on how stuttering affects individuals after they complete undergraduate and graduate school. This is a disconnect I hope to call attention to in my story.

Purpose of this Chapter

The purpose of this autoethnographic chapter is to add to the body of literature regarding the impact of student loan debt on people with communicative disorders. This chapter is written through an autoethnographic lens in order to shed light on my experiences as a stuttering adjunct professor with defaulted student loans. In light of the scarcity of research on this subject, the second purpose of this chapter is to help readers gain an in-depth understanding of how the narrow communication methods of ED loan servicers can cause borrowers with communicative disorders to default on their student loans. While my experience is with FedLoan Servicing, the loan servicer of the Pennsylvania Higher Education Assistance Agency (PHEAA), hereafter referred to as FedLoan, my story is vital for encouraging all student debt collecting entities[1] to provide reasonable communication accommodations for a population whose members are unable to effectively communicate by telephone. Although one single personalized autoethnographic chapter cannot account for all persons with communicative disabilities, the story can raise awareness for consideration.

The Beginning of My Student Debt

As I reflected upon the beginning of my experience with student loans, I realized that it linked back to my primary schooling experiences. While in primary schools, I was known as an introvert. Due to being teased and bullied (being called names like "stutter butter") I constantly stayed to myself. In light of my being an extreme introvert, many of my teachers and school administrators questioned whether I was mentally retarded (now known as intellectually disabled). When it was my turn to read aloud or verbally participate in class, the words that were in my brain would not come through my mouth.

Although my teachers knew that I was speech impaired, they would still call on me to verbally participate. Many of them stated that they were preparing me for the real world, where verbally speaking is a requirement. In essence, they were correct, as in the late 1980s and early 1990s, assistive technology for persons with speech impediments was almost nonexistent. Even in the year 2017, there are few technologies available for persons with speech impediments, with only online chatting and text messaging being options. However, based on my communication with student loan providers, online chatting and text messaging options are not used by student loan providers because of security measures.

I remained an introvert throughout primary and secondary school and, in many ways, into my adulthood. I still avoid situations and environments where I feel that I would be required to verbally communicate at length. For example, my friends and family know that I rarely answer the phone when they call. Instead, I refrain from answering the phone and immediately follow-up the call with a text message. To this extent, although all of my friends and family are aware that I am speech impaired, even some of them still insist on calling.

How does any of this connect to the beginning of my student debt? There is a direct correlation because we are living in a fluency-dominated culture (Hartlep & Ellis, 2012). Because there are only roughly three million people in America who stutter, most people tend to disregard stuttering and not take it seriously. When I ask people to text me instead of calling me, I often get responses such as, "Just take your time; breathe and think about you want to say; I can wait until you get the words out; and your stuttering doesn't bother me." In my experience, it appears that most people have normalized verbal communication fluency such that they are willing to inconvenience the person with the stuttering disability.

Based on pressure from others to be fluent, I was pushed more toward being a fearful introvert. Because of that, while in primary school, I began being truant because of my fear of coming to school. Eventually, my truancy caused me to fail the second and fifth grades. While my verbally fluent peers were in class learning, I was roaming the streets or hiding out in the school restrooms. My truancy caused me to miss out on valuable academic instruction and exposure. During the times when I would come to class, I was unable to focus, due to being scared and nervous about being called on to participate verbally. During those times, I would be more focused on my fear of being called on than on paying attention to what my teachers were teaching.

My truancy, combined with the fear that I constantly felt in the educational environment, particularly in high school, is the foundation of my student loan debt. First and foremost, because I rarely attended class, my grade point average was too low for me to earn academic scholarships. The only scholarship I qualified for was a partial marching band scholarship. Second, I didn't attend the workshops and trainings about how to apply for college and avoid student loan debt pitfalls, which my peers were attending, because I was afraid of being asked to introduce myself verbally.

Lastly, although my family didn't have the experience base to assist me, I also didn't communicate with my teachers or guidance counselors about college and how to pay for it because I knew it would require a heightened amount of verbal communication. In light of my fear to speak and being a first generation college student, after I exited high school I blindly applied for student loans without much guidance.

Communication Disorders and Student Loan Debt

The courts are presently divided on whether student loans are considered to be consumer debt. Assuming they are, student loans are the second largest category of consumer debt behind home mortgages. The student loan market has grown rapidly over the last decades (Collinge, 2009). In 2014, there were more than 40 million federal and private student loan borrowers and collectively these consumers owed more than $1.3 trillion (Best & Best, 2014). The market is now facing an increasing number of borrowers who are struggling to stay current on their loans. For many indebted college graduates, repaying a student loan is their first experience in the financial services marketplace.

Student loans will play a pivotal role as they seek to establish their creditworthiness and, eventually, finance their first major purchases, typically a car and a home. This potential impact on millions of Americans' lives only heightens the student debt stress borrowers face. According to *The State of the Nation's Housing* (2015) published by the Joint Center for Housing Studies at Harvard University, high amounts of student loan debt make it challenging for millennials to purchase homes because having high amounts of student debt undermines saving for down payments that are necessary for transitioning from renting to owning.

While student loan debt is a life-altering challenge for most persons, there is another hurdle that comes along with student loan debt. After leaving or graduating from college or graduate school, those with student loans must contact their loan providers to set up a payment plan or to request a deferment. While much of this can be done online, phone contact is necessary whenever problems are encountered. For most debtors this is easy enough, even if it's a hassle; but communicating with a student loan representative over the phone is nearly impossible for a person with a verbal communicative disorder.

James, Brumfitt, and Cudd (1999) surveyed 223 people with stuttering impairments on their attitudes toward using the telephone. Their survey results determined that *making* a telephone call was judged to be more problematic than *answering* a telephone call by those who stutter. Additionally, avoidance behaviors, such as writing or using alternatives to the telephone, or asking someone else to make a phone call, were reported more in younger than older stutterers.

Last, people who rated their stutter as "severe" reported using the telephone the least frequently. While I consider myself young and with a relatively severe stutter, I find avoiding phone calls nearly impossible, especially when it comes to communicating with FedLoan. Unfortunately, based on my personal experiences, the only way to communicate in a timely fashion with FedLoan is via telephone.

Being a Speech-Impaired Adjunct Professor With Student Debt

In light of fiscal constraints (Gappa, Austin, & Trice, 2007) and calls to lower the cost of an undergraduate education (Kezar, 2012; Webber & Boehmer, 2008), colleges and universities have become increasingly reliant on adjunct faculty (NCES, 2013). Based on the ED's National Center for Education Statistics (NCES) Digest on Educational Statistics (2013), of the 1.54 million faculty employed in the United States in 2013, barely half (51.3%) were full-time professors, a steady decrease since this statistic was first kept in 1970, when 77.8% of professors were full-time. And there are 3.25 times more post-secondary faculty members today than in 1970. Furthermore, research shows that undergraduate student enrollments are expected to increase by 15% by 2020 (Werf, 2009). Therefore, the use of a lower-cost adjunct faculty pool is likely to increase.

Because their pay is so low, adjunct faculty members often try to teach as many courses as possible to make enough income to pay their necessary expenses. Indeed, many teach five to fifteen courses annually at different higher education institutions (see Chapters 5–7, this volume). Most adjuncts are paid per course, and the median salary is between $3,300 and $4,500 for each three-credit course. In addition, adjunct faculty are very seldom provided benefits and have no real job security. Generally, their contracts are per term and they have to (re)apply for their jobs the following term. Moreover, classes can be canceled up to the first day of the semester. If a course is canceled, the adjunct most likely will not be paid for the class and/or the preparatory work s/he may have already done.

Given the national state of affairs regarding the push for cheap contingent faculty, I landed an adjunct position at a liberal arts college in South Carolina instead of the full-time tenure-track position for which I had prepared and hoped. My long-term intention for pursuing a doctoral degree in educational leadership and policy studies was to become an educational administrator (i.e., assistant principal, assistant school superintendent, school district office employee, educational leadership tenure-track professor, etc.). After decades of experiencing bullying and being marginalized as a student who stuttered in K–12 and higher-education classrooms, I am now experiencing what it's like to be someone who has a stutter as an adjunct college professor who has also defaulted on his student loans.

Upon completing my doctoral degree in 2013, I immediately started reaching out to my student loan servicers via e-mail in order to request a loan deferment because my income was insufficient to cover the payments due. In my e-mails I also disclosed that I was speech impaired, and that I needed a way to communicate with them via e-mail or, preferably, an instant chat option. However, neither option was made available. To my dismay, every time I e-mailed them, I received an automated response with a list of phone numbers to call.

After going through this vicious cycle for approximately two years, my loans defaulted. Thereafter, I was forced to ask my friends to call my debt collectors for me. While this was not my preferred option, I felt forced to take this route because no alternative options were made available, and interest and late fees were accruing. Along with asking people to call my loan collectors for me, I had to give the callers my personal information, such as my social security number, date of birth, previous work history, and loan amounts. Even though I asked people whom I trusted to call for me, there still were apprehensions in the back of my mind about disclosing personal information.

Not only did I ask my friends to call the debt collectors, I also went to a local university's Office of Disability Services for support. During this time, after I explained why my student loans defaulted, the director immediately called FedLoan on my behalf. She admitted that she never thought about how a verbal communication disorder could impact a person's ability to communicate with student loan collectors. While the director was talking with the loan representative over the phone, she explained to them who she was and why she was calling on my behalf. Even after being informed that I'm speech impaired, the FedLoan representatives still insisted that I speak with them over the phone. They made it clear to the director that e-mailing or instant chats were not available options. The only options they would approve were for me to call them or for me to sign a form approving someone else to call on my behalf. For me, neither of these options was reasonable.

During this time, my self-efficacy and feelings of self-worth plummeted. Before my student loans defaulted, I was already earning a very low income as an adjunct professor. At one point, I was earning only $257 every two weeks for teaching one course. This salary is less than what most fast-food employees earn during the same period of time. Making my situation worse, the FedLoan started to garnish 15% of my already low salary. Because of my low salary, combined with the wage garnishments, I experienced homelessness for months and my car was repossessed. Nevertheless, in the midst of my less than ideal economic condition, the university expected me to, and I expected myself to, effectively and optimistically teach students who were studying to be teachers and even college professors. As much as I love the study of education, it was physically, mentally, and emotionally stressful to teach about a system that I felt was neither safe nor accommodating to persons with communication disorders. Nevertheless, I persisted. It is also one reason I am writing my autoethnographic story here—hopefully, someone will read and learn something from my storytelling.

Regardless of my educational attainment and academic accolades,[2] I am constantly emotionally and mentally weighed down because of my high student loan debt (Walsemann, Gee, & Gentile, 2015; White, 2015). Researchers suggest that there are a number of health consequences associated with possessing debt, including anxiety and stress, depression, self-harm, and suicidal ideation (Barron, 2012; Johannsen, 2012). Meltzer et al. (2011) conducted a study that included questions that were used to assess suicidal thoughts, based on the work of Paykel, Myers, Lindenthal, and Tanner (1974). When participants were questioned about the impact of debt on their lives, 4.3% of adults considered committing suicide in the past year due to debt, ranging from 1.8% of men 55 years of age and younger to 7.0% of women aged 35–54 years old. Based on the article, other adjectives included to explain the feelings of those who reported being in debt were humiliation, entrapment, and hopelessness. In light of these findings, we can conclude that financial crisis correlates with suicidal ideation.

In the middle of 2015, I had suicidal thoughts because of my student loan debt and the embarrassment that came along with having defaulted on my loans. Most people who have student loan debt are able to take care of it without getting other people involved; however, because my student loan debt collectors refused to provide reasonable accommodations for me to communicate with them directly, I was forced to depend on someone else to communicate with them on my behalf. At this point, I began to wonder if my primary school teachers were correct. What if I can't comfortably survive in this world independently without being able to communicate verbally with fluency? Do I want to always have to depend on another person to communicate my personal business? As I asked myself these questions, among others, my response was not favorable. I do not want someone else to always have to be involved in communicating with my student debt collectors for me.

Student debt also brings with it other social consequences, such as isolation and exclusion, shame, depression, and a sense of personal failure and futility. In light of my student loan debt and the lack of accommodations from FedLoan, my passion for teaching diminished. However, I managed to appear happy and mentally healthy for the sake of my students. While the majority of my students admire my courage to pursue teaching in traditional educational spaces regardless of my communication disorder, they have no idea how my decision negatively impacts my quality of life. In addition, many of my students view all college professors the same, with the exception of understanding the authority of the dean and department chair. Otherwise, they don't pay much attention to the differences between adjunct, assistant, associate, and full professors. Therefore, in their minds, I became the model person with a communication disability who made it to the top successfully. Nevertheless, the inconvenient truth is that many of my students earn more from their night and evening jobs than I do as an adjunct professor. Such a reality is demoralizing and disillusioning not only for me but for most educators in so-called higher education.

As previously mentioned, adjunct professors typically take on as much (often more) teaching as full-time tenure-track professors, yet adjuncts are compensated significantly less. Because of that, while I was teaching multiple courses, bearing the responsibility of grading assignments, and supporting students with recommendations for internships and employment opportunities, I decided to search for an additional job for more income. Although I was an adjunct professor with a doctorate in the field of higher education, I applied to work at local grocery stores, restaurants, and local bars. Unfortunately, similarly to my student loan collectors, employers seemed not to be supportive of people with a stutter. The cycle of applying for jobs and being rejected at job interviews became a vicious and taunting cycle.

When I applied for jobs online, I was constantly told that I qualified for the available position regardless of my disability, until I arrived for the interview and they noticed the extent of my stuttered speech. At the end of each interview, the interviewers made generic comments such as "if anything becomes available, we will call you." Thankfully, after the local university Director of Disability Services communicated with a FedLoan representative, they allowed me to pay $5/month toward my student loans, which, at the time of writing this chapter, exceed $100,000. However, the representative indicated that I must pay $5 on time for ten months consecutively before they could terminate my default status. While this payment plan is helpful, it still doesn't address the systemic reason why my loans defaulted. The FedLoan payment plan seems to be a treatment for the issue, but not a long-term cure for myself (and others) with verbal communicative disabilities (like those persons who stutter).

Conclusion

I conclude my story with one recommendation for student loan servicers and higher-education funding policy. As a special educator, I feel obligated to advocate on behalf of all students with disabilities; however, for the sake of this chapter, I was intentional about highlighting that and how student debt neoliberalism disproportionately impacts persons with stuttering disabilities. I recognize that this topic is rarely, if ever, discussed in academic research. Most of the existing research on stuttering focuses on theory, pathology, and therapy. Therefore, I consider it my professional duty and moral obligation to let my voice be heard through qualitative narratives about this population and how our maltreatment intersects with other marginalized or oppressed populations or other aspects of our own identities.

While this chapter primarily focuses on my experiences, I argue that my experiences represent the voices of those who dropped out of school because of constant embarrassment, who don't have access to write book chapters, who feel silenced in society even through being forced to vocalize, or who died in the struggle by natural death or suicide. In light of my personal experiences, my single recommendation is that student loan collection agencies utilize secured technological tools that would allow their clients with speech and language disabilities to communicate with them directly, as opposed to giving them the run-around, and then forcing this population of clients to divulge all of their personal information to someone else to communicate on their behalf.

Providing a tool for secured online communication will allow speech- and language-impaired persons to maintain their financial privacy and human dignity. This is not too much to ask; indeed, we all expect and deserve nothing less.

Notes

1 There are currently nine loan servicers for federally held loans made through the William D. Ford Federal Direct Loan (Direct Loan) Program and the Federal Family Education Loan (FFEL) Program. See information online @ https://studentaid.ed.gov/sa/repay-loans/understand/servicers. FedLoan Servicing is @ https://myfedloan.org/.
2 I have an earned Ed.D., and in 2013 I received an Outstanding Alumni Award from the Howard University School of Education in the category "Leader of Change."

References

Barron, L. (2012, July 6). *Student loan debt spurring record number of suicides.* Retrieved from www.mintpressnews.com/student-loan-debt-spurring-record-number-of-suicides/32086/
Best, J., & Best, E. (2014). *The student loan mess: How good intentions created a trillion-dollar problem.* Berkeley, CA: University of California Press.
Collinge, A. M. (2009). *The student loan scam: The most oppressive debt in U.S. history—and how we can fight back.* Boston: Beacon Press.
Corcoran, J. A., & Stewart, M. (1998). Stories of stuttering: A qualitative analysis of interview narratives. *Journal of Fluency Disorders, 23*(4), 247–264.
Gappa, J. M., Austin, A. E., & Trice, A. G. (2007). *Rethinking faculty work: Higher education's strategic imperative.* San Francisco: John Wiley and Sons.
Giroux, H. A. (2014). *Neoliberalism's war on higher education.* Chicago: Haymarket Books.
Hartlep, N. D., & Ellis, A. L. (2012). Rethinking speech and language impairments within fluency-dominated cultures. In S. O. Pinder (Ed.), *American multicultural studies: Diversity of race, ethnicity, gender, and sexuality* (pp. 411–429). Thousand Oaks, CA: Sage Publications.
Harvey, D. (2005). *A brief history of neoliberalism.* Oxford, UK: Oxford University Press.
James, S. E., Brumfitt, S. M., & Cudd, P. A. (1999). Communicating by telephone: Views of a group of people with stuttering impairment. *Journal of Fluency Disorders, 24*(4), 299–317.

Johannsen, C. C. (2012, September 1). The ones we've lost: The student loan debt suicides. *Huffington Post*. Retrieved from www.huffingtonpost.com/c-cryn-johannsen/student-loan-debt-suicides_b_1638972.html

Joint Center for Housing Studies of Harvard University. (2015). *The state of the nation's housing*. Cambridge, MA: President and Fellows of Harvard College. Retrieved from www.jchs.harvard.edu/sites/jchs.harvard.edu/files/jchs-sonhr-2015-full.pdf

Kezar, A. (Ed.). (2012). *Embracing non-tenure track faculty: Changing campuses for the new faculty majority*. New York: Routledge.

Meltzer, H., Bebbington, P., Brugha, T., Jenkins, R., McManus, S., & Dennis, M. S. (2011). Personal debt and suicidal ideation. *Psychological Medicine*, 41(4), 771–778.

National Center for Education Statistics (NCES). (2013). *Digest of educational statistics*. Retrieved from https://nces.ed.gov/programs/digest/d14/tables/dt14_315.10.asp?current=yes

National Institute of Deafness and Other Communication Disorders. (2016). *Quick statistics about voice, speech, language*. Retrieved at https://www.nidcd.nih.gov/health/statistics/quick-statistics-voice-speech-language

National Stuttering Association (NSA). (2012). *Basic facts about stuttering*. Retrieved from www.westutter.org/whoWeHelp/Basic-Facts.htm

Paykel, E. S., Myers, J. K., Lindenthal, J. J., & Tanner, J. (1974). Suicidal feelings in the general population: A prevalence study. *British Journal of Psychiatry*, 124(582), 460–469.

Prud'homme, P., & Hensley, B. O. (2013). It takes more than public speaking: A leadership analysis of "The King's Speech." *Journal of Organizational Learning and Leadership*, 11(1), 19–28.

Walsemann, K. M., Gee, G. C., & Gentile, D. (2015). Sick of our loans: Student borrowing and the mental health of young adults in the United States. *Social Science & Medicine*, 124, 85–93.

Webber, K. L., & Boehmer, R. G. (2008). The balancing act: Accountability, affordability, and access in American higher education. *New Directions for Institutional Research*, 2008(S2), 79–91.

Werf, M. V. (2009, June). The college of 2020: Students. *Chronicle Research Services*. Retrieved from www.uwec.edu/CETL/bundles/upload/college2020-dl.pdf

White, G. B. (2015, February 2). The mental and physical toll of student loans. *The Atlantic*. Retrieved from www.theatlantic.com/business/archive/2015/02/the-mental-and-physical-toll-of-student-loans/385032/

Yairi, E., & Ambrose, N. (2013, June). Epidemiology of stuttering: 21st century advances. *Journal of Fluency Disorders*, 38(2), 66–87. Retrieved from http://dx.doi.org/10.1016/j.jfludis.2012.11.002

10 "Golden Years" in the Red

Student Loan Debt as Economic Slavery

Kay Ann Taylor

Introduction

Because of my age in 1996 (47)—in concert with the intersectionality (Crenshaw, 1989, 2016) of my gender, parents' educational and socioeconomic levels, welfare status, single parenthood, and other sociopolitical factors—I did not incur my Student Loan Debt (SLD) by design, but rather as a last resort. In that year, I learned that the Clinton administration passed a five-year limitation for welfare benefit recipients (Edelman, 1997). Desperate for socioeconomic uplift, I sought higher education as a vehicle for survival and providing a better life for my three children and me. Although I was on welfare, I had no outstanding debt prior to entering graduate school in the fall of 1996.

SLD affects lives, families, wellbeing, and futures in vastly different ways (Hartlep & Eckrich, 2013). The intersection of students' unique characteristics complicates the impact of SLD profoundly. We each become embroiled in SLD under different circumstances and at different times in our lives (Hartlep & Eckrich, 2013). With no accumulated wealth (Brown et al., 2003), I bought into the time-worn myth of formal education affording social and economic mobility through meaningful work and credentials. The predatory (Collinge, 2009) neoliberal capitalist (Biebricher & Johnson, 2012) lending practices that now bind many post-secondary students in economic slavery put our lives and futures in jeopardy because of debt-based education (Williams, 2015). I view SLD as economic slavery because it binds our labor as the legal property of our lenders, whom we are forced to pay far more than we ever borrowed.

Indebted students, like me, placed their trust in a flawed and imbalanced system disguised as opportunity and uplift—lauded by the federal government—to pursue higher education. Through the neoliberal capitalist agenda, which has been escalating for decades, college is viewed not as a venue to pursue intellectual curiosity or learning, but instead as a means to economic human capital that determines which cog we fill in the oppressive, undemocratic neoliberal privatization scheme (Giroux, 2014). Being a SLD slave parallels the dehumanizing treatment I experienced while I was on welfare.

We are embroiled in a system that is intended to keep us down, just like welfare (Taylor, 2009). While most people are familiar with the accumulation of assets (e.g., through investments, buying a home, savings, IRAs), disaccumulation receives less attention. Disaccumulation may be viewed as suffering financially from not benefiting from economic opportunities, e.g., gendered wage discrimination, lack of access to secure employment. Therefore, disaccumulation, like accumulation, increases over time depending on where one is situated within our private-interest-driven debt-based economy (see Chapter 4, this volume). When launched into disaccumulation, due to economic hardship, we are not positioned to accumulate assets or advance (Brown et al., 2003; Cook, 2007; Sahn & Brohn, 1986) out of the SLD prison.

Postlude and Prelude

In my current position as a 66-year-old Associate Professor of Curriculum and Instruction, there are unspoken assumptions regarding my background, status, and experiences. Most of my colleagues completed their doctoral studies at an age considerably younger than I and have been employed steadily for an extended period with regular retirement contributions and salary increases (allowing them to accumulate assets). My colleagues of similar age are retired or making plans for retirement. Most have financially comfortable and secure retirements, especially those in dual-income families. Meanwhile, my retirement has had less time to accumulate—only in the last 10.5 years at my current institution.

My Social Security income is meager due to embedded *gender wage differentials* and inflation over time. My Social Security and retirement income diminish drastically after deducting income tax, gap health insurance, dental and vision insurance, and living expenses, leaving nothing but precarious day-to-day survival. I am not eligible for my former spouses' Social Security benefits because I was not married to anyone for the required 10-year period.

Before delving deeper into my experiences with SLD, I first share a little about my life's background—circumstances that influenced me and my point of view. My chapter references primary documents from my personal records, such as income tax returns, SLD documents from Direct Loan Services, CornerStone Education Loan Service, and the Social Security Administration.

I was adopted at approximately six months of age by a farming couple in the Midwest. My father had an eighth-grade education and my mother had some high school education. Education was important to them; attending college was expected for me. There were events early in my life that foreshadowed the tentacles of neoliberal capitalism's impact: school consolidation (Elliot, 2012) and eminent domain (Gibson, 2010).

My rural school was consolidated in 1959. My father was president of the school board at the time. Economics via neoliberal capitalism dictated the school board's actions instead of community accountability. This was a personal lesson in the politics and economics of public schooling, although I didn't realize it until years later.

Further devastation came when our family's farm was condemned via eminent domain for the interstate highway system. I remember vividly one of my first acts of resistance. When the surveyors left their day's work, I ran into our pasture, pulled up the surveyors' stakes, and threw them under our front porch. This marked my first memorable encounter with an oppressive government. The summer of 1963, we were forced from our home. Our farmland was split and our beautiful rolling hills were bulldozed into submissive valleys and a concrete maze was left as proof that we were dispossessed.

I still recall our loss. Nevertheless, I graduated from a new high school, went on to college, earned a teaching degree, and was certified as an elementary teacher.

Moving to Adulthood and Economic Slavery

In the fall 1972 I began my first public school teaching job in a rural Midwestern community. After teaching a few years in two rural Midwestern cities, I left K–12 education and worked elsewhere until 1977. I was a full-time mother for two years, and returned to work in the fall of 1979. From 1979–1984, I was employed in several positions in different arenas. A brief period of economic uplift was followed by disaccumulation and underemployment. My first experience with unemployment started during 1984 for approximately 18 months. Income averaging was allowed at that time, which meant that I could spread out my tax liability by averaging my income over time. I benefited from receiving tax refunds I otherwise would not have been eligible to receive; the Tax Reform Act of 1986 repealed this. During this same period of time, I learned what "overqualified" meant. By 1985, I was on my own after the death of my father in 1969 and my mother in 1985.

From 1985–1989 I continued my quest for socioeconomic uplift. I was a single mother with three children: ages 3, 4, and 8. Around 1988, I was audited by the IRS because my husband omitted a form for $200 of income. Shortly after our 1989 divorce, my ex-husband filed for bankruptcy. I also filed for bankruptcy to avoid his creditors coming after me. This left me with no car and no credit. The bankruptcy stayed on my record for a decade.

During these ten years I continued to work and search for meaningful work that could support my family. In 1989 (at age 40), I secured employment with a non-profit organization—a place from which I hoped to retire. I advanced within the non-profit. They provided benefits and a retirement package. After a couple of years working there, I began experiencing hostility and increasing stress and, as a result, I left the agency. I attempted to claim unemployment, but it was challenged and I received no benefits. At age 44, I was an unemployed single mother with two children to support (my oldest son, when he turned 14, went to live with his father, as per our joint custody divorce agreement), no child support, no income, no family for support, and no money to pay my expenses.

1994—Welfare Mom

I applied for welfare benefits in 1994. Although there was a sign in the office stating that clients were to be treated with dignity and respect, this was not my experience. During the interview, I was asked if I had a retirement fund. I replied that I had a small amount from my previous employer. I was informed that I was ineligible for benefits until the retirement account was depleted or I found work, whichever occurred first. I sought employment actively with no results. I cashed in my retirement benefits, budgeted the money for my family, and continued seeking work. When the money was gone, I returned to the welfare office to file for benefits.

Being a welfare recipient introduced a new level of personal humiliation. I experienced this as a system executed through control and fear. The stress induced for meeting their demands and surviving on so little was debilitating (Dodson, 1999; Reich, 2005). The longer it continued, the more hopeless and worthless I felt. My self-confidence plummeted.

1996

Around April of 1996 I had a job interview with a private human services organization for an office position. I received not one but two rejection letters. Shortly thereafter, I received a phone call asking if I was still interested. I indicated that I was. They invited me back to the office and offered me the job. I would be paid approximately $6.35/hour ($13,208 annually). My welfare benefits were reduced, but I remained eligible. Medicaid for my children and me was critical for survival. As Table 10.1 demonstrates, I experienced a brief period of self-sufficiency through wages in 1981 and 1983 and again from 1985–1993. There was a sharp decrease from 1994–2001, whereas in 2002 my income was slightly higher than in 1993. My financial situation and future worsened in 1994. Wage discrepancies due to gender are ingrained in the economic system, as evidenced by women currently and historically earning less than men. Current figures indicate that women make from 76 to 79 cents for every one dollar men earn (AAUW, 2015; Taylor, 2009).

Graduate School

With no better employment prospects in sight, and Clinton's welfare limits now in force, I decided to apply to graduate school to improve my employability. I remember visiting with the Department Chair before applying for admission to graduate school to pursue my Master of Science in Curriculum

Table 10.1 Taxable Earnings from Ages 15–55, with 2014 Equivalence Adjusted for Inflation

Year	Age	Taxable earnings	2014 dollars	Inflation rate
1965	15	$78.00	$586.20	651.50%
1966	16	$0.00		
1967	17	$680.00	$4,819.77	608.80%
1968	18	$907.00	$6,170.00	580.30%
1969	19	$1,991.00	$12,843.09	545.10%
1970	20	$1,154.00	$7,041.07	510.10%
1971	21	$795.00	$4,647.04	484.50%
1972	22	$3,099.00	$17,551.31	466.50%
1973	23	$7,379.00	$39,344.03	433.20%
1974	24	$7,874.00	$37,810.53	380.20%
1975	25	$4,659.00	$20,500.99	340.00%
1976	26	$2,550.00	$10,609.43	315.10%
1977	27	$1,040.00	$4,062.80	290.70%
1978	28	$0.00		
1979	29	$2,675.00	$8,722.71	226.10%
1980	30	$7,400.00	$21,260.27	187.30%
1981	31	$20,589.00	$53,621.09	160.40%
1982	32	$14,851.00	$36,432.81	145.30%
1983	34	$25,735.00	$61,168.68	137.70%
1984	35	$2,000.00	$4,557.00	127.80%
1985	36	$12,250.00	$26,951.82	120.00%
1986	37	$12,065.00	$26,060.40	116.00%
1987	38	$15,499.00	$32,299.04	108.40%
1988	39	$16,275.00	$32,568.71	100.10%
1989	40	$17,249.00	$32,921.12	90.90%
1990	41	$18,437.00	$33,394.81	81.10%
1991	42	$19,828.00	$34,464.03	73.80%
1992	43	$22,750.00	$38,387.34	68.70%
1993	44	$25,500.00	$41,776.94	63.80%
1994	45	$7,910.00	$12,635.50	59.70%
1995	46	$360.00	$559.22	55.30%
1996	47	$7,643.00 (Began Graduate School)	$11,532.02	50.90%
1997	48	$4,373.00	$6,450.13	47.50%
1998	49	$0.00	$0.00	
1999	50	$0.00	$0.00	
2000	51	$11,378.00	$15,642.17	37.50%
2001	52	$3,000.00 (Year of Graduation)	$4,012.47	33.70%
2002	53	$28,949.00	$38,094.89	31.50%
2003	54	$35,527.00	$45,709.35	28.70%
2004	55	$33,797.00	$42,355.57	25.30%

Note: Medicare began in 1966

Source for years and taxed Social Security earnings: Estimated Benefit Report Retrieved from: www.ssa.gov/retire2/estimator.htm Inflation Calculator Source: www.usinflationcalculator.com/

and Instructional Technology Degree. I was on welfare, but I didn't carry any debt. I asked about scholarships and any debt-free financial assistance available. She told me there was nothing. My subsequent tears represented my despair and fear.

I submitted my application to graduate school after I began my job in April of 1996 and was admitted to the Master of Science (M.S.) program in the fall of 1996. I struggled through the obscure and infuriating Free Application for Federal Student Aid (FAFSA) application process. I was fortunate to be able to apply for subsidized loans because, since 2012, graduate students are not offered subsidized loans, which exacerbates their debt burden (Hartlep & Eckrich, 2013).

I recall my astonishment during our graduate student orientation. We were handed, without application or question, a U.S. Bank MasterCard with a $500 credit limit. Ever since my 1989 bankruptcy filing, I had no credit cards. Yet, here one was handed to me, nonchalantly. I used the card sparingly, charging small amounts I could pay off in full at the end of the bill cycle to avoid interest. Slowly, I began to rebuild my credit.

My subsidized federal loan accommodated dependents. Because I was fighting for survival and for my children, I signed the promissory note each semester without question. I budgeted the remaining money after tuition, fees, and books into a monthly amount for our living expenses. In combination with my meager income and the support of reduced welfare, my family was better off financially than when I was dependent solely on welfare.

My first student loan for fall 1996 was in the amount of $4,250 ($8,500 for the academic year, disbursed by semester). I failed to notice that the federal government deducted a "Loan Fee" from every disbursement. This is money I never received but for which I have been making payments and which has accumulated interest. After deducting fees and tuition, I received $2,408 each semester and I still had to pay for my books and parking permit, leaving me with about $600/month for my family's living expenses. My journey into debt-based education and becoming an SLD economic slave had begun.

1997–2001

In the fall of 1997, I was offered a Graduate Assistantship (GA). Combined with my student loans, it provided enough income for me to resign my job and pursue a doctorate. It offered reduced tuition, which increased the amount from my student loans for living expenses. Our family continued to receive reduced welfare benefits and Medicaid.

Each semester, I signed the promissory note. I also took out unsubsidized loans twice: Once to purchase a new computer to complete my M.S. degree and the other to present at an American Educational Research Association Annual Meeting as a doctoral student. I paid the interest on the unsubsidized loans when I received the bills; however, several years later there is no noticeable reduction in the balance. The total amount of interest paid through May 5, 2005, on my unsubsidized loans was $2,137 for a loan amount of $5,339.70. The balance as I write this chapter is $5,199.31.

Welfare Mom, Ph.D.

I completed the obligatory exit financial counseling during my last semester in December of 2001. I signed and submitted my "Rights and Responsibilities Summary Checklist" (USDOE, 2000) on November 19, 2001. This letter stated the following: "You should try to spend no more than 5 to 15 percent of your net income for monthly payments on student loans and consumer debts" (p. 24). The only debt I had was my SLD. Table 10.2 displays my GA income. Upon graduation, I hoped my efforts provided a role model for my children of survival and determination.

Table 10.2 Graduate Student Assistantship Income

Date	Appointment	Monthly stipend	Total stipend
5/9/98–6/30/98	0.50	$1,083.33	$1,857.18
6/1/98–6/30/98	0.50	$1,083.33	$1,083.33
7/1/98–8/31/98	0.50	$1,083.33	$2,166.66
8/16/98–12/31/98	0.25	$600.00	$2,714.29
8/24/98–5/7/99	0.25	$541.66	$6,500.00
8/16/98–5/15/99	0.50	$1,088.00	$9,792.00
6/1/99–6/30/99	0.50	$1,088.00	$1,088.00
8/16/99–5/15/99	0.50	$1,156.00	$10,404.00
8/16/00–5/15/01	0.75	$1,797.00	$16,173.00
1/1/01–5/15/01*	0.75	$1,797.00	$16,173.00
1/1/01–5/15/01*	0.50	$1,198.00	$10,539.00
8/16/01–12/31/01	0.50	$1,245.00	$5,602.00
8/16/01–12/31/01	0.25	$622.00	$2,801.00

Source: University, Letters of Intent, Personal Files

No Debt Advice or Counsel

I do not recall any institutional financial advisor or faculty member offering caution or advice regarding my SLD. I was 52 years old when I graduated with my Ph.D. in December of 2001. One of my professors informed me that the maximum annual salary I could expect to earn as an Assistant Professor on the tenure track in my field would be $42,000. This small salary was unsettling to me due to my SLD investment for uplift.

While my graduate student tuition increased from $1,467 in the fall of 1996 to $1,851 during my last semester in the fall of 2001 (an increase of approximately 26.17%), my student loan disbursement remained more constant. The Graduate College financial credit to my university account began at $762 in 1997 and ended at $863 in 2001—an increase of 13.25%. Clearly, the university's contribution did not match the tuition increases. Table 10.3 indicates my tuition amount, 2014 inflation rate, and equivalent.

Post-Graduation

I did not secure a tenure-track position immediately following graduation. After the six-month grace period for student loans following graduation, I filed to defer my loans on June 20, 2002. The deferment document states the following: "Maximum cumulative eligibility is 36 months" (Direct Loans, Revised 5/99, p. 1). At the time I deferred my loans, the total amount I owed for my SLD was $68,573. I also requested deferment and signed forms on June 13, 2003, and again on June 24, 2004, when I reached the "maximum cumulative eligibility" of 36 months.

For the 2002–2003 academic year, I accepted a one-year visiting position at a private university. The salary was $41,000/year. From the $42,000 salary expectation provided by one of my professors, it seemed reasonable. In 2003–2004, my M.S. major professor again assisted in ensuring that I was employed.

I consolidated my loans on July 19, 2004, according to the consolidation notice I received from Direct Loans (10817571, RLN229, LCCL9V03). Fortunately, compared to current interest rates, my loans were consolidated

Table 10.3 University Graduate Tuition and Increases FY'96—FY'01, with 2014 Equivalence Adjusted for Inflation for the Same Period

Year	Tuition amount		2014 dollars	% Inflation
Fall 1996	$1,467.00		$2,213.46	50.90%
Spring 1997	$1,467.00		$2,163.81	47.50%
Fall 1997	$1,524.00		$2,247.89	47.50%
Spring 1998	$1,524.00		$2,213.41	45.20%
Fall 1998	$1,583.00		$2,299.10	45.20%
Spring 1999	$1,583.00		$2,249.49	42.10%
Fall 1999	$1,654.00		$2,350.31	42.10%
Spring 2000	$1,654.00		$2,273.88	37.50%
Fall 2000	$1,726.00		$2,372.86	37.50%
Spring 2001	$1,726.00		$2,308.51	33.70%
Fall 2001	$1,851.00		$2,475.70	33.70%
Total % increase		~26.17%		
Loan amount remained constant				
Graduate College Financial Credit to my university account: Began at $762.00, Ended at $863.00				
Total % increase		13.25%		[12.92%]
Inflation Calculator Source: www.usinflationcalculator.com/				

Source: Compiled from personal financial and university records.

at a 3.125% interest rate. Regardless of the interest rate, however, the neo-liberal loan repayment regime, which requires paying off the interest compounded for the life of the loan prior to paying off the principal, makes it impossible to pay down the principal when one's income is not sufficient to cover the upfront interest and still have enough to live on.

2004

In the fall of 2004, I began my first tenure-track position. My initial salary was $48,000/year. Because I now had relatively stable and predictable employment, I consolidated my loans as noted above. During the 2005 academic year, I accepted a different tenure-track position in the Midwest. During my negotiation for the new position, I requested they pay my SLD because a friend informed me that some institutions of higher education would do so. My new institution did not consider my request. Without financial accumulation, I did not have the money to purchase a home in either location. My financial struggle continued.

Adding to my ongoing financial stress, I learned after my first two years at my university that pay was not offered on a 12-month basis. All 9-month faculty members (typical of tenure-track positions) receive their pay only over the academic year. Although the first two summers of my employment were guaranteed, thereafter, it was necessary to save money during the year to have enough money to live on during the summer months. Every academic year, I begin again saving money to live on during the summer. Merit raises, when we received them, did not match the cost-of-living increases. Years in which there were no merit raises resulted in even more lost purchasing power. As I write this chapter, we are faced with another year of no merit raises.

Entering Repayment

Payment Options

At the time my loans were consolidated, I had four payment plan options: (a) Standard, (b) Extended, (c) Graduated, or (d) Income Contingent (Direct Loans, 2003). In the exit interview in November of 2001, the booklet provided a table with examples of debt levels, beginning monthly payments, and total amounts repaid under each Direct Loan Payment plan. The Graduated plan seemed manageable based upon my income. What remains alarming, and untenable, is that I was almost 55 at the time, which meant that I would have to work until I was 80 to pay back all of my SLD.

Based on the exit counseling's guideline of paying no more than 5–15% of my net income on student loans *and* consumer debt, my recommended *total* debt payment estimates for my initial tenure track $48,000 salary, assuming a 25% tax bracket, are:

Net income = $36,000
5% of $36,000 = $1,800/year or $150/month for total debt payments
10% of $36,000 = $3,600/year or $300/month for total debt payments
15% of $36,000 = $5,400/year or $450/month for total debt payments

At the full 15%, my recommended *total* debt payments at $450/month fell below the Graduated repayment plan's $526/month SLD payment and left nothing for other debt payments. Today, even with a higher salary, I cannot afford $526/month.

First Bill

Somewhere in the endless maze of documents from incurring SLD, it was stated that, after consolidation, I should receive my first bill in approximately 60 days. My financial records indicate that my total consolidated loan amount was: $69,299.32. My records reveal that I did not receive or pay my first bill until July 16, 2005. This is one year after my consolidation and lost time in terms of paying down my loan and certainly not within the 60-day time frame stated by Direct Loans. I was not aware of this delay until now and have no idea how or why it happened. The records I requested from my current loan service provider, CornerStone Education Loan Service, confirm this payment date. (In a form letter I noted as received on March 30, 2012, Direct Loan Servicing Center assigned my loans to CornerStone Education Loan Service.)

I have never missed a payment. I have never made a late payment. As of October 24, 2015, my outstanding SLD balance is $60,054.27. This is scant progress in paying down an original amount of $69,299.32 over the last 10-plus years. According to my records, I have paid $32,456.50 in student loan payments (as of October 2015), which includes $2,137 in interest I paid prior to consolidation for my unsubsidized loans. However, the loan balance has declined by only about $9,200. The 3.125% interest accrues daily. Even with a 3.125% interest rate, the bulk of my payments go toward interest, which continues to accumulate faster than my ability to pay down the principal with no relief or end in sight. This is predatory lending.

Paying More than the Amount Due: Inconsistent Information

Since April of 2014, I have paid more than the amount due on my loan statements. I called CornerStone and asked: "If I paid in excess of the amount due, would the extra amount be applied toward the principal?" I was informed that it would. After several months of seeing no movement in the loan principal, I called them back. This time I was told that the previous person misinformed me and extra payments are not applied to the principal until the interest is satisfied. The person was unable to provide a definite statement other than that, if I continue to pay in excess of the amount due for the next two years or so, then I should see a decrease in the principal.

If I pay more than the payment amount on my car loan and apply it to the principal, the loan is paid more quickly.

Confounding the payment issue further, since I began paying more than the amount due, my last 11 statements indicate: "Total Amount Due: $0.00." I continue to pay the increased amount, even though it makes little sense if my principal balance remains stagnant. It is tempting, when receiving a statement that says $0 due, to ignore it and not pay. I know better!

Income Tax, SLD Interest Credit, and Phase Out

Added to the deleterious effects of SLD is that, as our earning power increases so, too, do our federal and state income taxes. Since 2002, my federal and state income taxes have continued to increase. However, my income did not make gains until 2005. What I now pay on student loans and in taxes takes a bigger chunk out of my earnings than before, minimizing the benefit to me of my increased earning power. I do not benefit from a two-person household income. One positive aspect is that I no longer work to support my childcare provider. Still, I have never had enough accumulated wealth to make a major purchase and pay for it outright.

The government entices us by stating that we receive a tax deduction for the interest paid on our student loans. However, I did not realize until 2015, after asking my income tax accountant, that the interest deduction is income-dependent. When my income (filing singly) reaches $65,000, the deduction is pro-rated until it reaches $0 at $80,000 income because my earnings will then surpass the amount to qualify for a deduction. This is called Phase Out (see https://www.irs.gov/publications/p970/ch04.html). I have never benefitted from other itemized deductions. Student loans punish me via Phase Out for making more money!

New SLD Repayment Plans

New repayment plans continue to emerge; however, they are misleading and the promise they offer is short-lived or benefits too few. I was hopeful when I learned about the Public Service Loan Forgiveness (PSLF) Program wherein SLD is forgiven after working for a public institution for 10 years. When I inquired about this repayment plan, I was informed that none of my previous payments applied because my payment plan was not one of the two approved to qualify for PSLF. I could move to this plan only by beginning my 10 years over from that day forward, and only if I made considerably higher payments. I could not afford the quoted amount. My hope and optimism for a payment plan to relieve my SLD were temporary.

Student Loan Service Providers

The Federal Student Aid website defines a service provider, or loan servicer, as "a company that handles the billing and other services on your federal student loan" (n.d., para. 1). The website notes 11 different loan servicers.[1] According to Hefling (2015), service companies typically receive a flat monthly fee for each account. Hefling quotes Richard Cordray, Director of the Consumer Financial Protection Bureau, as stating, "Student loan servicers often make more money when they spend as little time as possible on each account, and they typically get paid more when a borrower is in repayment longer" (para. 4). There are disturbing implications of predatory lending from loan servicers' practices. Collegians are being taken advantage of and misled when it is in the interest of the loan servicers to prolong payments so they make more money while providing minimal service. The prospects for borrowers are dismal.

Default: The Misdirected Greater Concern

On April 21, 2013, I shared my situation on http://studentdebtcrisis.org/read-student-debt-stories/, one of over 420 SL debtors to do so through November 2015, with another 310 submissions by February 2017. I was prompted by Patton's (2013) article in *The Chronicle of Higher Education*. The General Accounting Office's (GAO) 2014 report regarding SLD garnered some national media attention. It emphasized the growing problem for my generation—Baby Boomers—because our SLD is increasing. The GAO (2014) report minimizes the gravity of the situation from the onset through the report's title: "OLDER AMERICANS: Inability to Repay Student Loans May Affect Financial Security of a *Small Percentage* [emphasis added] of Retirees." The GAO's concern minimizes the plight of senior citizens because, although it's surely rising, currently they are few in number when compared to overall SLD ranks. They state that, whereas three percent of seniors, approximately 706,000 households, are saddled with SLD, this compares to 24%, approximately 22 million, of households headed by someone under 65 (p. 6). However, some insight into the seriousness for some seniors is provided: "Available data indicate that borrowers 65 and older hold *defaulted* [emphasis added] federal student loans at a much higher rate, which can leave some retirees with income below the poverty threshold" (n.p.; see also p. 12). Note the emphasis on defaulted loans. The 1996 policy to garnish Social Security and disability payments of seniors with SLD thrusts them into an even more indefensible financial position.

> From 2002 through 2013, the number of borrowers whose Social Security benefits were offset has increased roughly 400 percent, and the number of borrowers 65 and over increased roughly 500 percent . . . In 2013, Social Security benefits for about 155,000 people were offset and about 36,000 of those were 65 and over.
> (GAO, 2014, pp. 17–18)

It is unconscionable to garnish Social Security benefits. For someone like me, who has worked her entire life with only a small retirement amount and Social Security payment (ungarnished) to show for it, maintaining even a meager life is put in jeopardy. The futures of Baby Boomers with SLD are bleak, but so too are the futures of everyone with SLD. Indebted collegians have no recourse because SLD is not eligible for bankruptcy except in rare circumstances/situations. Indebted collegians are controlled through manipulation and fear and cast into a bottomless pit of economic slavery. Neoliberal capitalism is concerned only with profit, not people (Chomsky, 1999).

The focus regarding SLD is misplaced. Like the GAO (2014) report, public media seem most concerned with those in default or late making payments. Ignored are the millions who are working and continue struggling to make payments. Having a home, family, and sustainable life are difficult at best when faced with meeting SLD obligations. Those making payments warrant concern equal to those in default. The predatory configuration of our monetary system guarantees that those of us paying now will be in default in the future.

A Call to Action and Relief

Economic justice is part and parcel of social justice. Martin Luther King, Jr., tackled economic injustice; but it has gotten worse than in his courageous lifetime. Having completed my doctorate at age 52, it is clear I will not live long enough to pay off my SLD. I am now a senior citizen and retirement is not economically possible. I probably will drop dead teaching in the classroom. People laugh, but it's closer to the truth than they realize.

Although Senators Elizabeth Warren and Bernie Sanders understand the severity of SLD, most members of Congress are in collusion with neoliberal capitalists with no conscience for the majority of citizens. According to Hart (2015), more than one-third of Americans "are paying or have paid student loans and a sizable number of them are delaying other major purchases because of it" (para. 1). College may not be the preferred choice for all after high school, but it should be a viable option for those who seek it without cementing them into economic slavery.

The federal government of the United States of America has been and continues to be complicit in my economic slavery, as was my state government. Having ceded its money creation power to the banks through the Federal Reserve Act of 1913 (and failing as yet to take that power back), our federal government is also dependent on and beholden to that banking system. This leaves me part of a growing underclass in the United States: educated, employed, and economic slaves to SLD. There are psychological, emotional, economic, and health implications for those of us now enslaved by the debt that will not go away (Walsemann, Gee, & Gentile, 2015). It is my position that we should be granted relief and forgiveness of our debt without the additional punitive measures of paying income tax on the balance forgiven. If my debt was interest-free, over half of it would be paid off. In the end, I traded one form of oppression and slavery—welfare—for another, SLD. My Golden Years are nonexistent as an economic slave with

SLD, and my reward after working most of my life is the reality that I will never be able to stop working (i.e., retire). American Dream assets (Best, 2012), particularly SLD, are the American Nightmare. Student Loan Debt is unsustainable and constitutes odious debt. Without economic justice, social justice will never be possible.

Note

1 As of March 2017, nine loan servicers are listed on Federal Student Aid website (https://studentaid.ed.gov/sa/repay-loans). Loan servicing for the U.S. Department of Education is undoubtedly a lucrative business, even for the "not-for-profit" entities listed on their website, one of which is CornerStone, Kay's current loan servicer, and surely for the four main companies one of which is "Navient/Sallie Mae" (https://studentaid.ed.gov/sa/about/data-center/business-info/contracts/loan-servicing). While there has been some social justice research into these companies and their intersecting relationships and lobbying arms, much more is needed.

References

American Association of University Women (AAUW). (2015, Fall). *The simple truth about the gender pay gap* (Fall 2015 ed.). Retrieved from www.aauw.org/research/the-simple-truth-about-the-gender-pay-gap/

Best, E. (2012). Debt and the American dream. *Social Science and Public Policy, 49*, 349–352. Retrieved from http://dx.doi.org/10.1007/s12115-012-9559-3

Biebricher, T., & Johnson, E. V. (2012). What's wrong with neoliberalism? *New Political Science, 34*(2), 202–211. Retrieved from http://dx.doi.org/10.1080/07393148.2012.676398

Brown, J. K., Carnoy, M., Currie, E., Duster, T., Oppenheimer, D. B., Shultz, M. M., & Wellman, D. (2003). *White-washing race: The myth of a color-blind society*. Berkeley, CA: University of California Press.

Chomsky, N. (1999). *Profit over people: Neoliberalism and global order*. New York: Seven Stories Press.

Collinge, A. (2009). *The student loan scam: The most oppressive debt in U.S. history— and how we can fight back*. Boston: Beacon.

Cook, C. (2007). Addressing vulnerability through asset building and social protection. In C. O. N. Moser (Ed.), *Reducing global poverty: The case for asset accumulation* (pp. 104–117). Washington, DC: Brookings Institution Press.

Crenshaw, K. (1989). Demarginalizing the intersection of race and gender. *The University of Chicago Legal Forum, 14*, 139–167.

Crenshaw, K. (2016, October). The urgency of intersectionality. *TED Women* 2016. Retrieved from https://www.ted.com/talks/kimberle_crenshaw_the_urgency_of_intersectionality

Direct Loans—William D. Ford Federal Student Loan Program. (2003). Federal direct consolidation loan borrower's rights and responsibilities. U.S. Government Printing Office 2003-521-154/99657.

Direct Loans—William D. Ford Federal Student Loan Program. (Revised 5/99). Economic hardship deferment request. ED FORM 40–700(SCH). OMB No. 1845–0011. Form approved, Exp. Date 07/31/2011.

Dodson, L. (1999). *Don't call us out of name: The untold lives of women and girls in poor America*. Boston: Beacon Press.

Edelman, P. (1997, March). The worst thing Bill Clinton has done. *The Atlantic Monthly*, 279(3), 43–58. Retrieved from www.theatlantic.com/magazine/archive/1997/03/the-worst-thing-bill-clinton-has-done/376797/

Elliott, P. W. (2012). School consolidation and notions of progress: Why community actors almost always lose the fight to keep local schools and how they can turn the tables—a review of the literature. *Education*, 18(1). Retrieved from http://ineducation.ca/index.php/ineducation/article/view/25/429

Federal Student Aid. (n.d.). *An office of the U.S. Department of Education*. Retrieved from https://studentaid.ed.gov/sa/repay-loans/understand/servicers

General Accounting Office (GAO). (2014). Testimony before the special committee on aging, U.S. Senate. *Older Americans: Inability to Repay Student Loans May Affect Financial Security of a Small Percentage of Retirees*. GAO 14–866T. United States Government Accountability Office.

Gibson, T. A. (2010). Primitive accumulation, eminent domain, and the contradictions of neo-liberalism. *Cultural Studies*, 24(1), 133–160.

Giroux, H. A. (2014). *Neoliberalism's war on higher education*. Chicago: Haymarket Books.

Hart, M. (2015). *A third of all Americans have dealt with student debt*. Retrieved from https://campustechnology.com/articles/2015/10/15/a-third-of-all-americans-have-dealt-with-student-debt.aspx

Hartlep, N. D., & Eckrich, L. L. T. (2013). Ivory tower graduates in the red: The role of debt in higher education. *Workplace*, 22, 82–97. Retrieved from https://works.bepress.com/nicholas_hartlep/19/

Hefling, K. (2015, May 15). Consumer agency opens inquiry on student loan services. *Seattle Times*. Retrieved from www.seattletimes.com/business/consumer-agency-opens-inquiry-on-student-loan-services/

Patton, S. (2013, April 15). I fully expect to die with this debt. *The Chronicle of Higher Education*, 59(32), A10–A11. Retrieved from http://chronicle.com/article/I-Fully-Expect-to-Die-With/138507/

Reich, J. A. (2005). *Fixing families: Parents, power, and the child welfare system*. New York: Routledge.

Sahn, D. E., & von Brohn, J. (1986). Yield variability and income, consumption, and food security. In P. B. R. Hazell (Ed.), *Summary proceedings of a workshop on cereal yield variability* (pp. 87–111). Washington, DC: International Food Policy Research Institute.

Taylor, K. A. (2009). Poverty's multiple dimensions. *Journal of Educational Controversy*, 4(1), 1–20. Retrieved from http://cedar.wwu.edu/jec/vol4/iss1/4/

U.S. Department of Education Office of Student Financial Assistance. (2000). *Exit counseling guide for borrowers* (Revised September 2000). Washington, DC: Author.

Walsemann, K. M., Gee, G. C., & Gentile, D. (2015). Sick of our loans: Student borrowing and the mental health of young adults in the United States. *Social Science & Medicine*, 124, 85–93. Retrieved from http://dx.doi.org/10.1016/j.socscimed.2014.11.027

Williams, B. (2015, April 26). *Elite universities are turning our kids into corporate stooges*. Retrieved from www.newrepublic.com/article/121644/elite-universities-are-turning-our-kids-corporate-stooges

11 Should I Go Back to College?

Melissa A. Del Rio

My College Dream

The dream doesn't always start in the same way. Sometimes I am in a hall-way. Other times I am in a lab or a classroom. There are faces surrounding me—some I recognize, some I don't—and there is only one thing I am sure of: I am completely unprepared for this. Sometimes there is a test being passed out. Sometimes I realize there is a big project due, or all of the sudden it is the end of the school year, and I have somehow forgotten or been un-able to attend class up until this moment. But now (in my dream) I am there, I am terrified, and I am not ready. I don't have a lot of recurring dreams, so these dreams in which I find myself back at school and completely off-guard have provided much fodder for self-analysis. But I haven't had to delve too deep into my psyche to come to the conclusion that I harbor some serious guilt for never having "finished" school.

As a child, I always loved learning and possessed a self-directed curiosity. I spent most of my youth living with my single mom. I was her only child, and she worked to support us while completing a community college pro-gram in healthcare to secure our financial future. Consequently, the ability to problem-solve and figure things out on my own, although not forced, was clearly valued in our household. I liked to explore and create, and my mother encouraged my inquisitive nature. By the age of five, I was proudly explaining to adults that I wanted to be an archaeologist when I grew up and reading to them out loud as a party trick.

In elementary school, I did well academically and picked up on things quickly. I consistently scored well on tests, be they our weekly spelling tests, the high-stakes achievement tests mandated by the district, or, eventually, the intelligence quotient tests given to children to qualify for gifted and tal-ented programs. I did so well that I got excited for them and really looked forward to seeing my scores. I participated and performed at the top of my class; I was the kid who always had my hand raised for the answer, the stu-dent who didn't mind reading aloud or going up to the board.

My high achievement and IQ test scores in elementary school led to my being categorized as "gifted" and enrolled in a specialized middle school.

The gifted school strove to provide a challenging curriculum, to correlate knowledge encompassing multiple subjects, and to offer unique opportunities for extracurricular and supplemental learning. Emphasizing rigorous research was an avenue by which they carried this out, and the academic expectations were much more extreme than any I had previously experienced, or would experience in high school and even in some of my college courses. Maybe the material was too challenging for me and I didn't know how to adapt, or maybe it was because I was going through a tumultuous period in my family, culminating in the divorce of my mom and ex-stepfather.

I wonder, too, about how different my cultural capital was from that of my peers and from the resources that the "special" school and its teachers assumed enrolled students would have. Looking back, I suspect that they didn't recognize the resources or funds of knowledge I *did* bring to class (González, Moll, & Amanti, 2005) or provide scaffolding for me to nurture the resources I lacked. I've come to think that this played a role in why I struggled there.

Contributing factors notwithstanding, middle school was a very stressful time, and during this period I developed into a very lazy student. It felt like the academic competition was too stiff, and I was not good at asking for or receiving help and discipline, so I inwardly renounced my drive to compete. I still enjoyed learning, but I was starting to feel that the point of school was more about my grades and less about how I thought, what I was interested in, or what lessons I was internalizing. So, through trial and error, I figured out how to do just enough for the B average that kept my parents and teachers appeased.

During high school I was placed on a track of enriched courses and ended up in one of the few Advanced Placement (AP) classes my school offered, but I flew under the academic radar in these programs. I was able to push myself and excel in the classes I was interested in. I did the extra credit reading in a class in which our instructor used themes in literature to teach us about examining media and the world, but not just to earn the "A" in a challenging class. Our instructor made it clear that the extra credit reading list had the "good stuff" he wasn't allowed to require, such as *A Clockwork Orange* and *One Flew Over the Cuckoo's Nest*. After being enrolled in AP American History due to a clerical error, I stayed in the class because I enjoyed discussing the historical context behind the practices and views of our day, and because my instructor told me she knew I could handle it when I mentioned dropping it for the history class I had intended to take. No one from that class ended up scoring a 5 on the AP test at the end of the semester, but I was one of three students who scored a 4.

The majority of my classes, however, I blew off as much as I knew I could get away with. I did as little homework as possible, treating my Anatomy coloring worksheets as the joke they appeared to be—if I could still get a decent grade on the test, why should I do the work? I would let my grades slip and then boost them up the next semester to average them out. I knew my moderately good grades were "enough" to get into a relatively "good" college or university. My indifference toward academic competition clouded any thoughts toward going to an elite, "top-tier" school, so I rarely felt motivated to do any better.

My ambition at that time was to become an actress. I was very involved in the theatre productions at my high school, as well as other performance-related extracurricular activities, including group interpretation and show choir. I felt extremely passionate about acting and performing, like it was my calling. I didn't feel that higher education was an absolute necessity to pursue acting, however. Experience, I believed, was the true key to developing my skills. Even so, my big dreams scared me, and when push came to shove, I wasn't ballsy enough to go "all in": to move to the Big City and try to Make It as an Actress. Instead, because I was bright and capable, it felt like the "right thing to do" per societal norms was to go to college and enroll in a program congruent to my long-term career goals. I realize now that I subscribed wholeheartedly to the neoliberal notion that higher education grows an individual's "human capital"—that college was a commodity that would put me "a degree above" others in competition toward any future endeavors (Giroux, 2014).[1]

A performer with a diploma would be more employable than one without. This sealed my reticent acceptance that the logical path was to pursue a Theatre degree while getting what performance experience I could, putting off seeking employment as an actress until I was "better degreed." Plus, I admitted in the back of my mind, to have a diploma was to have an inherent Plan B, in case acting didn't work out.

My mother was extremely supportive of whatever it was I chose to do. She let me guide myself in decision-making for my future, even so far as shielding me from (and trying to balance out) the opinions of less supportive family members. Although I am grateful to my mother for her unwavering support, I had little confidence in my chosen path, and I felt completely lost as I was embarking upon it.

I had no idea what I was doing or what I wanted in a college; I just wanted to earn a degree in Theatre. I don't recall having any conversations about choosing a college until the time came that I needed to apply. Perhaps school thought home was guiding me, and my mom thought school was guiding me, but I had no experience or knowledge of the variables involved in figuring out the right program or school for me. A strong ACT score led to a daily bombardment in the mail of pamphlets and brochures from schools, but I felt more overwhelmed than empowered by this plethora of information and propaganda.

They all seemed to advertise the same kind of generic, student-centered experience. Although in retrospect I fault myself for not seeking out more resources to help me in this venture, it still frustrates me that college had always been propped up to be the most important step in my life as a young adult but I was given so few tools to guide me as to how and where to make this huge investment. After I expressed to my mom my plan to pursue higher education, she did gently suggest that I consider the local community college, but my one stubborn vision of myself in college was that of living on campus, being immersed in the sort of experience illustrated in the materials at my disposal. Propaganda indeed.

Thrust into creating my own criteria for deciding on a school, I made my own shoddy framework. I didn't feel comfortable with the idea of large crowds (and thus a large campus) and had already established that I wasn't ready to go too far from home. The financial implications of where I would end up weighed upon me. I knew my mother would help me and that there were various forms of financial aid available, but I had been raised in a frugal, lower-middle class family and tuition rates were almost too dizzying to make sense of. While my mind was considering dollar amounts that were well beyond my means, it was easy to fall into an elitist, neoliberal, capitalist train of thought concerned with getting what I was paying for. Surely, there must be inherent advantages to going to a private institution over a public one; surely, a higher cost must be directly related to the quality of the education, experience, and opportunities afforded to students, right?

Anxious and overwhelmed, and hoping to find something affordable but still of the "quality" I was imagining, I ended up applying to and being accepted at just one institution of higher learning; a small, private, liberal arts school that a few of my friends attended. I'd been to a party there once in high school. It was fun enough, and my friends seemed to like it there. It satisfied my criteria, thus concluding the vetting process for the most important investment I had ever made.

My College Reality

I received financial aid in the form of academic and theatre scholarships and a Pell Grant, but the cost of my education was still over $15,000 a year. I don't recall the details of the breakdown of the balance or of the loan itself, nor how it was decided that my mother would be responsible for roughly 75% of the repayment and I for the remainder. I do remember having heart palpitations as we skimmed over and signed the paperwork. This was it; this was the path I had chosen for myself. I was anxious and hopeful that I was doing the right thing.

It didn't take me long to regret my decision. The feeling of aimlessness I had started feeling in high school was progressively getting worse, and the abstract idea I had of what college was supposed to be like was nothing like what I was experiencing. The small population contributed to a cliquey atmosphere I had not been expecting, and I although I got along with my fellow students, I generally felt more isolated than independent. In accordance with the terms of my theatre scholarship, I was involved in every production in some capacity, and I was cast in the first major theatre production of my freshman year. I do credit the department for trying to provide a well-rounded program of study. I assisted with lighting, costumes and makeup, set building and set design on various projects. But the experience still felt lacking.

My theatre cohort seemed to get a lot out of the program, but I was underwhelmed and unfulfilled. They raved about the instructors and directors, but it seemed that a lot of their praise was the result of strong interpersonal relationships that I did not feel privy to. I didn't recognize my depression, and it is still hard for me to discern the extent to which my feelings of disengagement were due to my mental health at the time, as opposed to the quality of the program.

There was one professor who taught one of the required freshman general education courses I took my first semester who showed genuine interest in my growth as a student. I may romanticize it in my head a bit, but I remember the incident as such: after I was unable to turn in an important paper in class due to a printer failure, she stated that I could meet her at her office at a later time and turn in a hard copy. After I turned it in, she asked me what my major was.

"Why are you a theatre major?" she asked, in mock exasperation.
"Because I think I'd like to be an actress."
"Well, I think you're a writer."

We made a deal that she would not take any points off my assignment for being late, provided that I pick up a minor in English. From that one positive interaction, I gained more encouragement, confidence, and inspiration than I did from the theatre program or institution collectively.

As time passed, however, I continued down the spiral of becoming more depressed and disengaged. I pledged a sorority but felt as detached from my future "sisters" as I had the theatre students. Overwhelmed by the feeling that I wasn't in the right place or doing the right thing, but not knowing what to do or what would make me feel better, I found out about an opportunity to do volunteer work in Africa through the university. Once my position on the trip was secured, I let the lethargy and malaise I was feeling toward my college experience take over. I skipped class to lie in bed and hope that being far away in a new, very different place would clarify things for me. During my first semester, I had been just shy of making the Dean's list; by the end of second semester, I was failing out.

I spent six weeks in Soweto, South Africa, that summer, living and volunteering at a group foster home and the pediatric ward of the local hospital. The details of that experience (which are worthy of describing, but won't be in this piece) were sufficiently moving to help catalyze my acceptance of the need for a change. The following fall, I was unable to go back to the university due to my grades and my disillusionment with its offerings and the program I'd been in. I was anxiously, guiltily aware that my mother and I had spent a small fortune on this one inauspicious year. I had to do everything differently.

I decided to enroll in the local community college as a part-time student. I had soured on the idea of pursuing acting in an academic fashion, or at all, really; my trip to Africa had helped inculcate the desire to be of service in the world, but I had not defined in what capacity. I'd heard of the difficulties in becoming a student again after taking time off from formal study, and I did not want to lose momentum. I looked at it as a second chance, and a way to regain my footing after an unsuccessful year. I reproached myself for my refusal to consider community college when my mother had brought it up previously . . . while still holding on to my elitist disdain toward it. I had heard it described as a glorified high school with ashtrays, among other pejorative terms. On a trip to the public library, I had watched another student from my high school—a student who was in the *remedial* classes—find out that he had been accepted. If the prestige of this *Junior* college left something to be desired, at least we would be able to pay for it without loans.

I took a wide variety of classes, not following any cohesive program, and changing my mind several times about the direction of my further education and what career I might pursue. Throughout my time there, I generally found instructors to be very engaging and willing to help, interested in my growth and my education, as well as in me as a person. Some of the incidental courses I took—just because the description piqued my curiosity and/or I needed to retain a full course load—ended up being the most thought-provoking to me, influential both in my thinking and motivations. In particular, after a semester of a creative writing course that enriched my knowledge of the tools and techniques of the art and my confidence in finding my voice in the written word, my instructor told me he'd like to see me get something published someday, and provided me with a list of literary journals and publications where I could submit my work (hey, it took me a while, but hi, Craig!).

I juggled working my shitty retail job part-to-full-time as I went to school part-to-full-time, and, after three years, I had acquired enough credits to graduate with an Associate's Degree of Arts and Sciences in 2007. I kidded with my friends about getting my "Asshole's Degree," and I didn't walk at graduation. I was less than dazzled with myself for having achieved this, as I considered graduating from community college as only the first baby step to my higher education goals—I still wanted to earn a bachelor's degree.

Though I did want to continue with my college education, the thought of having to take out more student loans and/or ask my mother to help with the cost seemed too burdensome without a specific goal or plan in mind. I figured that I would just continue working my shitty retail job until I had a more concrete idea of what I wanted to do. Eventually, my peers started graduating with their bachelor's degrees, and I pined for a more "grown up" job and began traversing the market of not-inconsequential positions for which a bachelor's degree is not required.

It would seem that handling the most delicate of personal information is deemed well within the realm of capabilities of someone without a bachelor's degree. As Goldrick-Rab (2016) notes, "Two-year associate degrees pay off" (p. 56). "And people with even a couple years of college make significantly more money, on average, than those with none" (Goldrick-Rab, 2016, p. 58). I was responsible for thousands of daily cash transactions as a bank teller, and then for retirement plan investments as a trading specialist at a benefits group. Always interested in the field of medicine, yet terrified at the prospect of having hands-on involvement in the physical health of another human being, I progressed into the office administration end of the healthcare field, where I remain to this day.

I haven't exactly done poorly for myself. But although my ascension through the ever-decreasing job positions for which a bachelor's degree is "preferred, but not required" has been steady, it is also tainted with insecurity, even a tad bit of desperation. Recently, I expressed interest in an open position within my office. I was originally told that I would be able to shadow the position, but the offer was then rescinded, and I was told that instead I should be due further compensation within my current role. However, upon a review, I was denied the raise. The reasoning given was that, based on my education and experience, and the fact that I was already making the midpoint wage for my position (.08 cents below it, actually, but who's counting?), they were simply unable to offer me more due to the tiered waging system my employer implements. This, while also praising my work, ideas, and leadership abilities within my current position, and insinuating the possibility of a future promotion.

It is hard to discern to what extent not having a bachelor's degree plays a part in these situations. The entrenched seed of fear for my future employability that sprouted my decision to pursue the theatre degree I wasn't sure I needed has come to fruition along this alternative route. Because I don't have a bachelor's degree, I feel pressure to prove my worth as an employee, especially in terms of being promoted or being able to seek out opportunities for growth within my employment. As demonstrated in my personal example of a tiered wage system, my work is worthy of praise, but apparently I merit less pay than I would if I had academic credentials. What does this say about the purpose and value of a higher education degree? If someone doesn't need a bachelor's degree to perform well in these fields—which I am living proof of—but those with degrees get paid more, does this compensation really speak to their value as an employee? Tiered wage systems perpetuate the neoliberal agenda of hierarchy because higher education is sold as a commodity that increases one's lifetime earnings. Whom does this really benefit?

Many of my bachelor's degree-holding peers whose career paths have paralleled my own do get paid more but are saddled with hundreds of dollars in monthly student loan payments that they will be making for years to come. In this neoliberal landscape of credentialism (Alvesson, 2014), competition, and hierarchy, degree holders are entitled to more compensation within the same career as someone without a degree, but so much of this extra income goes toward student debt. This raises the question of whether students are getting true value out of their education or are simply unwitting participants in a cycle of money exchange largely on behalf of the student loan industry, the government, and higher education administrators. While I admit that there are jobs for which advanced education is genuinely necessary, they are arguably far fewer than the U.S. system of public and private higher education and its financing will admit. Far too many, and a disproportionately higher percentage of, lower-income students are being underdeveloped at the secondary level and/or borrowing to pay for unnecessary or poorly focused higher education in ways that benefit others financially far more than themselves. Who pays for and who benefits from such exchange relations is—or should be—increasingly apparent.

Now, in an anticlimactic turn, I find myself almost 10 years out of school, still cut by the double-edged sword of never having finished my Bachelor's degree. I think about it, fret about it, dream about it. Not going back to school puts a bow on the undeveloped potential I have been wrapping in underachievement for most of my life. It embarrasses me. However, even in considering my experience of the ramifications of not having my B.A. or B.S., the reality of going back to school is daunting.

I had my student loan debt paid off by 2010, and I was basically debt-free before getting married in 2014. My spouse, an academic who just completed his Ph.D., is in the opposite position. He has had to live off of credit and student loans throughout graduate school, and the idea of adding potentially thousands of dollars more debt to this is even more abhorrent to me now than it was before, when my perspective was blessed with financial naïveté. Additionally, to go back to school now would also mean a significant change in lifestyle. I work full time with a lot of overtime, and do not have flexible work hours, so at some point my current career would need to be sacrificed to be able to complete my courses in a bachelor's degree program. Although I do still fantasize about a career that would fulfill my desire to be of service to the world, the careers that I find desirable don't make a lot of money, not without a graduate degree anyway, the pursuit of which would further entrench me within this cycle.

It seems that my fears about the difficulty of going back were not unfounded, but perhaps not for the exact reasons I had anticipated. Here I remain, feeling stuck inside my head, stuck with my conflicting feelings about going back to school, questioning my role within the higher education system and the broader implications of the system itself. I want to go back to school, to gain more knowledge for the sake of self-actualization, for my own personal growth, and to be able to contribute more to the world in turn, but this is not possible without having to risk my livelihood and go deeper into debt. I want everyone to be able to do this, for the world to be rich in learning opportunities for potential students, instead of having a system that sees students as potential opportunities to benefit the rich few at the top of the neoliberal model with its fanaticism of degrees, ranking, hierarchy, and constant anxiety of not "stacking up."

I want an education system that emphasizes making the most of oneself for the betterment of society, in whatever capacity that may be. Realistically, however, until this happens, my dreams of going back to school will be just that—dreams. However, in the meantime or even after such systemic change, there is little (except overtime work to pay current bills) stopping me from pursuing my own education outside of school, whether through what Kamenetz (2010) calls "DIY U" and/or through community theatre or other self-initiated pursuits of my own choosing, online, at home, or in my larger community.

Note

1 The work of Henry A. Giroux and a quote from Robert McChesney best encapsulate how I have come to define neoliberalism, which I see as "the policies and processes whereby a relative handful of private interests are permitted to control as much as possible of social life in order to maximize their personal profit. Associated initially with Reagan . . . neoliberalism has been the dominant global political economic trend adopted by political parties of the center and much of the traditional left as well as the right" (as cited in Chomsky, 1999, p. 7).

References

Alvesson, M. (2014). *The triumph of emptiness: Consumption, higher education, and work organization.* New York: Oxford University Press.

Chomsky, N. (1999). *Profit over people: Neoliberalism and global order.* New York: Seven Stories Press.

Giroux, H. A. (2014). *Neoliberalism's war on higher education.* Chicago: Haymarket Books.

Goldrick-Rab, S. (2016, Winter). The economy needs more workers with associate degrees. *Education Next, 16*(1), 54–60. Retrieved from http://educationnext.org/files/ednext_XVI_1_forum.pdf

González, N., Moll, L. C., & Amanti, C. (Eds.). (2005). *Funds of knowledge: Theorizing practices in households, communities, and classrooms.* New York: Routledge.

Kamenetz, A. (2010). *DIY U: Edupunks, edupreneurs, and the coming transformation of higher education.* White River Junction, VT: Chelsea Green Publishing.

Part III

Alternatives to American Neoliberal Financing of Higher Education

12 Free Tuition

Prospects for Extending Free Schooling Into the Postsecondary Years

James C. Palmer and Melissa R. Pitcock

Introduction

In the two decades following World War II, policymakers faced a tremendous challenge: How could demands for postsecondary education (made evident by the high proportion of World War II veterans who used education benefits of the GI Bill) be met in a cost-effective manner? Public two-year colleges were a big part of the answer. Known in the 1940s as *junior colleges*, they were usually operated by school districts as extensions of high schools into grades 13 and 14 (Cohen, Brawer, & Kisker, 2013). Why not, many policymakers asked, encourage the further development of these institutions, creating statewide systems of two-year colleges that would serve local communities and extend free public schooling for all through grade 14 (President's Commission on Higher Education, 1947)? This would expand opportunity for postsecondary study at per-student costs to the state that were much lower than those at universities and, at the same time, buffer the universities from the anticipated onslaught of students that might otherwise threaten their standing as selective institutions and deflect attention from upper-division and graduate study (Illinois Association of Junior Colleges, 1956). It would also make college more affordable for students and their families.

The idea of "free" schooling at what came to be called *community colleges* never took hold. Most states didn't have the resources needed to fully fund their growing community college systems, and although California maintained a no-tuition policy up to the mid-1980s, the growing fees paid by students for labs and other services foretold its eventual demise in the mid-1980s (Lindsey, 1982; Lombardi, 1976). Since then, periodic recessions, increased competition for state monies needed to support other public obligations (e.g., K–12 schooling, corrections, and health care), and the growing influence of fiscal conservatism in the nation's political scene have further weakened the capacity of states to fund higher education, causing community colleges (like other segments of the higher education system) to become more dependent upon tuition (Archibald & Feldman, 2011; Palmer, 2013). Between 2001 and 2011 (when the economy was just starting to recover from the Great Recession of 2007–2009), state and local government appropriations per full-time-equivalent (FTE) student at community colleges declined by 23% nationwide (in constant 2011 dollars), while tuition revenues per FTE student increased by 42%. The shift from public subsidies to tuition was more pronounced during the same time period for public four-year institutions, where state and local funding levels declined by 28% and 26% at public research and public master's institutions, respectively, and tuition and fees rose by 64% and 59% (Romano & Palmer, 2015).

But as relentless tuition increases become politically untenable—especially in the face of an emerging consensus that the nation's economic competitiveness will require higher rates of postsecondary degree completion—the idea of free schooling through grade 14 has re-emerged. This can be seen in the many grassroots *promise* initiatives that cover all or some of the tuition costs of high school graduates who attend the local community college, in emerging state initiatives to revisit the possibility of making community colleges tuition free, and in recent proposals to involve the federal government in financing schemes that would essentially make the first two years of postsecondary education free for any student at a community college or even public university nationwide.

This chapter reviews these nascent steps toward what has been called a *free tuition* approach to higher education funding, acknowledging its laudable goals but noting two concerns. First, we wonder whether free tuition will make a significant difference in higher education affordability, especially in light of the already low net cost of community colleges (toward which many of these initiatives are targeted). Second, we are concerned with the fact that free tuition treats unequal students equally by subsidizing the wealthy as well as those from low-income families. Policymakers considering the free tuition option must therefore weigh the potential benefits of eliminating tuition against the cost of redirecting scarce funds from those who need them the most to those who need them the least.

Local Initiatives

The contemporary push for tuition-free education beyond high school stems not from the top-down advocacy of national leaders, but from the bottom-up actions of local promise programs that augment state and federal financial aid monies received by community college students with what Miller-Adams (2015) calls "place-based scholarships" (p. 1). These programs take many forms. Some are very expansive. The Kalamazoo Promise, established in 2005 and considered by many to be the starting point of the promise movement, is an example. It covers all or part of the tuition costs of high school graduates from the Kalamazoo public school system in any public institution of higher education in Michigan (as well as in selected private institutions), as long as the student maintains a minimum 2.0 grade point average; the amount of subsidy depends on how long the student had been enrolled in the Kalamazoo schools (Miller-Adams, 2015). But many are more restrictive, sometimes limiting scholarships to those who meet certain academic thresholds in high school (e.g., maintaining a specific grade point average) or to those who attend specific institutions.

Regardless of scope, all share two characteristics: (a) the award of scholarships on the basis of "long-term attendance (and often residency) in a specific school district," as opposed to the need- or merit-based emphasis of state and federal financial aid programs, and (b) the pursuit of broad community goals, including increased educational access to postsecondary education within the local community, the development of a "college-going culture in the school district and surrounding community," and enhanced economic development through educational attainment (Miller-Adams, 2015, pp. 7, 10). The promise programs are not simply local financial aid initiatives. As Miller-Adams (2015) points out, "Promise stakeholders have made it clear that these initiatives are not just about students and schools; they are also about transforming the communities in which the schools are located" (p. 11).

The promise of free or reduced tuition at community colleges is a central feature of many of these programs, foreshadowing President Obama's proposal to make community college tuition-free (White House, 2015). In fact, of the 83 local promise initiatives identified in a database compiled by the W. E. Upjohn Institute for Employment Research (2016), 48 subsidize the tuition and fees (either wholly or partially) of students attending specific community colleges in local areas. Examples include the Galesburg Promise, which provides subsidies for up to 64 credit hours for graduates of Galesburg (IL) High School who attend the local community college, and the Jackson Legacy, which provides high school seniors in Jackson County, MI, with a one-time grant of $1,000 for use at Jackson College as well as at two other local institutions (W. E. Upjohn Institute for Employment Research, 2016). Another 29 programs offer subsidies to local high school graduates who attend any community college nationally or within a specific state higher education system. (The remaining six programs target subsidies to those attending specific four-year colleges in the local area.) Most rely primarily on privately raised monies to provide last-dollar subsides, "meaning they provide scholarships after all state and federal financial aid, like Pell Grants, are taken into account" (Smith, 2016, para. 17).[1] This private money is typically raised by soliciting donations from local philanthropists and businesses, or from fundraisers hosted by local organizations (Smith, 2016). However, some programs depend upon a combination of private and public funding, and have levied property or sales taxes to provide part of the necessary funds. For example, the Galesburg Promise draws upon a 2% hotel tax as well as funding from the Galesburg Community Foundation (Carl Sandburg College, 2014).

Beyond the baseline requirement that beneficiaries must be area residents who have been enrolled in specific school districts (sometimes for specific lengths of time), eligibility criteria vary across the 83 programs listed in the W. E. Upjohn database. Many (37) have universal eligibility for recent high school graduates in local areas. But others apply selection criteria that generally fall into two categories. First, many promise programs subsidize students on the condition that they maintain satisfactory levels of academic achievement (i.e., merit) in high school, as evidenced, for example, by their attendance records and grade point averages. Second, a smaller number of programs also tie funding to what might be called responsible behavior. This is evident in the programs that require community service activities while in high school and, in the case of at least one program (the Great River Promise), a record that is free of drug offenses or convictions for driving while intoxicated (Arkansas Northeastern College, n.d.).[2]

The explicit reference to criminal behavior in the Great River program, although absent from most other promise initiatives, reflects the underlying intent of the promise movement to, among other goals, provide students with incentives for hard work and educational achievement. The Horatio Alger *mythos* is evident. As the website for the Great River Promise explains,

> If you want a college education . . . You can have one! Stay in school, stay out of trouble, work hard, earn your high school diploma, and there will be money to cover your full tuition and mandatory fees to Arkansas Northeastern College.
> (Arkansas Northeastern College, n.d., para. 1)

But what's less evident is a focus on income inequality. Only 14 of the 83 programs listed in the W. E. Upjohn database include income as an eligibility criterion, reflecting the broad intent of creating a college-going culture for all and not simply providing financial aid for low-income students. Indeed, it is curious to consider that the income-blind approach of these programs may inadvertently exacerbate income inequalities, especially in the case of programs that provide last-dollar subsidies after other financial aid is applied. In those cases, students with incomes high enough to disqualify them from need-based student financial aid (e.g., Pell grants) may receive a greater proportion of local promise monies than lower-income students whose subsidies reflect the difference between tuition charges and what government financial aid programs provide. And when one considers that for many low-income students, financial aid actually covers 100% or more of the relatively low tuition rates charged by community colleges, the proportionately greater benefit streaming to higher-income students becomes even more evident, and the prospect that promise funds will make college more affordable for low-income students becomes questionable (Miller-Adams, 2015; Romano & Palmer, 2015).

Still, promise programs might increase the proportion of low-income students who attend college if the process of promoting the promise initiative creates a culture of college going in local school districts, provides students with additional help in filling out the Free Application for Federal Student Aid (FAFSA) form, and, as a consequence, increases the number of low-income students who ultimately receive the state and federal aid needed to cover tuition expenses. But this will come at the cost of a subsidy to students from middle- and higher-income families.

State Initiatives

These concerns notwithstanding, the last-dollar, incentive approach to free tuition pioneered by the promise movement has had great appeal. Indeed, the recently implemented Tennessee Promise initiative (begun for the state's 2015 high school graduates) has moved this approach from the relatively obscure realm of local philanthropy to the more visible realm of state financial aid policy. Operated by the Tennessee Student Assistance Corporation, the Tennessee Promise is an ambitious program offering last-dollar assistance (after application of any Pell grant, state lottery scholarship, or grant from the Tennessee Student Assistance Award program) to high school graduates who enroll full-time in any of the state's community colleges or colleges of applied technology. Students enrolling in Associate's degree programs at four-year institutions are also eligible, although their subsidy is capped at the average tuition charge of the state's community colleges and may therefore not cover full tuition costs (Tennessee Promise, n.d.).

The process of applying for the Tennessee promise subsidy begins in the student's senior year of high school, when he or she is connected with a mentor from a partnering non-profit organization (that operates without state funds) who will help with filling out the FAFSA form and applying for admission to the college. Students must maintain satisfactory academic progress while in college, and they are expected to complete a certificate or associate's degree within five semesters. In addition, students must complete eight hours of community service work before enrolling in college and each year thereafter (Tennessee Promise, n.d.). This requirement, like the obligation to study on a full-time basis and maintain satisfactory progress, reflects the program's emphasis on degree completion and civic engagement. As Tennessee Promise Executive Director Mike Krause put it in a 2014 interview, "students who serve in their communities are more engaged and more successful, and it's a great lesson to teach them—that while we're engaged in assisting you in your higher education goals, we're also asking you to give back" (Kim, 2014, question 7).

Krause also noted a key criterion for judging the Tennessee Promise: the extent to which it boosts the college-going rate of students who might otherwise have opted not to continue their education after high school graduation. The "Tennessee Promise," he pointed out, "is built for students who aren't entering higher education at all" (Kim, 2014, question 5). And in response to those arguing that this goal might be better met through targeted financial aid that focuses on those with demonstrated need, he points out that low-income students retain the benefit of need-based financial aid, which often covers 100% of community college tuition, and urges that the larger goals of the Tennessee Promise—including the development of a mindset that "college is an option for everyone"—be kept in mind (Deruy, 2015, para. 20). This reflects the universal strategy of the promise movement, which implies that the best way to make college possible for students who might otherwise opt out of postsecondary study is to reinforce its importance for all, even to the extent of assisting those who do not qualify for need-based aid at current levels.

Whether this strategy is working remains an open question. Preliminary data for the fall of 2015 show an uptick in the enrollment of first-time freshmen at community and technical colleges, along with a decline at public four-year institutions. The underlying causes cannot yet be determined (Smith, 2015b). Perhaps the Tennessee Promise funding caused some students who might otherwise have enrolled in four-year colleges to begin their postsecondary studies at two-year colleges. Or perhaps the increased enrollments at community colleges and colleges of applied technology reflect a positive influence of the Tennessee Promise on students who might initially have been uncertain about whether to go to college in the first place. Other unanticipated influences might also be at work. An aggressive research agenda will undoubtedly be undertaken in the years ahead to answer these questions.

Until this research is completed, it is doubtful that many other states will attempt their own promise programs. Although "tuition-free college" bills have been introduced in at least 11 state legislatures (National Conference of State Legislatures, 2016), only Oregon has, as of this writing, joined Tennessee in providing free tuition at community colleges.[3] Oregon's recently enacted program will begin with students who graduated from high school in 2016 and enrolled in a community college within six months. The Oregon Promise differs from the Tennessee initiative in that eligible students must have earned a minimum 2.5 grade point average while in high school and pay a $50 per term copayment. In addition, the Oregon Promise provides a minimum annual benefit of $1,000 (regardless of financial aid received) that can be used for books or living expenses of students with federal or state grants covering the full tuition cost (National Conference of State Legislatures, 2016; Office of Student Access and Completion, 2015).[4] The Oregon program does not include a mentoring or community service component and is therefore much easier to administer. But behind these technical nuances is the narrative of good behavior that prevails across all promise programs. As a senior member of the Oregon Legislature put it, "We are saying to our young people that if you finish high school, keep up your grades and stay out of trouble, we promise to provide you with an opportunity to reach the middle class on your own" ("Oregon Students," 2015, para. 6).

National Proposals

However ambitious the Tennessee and Oregon initiatives are, they pale in comparison to two proposals that would extend free tuition through grade 14 across the country. In contrast to the promise programs, both offer first-dollar approaches that would totally cover tuition costs, leaving students free to use other aid, including loans, for living expenses. In addition, both would allocate federal monies directly to institutions (rather than indirectly through financial aid), thereby altering the federal role in higher education. Their implementation would also make "existing two-year Promise programs . . . redundant," perhaps causing the latter to "shift their attention to funding four-year options for eligible students, providing support for college costs beyond tuition, or investing in college access and preparedness initiatives" (Miller-Adams, 2015, p. 94).

The more visible of the two national proposals is encompassed in the America's College Promise Act of 2015. Backed by the Obama administration, this legislation authorizes states to apply for federal grants that would be used to waive all tuition costs for first-time community college students, regardless of income, who enroll in vocational or transfer programs. The state share of these grants would account for 25% of the average resident tuition and fees per student across community colleges nationwide, thereby making the federal government responsible for the remaining 75%. Many strings are attached, including provisions that colleges adopt "promising and evidence-based institutional reforms and innovative practices to improve student outcomes"; that states report how they are aligning K–12 schooling with postsecondary education, as well as two-year colleges with four-year colleges; that states employ performance-based funding mechanisms, along with other policies that "promote the improved performance of public institutions of higher education"; and that states maintain fiscal support for higher education at a rate that equals or exceeds the average funding provided to colleges and universities over the past three years (America's College Promise Act of 2015). These provisos reflect the legislative intent not only to make community colleges tuition free but to assure that increased federal funding does not supplant and further weaken state support for higher education, which is a primary cause of tuition increases. In addition, they address concerns that the increased access to community colleges afforded by the new federal subsidies could be meaningless without structural reforms needed to strengthen the curricular pathways and attendant services that help students to complete credentials or transfer to four-year schools.

The second and even more ambitious approach stems from the free two-year college option (F2CO) proposed by Sara Goldrick-Rab and Nancy Kendall (2014).[5] Under this plan, federal monies now spent on student financial aid and higher education tax credits would be redirected to public institutions—both two-year and four-year—which would use those funds (along with state and local monies) to waive tuition for all students (regardless of income) at the 13th and 14th grade levels, cover the cost of books and materials for these students, subsidize work-study programs that provide on-campus or community-service employment, and award stipends in amounts equal to 15 hours per week of living-wage employment in the local area for living expenses. Unsubsidized loans "equal to 5 hours/week of living wage employment in [the] local area" would be available to augment monies for living expenses, but repayment would be contingent on income, and they would be "dischargeable in bankruptcy" (p. 20). In addition, institutions serving large numbers of low-income or special-needs students would receive additional "top-up" allocations combined with performance-based funding for "holistic social services," including "medical, dental, and health" services, "housing . . ., free breakfast and/or free lunch programs . . ., childcare . . ., public benefits screening . . ., case management . . ., transportation services, or . . . supplementary instructional assistance" (pp. 19, 21). All institutions with selective admissions policies would be required to "report on enrollment and graduation rates of disadvantaged students" (p. 20).

Thus, like the GI Bill of 1944 (which was admittedly much more expansive, at least for the targeted population of veterans, covering expenses at all undergraduate and graduate levels), the F2CO proposal covers not just tuition, but living expenses as well, thereby emphasizing that college is not truly "free" if subsidies cover only tuition. Still, Goldrick-Rab and Kendall (2014) admit that their proposal will have several consequences that many might be concerned with. The F2CO plan, for example, would privilege public institutions, potentially limiting opportunities for low-income students to study in the private sector and possibly hurting the bottom line of non-profit and for-profit private colleges that have grown accustomed to having publicly subsidized students attend their institutions. It would also raise the question of how to fund upper-division education for those pursuing the bachelor's degree. In response, they note that private institutions could seek out their own funding and would indeed be driven to do so as they face pressures to diversify their student clienteles. Indeed, Ivy Leagues and most liberal arts colleges are already well endowed and pay no taxes on those foundation funds. They also note that upper-division study could be funded through the establishment of a need-based grant system "for F2CO students who qualify by establishing a record of success during their first two years of college, perhaps drawing largely on institutional and private scholarships" (p. 24).[6]

But their ultimate argument is that whatever the faults of the F2CO proposal might be, the current financial aid system is irretrievably broken. It has not eliminated income disparities in higher education access and achievement, and, although it may cover tuition costs for many low- and middle-income students, it leaves them dependent on loans to cover living expenses. In addition, they argue, the system of need-based aid is costly, cumbersome, and divisive. It imposes special burdens on low-income students who, unlike their more well-off peers, must navigate its bureaucratic procedures. Furthermore, it inspires little confidence in government and may diminish the impetus to civic engagement. Rather than structuring financial aid as a "poverty program" targeting low-income students specifically, financial aid under the F2CO plan would be reconfigured as a broader social policy. As Goldrick-Rab and Kendall (2014) note:

> A move to a broader-based policy that makes support available to all Americans in equitable ways will return financial aid policies to their original intention, and like the remarkably successful GI Bill, has greater potential to generate long-lasting benefits as generations of successful college graduates become involved participants in their nation's future.
>
> (p. 27)

Unanswered Questions

The remarkable evolution of the contemporary "free tuition" idea from local, often privately funded promise initiatives to proposals for the wholesale reform of higher education funding bespeaks a renewed consensus among many policymakers and scholars that free (or close to free) schooling should be extended beyond the 12th grade. One could also argue that it reflects a backlash against the view of education as a process that yields primarily private benefits and therefore requires few public subsidies (Cottom, 2015). Even the local and state promise initiatives that tout the value of individual effort and upstanding behavior ultimately concede the social benefits of increased participation and achievement in higher education, if only in the form of regional economic development and the attendant outcomes of enhanced civic engagement, reduced crime rates, and other desired goals. But these laudable aims notwithstanding, two crucial questions need to be answered before states (or the nation) move to a tuition-free community college enterprise.

First, will those proposals that focus primarily on the elimination of tuition at community colleges (e.g., local and state programs, as well as the America's College Promise Act) really make a significant difference for affordability? By several measures, community colleges are—as they currently stand—the most affordable higher education sector in the United States. They compare favorably to other sectors in terms of (a) their reliance on tuition as a revenue source per full-time equivalent (FTE) student, which grew by only 42% from 2001 to 2011 compared to 64% at public research universities, 59% at public master's universities, and 62% at public bachelor's degree institutions; (b) the average national sticker price (before financial grant aid is factored in) for full-time students, which grew between 1993–1994 and 2013–2014 at an inflation adjusted rate of 62% at community college, compared to 116% at public four-year colleges; and (c) the average national net price (tuition minus tax credits and grant aid from all sources) charged to full-time students, which actually declined dramatically at community colleges by an inflation adjusted 358% between 1993–1994 and 2013–2014, compared to an increase of 53% at public four-year colleges (Romano & Palmer, 2015). In addition, although community college attendees accounted for 29% of all FTE students (both undergraduate and graduate) in the fall of 2013, they accounted for only 6% of the aggregate outstanding federal student loan balances in 2013–2014. In contrast, 37% of this aggregate outstanding loan debt was accounted for by students from public four-year colleges, where 41% of all FTE students were enrolled; 34% was accounted for by students from private non-profit four-year colleges, where 22% of all FTE students were enrolled; and 21% was accounted for by students from for-profit institutions, where only 9% of all FTE students were enrolled (College Board, 2015b).

Admittedly, these national averages mask considerable variations across the states. Indeed, average in-district tuition charges at community colleges for full-time students over the course of the nine-month academic year in 2015–2016 ranged from $1,420 in California (a state that enrolls 15% of all community college students nationwide) to $7,530 in Vermont (College Board, 2015a). But overall, the community colleges have served their intended purpose—to provide an affordable option for higher education. Offering "free tuition" at these institutions may, in many states, do little to increase the number of students who participate in postsecondary education. In addition, free tuition for community college students alone may do little to enhance the overall affordability of higher education or reduce overall debt loads unless the increased community college subsidy diverts students from four-year institutions into the two-year sector, thereby reducing the diverted student's overall cost of obtaining a four-year bachelor's degree.

But even if local promise programs or the provisions of the America's College Promise Act (were it to be enacted) encouraged more students to begin postsecondary study at community colleges rather than four-year institutions, other costs could arise, including damage to the fiscal viability of masters-level public universities from which students are diverted (students aiming for the Ivy League or for flagship universities are less likely to be diverted); the potentially lower probability of students attaining a bachelor's degree, given evidence that students starting postsecondary study at community colleges are less likely to complete a four-year program than students who start at four-year colleges, all other things being equal; and increased strain on already overtaxed community colleges that would see enrollment increases without attendant increases in per-student state subsidies needed to finance curricular reforms required for student success (Romano & Palmer, 2015; Scott-Clayton & Bailey, 2015).

All of this suggests that targeting subsidies to students at four-year colleges as well as two-year colleges, a key feature of the F2CO proposal, will be essential if affordability is to increase and debt loads are to decrease. The F2CO proposal appears even more compelling in its attention to living expenses as well as tuition. Yet, like the local, state, and national promise programs, the F2CO framework begs the second question that must be considered: Is it necessary to subsidize education through grade 14 for all students regardless of income? As Miller-Adams (2015) notes, this puts the free tuition issue squarely in the classic debate about "whether social programs are most effective if they are designed to reach an entire population or targeted toward a specific group" (p. 47). Those who favor "universal" programs argue that they are "more feasible, or likely to reach all segments of the highest-need population, and non-stigmatizing" (p. 47). This clearly undergirds the arguments advanced by Goldrick-Rab and Kendall (2014) in support of the F2CO proposal, and it can be seen in the underlying intent of many local promise initiatives and the Obama-supported America's College Promise Act. But those favoring targeted or means-tested programs argue that they are more efficient "in that they distribute scarce resources to the population that needs or deserves them the most" (Miller-Adams, 2015, p. 47).

It is the latter argument that leads us to view the free-tuition movement cautiously. We recognize the arguments of those who favor the universal approach, particularly the arguments of those who maintain that the promise movement is not simply a way of increasing affordability for individuals, but also a wider social initiative undertaken to enhance a culture of college going among students generally. Yet, however worthy the goal, economic reality still applies: resources are limited, and funds used for one purpose cannot be used for another, perhaps equally compelling, purpose (Cochrane, 2015). Under the universal approach, addressing the goal of increased opportunity and participation rates for low-income students comes at a cost: subsidies to the relatively wealthy students and families. For example, promise programs providing free tuition to community college students regardless of income would subsidize not only low-income students, but also those from families with incomes of $100,000 or more, a group that accounted for 25% of all community college students in 2013–2014 (Sallie Mae, 2014). The subsidy to well-off students increases if free tuition were extended through grade 14 to students at public four-year colleges, where 40% of all students come from families with incomes of $100,000 or more (Sallie Mae, 2014).

These subsidies to the well-off are monies that might be better spent on childcare services, universal healthcare, K–12 education, and greater funding for the Pell grant program—to name just a few of the competing demands made on scarce government funds for programs that have a bearing on the ability of individuals to take advantage of opportunities for a college education. They also represent monies that could be used to increase the proportion of full-time faculty members at community colleges, hire additional advising staff at those institutions, initiate curricular reforms leading to stronger pathways toward transfer and/or credential attainment, or subsidize any number of efforts to enhance community college work with students.

This is not to say that we should turn a blind eye to and accept the overarching economic and policy structures that shape the fiscal scarcity with which we live. This scarcity is the product of policy decisions, not an inalterable feature of higher education funding nor its underlying monetary system. We can make better decisions, routing more resources to education in more equitable ways. For example, state capacity to increase funding for higher education could be enhanced to the extent that antiquated sales-tax laws were modified to focus less on the purchase of goods and more on the purchase of services that characterize the modern economy; this assumes, of course, that progressive income-tax policies are also in place to offset the potentially unfair burden that might be borne by low-income citizens (Leachman & Mazerov, 2013). At the national level, efforts can be made to reverse the long history of neglect that has characterized financial aid policy and left it inadequate to the task of making college affordable for all, regardless of income (Mettler, 2014). In addition, steps can be taken to avoid what Mumper (2003) called the "subsidy creep" phenomenon that thwarts the goals of both universal and targeted initiatives through the creation of "supplemental programs" such as merit aid and tuition tax credits that redirect funds away from the "needy and toward middle income students" (p. 55).

But in the end, these efforts, although necessary and helpful, simply make resources for higher education "less scarce." Claims on resources are endless. As a consequence, there is no escaping the need to weigh the potential benefits of "free tuition" for all against the considerable opportunity costs of the universal approach mentioned above. Before accepting free tuition for all, policymakers should at least investigate targeted and less expensive approaches to making college affordable. At the community college level, for example, much could be done if institutions were to "renew their efforts to smooth the process of applying for financial aid and . . . locate eligible students on their own campuses needing help through this process" (Romano & Palmer, 2015, p. 45). These efforts are especially needed in light of research indicating that only 58% of Pell-eligible students at community colleges actually fill out the Free Application for Federal Student Aid (FAFSA) form, compared to 99.5% at for-profit two-year colleges (Kantrowitz, 2009). And within the system of higher education generally, including four-year colleges, simplifying the FAFSA form and the process for obtaining Pell grants along the lines suggested by Rueben, Gault, and Baum (2015) might go a long way, as could enhanced efforts to inform students of financial aid opportunities. Here we could learn a lot from the efforts of local promise initiatives, as well as the Tennessee Promise, about how to help high school graduates fill out the FAFSA and secure the grant aid to which they are entitled. Indeed, the proportion of high school seniors in Tennessee who filled out the FAFSA form rose from 42% in 2014 (the year before implementation of the Tennessee Promise) to 61% in 2015 (Smith, 2015a). Certainly this sort of assistance can be provided in an effective manner without wholesale subsidies to higher-income students.

It is encouraging that policymakers are revisiting the idea of extending free schooling into the postsecondary years. This is a refreshing response to rising tuition rates and student debt levels. But we need to consider whether contemporary plans to eliminate tuition for the first two years of college may unintentionally exacerbate inequities in educational opportunity, especially if scarce resources are diverted from investments in social programs and improved community college services to subsidies for the relatively well off. As counterintuitive as it may seem, the free-college-for-all approach—although perhaps more likely to garner broad-based public support than a targeted, means-based program—may reinforce rather than work against neoliberal tendencies in higher education. Targeting funds to lower-income students and simplifying the processes used to apply for needed grant aid may move us further along the way toward a more equitable higher education system.

Notes

1 The extent to which loans count as aid in the calculation of last-dollar promise grants is an open question, at least in terms of information provided on program websites. While some promise program websites specify that awards are made after all financial aid "grants" are used (e.g., City of Lansing, n.d.; Garrett College, 2014), others simply note that applying for aid by filing a FAFSA form is a prerequisite for receiving a promise grant, or that grant totals are calculated after all federal and state financial aid is used (e.g., City Colleges of Chicago, 2015). However, Miller-Adams (2015) notes that "most promise programs . . . are 'last dollar' programs, meaning that the Promise scholarship is awarded after other grant aid is calculated" (p. 7).

2 Most programs also require students to enroll full time and maintain satisfactory academic progress once in college.

3 Programs in two other states are on the immediate horizon. Kentucky's Work Ready Scholarship Program, not scheduled for implementation until the 2017–2018 academic year, will offer last-dollar subsidies to high school graduates who enroll in certificate, diploma, or associate's degree programs at public or private two-year or four-year institutions immediately after high school graduation; starting in 2020–2021, students will have had to complete dual-credit courses while in high school in order to be eligible (Kentucky Legislature, 2016; National Conference of State Legislatures, 2016). Minnesota has established a two-year pilot program, the MnSCU Two-Year Occupational Grant Pilot Program that began in the fall of 2016 and provides last-dollar subsidies to high school graduates pursuing certificate, diploma, or associate's degrees in occupational fields that have been designated by the state as being in high demand. Like the Tennessee Promise, the Minnesota pilot includes a mentoring component. Free-tuition benefits may be extended to a broader range of students to the extent that the pilot "succeeds in attracting new students and helping them complete their programs" (Lerner, 2015). Information is at https://www.ohe.state.mn.us/mPg.cfm?pageID=2163

4 The ultimate extent of the Oregon Promise is unknown. Blumenstyk (2015) noted that the "program will start in the 2016–2017 academic year, but with just a $10-million budget allocation, it remains to be seen how extensive the program will be" (para. 12). This reflects the nascent character—as of this writing—of free tuition as a state financial aid strategy.

5 Readers should note that since this chapter was written, Goldrick-Rab has published a subsequent analysis entitled *Paying the Price: College Costs, Financial Aid, and the Betrayal of the American Dream* (Goldrick-Rab, 2016).
6 Another intriguing possibility is that local promise efforts made redundant by the F2CO plan might instead subsidize students who move on to the upper division.

References

America's College Promise Act of 2015, H.R. 2962, 114th Cong. (2015). Retrieved from https://www.congress.gov/bill/114th-congress/house-bill/2962

Archibald, R. B., & Feldman, D. H. (2011). *Why does college cost so much?* New York: Oxford University Press.

Arkansas Northeastern College. (n.d.). *The great river promise.* Retrieved from www.anc.edu/promise/

Blumenstyk, G. (2015, July 8). When college is free, or free(ish). *Chronicle of Higher Education.* Retrieved from http://chronicle.com/article/When-College-Is-Free-or/231421

Carl Sandburg College. (2014). *Galesburg promise offers Sandburg scholarships to district 205 graduates.* Retrieved from http://sandburg.mycareerfocus.org/2014/04/03/galesburg-promise-offers-great-opportunity-district-205-graduates/

City Colleges of Chicago. (2015). *Chicago star scholarship.* Retrieved from www.ccc.edu/departments/Pages/chicago-star-scholarship.aspx

City of Lansing. (n.d.). *H.O.P.E. scholarship compact.* Retrieved from www.lansingmi.gov/faq2

Cochrane, D. (2015, January 9). *Why "free community college" is a wolf in sheep's clothing* [Blog]. Retrieved from http://ticas.org/blog/why-%E2%80%9Cfree-community-college%E2%80%9D-wolf-sheep%E2%80%99s-clothing

Cohen, A. M., Brawer, F. B., & Kisker, C. B. (2013). *The American community college* (6th ed.). San Francisco: Jossey-Bass.

College Board. (2015a). *Trends in college pricing 2015.* Retrieved from http://trends.collegeboard.org/sites/default/files/trends-college-pricing-web-final-508-2.pdf

College Board. (2015b). *Trends in student aid 2015.* Retrieved from http://trends.collegeboard.org/sites/default/files/trends-student-aid-web-final-508-2.pdf

Cottom, T. M. (2015). Why free college is necessary. *Dissent Magazine, 62*(4), 115–117.

Deruy, E. (2015, July 27). The debate over free community college. *The Atlantic Magazine.* Retrieved from www.theatlantic.com/education/archive/2015/07/free-community-college-mixed-reviews/399701/.

Garrett College. (2014, March). *The Garrett county scholarship program: Report to the Garrett county commissioners.* Retrieved from https://www.garrettcounty.org/resources/commissioners/pdf/Garrett-County-Scholarship-Program-2014.pdf

Goldrick-Rab, S. (2016). *Paying the price: College costs, financial aid, and the betrayal of the American dream.* Chicago: University of Chicago Press.

Goldrick-Rab, S., & Kendall, N. (2014). *F2CO redefining college affordability: Securing America's future with a free two-year college option.* Retrieved from https://www.luminafoundation.org/files/publications/ideas_summit/Redefining_College_Affordability.pdf

Illinois Association of Junior Colleges. (1956). *Illinois public junior colleges invite you to read this report.* Belleville, IL: Author.

Kantrowitz, M. (2009). *FAFSA completion by level and control of institution.* Retrieved from www.finaid.org/educators/20091014fafsacompletion.pdf

Kentucky Legislature. (2016 Regular Session). *House Bill 626EN: An act relating to the development of a highly trained workforce in the Commonwealth and making an appropriation therefor*. Retrieved from www.lrc.ky.gov/record/16RS/HB626/bill.pdf

Kim, A. (2014, June). Tennessee promise: Offering free community college to all students. *Republic 3.0*. Retrieved from http://republic3–0.com/tennessee-promise-free-community-college-for-all-students/

Leachman, M., & Mazerov, M. (2013). Four steps to moving state sales taxes into the 21st century. *Center on Budget and Policy Priorities*. Retrieved from www.cbpp.org/research/state-budget-and-tax/four-steps-to-moving-state-sales-taxes-into-the-21st-century?fa=view&id=3987

Lerner, M. (2015, May 22). Minnesota pilot project offers free ride to technical college. *StarTribune*. Retrieved from www.startribune.com/minnesota-pilot-project-offers-free-ride-to-technical-college/304787961/.

Lindsey, R. (1982, December 28). California weighs end of free college education. *New York Times*. Retrieved from www.nytimes.com/1982/12/28/science/california-weighs-end-of-free-college-education.html

Lombardi, J. (1976). *No- or low-tuition: A lost cause* (Topical Paper No. 58). Los Angeles: ERIC Clearinghouse for Junior Colleges. ERIC database (ED129353). Retrieved from http://files.eric.ed.gov/fulltext/ED129353.pdf

Mettler, S. (2014). *Degrees of inequality: How the politics of higher education sabotaged the American dream*. New York: Basic Books.

Miller-Adams, M. (2015). *Promise nation: Transforming communities through place-based scholarships*. Kalamazoo, MI: W. E. Upjohn Institute for Employment Research.

Mumper, M. (2003). Does policy design matter? Comparing universal and targeted approaches to encouraging college preparation. *Educational Policy, 17*, 38–59.

National Conference of State Legislatures. (2016, April 24). *Free community college*. Retrieved from www.ncsl.org/research/education/free-community-college.aspx

Office of Student Access and Completion. (2015). *Oregon promise*. Retrieved from www.oregonstudentaid.gov/oregon-promise.aspx

Oregon students get tuition help from 'promise.' (2015, 7 July). *Portland Tribune*. Retrieved from http://portlandtribune.com/pt/9-news/265892–139687-oregon-students-get-tuition-help-from-promise

Palmer, J. C. (2013). State fiscal support for community colleges. In J. S. Levin & S. T. Kater (Eds.), *Understanding community colleges* (pp. 171–84). New York: Routledge.

President's Commission on Higher Education. (1947). *Higher education for American democracy*. Washington, DC: U.S. Government Printing Office.

Romano, R. M., & Palmer, J. C. (2015). *Financing community colleges: Where we are, where we're going*. Lanham, MD: Rowman & Littlefield.

Rueben, K., Gault, S., & Baum, S. (2015). *Simplifying federal student aid: How do the plans stack up?* Retrieved from www.urban.org/research/publication/simplifying-federal-student-aid-how-do-plans-stack/view/related_publications

Sallie Mae. (2014). *How America pays for college*. Washington, DC: Author. Retrieved from http://news.salliemae.com/files/doc_library/file/HowAmericaPaysforCollege2014FNL.pdf

Scott-Clayton, J., & Bailey, T. (2015, January 20). The problem with Obama's "free community college" proposal. *Money*. Retrieved from http://time.com/money/

3674033/obama-free-college-plan-problems/?utm_source=free+college&utm_campaign=UA-2832117–7&utm_medium=email

Smith, A. A. (2015a, March 17). The impact of free tuition. *Inside Higher Ed*. Retrieved from https://www.insidehighered.com/news/2015/03/17/high-tenn-promise-participation-numbers-boost-fafsa-completion-rates-state

Smith, A. A. (2015b, November 24). Promise provides enrollment boost. *Inside Higher Ed*. Retrieved from https://www.insidehighered.com/news/2015/11/24/promise-program-sharply-lifts-tennessee-college-freshman-enrollment

Smith, A. A. (2016, April 21). Public good, private money. *Inside Higher Ed*. Retrieved from https://www.insidehighered.com/news/2016/04/21/private-donors-and-businesses-are-backing-free-community-college-campaigns

Tennessee Promise. (n.d.). *School resource guide, 2015–2016*. Retrieved from http://tennesseepromise.gov/files/TNPromiseHandbook081715.pdf

University of Chicago Press. (n.d.). *Paying the price* (advertisement). Retrieved from http://press.uchicago.edu/ucp/books/book/chicago/P/bo24663096.html

W. E. Upjohn Institute for Employment Research. (2016, June). *Local, place-based scholarship programs*. Retrieved from www.upjohn.org/sites/default/files/promise/Lumina/Promisescholarshipprograms.pdf

White House. (2015, January 8). *President Obama announces free community college plan*. Retrieved from https://www.whitehouse.gov/photos-and-video/video/2015/01/09/president-obama-announces-free-community-college-plan

13 "Work Colleges" as an Alternative to Student Loan Debt

Nicholas D. Hartlep and Diane R. Dean

Introduction[1]

We begin this chapter by contextualizing the American student debt problem. The national student debt "bill," at $1.4 trillion and growing by an estimated $3,000 each second, is the second highest form of consumer debt behind home mortgages (Berman, 2016; Best & Best, 2014). Next, we define and situate "Work Colleges" within this context, analyzing Work Colleges as an alternative to student borrowing. Using 2008–2009 through 2012–2013 data from the Integrated Postsecondary Education Data System (IPEDS), we examine the amounts of federal debt reported by students who graduate from Work Colleges. Similar to, and updating the work of, Wolniak and Pascarella (2007), we find that Work College graduates borrow fewer and lower amounts of loans than their peers who graduate from non-Work Colleges.

Contextualizing the American Student Debt Problem

More than 20.4 million students are enrolled in the nation's 4,665 colleges and universities, a statistic that has grown by 31% since 2000 (NCES, 2016). The majority of these students (62%) are enrolled full-time (NCES, 2016). Among traditional-aged undergraduates (18–21 years old), however, that figure is higher. About 80% of young undergraduates enroll full-time (Payea, Baum, & Kurose, 2013). Conversely, part-time enrollment is the norm (63%) among older undergraduates (22 years and older) (Payea et al., 2013). We should celebrate this growth, and continue to push for the higher college participation and completion rates needed to meet President Obama's 2020 goal for the United States to reclaim its lost prominence of having the highest proportion of college graduates in the world (Lee, 2014; Obama, 2009).

While there is often confusion and disagreement about the costs and benefits of a college education (Baum, Kurose, & Ma, 2013), a review of the literature consistently demonstrates significant, strong returns to both individuals and the public from an individual's increased years in higher education. Amount of education is positively correlated with economic returns, such as reduced unemployment rates, higher individual income earnings, likelihood of being employed in a job with pension plan coverage, higher public tax revenues, higher payroll contributions to public social service programs, increased output of goods and services, and greater over-all economic growth due to the creation, diffusion, and transmission of knowledge (Baum, Ma, & Payea, 2013; Hearn & Bunton, 2001; U.S. Congress, 2000). Higher amounts of education are also positively correlated with important non-economic returns, such as individuals having greater interest in political issues; increased civic behaviors such as democratic attitudes, volunteerism, voting, and supporting free speech; an appreciation for human diversity; better informed consumer decision-making; the pleasure of reading, learning, and attending cultural events; and healthier habits such as reduced smoking, obesity, and disability rates, increased aerobic exercise, and greater likelihood of being employed in a job with employer-provided health insurance (Baum, Ma, & Payea, 2013; Dee, 2004; Hearn & Bunton, 2001; U.S. Congress, 2000). These correlations hold true across race, gender, and age, despite between-group differences. Such wide-ranging outcomes benefit the individual, his or her family, and society as a whole.

Despite the clear collective economic and non-economic societal benefits of having a higher educated populace, public discourse tends to focus primarily on the economic returns to the individual. Millions of undergraduates annually enter college, faithfully believing that the more a student "learns" the more s/he "earns." It is a behavior fueled by the tenets of human capital theories of socioeconomic mobility, which view higher education as a "private" benefit (a reward) that requires a "personal" financial investment (a risk). This is problematic because multiple assumptions, "concepts and complexities . . . underlie analyses of the benefits of postsecondary education" (Baum, Kurose, & Ma, 2013, p. 6). The majority of what we know about higher education's benefits focuses on aggregate data. But, despite the significant benefits for majorities of students, there are undeniably disappointing outcomes for some (Baum, Kurose, & Ma, 2013, p. 6).

Moreover, the cost of that investment continues to rise at rates beyond many students' ability to pay (Dickeson, 2004; Immerwahr, 2004; Immerwahr & Johnson, 2010; Mumper & Freeman, 2011). According to the White House (2014), "Over the past three decades, the average tuition at a public four-year college has more than tripled, while a typical family's income has increased only modestly" (para. 1). The average annual total tuition, fees, room, and board charged by all colleges and universities in 2014 was $21,003; but this figure was higher for private ($35,987) than for public ($15,640) institutions, and higher for four-year ($24,706) than for two-year ($9,888) institutions (NCES, n.d.f). In their analysis of how full-time undergraduate college students and their families paid for college costs, Payea et al. (2013) found that parents and students pay 38% of the total charges out of their own pockets, use grants and tax benefits to cover 36%, and borrow money to cover the remaining 26%.

As the need and demand for financial aid has outstripped the available amount of scholarships and grants, students and their families have increasingly relied on borrowing to close the gap (Akers & Chingos, 2014; Cunningham & Kienzl, 2011). The largest borrowing source is the federal government, through an array of programs such as federal student loans (which are awarded directly to students to use at their chosen college), Parent Loans for Undergraduate Students (PLUS loans, which are awarded to parents of undergraduates), and Perkins loans (which are awarded to institutions that then distribute awards to their eligible students) (ACE, 2013). In 2014–2015, undergraduates borrowed a collective $62 million from these programs to pay for college: This staggering amount represents an increase of 39% over the previous decade (College Board, 2015). In contrast, education loans from nonfederal sources such as banks, credit unions, states, and institutions, although enormous at $10.1 billion, actually declined by 43% in the same period (College Board, 2015).

Due to extensive borrowing, students are leaving college with increasingly higher levels of debt. A majority (60%) of bachelor's degree recipients graduate with an average debt of $25,500 (College Board, 2015). However, actual borrowing patterns vary greatly according to institutional type and student demographics. Among four-year institutions, higher proportions of students borrow loans at for-profit institutions (65%) and borrow higher average amounts ($8,237) than do students at private non-profit colleges (56% borrowing, $7,551 average loan amount) or public colleges (45.8% borrowing, $6,903 average loan amount) (*Chronicle of Higher Education*, 2016). Among two-year institutions, patterns were similar. More students borrowed at for-profit two-year colleges (66.2%), and their average loan amounts were higher ($7,423), compared to private non-profit two-year colleges (57.1% borrowing, $7,040 average loan) and public two-year colleges (19.3% borrowing, $5,222 average loan) (*Chronicle of Higher Education*, 2016). Regardless of college attended, Black students are the most likely to have student loan debt (81%), and Asian students are least likely (60%); whereas White (74%) and Hispanic/Latino students (77%) are nearly equally likely to have loan debt (Baum & Steele, 2010).

The more serious issue underlying borrowing, however, is students' ability to repay. Much has been written about the burdens of student loan debt. Research has found that up to 80% of indebted college students underestimate the number and amount of loans they have taken out (Andruska, Hogarth, Fletcher, Forbes, & Wohlgemuth, 2014; King & Frishberg, 2001), and, thus, unwittingly acquire more debt than they can manage (Baum & Steele, 2010). Regrettably, students who graduate from majors in the least-paying career fields—such as theology, education, public administration, and the applied arts—are more likely to have higher federal student loan debt than students who graduate from majors in higher paying career fields, such as engineering, mathematics, architecture, and the biological and physical sciences (Vedder, Denhart, & Hartge, 2014).

The proportion of college graduates devoting too high a percentage of their annual income to repay student loan debt continues to rise (Kantrowitz, 2016). Fortunately, the government has established a series of income-based repayment plans that link and limit student loan payments to a fixed proportion of graduates' discretionary income. These include the Pay as You Earn (PAYE) and Revised Pay as You Earn (REPAYE) Plans, and the Income-Based (IBR) and Income-Contingent (ICR) Repayment Plans. One-fifth (20%) of student loan borrowers who are in repayment (no longer in school or any other type of deferment status) participate in such plans (College Board, 2015). Unfortunately, a nearly equal amount (22%) of borrowers are unable to make their payments and default on their loans (College Board, 2015). In fact, the dollar level of seriously delinquent student loans in the United States has outstripped dollar levels of delinquency on auto loans, credit cards, home equity loans, and mortgages combined (Vedder et al., 2014).

Defaulting on any kind of debt has serious consequences. It lowers an individual's credit rating, which in turn hinders the ability to secure mortgages, auto loans, and credit cards, and raises the interest rate charged on such borrowing. Negative credit ratings can also have detrimental consequences on job hiring, the ability to rent an apartment, and the ability to secure payment-based purchases or services such as cell phones, utilities, and insurance. "As the burden of student debt [soars, it makes] . . . the prospect of individual economic progress more daunting than a few generations ago" (Vedder et al., 2014, p. 9).

As with overall borrowing patterns and amounts, student loan default rates differ by institutional type and race. They are "consistently two to three times as high for borrowers who attend[ed] for-profit and public two-year institutions as for those who attend[ed] private nonprofit and public four-year institutions" (College Board, 2015, p. 22). Regardless of institutional type attended, students who do not graduate have the greatest difficulty repaying their loans (Cunningham & Kienzl, 2011). Such students incur the same obligation of repaying the loan, but without the economic benefits of having earned a degree.

The student debt crisis in the United States has impacted many families: As of 2012, one in five American households owes student loan debt (Fry, 2012). It is likely higher now. Clearly, income-based repayment plans and other forms of debt relief do not serve all students' needs or address the debt crisis. The best approach, logically, is to simply borrow less while in college. Students take many approaches toward that goal: postponing college in order to work and save up for it, living at home with parents and commuting to college, working a full-time or near full-time job while in college, attending part-time, and attending a lower-priced community college for a few years and then transferring to a four-year institution. Yet these strategies are problematic. National studies show that only 7.8% of part-time students at two-year colleges finish their associate degrees, and only 24% of part-timers at four-year colleges or universities finish their bachelor's degrees (Complete College

America, 2013). The odds of graduation are worse for part-time students who are Black, Hispanic, or poor (Complete College America, 2013). As for aspiring to transfer, only 14%—one in seven—of community college students successfully transfer and complete a four-year degree (Kolodner, 2016). Looking at those who do transfer, the savings are illusory. González Canché (2014), using data from the National Education Longitudinal Study (NELS: 1988/2000), compared the loan debts of bachelors' degree recipients who started in two-year colleges and transferred to four-year colleges for completion, versus those who initially enrolled and remained at four-year colleges. He found that there were no debt savings for starting at a lesser priced two-year college. Both types of students had commensurate loan balances owed.

In the next section of this chapter, we introduce a different alternative to loan-funded education. We explore Work Colleges, an established but as yet still unconventional alternative means for higher education centered on the premise that students can "earn" their way through college while they "learn," and thus avoid significant student debt.

Working Through College as an Alternative to Borrowing

In the 1960s and 1970s, students pursuing a bachelor's degree could work their way through school and graduate with slight debt, if any at all (Carnevale, Smith, Melton, & Price, 2015). However, those are realities of a bygone era, seemingly out of the question for the Millennial Generations—the demographic cohorts since Generation X (Y & Z) who came after the baby boomers (Grant, 2015; *New Republic*, 2015). According to Appel and Taylor (2015), "Over the last three decades, the price of a year of college has increased by more than 1,200 percent" (p. 31). Making matters more financially burdensome, the majority of American college students do not graduate "on time"—meaning within four years (Complete College America, 2013). The combination of increased tuition and fees, state disinvestment from public higher education, and increased time-to-completion results in bachelor's degrees costing considerably more money to attain than they did in times past.

Figure 13.1 illustrates why nowadays it is impossible for "traditional" (full-time, 18–21 years old) college students to work during the summer and earn enough money to finance their college education. Because of this, many college students work 15–40 hours while they are in school and/or turn to loans to pay for their higher education. Carnevale et al. (2015) state the following:

> A generation ago, students commonly saved for tuition by working summer jobs. But the cost of college now makes that impossible. A student working full-time at the federal minimum wage would earn $15,080 annually before taxes. That isn't enough to pay tuition at most colleges, much less room and board and other expenses.
>
> (p. 11)

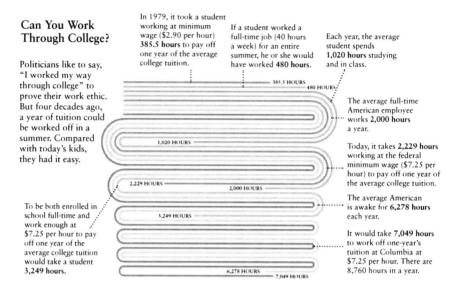

Can You Work Through College?

Politicians like to say, "I worked my way through college" to prove their work ethic. But four decades ago, a year of tuition could be worked off in a summer. Compared with today's kids, they had it easy.

In 1979, it took a student working at minimum wage ($2.90 per hour) **385.5 hours** to pay off one year of the average college tuition.

If a student worked a full-time job (40 hours a week) for an entire summer, he or she would have worked **480 hours**.

Each year, the average student spends **1,020 hours** studying and in class.

385.5 HOURS
480 HOURS
1,020 HOURS
2,229 HOURS
2,000 HOURS
3,249 HOURS
6,278 HOURS
7,049 HOURS

To be both enrolled in school full-time and work enough at $7.25 per hour to pay off one year of the average college tuition would take a student **3,249 hours.**

The average full-time American employee works **2,000 hours** a year.

Today, it takes **2,229 hours** working at the federal minimum wage ($7.25 per hour) to pay off one year of the average college tuition.

The average American is awake for **6,278 hours** each year.

It would take **7,049 hours** to work off one-year's tuition at Columbia at $7.25 per hour. There are **8,760 hours** in a year.

Figure 13.1 Can You Work Through College?

Source: Reproduced and reprinted from "How Many Hours Would It Take You to Work Off Today's College Tuition?" from *The New Republic*, 10/6/2015. Graphic: in context as originally published.

"Earning" While "Learning"

National data indicate that now, more than ever before, college students are balancing non-academic work and college coursework (Perna, 2010). Employment (part-time or full-time) while attending college as at least a half-time student may mitigate the amount of student loans a student takes out to fund his/her education; however, holding a job while in college may be costly to academic performance. Research has found that working more than 20 hours as a full-time student may harm a student's G.P.A. (Carnevale et al., 2015) not to mention his/her academic learning. However, the type of work a student does may matter. Tinto's (1975) student integration model, for example, implies that students who work on campus in programs such as work-study may actually benefit from the experience, because this form of work does not separate the student from the campus. Rather, it integrates students more firmly into the institution's operational, academic, and social life (DesJardins, Ahlburg, & McCall, 2002). Work Colleges do this, creating learning environments where work serves as part of the educational experience, not an external activity, and, according to the *Work Colleges Consortium* (2012), "Work College graduates have some of the lowest student debt in the nation" (p. 3).

Meet the Work Colleges

At the time of this research, there are seven colleges/universities that comprise the *Work Colleges Consortium* (www.workcolleges.org). According to the U.S. Department of Education, a "Work College" is a public or private non-profit, four-year degree-granting institution where student work is an integrated, essential, and federally required core component of the educational work-learning-service program (David, 2007). Figure 13.2 presents a map with their geographic locations.

The seven Work Colleges are (1) Alice Lloyd College in Pippa Passes, Kentucky; (2) Berea College in Berea, Kentucky; (3) Blackburn College in Carlinville, Illinois; (4) College of the Ozarks in Point Lookout, Missouri; (5) Ecclesia College in Springdale, Arkansas; (6) Sterling College in Craftsbury Common, Vermont; and (7) Warren Wilson College in Asheville, North Carolina. Work Colleges have existed for over 150 years (Hamilton, 2005)[2] but, interestingly, have not received much attention in the higher education finance literature. The following sections provide brief introductions to each.

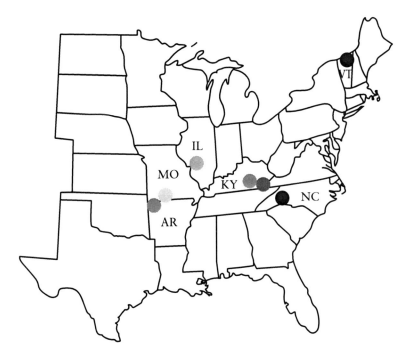

Figure 13.2 Locations of Work Colleges in the United States

Source: www.workcolleges.org/node/30

Alice Lloyd College

Alice Lloyd College (ALC) is a 90-year-old private liberal arts college in rural Kentucky that focuses on educating residents from a specific 108-county region of Appalachia (Alice Lloyd College, n.d.). The majority (96%) of the college's 628 students come from Kentucky, are predominantly White (97%), and are the first in their families to attend college (70%).

With selective admissions (10%), the average ACT score for incoming students is 20 (ALC, n.d.; National Center for Educational Statistics [NCES], n.d.a). The college's curriculum focuses on small class sizes (20 students per class), leadership, service learning, and Christian values (ALC, n.d.). Two-fifths of its 17 majors are teaching degrees (ALC, n.d.). The college's retention rate (75%) slightly exceeds national averages (73.8%) for full-time undergraduates, although its six-year graduation rate (36%) is poorer than the national average graduation rate (54.5%) at four-year institutions (NCES, n.d.a, n.d.i).

Alice Lloyd's published tuition and fees price for the 2015–2016 academic year was $11,460, and its published room and board was $5,940 (NCES, n.d.a). All students in Alice Lloyd's target service area attend school tuition-free, made possible through a $37-million-dollar endowment and generous private giving (ALC, n.d). However, students are expected to pay for their room, board, student fees, and other educational expenses. Numerous scholarships and grants are applicable toward these costs. Given that it is a Work College, all full-time students are expected to work 10–20 hours per week in an array of positions, such as grounds and janitorial staff, the campus radio station and computing services, the library, office positions and teaching assistants, and residence hall advisors (ALC, n.d.).

Berea College

Berea College is a 161-year-old private liberal arts college also located in rural Kentucky and focused on educating Appalachian students (Berea College, n.d.). With selective admissions (33%), an average incoming ACT score of 25, and small class sizes (11 students per class), Berea offers 28 majors and a core curriculum focused on leadership, service learning, sustainability, diversity, and Christian values (Berea College, n.d.).

Berea College claims the honor of being the first interracial and co-educational postsecondary institution in the south. A third (36%) of its students are from a racial category other than "White/non-Hispanic," and the college also enrolls students from 40 other U.S. states and international students from 60 countries. Retention rates (84%) are stronger than the national average (73.8%), as is the six-year graduation rate (66%, versus the national average of 54.4%) (NCES, n.d.b, n.d.i) Over a third (34%) of students study abroad (Berea College, n.d.).

Berea's 2015–2016 published tuition and fees totaled $24,780, with room and board at $6,410 (NCES, n.d.b). Students are expected to pay only for their room, board, student fees, and other extracurricular expenses. Tuition at Berea is "free" (zero net cost), made possible through a combination of federal, state, and private grants, a labor grant, and institutional financial aid from Berea's massive $1-billion-dollar endowment (Berea College, n.d.). The financial model is crucial to the college's 1,623 students, the majority of whom come from low-income families, and half of whom have an Expected Family Contribution (EFC) of zero.[3]

Advertising itself as "the best education money can't buy," all Berea students are expected to work in its labor program, which is integrated into the academic curriculum and for which students receive a $6,000 credit toward tuition (Berea College, n.d.). Students receive a documented work performance history and outcomes on their Labor Learning Goals for working 10–15 hours per week in approved jobs on campus, such as administrative assistants, teaching assistants, lab workers, buildings and grounds staff, janitors, library aides, forestry aides, and hundreds more.

Blackburn College

Blackburn College, founded 175 years ago, is the oldest of the seven Work Colleges. Its work program recently celebrated its 100th anniversary (Blackburn College, n.d.). Located in rural Illinois, the institution does not focus on one geographic service region, although 88% of its predominantly White (82%) 550 full-time students are Illinois residents.

Blackburn's liberal arts curriculum is challenging, focusing on critical thinking, leadership development, service, lifelong learning, and sustainability (Blackburn College, n.d.). With an acceptance rate of 55%, its average ACT score for incoming students is 22 (NCES, n.d.c). It offers over 40 majors and minors, including 18 different education majors. As with other Work Colleges, Blackburn maintains small class sizes (13). Retention rates (62%) are lower than the national average (73.8%), as are its six-year graduation rates (45%, versus national averages of 54.4%) (NCES, n.d.c, n.d.i). Although affiliated with the Presbyterian Church, the college's curriculum does not have the same overt Christian mission as do Work Colleges such as Alice Lloyd, Berea, College of the Ozarks, and Ecclesia.

Blackburn's 2015–2016 tuition and fees were $20,364, with room and board of $7,034; but all students receive a $2,640 work credit for participating in the mandatory work program (Blackburn College, n.d.; NCES, n.d.c), as well as an array of grants and scholarships from its $21.2-million-dollar endowment and national, state, and private sources.

Blackburn's work program is the only one of the seven Work Colleges that is completely student managed (Blackburn College, n.d.). All students typically work 10–15 hours per week on campus, with a minimum of 160 hours each semester. The positions are typical of those found in other Work Colleges: academic, administrative, and athletic services; the campus bookstore and dining facilities; buildings, grounds, maintenance, and custodial services; and technology services. However, the majority of student orkers report to student managers who oversee services, supervise staff and are responsible for job training, scheduling, performance reviews and disciplinary actions. This creates career progression opportunities within the program and provides valuable managerial experience for students. In addition to their academic transcripts, students receive a second transcript that records their job skills and managerial experiences.

College of the Ozarks

Founded 100 years ago in 1906, College of the Ozarks is a small, Interdenominational Evangelical Christian college located in rural Point Lookout, Missouri. "C of O," as it is colloquially known, defines its mission as follows:

> Christian values and character, hard work, and financial responsibility comprise the fundamental building blocks of the "Hard Work U" experience. At a time when there is much talk about what is wrong with the nation, College of the Ozarks exemplifies what is *right* with America. C of O is committed to its founding mission of providing a quality, Christian education to those who are found worthy, but who are without sufficient means to obtain such training. Instead of paying tuition, all full-time students work campus jobs to defray the cost of education.
>
> (College of the Ozarks [C of O], n.d.)

Showing financial need (90%) and having a high ACT score (23 on average) are among the qualifications needed to join the 1,593 students enrolled at C of O (NCES, n.d.d, USNWR, n.d.a). Only 8% are accepted each year, most of whom are White (92%) and from Missouri (80%).

College of the Ozarks offers 27 majors in a curriculum that is "intentionally Christ-centered, . . . taught from the perspective of a biblical worldview, which provides a broad and robust understanding of the world that a secular worldview cannot provide" (C of O, n.d.).Vocational goals (to develop a strong work ethic), patriotic goals (to foster an understanding of American heritage, civic responsibilities, and a willingness to defend the country), and cultural goals (to cultivate an appreciation of the fine arts) accompany its academic and Christian goals. The end result is "to develop citizens of Christ-like character who are well-educated, hard-working, and patriotic" (C of O, n.d.). Selective admissions and a focused program work well for C of O, whose 88% retention rate is above the national average (73.8%), as is its six-year graduation rate (62%, versus the national average of 54.4%) (NCES, n.d.d, n.d.i).

C of O's 2015–2016 tuition and fees were $18,730, although—as is the norm for Work Colleges—the money earned from their mandatory jobs helps to defray this, along with scholarships and grants from the college's $442-million-dollar endowment along with government, and private sources (USNWR, n.d.a). Students work an average of 15 hours a week in the college's work program, earning approximately $4,284 annually in 80 different employment options. The college takes its integration of work and academics seriously, and work performance records are maintained by a Dean of Work, who issues work performance grades each term. In addition to the general quality of their work, students are evaluated for skills such as communication and teamwork, and for dispositions such as reliability, motivation, and responsibility. Students earning a C- or less in their work performance can be placed on probation or dismissed (C of O, n.d.).

Ecclesia College

The youngest (41 years) of the seven Work Colleges, Ecclesia College is classified as a theological seminary (NCES, n.d.e). Located in rural Springdale, Arkansas, with an enrollment of 217, the institution offers just two majors (business administration and sports management), and five theologically related certificates in areas such as Biblical studies, music ministry, Christian counseling, and Christian leadership (Ecclesia College, n.d., NCES, n.d.e.). No college admissions scores are reported for Ecclesia, although the institution is modestly selective, with an acceptance rate of 64% (NCES, n.d.e). Only 59% of the student body is White.

As a theological seminary, Ecclesia (n.d.) is overt in its Christian mission, stating the following:

> [T]he whole EC educational experience focuses on developing and living out the character of Christ in order to display His glory and bring about His kingdom 'on earth as it is in heaven.' . . . [A]ll education . . . is done from the Biblical perspective . . . [as] true knowledge comes on the foundation of faith and character (2 Peter 1:5). . . . [EC promises to work with students, their] parents and home pastor to help . . . [each student find his or her] place and purpose in God's Kingdom. . . .

Unique among the seven Work Colleges, up to 20% of the students attend part time, and 30% attend online (Ecclesia, n.d.; NCES n.d.e).

Ecclesia's work learning program promises to develop students' job skills and experience, enable them to follow the mission of Jesus Christ through service, and provide a practical means to offset tuition costs that is concordant with Christian values (Ecclesia, n.d.). Students work an average of 15 hours per week at an array of service and clerical jobs on campus, earning $9 to $12 per hour, which is credited toward tuition costs (Ecclesia, n.d.). Participation is mandatory only for the 70% of students who attend full time and reside on campus (Ecclesia, n.d.).

Tuition and fees at the college were $15,140 in 2015–2016, and room and board was $5,010 (NCES, n.d.e).[4] Ecclesia's retention rate (43%) is the lowest among Work Colleges, and only a little over half that of the national average (73.8%) (NCES, n.d.e, n.d.i). Its six-year graduation rate (33%) is also very low, not quite reaching two-thirds of the national average (NCES, n.d.e, n.d.i).

Sterling College

Founded in 1958, Sterling College in rural Craftsbury Common, Vermont, is the only Work College that has secular origins. Sterling's mission is also unique. The tiny 59-year-old college focuses exclusively on what it calls an "experiential place-based liberal arts academic program to aspiring environmental stewards" (Sterling College, n.d.). Only five majors are offered: ecology, environmental humanities, sustainable agriculture, sustainable food systems, and outdoor education; plus one design-your-own major.

With its 98% admissions rate, Sterling classifies as a nearly open-access institution (NCES, n.d.g) and reports no college admissions test scores. The student body of 168 is 72% White and primarily from out-of-state (89%) (NCES, n.d.g). Sterling's 82% retention rate is above the national average (73.8%), although its six-year graduation rate (57%) is on par (national average, 54.4%) (NCES, n.d.g, n.d.i).

At $34,800 in published tuition and fees for 2015–2016 and $9,104 in room and board, Sterling is among the most costly of the Work Colleges. Although students do receive various forms of grants and scholarships and work in campus-based jobs to offset their college costs, Sterling lacks a large enough endowment to provide much institutional support of its own. Its endowment is slightly over $1 million, although a $9-million capital campaign is underway (Shilton, 2014; Sterling College, n.d.). Sterling's work program includes interesting offerings unique to its mission, such as caring for livestock, an array of agricultural positions, and making maple syrup.

Warren Wilson College

Warren Wilson College is the least-rural of the seven Work Colleges. Although situated in the mountains of North Carolina, Warren Wilson makes its home among the half-million residents of metropolitan Asheville (Asheville Chamber of College, n.d.). Founded 123 years ago by Presbyterians in 1894, the college's original mission was to provide for the education of Appalachian area residents. Today, only 25% of its student body are from within state.

The college is unselective, with an admissions rate of 71%, yet attracts a highly talented student body whose median ACT score is 25 (NCES, n.d.h). The majority (80%) of its small student body (882 undergraduates) is White. Warren Wilson offers 34 majors, and describes its curriculum in the following way:

> . . . academics, work and service [called the Triad] in a learning community committed to environmental responsibility, cross-cultural understanding and the common good. . . . The mission of Warren Wilson College is to provide a distinctive undergraduate and graduate liberal arts education. [Its] students graduate not only with a rigorous liberal arts education, but also with skills such as problem-solving and team leadership that equip them for life.
>
> (Warren Wilson, n.d.)

The college's retention rate (66%) is below the national average (73.8%), although its six-year graduation rate (57%) is on par (national average, 54.4%) (NCES, n.d.h, n.d.i).

In 2015–2016, an undergraduate education at Warren Wilson cost $32,560 in tuition and fees and $9,900 in room and board (NCES, n.d.h). At least half of the cost is covered through various sources of scholarships and grants, including the college's $54.8 million endowment (USNWR, n.d.b, Warren Wilson, n.d.). Students work 10–20 hours per week, at jobs similar to those at other Work Colleges. However, jobs also include harvesting timber, raising grass-fed cattle, and updating the institution's global information systems. Rather than offering a set stipend, the college pays students minimum wage and credits the amount toward their student account. The institution also maintains and provides official Work Transcripts, including a form of a work G.P.A. calculated from performance evaluations.

Key Commonalities Among Work Colleges

Although the seven Work Colleges each have unique attributes, four commonalities stand out. First and foremost is their work programs, which help defray college costs but differ from other forms of working while in college in that they are mandatory, income is credited directly in students' accounts, and they are integrated into the overall academic experience and have their own intended learning outcomes. The most innovative work programs offer evaluative report cards, skills transcripts, and opportunities for advancement and managerial experience.

The second commonality is that, structurally, these are very small and rural programs. Creating mandatory jobs for all students may be a more feasible undertaking for these institutions, with enrollments ranging from just 128 to 1,623, than it would be for colleges or universities with enrollments of 12,000 to 16,000. Operating expenses for Work Colleges in rural locations may be lower than for institutions in more heavily populated or urban areas.

Third, the majority (five of the seven) of Work Colleges are well-endowed. It takes tremendous resources to offer "free" tuition, and Work Colleges have it. The American Council on Education (2014) reports the median endowment size for private colleges and universities is approximately $7.9 million (in 2012 dollars), with over half (53%) of private colleges having endowments of less than $10 million. Yet nearly all (five) of the Work Colleges exceed that average. Nearly half (3) of the Work Colleges reviewed have endowments that exceed $50 million, an echelon they share with only 16% of all public and private non-profit colleges and universities in the country (ACE, 2014). Moreover, one Work College—Berea—joins the most exclusive group of all: the tiny sliver (1.6%) of the nation's public and non-profit colleges and universities ($n = 62$) with endowments that exceed $1 billion (ACE, 2014).

Fourth, six of the seven Work Colleges were founded by Protestant Christian denominations with missionary goals to impart the tenets of their faith while helping poorer students earn their way through college. This Protestant work ethic—hard work, discipline, thrift, and faith—still pervades the missions and visions of Work Colleges, and is an overt cornerstone in more than half of the seven. This distinct identity has implications for who is recruited and attracted to work, teach, and study at these institutions, as well as implications for the donor identification and fundraising strategies that underlie their large endowments.

Work Colleges as an Alternative to Borrowing

We sought to test the previously described "earning while learning" philosophy using data procured from the Integrated Postsecondary Education Data System (IPEDS), with the goal of determining whether or not being educated at Work Colleges "can help students graduate without big debt" (Young & Hobson, 2011). First, we explain our data source and methods of analysis.[5] Next, we present the study's results. Last, we discuss the transferability of the Work College model and suggestions for further research.

Methodology

Attracted by claims that being educated at Work Colleges can help students graduate without large amounts of student debt (Funk, 2015; Wolniak & Pascarella, 2007; Young & Hobson, 2011), we were interested in Work College students' use and accumulation of federal student loan debt to finance their higher education in comparison to that of other undergraduates. According to Snider (2015), three Work Colleges—College of the Ozarks,

Berea College, and Alice Lloyd College—are among the top-10 in colleges whose graduates have the least student debt. Consequently, we sought to determine whether or not students who attend any of the Work Colleges do, in fact, borrow less federal loans than those students who attend other types of colleges and universities using a data source that none of the prior studies had used.

Study Population, Data Source, and Sample

As indicated earlier, Work Colleges are four-year, baccalaureate degree-granting institutions. Therefore, the study population included under-graduates at the universe of similar colleges and universities: four-year, public and private, non-profit and for-profit, degree-granting colleges and universities in the 50 United States and the District of Columbia. We excluded two-year colleges, tribal colleges, and specialized colleges, medical schools, and theological seminaries. However, we retained one theological seminary—Ecclesia College—in the sample because it is one of the seven Work Colleges. We also removed institutions from the sample that were upper-level transfer institutions,[6] or that otherwise lacked sufficient IPEDS data for analysis. Finally, because this study was interested in student loan debt, we also excluded colleges that do not accept federal financial aid.

To create the study sample, we relied on cross-sectional data drawn from the Integrated Postsecondary Education Data System (IPEDS), maintained by the U.S. Department of Education's National Center for Education Statistics (NCES),[7] for academic years 2008–2009 through 2012–2013. We purposefully used five years of data in order to account for any annual fluctuations or differences in loan borrowing. For example, our data include years before and after a major change in how federal student loans are done. Prior to 2010, under the Federal Family Education Loan Program (FFELP), "private lenders provided loans to students that were guaranteed by the federal government," including federally subsidized and unsubsidized loans (U.S. Department of Education, n.d.). The Health Care and Education Reconciliation Act (2010) eliminated FFELP, replacing it with the Direct Loan program in which the federal government is the lender. We established 2012–2013 as the cut-off year in our analysis because this was the most recent and most complete dataset available at the time of the study.

To create the study sample, we used the variables "level of institution," "control of institution," and "degree-granting status." We then used the variable "2010 Carnegie Classification: Basic" to identify and remove excluded institutional types. The resulting sample size was 1,636 colleges and universities (including the seven Work Colleges). The majority of the sampled institutions (56%, N = 918) were private, not-for-profit; a little more than a third (34%, N = 548) were public, and the remainder (10%, N = 170) were private, for-profit (see Figure 13.3).

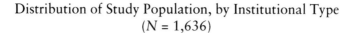

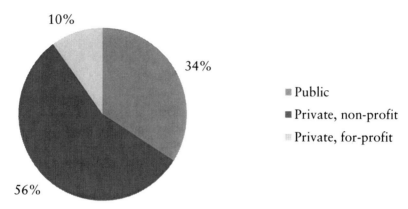

Figure 13.3 Distribution of Study Population, by Institutional Type

Methods of Analysis

To examine student loan borrowing at Work Colleges, we asked, "Are there significant differences in the average annual amount of federal student loan aid borrowed by undergraduates at Work Colleges versus at other four-year colleges and universities?" As defined by the IPEDS dataset, "federal student loan aid" includes all Title IV subsidized and unsubsidized loans. "Undergraduates" includes all students enrolled in an undergraduate degree program, whether they attend full-time or part-time, and whether they are first-year, transfer, or returning students.[8]

Statistical Tests

To test our question, we employed a factorial analysis of covariance (AN-COVA), examining the research question for each of the five years' of data (2008–2009 through 2012–2013). The single, discrete independent variable in each test was whether the institution was one of the seven Work Colleges (yes/no). The continuous dependent variable was the average amount of federal student loan aid received by all undergraduates who had received loans (full- and part-time, first-year, transfer, and returning).

Our null hypothesis, H_0, was that there were no significant differences: Attending a Work College *does not* predict the variance (or difference) in the amounts of federal student loans borrowed by undergraduates. Our alternative hypothesis, H_1, was that there were significant differences: Attending a Work College *does* predict the variance (or difference) in the amounts of federal student loans borrowed by undergraduates.

Covariates

The differentiation and complexity of U.S. higher education is tremendous, and comparing phenomena across institutions is not always a straightforward task. Case in point: the Carnegie Classification system divides U.S. colleges and universities into 30 different basic types, based on dimensions such as level of control, degree offerings, scope, and location. Further layers of classifications in the Carnegie system, such as the undergraduate profile, size, and settings, quickly multiply the array of institutional distinctions. We believe that research on U.S. higher education, when done well, seeks to acknowledge and account for such nuances and complexity.

A number of contextual circumstances—including both institutional differences and individual student differences—influence the amount of loan aid that students borrow to pay for their education and were at play in this study. For example, the tuition and fees that each college or university charges is the result of variations in its financial circumstances, such as its sources and amounts of institutional revenue, and how much each contributes to its overall budget. Variations in its context, such as size, geographical location, and setting; and variations in its own nature, marketing and branding, such as the types of academic programs it offers and academic selectivity, also have an influence on tuition pricing. At public institutions, a student's residency status ("in-state" or "out-of-state") further triggers variations in tuition and fee pricing.

Students borrow money to pay for their overall total cost of attending colleges, not just their tuition and fees. The overall total cost of attendance also includes expenses such as books and supplies, room, board, and other outlays needed for successfully supporting academic study. These additional expenses, in turn, vary according to the contextual circumstances of individual students. For example, charges differ depending on whether a student lives "on campus" or "off campus" and lives independently, in shared situations, or with family. Such lifestyle choices reflect the availability of housing options, the market price of room and board, institutional policies that may require on-campus residency, and also individual student preferences and constraints.

Finally, what ultimately determines how much money a student borrows to pay for college is not the sticker price of tuition and fees, nor the total cost of attendance, but rather the net price that s/he is charged, and—importantly— her/his ability to pay that net cost. "Net price" is the total cost of attendance minus any non-repayable need-based or merit-based grants and scholarships, the sources of which are public (federal, state, or local aid), institutional (endowment), and/or external (i.e., rotary, foundations, professional associations, unions, etc.). Again, contextual circumstances mediate the situation. For example, the number and size of financial aid programs in the institution and state will shape how much need-based or merit-based aid is available. A student's level of cultural capital may influence his or

194 Nicholas D. Hartlep and Diane R. Dean

her awareness of, application for, and competitiveness in available aid programs, and his or her individual eligibility will influence whether and how
much aid is awarded. Similarly, a student's "ability to pay" reflects both his
or her family's income level and savings available for college.

To account for these many contextual differences and to minimize their
influence on the dependent variable of interest (the average amount of federal loan aid borrowed), we included a covariate independent variable. In an
Analysis of Covariance (ANCOVA), the covariate reduces the variance (or
difference) in the dependent variable (student loan use) that is explained by
the independent variable (whether the institution is a Work College or not).
With less variance to explain, we can more accurately understand whether
Work Colleges are significantly different from other (or what we are here
referring to as neoliberal) colleges and universities.

As already explained, when considering student loan use, reflects both
the "net price" of attendance is and the individual's ability to pay. It reflects
the distillation of an array of institutional and individual circumstances.
Therefore, we used the IPEDS variable "average net price of attendance for
full-time, first-year (FTFY) undergraduates receiving grant or scholarship
aid" as a covariate. IPEDS generates "net price" by subtracting the average amount of federal, state, local government, or institutional grants and
scholarships from the total cost of attendance. This variable applies only to
the population of FTFY undergraduates and not to the entire undergraduate
student population. However, the scope of the variable is sufficient for the
model to demonstrate and to control for the influence of institutional and
individual circumstances.

Limitations

The present analytical approach, although robust, does have limitations associated with using the Integrated Postsecondary Data System as a data
source. First, IPEDS is limited in the currency of its data. The National
Center for Education Statistics releases information cyclically at the end of
academic semesters, academic years, and fiscal years, but the available data
lag several years behind the current year.

Second, IPEDS focuses on institutions and thus reports aggregated student
data. For financial aid related data, IPEDS reports some variables aggregately
for all undergraduates and other variables aggregately for full-time, first-time
undergraduates. This can obscure information for continuing students, those
attending part-time, those returning, and transfer students. Third, IPEDS
reports only on loans made directly to students. It does not track information
on PLUS or other loans made directly to students' parents (such as borrowing
through home equity lines of credit, HELOCs) or accumulated credit card
balances, even though these are important for understanding the full picture
of student loan use. Finally, IPEDS relies on the completeness of the data
reported by—and the accuracy of data entered by—participating institutions.

The 1,636 institutions in our study sample results from data entry by at least 1,636 different individuals with occasional intentional omissions and accidental errors. Despite these limitations, IPEDS data are a nationally trusted source of higher education information used by scholars, professionals, policymakers, and the public; they are an appropriate source for this study.

Model Assumptions

Our selected method of analysis, ANCOVA, relied upon several assumptions about the data. First, the independent variable (Work College = yes/no) describes two categorical groups. Second, each institution in the sample appeared in only one of these two groups (independence of observations). Third, there was homogeneity of population variances (homoscedasticity). Fourth, the dependent and covariate variables are continuously, normally distributed, with no significant outliers. Finally, the covariate (average net price of attendance) had a linear relationship with the dependent variables (student loan usage), but not a significant interaction with the independent variable (Work Colleges). These assumptions were satisfied in the model.

Results

We initially looked at student loan use across the entire sample of 1,636 four-year colleges and universities. This provided a staggering picture of student loan consumption in the United States, which we present below. Then we explored the ANCOVA results for each of the five academic years in the dataset. We begin by sharing the descriptive data and, after that, the significance tests of the ANCOVA results.

Descriptive Data

Total Undergraduate Federal Student Loan Borrowing

Across the five years of the dataset (2008–2009 to 2012–2013), students at the 1,636 institutions in the study sample borrowed a cumulative $172.6 billion in federal student loans (see Figure 13.4). This figure is an astronomical amount. To put it into context, their annual federal student loan borrowing of $31–35.9 billion surpasses the 2014 gross domestic product of half of the 190 countries in the International Monetary Fund world database.[9] Remarkably, this is only a snapshot of federal student loan borrowing, limited to the types of institutions and loans included in our study sample. The complete picture of student loan borrowing in the United States actually is vastly higher, when all post-secondary institutions and loan types (i.e., PLUS loans, parental HELOCs, private loans, unpaid credit card balances, etc. are included. Figure 13.4 breaks down the annual borrowing based on institutional type.

For the individual institutions in the study, the annual total amount of federal student loans that undergraduates borrowed over this five-year time period ranged from $60,000 (at American Jewish University, in 2010–2011) to an astonishing $3.8 billion (at the University of Phoenix, in 2009–2010). In fact, University of Phoenix—the private, for-profit behemoth founded in 1976—consistently ranked as the largest single consumer of total undergraduate federal student loan debt in the country for each year of the study, annually racking up billions of loan dollars (see Table 13.1). Of the annual top-10 student loan consuming institutions, half or more were private for-profit colleges and universities (Table 13.1).[10] In contrast, the seven private, non-profit Work Colleges in the United States generated only a modest $8 to $9 million in federal student loans each year, or an average of slightly over $1 million per college, a small fraction of the top federal student loan consumers. The largest loan consuming universities also enroll massive numbers of undergraduate students, whereas Work Colleges maintain small (128 to 1,623) enrollments. Notwithstanding, our research question and analyses controlled for these differences, focusing on behaviors of students (average amounts borrowed) rather than aggregate institutional totals.

Percentages of Students Borrowing Federal Loans

Across the five years of the dataset, the mean percentage of undergraduates receiving federal student loans at four-year colleges and universities

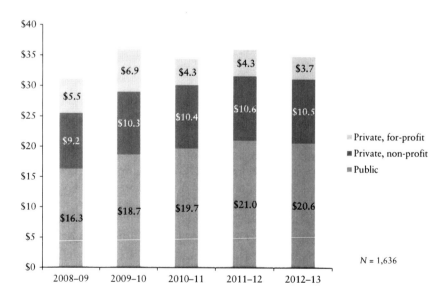

Figure 13.4 Total Amounts of Undergraduate Federal Student Loans Borrowed Annually at Four-Year U.S. Colleges and Universities by Institutional Type (in Billions)

Table 13.1 Top-10 Student Loan Consuming Universities 2008–2013 with Annual Total Student Loan Consumption

Rank	Academic year				
	2008–2009	*2009–2010*	*2010–2011*	*2011–2012*	*2012–2013*
1	University of Phoenix* $3,227 million	University of Phoenix* $3,821 million	University of Phoenix* $1,830 million	University of Phoenix* $1,735 million	University of Phoenix* $1,363 million
2	Kaplan University* $678 million	Kaplan University* $872 million	Ashford University* $327 million	Ashford University* $406 million	Ashford University* $393 million
3	Colorado Technical University* $176 million	Everest University* $409 million	Kaplan University* $333 million	Everest University* $362 million	Everest University* $343 million
4	Everest University* $160 million	Colorado Technical University* $218 million	Everest University* $273 million	Arizona State University $224 million	Liberty University $241 million
5	American InterContinental University* $156 million	Ashford University* $200 million	Arizona State University $204 million	Liberty University $219 million	Kaplan University* $190 million
6	Pennsylvania State University $135 million	American InterContinental University* $180 million	Colorado Technical University* $284 million	Kaplan University* $166 million	University of Central Florida $166 million
7	Temple University $132 million	Arizona State University $165 million	Liberty University $181 million	University of Central Florida $159 million	Full Sail University* $163 million
8	Michigan State University $131 million	Temple University $147 million	Grand Canyon U.* $160 million	Rutgers U., New Brunswick $154 million	Grand Canyon University* $155 million

(*Continued*)

Table 13.1 (Continued)

Rank	Academic year				
	2008–2009	2009–2010	2010–2011	2011–2012	2012–2013
9	Arizona State University $130 million	Pennsylvania State University $145 million	Pennsylvania State University $143 million	Colorado Technical University* $153 million	Colorado Technical University* $143 million
10	Ashford University* $127 million	Liberty University $139 million	Michigan State University $136 million	Central Michigan University $152 million	Pennsylvania State University $141 million

Total annual student loans consumed by the top-10 consuming universities and percentage of overall student loan consumption by the 1,636 four-year universities in the study.

	2008–2009	2009–2010	2010–2011	2011–2012	2012–2013
	$5,056 million 16%	$6,256 million 17%	$3,787 million 11%	$3,734 million 11%	$3,302 million 9%

* = Denotes a private, for-profit university

was 61.7%, remaining consistent over the years, with a relatively small range of 59.5% in 2008–2009 to 62.8% in 2011–2012 (see Figure 13.5). The same was true when looking at five years of data for each institutional type (public, private non-profit, and private for-profit) in the sample population. Means held relatively consistent across the years.

However, when looking at differences between institutional types, important distinctions were seen (see Figure 13.5). At public colleges and universities, the mean five-year federal student loan-borrowing rate among students was 53%. At private non-profit colleges and universities, the mean rate was higher, at 64%. Among private for-profit institutions, the mean rate was highest of all, at 77%. This variance reflects what is known about the basic differences in the financial models of these institutions. At private non-profits, endowments and relatively high tuition support the cost of operations and instruction. At public universities, the actual total cost—or expense— of operating the institution and educating students is partially subsidized by state appropriation money, relatively low tuition, and, in some cases, endowment revenues. In contrast, in the case of private for-profits, part of the mission of the institution is to be a profit-generating business. Students not only pay for the full cost of operations and instruction, but also provide a profit margin (see Norris, 2012).

Not surprisingly, the percentages of students who borrow federal loans at Work Colleges are below the national average (see Figure 13.5). Yet, within that group of institutions, the results for individual institutions vary

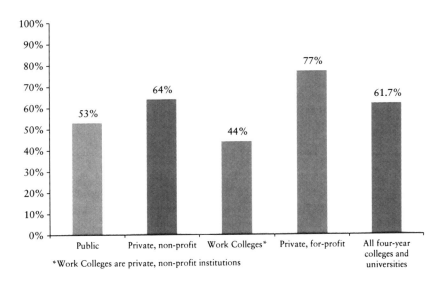

Figure 13.5 Mean Percentage of Undergraduates Borrowing Federal Student Loans at Four-Year U.S. Colleges and Universities, by Institutional Type (2008–2009 through 2012–2013)

widely (Figure 13.6). Several Work Colleges (Blackburn College, Sterling College, and Warren Wilson College) exceed the national average, whereas one—College of the Ozarks—holds the distinction of being the only institution in the entire 1,636 sample population to have completely zero federal student loan borrowing. The only other institutions that can claim consistent, extremely low borrowing rates are Harvard, Princeton, and Yale (see Figure 13.6), a recent phenomenon others have written about and documented (see Snider, 2015).[11] The takeaway points from this descriptive information are that Work Colleges are not monolithic, and they show promise when compared to public, private, and for-profit colleges and universities.

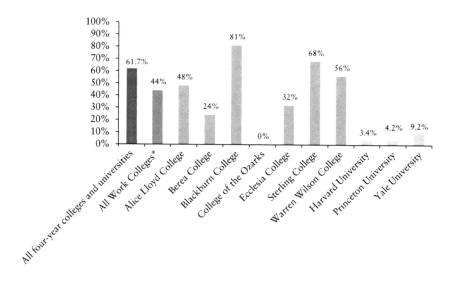

Figure 13.6 Mean Percentage of Undergraduates Borrowing Federal Student Loans at Selected Four-Year U.S. Colleges and Universities (2008–2009 through 2012–2013)

Average Amount of Federal Student Loans Borrowed

Rates of loan borrowing provide insight into the scale of how many students across the United States are borrowing to finance their higher education. A sharper picture emerges when considering the average amount of federal student loan aid borrowed. Between 2008–2009 and 2012–2013, undergraduate students at four-year colleges and universities in the sample borrowed an average of $7,326 in federal loans each year (see Figure 13.7). At individual institutions, the amounts varied widely, from a low of zero federal loans borrowed each year at College of the Ozarks (a Work College) to a high of $15,349 on average borrowed at

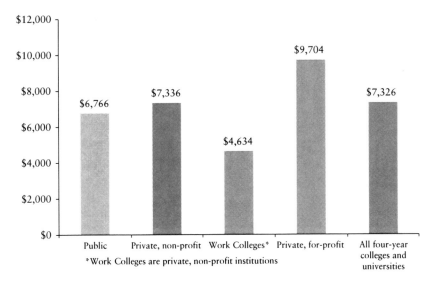

Figure 13.7 Average Amount of Federal Student Loans Borrowed Per Year by Undergraduates at Four-Year U.S. Colleges and Universities, by Institutional Type (2008–2009 through 2012–2013)

Platt College (a private for-profit college) in 2011–2012 and 2012–2013. Comparing across institutional types the average amount of student loans borrowed annually was highest among private, for-profit institutions ($9,704), lower among private, non-profits ($7,336), further reduced among public institutions ($6,766), and was lowest among the Work Colleges ($4,634).

Although average amounts also varied within the Work Colleges cohort, they were consistently below the national average (Figures 13.8). This suggests a key relationship between the Work College model and reduced student loan borrowing, a relationship that was tested with ANCOVA analyses in the subsequent section. It is notable that although the dollar amounts of average federal student loans are low among undergraduates at Work Colleges, these are not the lowest rates in the population sample. The "Big Three"—Harvard, Princeton, and Yale—had borrowing averages lower than four of the seven Work Colleges (Figure 13.8). Given their higher tuition rates, and their contrasting low percentages of loan borrowing, the low rates and average amounts of loans at these elite "Ivy League" universities reflect their vast wealth and available institutional aid, although it should be noted that they also benefit from federal financial aid through enrolled students who qualify.

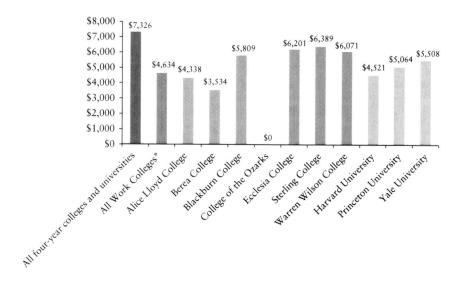

Figure 13.8 Average Amount of Federal Student Loans Borrowed Per Year by Undergraduates at Selected Four-Year U.S. Colleges and Universities (2008–2009 through 2012–2013)

ANCOVA Results: Test of Significance

It is clear that the descriptive data convey differences in federal student loan borrowing patterns relative to institutional type, with students at Work Colleges engaging in relatively lower rates of borrowing and receiving smaller average loan amounts. However, the descriptive data do not tell us whether that relationship (loan borrowing and institutional type) is significant. Further, the visual data cannot tell us whether the differences are, in fact, attributable mainly to institutional type and not to an intervening variable (e.g., any one of the myriad related institutional or individual contextual circumstances that influence college costs, net price, and resultant student loan borrowing that we wrote about earlier in the chapter).

The one-way ANCOVA model addresses these questions. It tests for a statistically significant relationship between loan borrowing and Work Colleges, while controlling for the differences in average net price. Our analyses rejected the null hypothesis, demonstrating a direct, linear relationship between Work Colleges and loan borrowing. For each of the five years in the dataset, attendance at a Work College did have a highly significant effect on the average amount of federal student loan aid borrowed by undergraduates, even after controlling for the effect of the average net price of attendance. Table 13.2 is a summary table that shows the specific results for each year.

The effects were consistently significant at the $p < 0.01$ level. In each test, the covariate (average net price) also was significantly related to the

Table 13.2 Tests of Between-Subjects Effects on Average Federal Student Loan Aid Received by FTFY Undergraduates by Year

Year	Variables	DF	Type III Sum of Squares	Mean Square	F-Ratio	Sig.
2008–2009 (Adj. R^2=.925)	Model	3	55590293810	18530097937	6745.284	.000
	npgrsio_0809	1	228750662.3	228750662.3	83.269	.000
	Work College	2	4539937085	2269968543	826.309	.000
	Residual	1633	4486045131	2747118.88		
2009–2010 (Adj. R^2=.926)	Model	3	62988004662	20996001554	6817.446	.000
	npgrsio_0910	1	457429192.5	457429192.5	148.528	.000
	Work College	2	4406012121	2203006060	715.321	.000
	Residual	1633	5029224815	3079745.753		
2010–2011 (Adj. R^2=.949)	Model	3	58956258111	19652086037	10128.182	.000
	npgrsio_1011	1	203368175.4	203368175.4	104.811	.000
	Work College	2	4789454925	2394727462	1234.181	.000
	Residual	1633	3168570394	1940337.044		
2011–2012 (Adj. R^2=.948)	Model	3	59615588238	19871862746	10034.843	.000
	npgrsio_1112	1	133689083.3	133689083.3	67.51	.000
	Work College	2	4914299809	2457149905	1240.805	.000
	Residual	1632	3231827201	1980286.275		
2012–2013 (Adj. R^2=.959)	Model	3	61556355930	20518785310	12882.516	.000
	npgrsio_1213	1	85824183.29	85824183.29	53.884	.000
	Work College	2	5463299782	2731649891	1715.039	.000
	Residual	1632	2599388092	1592762.311		
2008–2009 (Adj. R^2=.925)	Model	3	55590293810	18530097937	6745.284	.000
	npgrsio_0809	1	228750662.3	228750662.3	83.269	.000
	Work College	2	4539937085	2269968543	826.309	.000
	Residual	1633	4486045131	2747118.88		

(Continued)

Table 13.2 (Continued)

Year	Variables	DF	Type III Sum of Squares	Mean Square	F-Ratio	Sig.
2009–2010 (Adj. R²=.926)	Model	3	62988004662	20996001554	6817.446	.000
	npgrsio_0910	1	457429192.5	457429192.5	148.528	.000
	Work College	2	4406012121	2203006060	715.321	.000
	Residual	1633	5029224815	3079745.753		
2010–2011 (Adj. R²=.949)	Model	3	58956258111	19652086037	10128.182	.000
	npgrsio_1011	1	203368175.4	203368175.4	104.811	.000
	Work College	2	4789454925	2394727462	1234.181	.000
	Residual	1633	3168570394	1940337.044		
2011–2012 (Adj. R²=.948)	Model	3	59615588238	19871862746	10034.843	.000
	npgrsio_1112	1	133689083.3	133689083.3	67.51	.000
	Work College	2	4914299809	2457149905	1240.805	.000
	Residual	1632	3231827201	1980286.275		
2012–2013 (Adj. R²=.959)	Model	3	61556355930	20518785310	12882.516	.000
	npgrsio_1213	1	85824183.29	85824183.29	53.884	.000
	Work College	2	5463299782	2731649891	1715.039	.000
	Residual	1632	2599388092	1592762.311		

Note: FTFY = full-time, first-year

average Federal loan amounts borrowed, also consistently at the $p < 0.01$ level. Moreover, with R-squared values for the five years ranging between 92.5 and 95.9, our model explains the differences in student loan borrowing among the 1,636 colleges and universities in the sample population between 92% and nearly 96% of the time.

Discussion

The rising costs of higher education exceed many students' and families' ability to pay. With limited personal resources and limited financial aid available, students are taking out more and larger student loans to finance their educations. The entrenched human capitalistic belief that greater investments (funded by loans) will yield greater returns (higher resultant salaries and economic status after graduation) fuels their behavior. Yet borrowing is no simple task. A preponderance of research indicates that the student loan industry is overly complicated and confusing for borrowers. Students lose track of the amount of debt they are accumulating (King & Frishberg, 2001) and graduate with massive amounts of debt (College Board, 2015), more than they can reasonably manage (Baum & Steele, 2010). Although the federal government offers an array of income-based repayment plans and forgiveness programs, many students are unaware of these options. An equal number of students default on their loan payments as those who use the income-based repayment plans (College Board, 2015). The impact of massive student loan debt has deleterious effects on college graduates' lives, and the effects are worsened for the increasing numbers who default on their loans. The best course of action would be to avoid accumulating debt altogether, and many students do undertake an array of strategies to avoid borrowing while in college. Yet many of these strategies—such as attending part time, working off-campus jobs while attending college, and enrolling in community colleges with the intent of transferring later—sabotage college retention and completion rates.

Student involvement theory (Tinto, 1975) suggests that work as a form of campus-based involvement might yield the same cost-reducing benefits without undermining retention and completion. The Work College model embodies this spirit. Offering campus jobs that help defray college costs, "work" is not just a means to financial ends: It is integrated into the overall academic experience and has its own intended learning outcomes, often with career-enhancing skills transcripts and opportunities for advancement.

In our examination of federal student loan usage at Work Colleges, we found that students enrolled in these institutions borrow fewer federal student loans than students at other institutional types, and borrow in lower amounts. In fact, federal loan borrowing among Work Colleges was paralleled only by Harvard, Princeton, and Yale. However, unlike these three Ivy League institutions, the unique missions and historical commitments of many Work Colleges center on educating first-generation and economically "poor" students.

Clearly, the Work College approach helps many students avoid the trap of federal student loan debt. However, the question remains as to whether this model offers a viable, replicable alternative to undergraduate education on a larger scale. There are some concerns with Work Colleges that need further investigation. First, retention and graduation rates are uneven. Average retention among Work Colleges (70%) trail national averages (73.5%) (NCES, n.d.f), ranging from lows of 43% and 45% to highs of 84% and 88%. Equally concerning, average graduation rates at Work Colleges (52%) trail national averages (54.5%) (NCES, n.d.f), while varying widely among individual Work College campuses, from lows of 33% and 36% to highs of 62% and 66%. The causes of variations in retention and graduation among Work Colleges merits further investigation. Moreover, the on-campus employment experiences, work and academic learning outcomes, and post-graduate employment and economic outcomes for Work College students have not been examined sufficiently.

Second, Work Colleges—while having a welcoming ethos—have arguably homogeneous student bodies. Overall, White students represent an average of 78% among all Work College enrollments. However, looking more closely, only a few have diverse student bodies (59%—64% White). The majority enroll predominantly White students (80–97% White). Additionally, the majority have geographic-centric missions intended to serve confined locales of the country. Additionally, the majority offer an overtly Christian-centered education with a missionary tenor that may not be appealing to all students, particularly those whose religious views differ. A better understanding of recruitment, admissions, and enrollment practices, as well as campus climate at Work Colleges is warranted before they may be considered as anything greater than a niche phenomenon.

Third, in terms of scalability, replicating Work Colleges may be problematic because these are very small and rural institutions:[12] The largest enrolls just 1,623 students. As discussed earlier, creating mandatory jobs for all students may not be feasible in institutions that have larger enrollments. Even scaling up to 5,000 students could prove unfeasible, let alone employing enrollments of 12,000 to 16,000. Moreover, operating expenses may be lower for institutions in rural locations than in heavily populated urban areas. Finally, half of the Work Colleges are relatively wealthy institutions with enviable endowments unparalleled by the majority of American colleges and universities. A deeper understanding of operational expenses and management of Work Colleges, in the context of their economic environments, is necessary before the model may be considered exportable to other locales and organizational contexts.

Despite these challenges, the Work College model is undeniably compelling and has withstood the test of time on these unique campuses. Although transforming entire existing colleges into this model may be unrealistic and improbable, interest is growing and it may be possible to create similar small programs on campuses to offer as an option alongside other forms of financial aid.[13] In the confusing and often disconnected mosaic of how students and their families pay for college, such clear and straightforward opportunities to avoid the student debt trap merit consideration.

Acknowledgments

While working on this chapter we reached out to many Work College personnel, such as David K. Tipton (Dean of Labor at Berea College), Judith Weckman (Director of Institutional Research and Assessment at Berea College), Theresa Lowder (Director of Student Financial Aid at Berea College), Brenda Boggs (Assistant Director of the Work Colleges Consortium), and Robin Taffler (Executive Director of the Work Colleges Consortium). Taffler pointed out that because the majority of Work Colleges are small, minor fluctuations in numbers (based on the circumstances of students at the time) can easily skew data from year to year.

Notes

1 This chapter is part of a larger study (Dean & Hartlep, under review).
2 Why attend a work college? Retrieved from www.workcolleges.org/students/why-attend-work-college
3 College financial aid offices use the "Expected Family Contribution" formula to determine how much financial aid to award. It considers a family's income, assets, and benefits against the cost of attending college, while factoring in family size and number of family members attending college.
4 Endowment information for Ecclesia College was not available.
5 We'd like to thank Dr. Derek A. Houston (University of Illinois at Urbana Champaign) who provided feedback on the tables presented in this chapter developed by Dr. Diane R. Dean.
6 Upper-level transfer institutions function as the inverse of community colleges, offering only junior and senior level courses leading to the completion of a baccalaureate degree.
7 National Center for Education Statistics. (n.d.). *Integrated Postsecondary Data System.* [Database]. Retrieved from https://nces.ed.gov/ipeds/datacenter
8 "Undergraduates" technically includes students enrolled in bachelor's and associate's degree programs, and in vocational or technical programs below the baccalaureate. However, the study sample was limited to four-year institutions or higher.
9 International Monetary Fund. (2014, October). *World Economic Outlook Database.* [Database]. Retrieved from www.imf.org/external/pubs/ft/weo/2014/02/weodata/index.aspx
10 Related to neoliberalism, according to Washburn (2005), "The University of Phoenix has no faculty governance and no tenure; it pays 'facilitators' $950 to teach a college-level course ($1,050 if the facilitator has a PhD)" (p. x).
11 Princeton was the first university in the country to institute a "no-loan" policy (see https://www.princeton.edu/pr/aid/pdf/1213/PU-Making-It-Possible.pdf). Harvard has a "no-loan" policy (see www.forbes.com/sites/ccap/2014/11/11/no-loan-policies-at-top-colleges-quell-student-debt/). Since 2008 Yale has not included

loans in its financial aid awards (see http://news.yale.edu/2015/02/27/faqs-about-financial-aid-and-student-borrowing-yale-college). The long-term elitism built into this policy, wherein beneficiaries of current largesse will earn returns via their elite degrees and, in turn, pay dividends to their alma mater to benefit future students, is another example of neoliberal ways. That these no-loan policies developed at the same time that some state legislatures (i.e., Connecticut) were eying these school's large endowments as being worthy of taxation may not be coincidental.

12 This reality may change, soon, however. Although Paul Quinn College (PQC) has not yet applied to nor been approved by the U.S. Department of Education as a Work College, it has embraced the model (see https://www.texastribune.org/2015/02/17/private-dallas-college-plans-get-work/). PQC is a private, Historically Black College (HBCU) located on 144 acres just south of downtown Dallas, Texas.

13 At the time of writing this chapter, Bethany Global University (BGU), located in Bloomington, Minnesota, was recently approved by the Department of Education to be a Work College. Though, the Work Colleges Consortium (WCC) is working closely with BGU, they are not a formal member of the WCC at this time.

References

Akers, B., & Chingos, M. M.. (2014). *Student loan safety nets: Estimating the costs and benefits of income-based repayment* [Executive Summary].

Alice Lloyd College. (n.d.). *Leadership U: Alice Lloyd College.* Retrieved from www.alc.edu/

American Council on Education. (2013). *Paying for college: How the federal higher education act helps students and families pay for a postsecondary education.* Washington, DC: Author. Retrieved from www.acenet.edu/news-room/Documents/Paying-for-College-Oct-2013.pdf

American Council on Education. (2014). *Understanding college and university endowments.* Washington, DC: Author. Retrieved from https://www.acenet.edu/news-room/Documents/Understanding-Endowments-White-Paper.pdf

Andruska, E. A., Hogarth, J. M., Fletcher, C. N., Forbes, G. R., & Wohlgemuth, D. R. (2014). Do you know what you owe? Students' understanding of their student loans. *Journal of Student Financial Aid*, 44(2), 125–148. Retrieved from http://publications.nasfaa.org/cgi/viewcontent.cgi?article=1222&context=jsfa

Appel, H., & Taylor, A. (2015). Education with a debt sentence: For-profit colleges as American dream crushers and factories of debt. *New Labor Forum*, 24(1), 31–36. Retrieved from http://dx.doi.org/10.1177/1095796014562860

Ashville Chamber of Commerce. (n.d.). *County population.* Retrieved from www.ashevillechamber.org/economic-development/research-and-reports/county-demographics-reports

Baum, S., Kurose, C., & Ma, J. (2013). *How college shapes lives: Understanding the issues.* New York: The College Board. Retrieved from https://trends.collegeboard.org/sites/default/files/education-pays-2013-how-college-shapes-lives-report.pdf

Baum, S., Ma, J., & Payea, K. (2013). *Education pays, 2013: The benefits of higher education for individuals and society.* New York: College Board.

Baum, S., & Steele, P. (2010). *Who borrows most? Bachelor's degree recipients with high levels of student debt.* New York: College Board.

Berea College. (n.d.). *Berea College: God has made of one blood all peoples of the Earth.* Retrieved from https://www.berea.edu/

Berman, J. (2016, January 30). Watch America's student-loan debt grow $2,726 every second: Introducing the national student loan debt clock. *MarketWatch.* Retrieved from www.marketwatch.com/story/every-second-americans-get-buried-under-another-3055-in-student-loan-debt-2015–06–10

Best, J., & Best, E. (2014). *The student loan mess: How good intentions created a trillion-dollar problem.* Berkeley, CA: University of California Press.

Blackburn College. (n.d.). *Blackburn College: Learn, work, earn.* Retrieved from https://blackburn.edu/

Carnevale, A. P., Smith, N., Melton, M., & Price, E. W. (2015). *Learning while earning: The new normal.* Washington, DC: Center on Education and the Workforce. Retrieved from https://cew.georgetown.edu/wp-content/uploads/Working-Learners-Report.pdf

Chronicle of Higher Education. (2016). Borrowers outstanding balances on student-loan debt 2005–15. *2016 Almanac of Higher Education.* Retrieved from www.chronicle.com/interactives/almanac-2016#id=39_252

College Board. (2015). *Trends in student aid: 2015.* New York: Author. Retrieved from http://trends.collegeboard.org/sites/default/files/trends-student-aid-web-final-508–2.pdf

College of the Ozarks. (n.d.). *College of the Ozarks: Hard work U.* Retrieved from www.cofo.edu/

Complete College America. (2013). *Four-year myth.* Indianapolis: Complete College America. Retrieved from http://completecollege.org/wp-content/uploads/2014/11/4-Year-Myth.pdf

Cunningham, A. F., & Kienzl, G. S. (2011). *Delinquency: The untold story of student loan borrowing.* Washington, DC: Institute for Higher Education Policy.

David, C. (2007). A working education. *University Business, 10*(12), 54–58.

Dean, D. R., & Hartlep, N. D. (under review). An exploratory study of financial aid use and student debt at Work Colleges. *Journal of Student Financial Aid.*

Dee, T. S. (2004). Are there civic returns to education? *Journal of Public Economics, 88,* 1697–1720.

DesJardins, S. L., Ahlburg, D. A., & McCall, B. P. (2002). Simulating the longitudinal effects of changes in financial aid on student departure from college. *Journal of Human Resources, 37*(3), 653–679.

Dickeson, R. C. (2004). *Collision course; rising college costs threaten America's future and require shared solutions.* Indianapolis: Lumina Foundation.

Ecclesia College. (n.d.). *Ecclesia College.* Retrieved from https://ecollege.edu/

Fry, R. (2012, September 26). *A record one-in-five households now owe student loan debt.* Washington, DC: Pew Social & Demographic Trends. Retrieved from www.pewsocialtrends.org/files/2012/09/09–26–12-Student_Debt.pdf

Funk, W. H. (2015). Free college for mountain folk. *Humanities, 36*(4), 44–49.

González Canché, M. S. (2014). Is the community college a less expensive path toward a bachelor's degree? Public 2- and 4-year colleges' impact on loan debt. *Journal of Higher Education, 85*(5), 723–759.

Grant, S. (2015, October 27). You can't work your way through college anymore. *Bloomberg Business.* Retrieved from www.bloomberg.com/news/articles/2015-10-28/you-can-t-work-your-way-through-college-anymore

Hamilton, K. (2005). All about the mission. *Diverse: Issues in Higher Education,* 22(15), 22–25.

Health Care and Education Reconciliation Act of 2010, Pub. L. 111–152, title II, §1029.

Hearn, J. C., & Bunton, S. A. (2001). *Economic and social returns of baccalaureate, graduate and professional degrees* (Policy Brief 01–01). Minneapolis: University of Minnesota/Postsecondary Education Policy Studies Center.

Immerwahr, J. (2004). *Public attitudes on higher education: A trend analysis 1993 to 2003.* San Jose, CA: The National Center for Public Policy and Higher Education.

Immerwahr, J., & Johnson, J. (2010). *Squeeze play 2010: Continued public anxiety on cost, harsher judgments on how colleges are run.* San Jose, CA: The National Center for Public Policy and Higher Education.

Kantrowitz, M. (2016, January 11). Why the student loan crisis is even worse than people think. *Time Money.* Retrieved from http://time.com/money/4168510/why-student-loan-crisis-is-worse-than-people-think/

King, T., & Frishberg, I. (2001). *Big loans, bigger problems: A report on the sticker shock of student loans.* (Research report). Washington, DC: The State PIRG's. Retrieved from www.uspirg.org/sites/pirg/files/reports/Big_Loans_Bigger_Prob lems_USPIRG.pdf

Kolodner, M. (2016, January 19). Fewer than one in seven community college students transfer and get a bachelor's degree—but there is new hope. *The Hechinger Report.* New York: The Hechinger Institute/Teachers College, Columbia University. Retrieved from http://hechingerreport.org/how-often-do-community-college-students-who-get-transfer-get-bachelors-degrees/

Lee, T. (2014, January 16). As college graduate rank falls, Obama unveils education push. *MSNBC.* Retrieved from www.msnbc.com/msnbc/college-graduate-rank-falls-obama-touts

Mumper, M., & Freeman, M. L. (2011). The continuing paradox of public college tuition inflation. In D. E. Heller (Ed.), *The states and public higher education policy: Affordability, access and accountability* (2nd ed., pp. 37–60). Baltimore: Johns Hopkins University Press.

National Center for Educational Statistics. (n.d.a). *Alice Lloyd College: Institutional profile.* Retrieved from https://nces.ed.gov/ipeds/datacenter/InstitutionPro file.aspx?unitId=acb0b1acb3b4.

National Center for Educational Statistics. (n.d.b). *Berea College: Institutional profile.* Retrieved from https://nces.ed.gov/ipeds/datacenter/institutionprofile.aspx?unitId=acb0b1adb4b0

National Center for Educational Statistics. (n.d.c). *Blackburn College: Institutional profile.* Retrieved from https://nces.ed.gov/ipeds/datacenter/institutionprofile.aspx?unitId=acafaeadb3b3

National Center for Educational Statistics. (n.d.d). *College of the Ozarks: Institutional profile.* Retrieved from https://nces.ed.gov/ipeds/datacenter/institutionpro file.aspx?unitId=acb2b3b1b4b2

National Center for Educational Statistics. (n.d.e). *Ecclesia College: Institutional profile.* Retrieved from https://nces.ed.gov/ipeds/datacenter/institutionprofile.aspx?unitId=afafb1adaeae

National Center for Educational Statistics. (n.d.f). *Fast facts: Tuition costs of colleges and universities.* Retrieved from http://nces.ed.gov/fastfacts/display.asp?id=76

National Center for Educational Statistics. (n.d.g). *Sterling College: Institutional profile*. [Web report]. Retrieved from https://nces.ed.gov/ipeds/datacenter/Institu tionProfile.aspx?unitId=adaeacabb4b0

National Center for Educational Statistics. (n.d.h). *Warren Wilson College: Institutional profile*. Retrieved from https://nces.ed.gov/ipeds/datacenter/institutionpro file.aspx?unitId=acb4b4b3b1b0

National Center for Educational Statistics. (n.d.i). *Trend generator* [Web database from the Integrated Postsecondary Education Data System]. Retrieved from http:// nces.ed.gov/ipeds/trendgenerator.

National Center for Educational Statistics. (2016). *Fast facts: Undergraduate enrollment* [Web page]. Retrieved from http://nces.ed.gov/programs/coe/indicator_cha.asp

New Republic Staff. (2015, October 6). How many hours would it take you to work off today's college tuition? *The New Republic*. Retrieved from https://newrepublic.com/ article/122814/how-many-hours-would-it-take-you-work-todays-college-tuition

Norris, F. (2012, May 24). Colleges for profit are growing, with federal help. *New York Times*. Retrieved from www.nytimes.com/2012/05/25/business/us-subsidies-to-for-profit-colleges-keep-growing.html?_r=0

Obama, B. (2009, February 24). Remarks of President Barack Obama, address to joint session of congress. *White House*. Retrieved from https://www.whitehouse. gov/video/EVR022409#transcript

Payea, K., Baum, S., & Kurose, C. (2013). *How students and parents pay for college*. New York: The College Board. Retrieved from https://trends.collegeboard. org/sites/default/files/analysis-brief-how-students-parents- pay-college.pdf

Perna, L. W. (Ed.). (2010). *Understanding the working college student: New research and its implications for policy and practice*. Sterling, VA: Stylus Publishing.

Shilton, A. C. (2014, December 14). These 3 colleges stopped investing in fossil fuels—one year later, their endowments are doing just fine. *Yes! Magazine*. Retrieved from www.yesmagazine.org/climate-in-our-hands/these-three-colleges-stopped-investing-fossil-fuels-endowments

Snider, S. (2015, February 24). 10 Colleges where graduates have the least student loan debt. *U.S. News & World Report*. Retrieved from www.usnews.com/ education/best-colleges/the-short-list-college/articles/2015/02/24/10-colleges-where-graduates-have-the-least-student-loan-debt

Sterling College. (n.d.). *Sterling College: Working hands, working minds*. Retrieved from www.sterlingcollege.edu

Tinto, V. (1975). Dropout from higher education: A theoretical synthesis of recent research. *Review of Educational Research*, 45(1), 89–125.

U.S. Congress. (2000). *Investment in education: Public and private returns*. Washington, DC: Joint Economic Committee of the United States Congress.

U.S. Department of Education. (n.d.). *Federal student aid: Glossary*. Retrieved from https://studentaid.ed.gov/sa/types

U.S. News & World Report (USNWR). (n.d.a). College of the Ozarks. *Best College Rankings*. Retrieved from http://colleges.usnews.rankingsandreviews.com/best-colleges/college-ozarks-2500

U.S. News & World Report (USNWR). (n.d.b). Warren Wilson College. *Best College Rankings*. Retrieved from http://colleges.usnews.rankingsandreviews.com/best-colleges/warren-wilson-2979

Vedder, R., Denhart, C., & Hartge, J. (2014, June). *Dollars, cents, and nonsense: The harmful effects of federal student aid.* Retrieved from http://centerforcollegeaffordability.org/uploads/Dollarsnonsense.pdf

Warren Wilson College. (n.d.). *Warren Wilson College.* Retrieved from www.warren-wilson.edu

Washburn, J. (2005). *University, Inc.: The corporate corruption of higher education.* New York: Basic Books.

White House. (2014). *Presidential memorandum—federal student loan repayments.* Retrieved from www.whitehouse.gov/the-press-office/2014/06/09/presidential-memorandum-federal-student-loan-repayments

Wolniak, G. C., & Pascarella, E. T. (2007). Initial evidence on the long-term impacts of work colleges. *Research in Higher Education, 48*(1), 39–71. Retrieved from http://dx.doi.org/10.1007/s11162-006-9023-6

Work Colleges Consortium. (2012). *Understanding and measuring success of work college graduates.* Retrieved from http://workcolleges.org/sites/default/files/attachments/WCC%202012%20Brochure.pdf

Young, R., & Hobson, J. (2011, December 22). Work colleges help students graduate without big debt. *Here & Now.* Retrieved from http://hereandnow.wbur.org/2011/12/22/work-colleges-students

14 It Takes More Than a Village, It Takes a Nation

Daniel A. Collier, T. Jameson Brewer, P. S. Myers, and Allison Witt

Neoliberalism, Individuality, and the Common Good

We understand neoliberalism to be "an ensemble of economic and social policies, forms of governance, and discourses and ideologies that promote individual self-interest, unrestricted flows of capital, deep reductions in the cost of labor, and sharp retrenchment of the public sphere" (Lipman, 2011, p. 6). In effect, neoliberalism is the favoring of markets and private gain over governments and the collective good.

For the last few decades, neoliberalism has dominated political discourse and policymaking in almost every social and governmental arena. And because equal education is seen as the mechanism through which the economic playing field is leveled for competition, both K–12 schooling and higher education are fields that have been redefined, reorganized, and appropriated by neoliberal philosophy and practice (Brewer & Myers, 2015). Indeed, higher education in the United States has proven to be an effective refuge for neoliberal philosophy and practices while simultaneously justifying and reinforcing socioeconomic stratification under the guise of equal competition and the myth of meritocracy (Giroux, 2002). Therefore, shifting public disposition away from notions of education for the collective good to a disposition that elevates individuality through meritocracy is anathema to traditional definitions of democracy. Even though the United States operates within the economic influences of capitalism, historically legislation has had socialist elements toward the collective good. Yet, while public investment in higher education increased with the GI Bill and the rapid expansion of colleges in the 1960s, the neoliberal proliferation of the 1980s began to challenge all manifestations of the public and collective good in postsecondary education. Opposing the neoliberal movement, Henry Giroux (2004) remarks:

> Under attack is the social contract with its emphasis on enlarging the public good and expanding social provisions—such as access to adequate health care, housing, employment, public transportation, and education—which provided a limited though important safety net and

a set of conditions upon which democracy could be experienced and critical citizenship engaged.

(p. xv)

The collective good—a disposition grounded in the idea that society improves together—is being subverted as "self-reflection and collective empowerment" are "reduced to self-promotion and self-interest" (Giroux, 2004, p. xv). The self-interest most glaringly supported by neoliberal tenets and practices is the self-interest of the wealthy and those who are in positions of power. Accordingly, in the 1970s many architects of neoliberalism sought to increase the wealth of the richest individuals by promoting neoliberal economic and social reforms (Harvey, 2005). Charged with a commonsensical discourse of personal freedom(s) and the myth of meritocracy, neoliberal ideology has proven itself an effective means of justifying growing socioeconomic stratification under the guise of individualistic competition and embedding neoliberal policies that benefit individuals with enormous wealth concentration (Piketty, 2014; Wilkinson & Pickett, 2010).

Neoliberalism and Higher Education

We understand neoliberalism to be an ideology and practice that is an affront to the historical perceptions surrounding higher education. Namely, although the pursuit of college degrees by individuals has long been seen as a benefit to the collective society (Friedman, 1955, 1962; Harris, 1953, 1962, 1967; Keppel, 1987; McMahon, 2009), the 1980s and 1990s saw a shift in both ideology and practice as related to funding higher education (Doyle, 2013; Dynarski & Scott-Clayton, 2013; Slaughter & Rhoades, 2004). That shift, informed by the neoliberal imagination, redefined the understanding of an individual's pursuit of a college degree to be largely an individualistic choice that should receive less funding by way of collective tax subsidies to offset tuition and other related costs (Best & Best, 2014). Thus, in short, the purposes for and logistics of financing higher education shifted from a view of education as a benefit to the society writ large to a view that education was an individual investment and benefit. Such a shift in perspective represents "roll-back neoliberalism," which, according to Ball (2012), refers to "the active destruction or discreditation of Keynesian-welfarist and social-collectivist institutions" (pp. 3–4).

Examining higher education through the logic of capitalist markets, Labaree (1988) asserts that "schools are producers of educational commodities— credentials—and must adapt themselves to meet the demands of the consumers who seek to acquire these commodities" (p. 4). Within the neoliberal imagination of higher education, students who are viewed as consumers are situated against one another, and the collective, while learning is reduced to a means to an end—the end being a credential to be used competitively on the job market (Bills, 2004; Labaree, 1997, 2007). Neoliberal thought advances the assumption that higher education credentials are individual goods that confer personal reward, challenging those who consider education to be a collective benefit and who know that education requires a personal investment that money can't buy—namely the investment of time and increasingly qualified effort to learn a subject and its requisite skills. Nonetheless, it is important to point out that the neoliberal understanding of individual benefits does not consider the collective. Individualized and competitive education fit within a neoliberal economic mindset that pays lipservice to collective good, manifested through beliefs and practices of supply-side or trickle-down economics. That is, as individuals are able to afford to benefit and improve their own lives—including their economic livelihood—spoils will naturally flow down the socioeconomic ladder. However, this practice is regularly shown to be at best ineffective (Hungerford, 2012) and, at worse, an oppressive platform that places the U.S. economic and sociopolitical structures in consistent danger (Holt & Greenwood, 2012; Stiglitz, 2013).

Because state governments have reduced subsidies to public universities, increased costs have been shifted to the individual student (Alexander, 2011; Alexander, Harnisch, Hurley, & Moran, 2010). Ever since President Reagan, the federal government has moved to strip the purchasing power of non-repayable aid such as grants (McMahon, 2009), including a defunding of the Federal Work-Study Program (Dynarski & Scott-Clayton, 2013). While the federal government enacted these policies they expanded the student loan system (Burdman, 2005; Williams, 2004). In 1992, under the first President Bush, the federal government introduced the unsubsidized student loan. Under this style of loan the government no longer pays for the interest while a student is attending school (Gladieux, 1995). The introduction of unsubsidized loans has significantly changed the structure of loans; subsidized loan eligibility is determined by financial need, whereas unsubsidized loans are meant for those considered above middle class or those who already borrowed the maximum allowed in subsidized loans (Gladieux & Hauptman, 1995). The growth of unsubsidized loans has been extreme: From 2003 to 2013, unsubsidized direct loans have grown by 108% and are now roughly double what is given in subsidized loans. In 2003, unsubsidized loans were roughly $25 billion and subsidized were $28 billion. Yet, in 2013, unsubsidized loans were $52 billion and subsidized were $25 billion; subsidized loans shrunk by 9% during this time frame (Baum & Ma, 2014b). In the modern era, with interest rates higher than inflation, "the federal government is in effect levying a new tax on college students in a program that already raises an obscene amount of money for the Treasury and is jeopardizing the financial future of a whole generation of young Americans" (Quirk, 2013, p. 34). What was once profit for the private lenders has become tens of billions in annual profit for the federal government (Congressional Budget Office, 2015).[1] As such, henceforth we no longer refer to student loans as "aid" in our chapter.

In the same time that the federal government pushed students toward increased reliance on student loans, state governments have reduced their financial pledges toward public higher education. Since the 1980s, state appropriations per full-time student have experienced significant decreases (McMahon, 2009), and, since the great recession, aggregate appropriations have deteriorated from a high of $90.5 billion in 2007 to $76.2 billion by 2013 (Baum & Ma, 2014a) despite increasing enrollment. As state policy-makers accept that costs will be shifted onto students upon removing state appropriations (Hovey, 1999), the expansion of the student loan system has arguably emboldened state legislative cuts and has played an integral role in the "price spiral in higher education" (Doyle, 2013, p. 5).

Obviously, as prices have increased and insufficient grant aid is avail-able, more students are borrowing, leading to annual increases in student loan balances. With increases in both borrowers and amount of average debt, defaults are expected to increase. Recently, the default rate has been hovering between 13 and 14%, with the aggregate number of people in default continuing to climb (Wright & Gallegos, 2014). Bankruptcy in the United States is governed under the United States Constitution. Yet, in the name of the social good, as promoted by banking sector lobbyists (Williams, 2004), in 1978, Congress applied special limitations to bankruptcy of stu-dent loan debt. This set of limitations is called *The Brunner Test* (Pardo & Lacey, 2009). Utilizing *Brunner*, courts individually determine (1) whether the debtor is able to maintain a minimal standard of living, (2) whether the debtor can prove sustained financial difficulty, and (3) whether the debtor has made enough of an effort to repay the debts.

Due to differing and inconsistent interpretations of the *Brunner Test*, the courts have applied the assessment unevenly (Hancock, 2009; Pardo & Lacey, 2009). These uneven applications have resulted in incredible rulings, such as in the case of Monic Stitt, a disabled woman receiving governmental assistance. In Stitt's case, the court ruled she did not make enough *effort* to repay her student debt, so her debts could not be discharged. However, she could enroll in an income-based repayment program where she would pay nearly zero dollars and the debts would be forgiven in 25 years, when she would be 70 years old (Rochelle & Kitroeff, 2015). After Stitt turned 70 she would be free from debt...or maybe not. That's because the balance of the "forgiveness" is considered taxable income. Thus, at the time of the "forgiveness," Stitt would still owe the IRS considerable money that she may not have.

Interestingly, an individual can rack up tens of thousands of dollars in credit card debt, making what are purchases to benefit only the individual, and the entirety of that debt can be discharged in bankruptcy. Contrary to such consumer debt provisions, student loan debt—even as a tangible manifestation of the neoliberal ideology that education is a consumerist endeavor—is not eligible for bankruptcy. And, despite the actual social ben-efits related to individuals attaining college degrees, student debt is uniquely the only debt that cannot be discharged in bankruptcy filings. In light of this discrepancy, it is entirely conceivable that an individual who achieves a college degree may be beneficial to an employer given the training and skills associated with higher education experience, yet at the same time, that employee may be so overburdened with personal debt that the only real beneficiary of the college degree is the employer and the banking system behind the student loan system. Thus, while an individual may take on tens or even hundreds of thousands of dollars of debt to improve his/her employment prospects, the residual debt may deliver net-benefits to the employer and the banks, but not the individual worker.

We feel confident in the argument that researchers, policymakers, and business leaders generally agree that (a) a more educated populace is beneficial to the collective good and (b) the early federal level policies aimed toward assisting more middle- to lower-income students in affording college. However, as touched upon in previous paragraphs, the nature of the aid has changed, resulting in these groups owning debilitating debt and widely contributing to various issues such as delay of marriages and home purchases (Stone, Van Horn, & Zukin, 2012), lowered net wealth (Fry, 2014), rise in delinquencies (Desilver, 2014), lowered credit scores (Yi, 2014), and increased affliction of various mental health issues (Dugan & Kafka, 2014).

The increased amount of student loan debt likely undermines many of the collective benefits of higher education as many are now struggling to repay the debt. To those ends, a 2015 *New York Times* op-ed (Siegel, 2015) encouraged readers to simply stop making payments on their educational debt. However, in a response, an article in *Slate* suggested the willful non-payment of student loans constituted "pick-pocketing the government" (Weissmann, 2015). The disposition reflected in the *Slate* piece reifies the neoliberal imagination of higher education.[2]

Crowdsourcing and Crowdfunding: A Brief Review

Using the collective resources of groups is not a new phenomenon. The engagement of groups through the Internet, quantitatively and experientially, differentiates crowdsourcing and crowdfunding from previous examples of group problem-solving, election contests, voting, fundraising, and pooling. In effect, the Internet changes who gets to be in the collective. Just as the collective tool is not new, neither is the study of it. Surowiecki (2005) explains that studies of pooling collective intellectual capabilities are historically established. Knight (1921), Klugman (1944), and Markey (1934) each present early studies into collective judgment and understanding. The desire to understand the capabilities of the crowd drives this research.

Crowdsourcing

Wired Magazine's Jeff Howe, as a combination of "outsourcing" and "crowd," coined the neologism "crowdsourcing" in 2006. Howe (2008) defines crowdsourcing as the act of taking a job traditionally performed by a designated agent (usually an employee) and outsourcing it to an undefined, generally large group of people in the form of an open call. While crowdsourcing has long been practiced in the private sector, recently, there has been a rise in the use of crowdsourcing for public benefit. For example, it was used at the University of Michigan to catalogue ancient Islamic texts (Kropf & Rodgers, 2009); the New York Public Library used similar methods in transcribing its popular culinary archives (Vershbow, 2013); and www.challenge.gov was introduced in 2010 to crowdsource innovation and improvement (Mergel & Desouza, 2013). Similarly, municipalities have used mobile Internet-based platforms to gather ideas and consensus (Desouza & Bhagwatwar, 2014). Citizen science projects, such as those used by NASA, involve observation, but also the passive use of computing power (Robson, 2012).

The most obvious and well-known example of crowdsourcing for the collective good is Wikipedia—an online open access encyclopedia that contains unlimited webpages of knowledge. While not considered scholarly, Wikipedia has become a source of information where individuals can uncover virtually any topic they desire, from quantum physics to higher education policy. The value of Wikipedia is that people now cite from where they have gained the information, making Wikipedia one of the world's most diverse library and citation sources. That said, issues of expertise have arisen and researchers have thought about how best to ensure data quality through various means.

An offshoot of crowdsourcing is "crowdfunding," which, instead of collecting intellectual capabilities, information, and general beliefs for the common good, focuses on gaining economic resources for the collective good.

Crowdfunding

Crowdfunding is an appeal to individuals—often disseminated via online media—to assist with financing projects (Kleemann, Vob, & Rieder, 2008). Using Kleemann et al.'s (2008) research as a foundation, Lambert and Schwienbacher (2010) expanded the definition by which they describe crowdfunding as an open call—essentially through the Internet—for the provision of financial resources, either in the form of donation or in exchange for some form of reward and/or voting rights, all in order to support an initiative for specific purposes. Crowdfunding, like the idea of crowdsourcing from which it arises, is not, in its simplest practice, a new idea. Rewards-based crowdfunding (such as Kickstarter.com) is similar to the advanced financing subscription and publication model of *praenumeration* used in 18th-century Germany (Ketoja & Pajunen, 2014). Mutual benefit purchasing cooperatives also serve as a model (both prior to and in the digital age) model for crowdfunding (Shaffer, 1999).

Hemer (2011) provides a typology for crowdfunding project objectives and embeddedness (pp. 11–12). Objectives include (a) not-for-profit projects that seek to impact the social sphere in varied areas, (b) for-profit projects with commercial aims, and (c) "intermediate" projects whose commercial prospects are unclear in the moment they are launched or are purposefully short-lived. Typologies of embeddedness include (a) independent projects, started and maintained through individual efforts; (b) embedded projects that exist within a larger organizational context; and (c) start-ups, which may begin as independent projects, but ultimately have the purpose of being the impetus for a larger organization.

Crowdfunding has also been used as a debt financing and loan repayment tool. These projects may exist as collective or peer-to-peer arrangements (Berger & Gleisner, 2014). As student loan debt has risen, crowdfunding organizations have proliferated. Several examples of these web-based organizations include Givling (2017), Piglt (2017), Rolling Jubilee (2017), and Zerobound (2017). Collectively these organizations are working toward eliminating student loan debt, and each has different models and methods of crowdfunding. For example, Zerobound (2017) matches borrowers as volunteers to non-profits and then they are sponsored by individuals in exchange for the volunteer work. Piglt is akin to Kickstarter for higher education finance. The Piglt (2017) platform has "dreamers" (students) promote themselves to "believers" (financiers) in hopes to gain funding.

Rolling Jubilee (2017) is described as "a network of debtors who liberate debtors through mutual aid." Here, money is donated and then the private student loan debt is bought for significantly less than what is owed. As of November 2014, Rolling Jubilee (2015) claims to have assisted 9,438 debtors at an average of $1,418 per person, totaling $13 million. While impressive, $13 million represents less than .001% of total student loan debt at $1.4 trillion. Givling is a trivia game app that is specifically designed to help people repay student loan debt. Essentially Givling crowdfunds by charging users to play the trivia game and for the winners, the money is distributed in two ways. Once Givling reaches $10 million, $5 million is redistributed back to the members who play, and $4 million is funneled to the highest scoring players (Janci, 2015). The remaining money is used for administrative costs. Each of the above programs is in their infancies, and, at this time, there has been little scholarly discussion of any of these new crowdfunding measures for indebted students.

While some may promote crowdfunding as an innovative, market-like solution toward relieving student loan debt, this method of easing student loan debt may pose some serious issues. One issue may be that, because crowdfunding allows for the choice to emotionally buy into a person or a cause, those who are able to craft excellent narratives or utilize rhetoric persuasively will find success in tapping into the generosity. Take Piglt, for example. If you have seen or read *The Hunger Games*, you might liken this process to the "dreamer" (Katniss) trying to impress the "believers" (people with money and influence) for gifts and advantages during the games. Essentially, Piglt may promote the ability to string together several nonsensical buzzwords designed to foster idealizations that, given that this person is able to confidently write with fancy words, he or she would clearly deserve the money because that would be a fantastic return on investment for society. Additionally, when thinking about Givling's model of charging debtors to play in hopes of a return of funds, we should ask, who does this model not include? It is obvious that those with higher debt cannot afford a "pay-to-play" model. As such, Givling may be helping only those with small to moderate levels of student debt, people who need less help than those more heavily afflicted by this debt.[3]

Under these models, individuals who may truly be in greater need may never gain access to the financial assistance ostensibly provided through this action. Undoubtedly, many Americans are generous people. Yet the differences between democratically accountable crowdfunding (taxation) and the private choice to individually crowdfund elicit great debate, as neoliberalism remains a prevalent belief system and people want to believe that they have a choice in how their collective money is spent.

Analyzing an Example of a Crowdfunded Debt Collective

The essence of this chapter is in the question, "Can crowdsourcing be a viable option to help ease student loan debt burden?" Recently, one of the authors had been approached by several administrators of an online community who wanted to test the viability of creating a debt collective for members of the group. To protect anonymity, as required by the terms of agreement for our research, we cannot fully describe this group. However, to give a general sense, this community is hosted on a popular social media website, has tens of thousands of members, and was developed to provide space for information sharing and promotion of political action in easing student loan debt. Sharing organizational reports, discussing current student loan debt news stories, and answering each other's questions are common events of the community.

After one member sparked a discussion on debt collectives and the potential for this type of activity to serve the group, an administrator who knew that one of the authors was collecting data on the group asked whether a debt collective policy could be viable. To begin, the members of the group decided to explore an extraordinary conservative model; if this initial conservative model was practical, then more advanced models would be explored. The conservative, safer model is what follows and what we analyzed.

The group pitched an idea similar to what you see on TV, the dollar-a-day, to save a tiger or feed a child, model. The terms of the model are as follows. First, each member of the group would "donate" two dollars per day, $730 per year. At the beginning of each month, the entire pool of money collected would be used to pay off student loan debt, saving an immense amount of interest on those loans. Those who had their loans repaid (early) would then pay $250.00 per month ($3,000 annually) for 15 years; these payments would begin immediately the month after the loans were cleared. Starting in the second month of the plan, both the two-dollar per day and $250.00 monthly revenue would be pooled to buy more debt.

After the initial plan was devised, additional assumptions had to be fleshed out. We understand these assumptions may be limiting; however, this is what the group wanted to explore. The first assumption is that growth in the group would continue at a similar rate. At the time of writing this chapter in 2016, this group had just over 13,000 members and in the past year grew at an average rate of 120 members per month. Although this growth may be unsustainable due to the difficulty of buying in while still repaying one's own debt, we defend this decision, as the group did ask whether this was viable given what we knew at the time about group dynamics. As previously stated, one author was in the process of collecting data on this group for another project. Based on that data, the average undergraduate student loan debt of the group was slightly over $42,000; therefore, the initial calculation of total undergraduate debt for the entire group was just under $550 million. This debt includes federal and private debt, with the private debt interest rates generally found to be slightly higher than the federal. Because most private loans have sliding inflation rates, we decided to use the federal 6.8% interest rate.

The model also assumes that people are paying down their debts at this monthly average; therefore, it subtracts the money that would be applied to the principal from total balance remaining. In a mortgage-like 25-year extended repayment plan with a 6.8% interest rate, the expected monthly payment started at $292 (FinAid, 2017). For new members, the monthly payment of the debt was calculated in accordance with the average loan debt with which they would have entered the group; for instance, in 2016, it would be $298. Finally, because the data the researcher collected on the group did not allow for indication of how the debt was growing, the model considered that the average debt of new group members would grow by only $1,000 per year. With these assumptions in place, the model was created and the results are interesting. Table 14.1 below provides an outline of the results, which indicate total members of the group with debt, total remaining student loan balance, money raised through the two-dollar-a-day scheme, money raised through the $250 per month scheme, and, finally, total amount of student loans that were paid off (at an average of $42,000).

As Figure 14.1 indicates, over 15 years, the group could raise $286 million in the two-dollar-a-day scheme and nearly $200 million in the $250 per month repayment. Throughout the course of the plan, they could clear 11,553 loans, at an average of $42,000. Additionally, as the group grows, which is necessary for generating more funds, so does the aggregate balance. By 2030, in this conservative estimation, the aggregate debt will be over

Table 14.1 Debt Collective Model Utilizing a Two-Dollar-a-Day and $250 Monthly Repayment Scheme

End of year totals	Number of group members with debt	Total balance remaining (millions)	Aggregate money raised through $2 a day (millions)	Total money raised through $3,000 a year (millions)	Aggregate loans paid off by end of the year
2015	14,377	600	10.0	.36	247
2016	15,817	660	11.1	1.1	290
2017	17,257	720	12.1	2.1	338
2018	18,697	780	13.2	3.1	388
2019	20,137	840	14.2	4.4	443
2020	21,557	900	15.2	5.8	500
2021	23,017	960	16.3	7.4	564
2022	24,457	1,020	17.3	9.2	631
2023	25,897	1,080	18.4	11.1	702
2024	27,337	1,140	19.4	13.3	779
2025	28,777	1,200	20.5	15.8	864
2026	30,217	1,260	21.5	18.5	952
2027	31,657	1,320	22.6	21.5	1,050
2028	33,097	1,380	23.7	24.8	1,155
2029	34,537	1,440	24.7	28.4	1,264
2030	35,977	1,500	25.8	32.4	1,386
15 Year Total			286.0	199.26	11,553

$1.5 billion. Theoretically, the group could raise large amounts of money and it would make such a small combined difference that, for the group, it might as well be no difference at all. For individuals, this type of plan may be seen as a godsend. Below, however, is a line-chart that clearly shows how ineffective this crowdfunding model is.

It is important to note that this model was predicated on *only* undergraduate debt. Consider this: a group of only 13,000 people holds just over $550,000,000 in *just* undergraduate debt. This debt is so unwieldy that, with all things considered, the collective effort could raise approximately $485 million dollars in 15 years and still gain next to nothing on total debts of the group. Beyond the gravity of the crushing debts, this crowdfunding model brings to light one of the most significant issues associated with self-contained crowdfunding efforts: In order to gain increased funds to clear more loans, the group always needs to grow. Yet, as the group grows, the debt also grows and, as the model in this chapter suggests, very few people will actually benefit from the scheme. A crowdfunding plan like this is essentially a pyramid scheme where the idealization of buying into the plan holds more promise than the actual engagement in or results from the practice.

Moreover, crowdfunding plans create many ethical and legal issues for the group administrators. Just like with other privatized debt collective efforts, the group must determine who will benefit from the effort and how

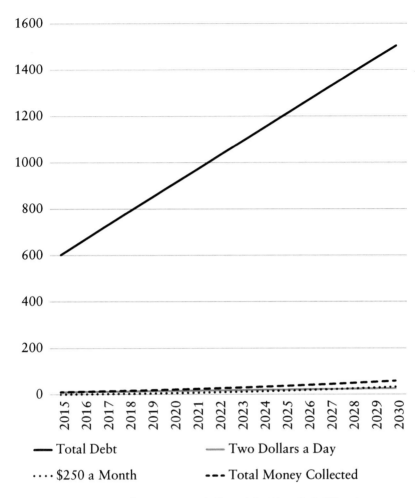

Figure 14.1 Aggregate Debt vs. Money Collected, by Year (in Millions)

they will benefit. For example, whose loans will be paid off first? Does everyone get a maximum up to $42,000—meaning those with debts over $42,000 get their loans only partially paid for? Will that solve most of their problems? Remember, these debtors would be paying into this plan as they are also struggling to pay their loan debts. Should the group target those who are paying a higher percentage of their income to student loan debt—a move that may mean repaying the debts of those who have higher yearly earnings but also more student loan debt? Does it hurt someone to pay 20% of their income to student loan debt if they are making $70,000 as much as it does someone paying 8% and making $20,000? Would the group take into consideration factors such as: (1) race, (2) single parent

224 Daniel A. Collier et al.

status, (3) those who have filed for bankruptcy but still own their student loan debts, and (4) those whose social security checks are being garnished to repay the debt? What happens to group members who leave the collective; is there a legally binding contract that compels them to pay (Vogel, 2015)? Is it really fair to force people who are struggling financially to pay for everyone's debt as they also try to pay their own down? Would the administrators legally compel those who leave the group to honor the contract? What about those who stop paying their 15-year commitment after their loans have been paid off?

For us, the component that is missing from this model, and likely from this group in its current form, is the inclusion of those with little to no debt buying into the plan. A group like this will absolutely have to recruit people who do not expect their own debts to be covered by the model. Nevertheless, with the various well-documented struggles of most students graduating with some level of student loan debt, stagnant wages, and increased prices of rent, homeownership, childcare costs, and necessities, how could this group be expected to effectively recruit such people and sign them up for long-term participation? It is unlikely that they would be able to recruit enough low- to no-debt donors to buy into their debt situations, except perhaps a few well-off grandparents, let alone sustain a model that encourages monthly payment. Realistically, the members of this group may be better served by paying to play on Givling or crafting buzzword-heavy, emotionally driven narratives for "believers" on Piglt.

Conclusion

Without a doubt, the neoliberal movement has prevailed in developing policies that have minimized the purchasing power of grants and scholarships and various governmental supports for higher education, thus creating an environment in which costs are increasingly shifting to students who now rely greatly on student loans to participate in higher education. With increasingly greater reliance on student loans and interest rates higher than inflation, some might think that only the more recent generation is at risk. But student debt extends through all current adult generations and will increasingly affect all future generations as long as we leave this debt-based system in force. For example, some baby boomers are having their social security checks garnished to cover outstanding balances on student loans (GAO, 2014). Their numbers are expected to rise over the coming decades.

Various neoliberal policy changes have shifted the higher education landscape, although not without resistance. As President Obama indicated in public speeches, "If we're serious about making sure America's workers and America itself succeeds in the 21st century, the single most important step we can take is to make sure that every one of our young people . . . has the best education that the world has to offer" (Horsley, 2010). We still live in a society that essentially tells youth that going to college is one of the most important choices citizens can make, not only for individual success but also for the economic and social advancement of *all* society. However, although this choice is often predominantly framed as a social good, the neoliberal practices connected with financial aid indicate that individuals are more responsible than society for financing this choice—even though the loan system has been exposed as predatory.

We believe that, because higher education is generally promoted as a social good, and societal messages reinforce this ideal among young adults, policymakers must make greater efforts to develop a tuition-less public education system. The financial onus needs to be on society to produce the financial means for students to engage in higher education. Stiglitz's (2013) book, *The Price of Inequality*, concludes by stating that the U.S. government should both raise enough money and decide to equalize many unequal systems—one system being higher education funding. One source of funding Stiglitz often targets in the book is ending the contemporary tax loopholes for the wealthiest earners and the largest corporations. He argues that tax loopholes for these groups ("rent-seekers") sap money from the middle- to lower-class and transfer it to higher earners and corporations. Additionally, these policies allow these groups to abdicate their social responsibilities by not returning money back to society. As policymakers are encouraged to work toward modifying tuition and financial aid schemes, they must also be pressured to find solutions that will subsidize current student loan debts. Given how woefully inadequate, even though valiant, collective efforts to crowd-fund are in the face of ever-growing mountains of student debt, our suggestions to provide immediate relief for this debt are radical: first, divert current corporate subsidies toward repaying this debt; next, enforce taxes on the large corporations; and, finally, seize assets of corporations found to harbor their profits in tax havens.[4] Each of these suggestions obviously rejects the protections that large corporations have enjoyed under neoliberalism. If neoliberals actually adhered to their ideology, they would also be in favor of our suggestions because such protections for top corporations arguably destroy the free market and create governmental dependencies.

Recently, Ted DeHaven (2012) of the CATO Institute suggested that corporate welfare cost taxpayers nearly $100 billion dollars a year (DeHaven, 2012). Whereas President Reagan once promoted the image of individuals as "welfare queens" so as to pass neoliberal reforms on to the poor in the 1980s, there is often little said by his devotees about the corporate "welfare queens" that take, on average, $6,000 per year from each taxpaying American family, of which $870 is linked with tax subsidies, $1,231 supports revenue lost from tax havens, and the rest is dispersed in specific sectors like banking and pharmaceutical and contributes to various other incentives programs (Buchheit, 2013). Key findings in two recent reports indicated that: (1) large corporations pay a tax rate of 19.4%, which is far below the expected 35%; (2) 26 major corporations effectively paid no federal income taxes from 2008–2012; (3) 93 corporations paid a tax rate of less than 10%; (4) many corporations that claim off-shore profits pay higher taxes in foreign counties than they do in the United States (McIntyre, Gardner, & Phillips, 2014); and (5) U.S.-based multinational corporations are hiding $2.1 trillion dollars offshore (Audit Analytics, 2014). One article suggests that closing various corporate subsidies would allow the government to reclaim more than $300 billion annually (Tasini, 2011). If such revenue was directed toward student loan debts, the system could be wiped clean in several years. Once the system is cleaned, the revenue not going to such subsidies can be used to finance tuition-less public higher education. Essentially, our first two suggestions argue to take back money from the corporate rent-seekers.

Our third suggestion is a radical argument to realign the expectations of private rewards with social contributions. This suggestion supports direct punishment for corporations' continued shady practices of hiding money from the United States, such as Walmart's practices of posting profit in countries where they have no stores (Clemente & Auerbach, 2015). We find no greater justification for this suggestion than within Stiglitz's (2013) writing: "some of the most important innovations in business in the last three decades have centered not on making the economy more efficient but on how better to ensure monopoly power or how better to circumvent government regulations intended to align social returns and private rewards" (p. 44). With these guiding words, we believe that the trillions of dollars hidden from the U.S. government should be fully seized and utilized to completely pay outstanding student loan debts and apply the remaining funds to serve as the base for tuition-less public education, as expressed in Bernie Sanders's proposal for eliminating student debt (Schramm & Stoetzer, 2015).

While these actions seem harsh, many corporations choose to engage in unethical, potentially illegal practices, helping to contribute toward polices that have broken social institutions like higher education and egregiously harmed many Americans. Therefore, our harshness is arguably justified, as the action would serve to help some individuals to reclaim their financial futures, and it would situate America for future economic and social success—success that should translate into increased productivity and profits for these very same corporate entities. Abandoning America's social good should be heavily punished to circumvent future practices and to send the message that the citizens of the United States will be protected and any private rewards will remain aligned with the social good. We feel it important to state that our arguments are not merely anti-corporation. We do not wish to break up large corporations, nor do we want to see the United States seize profits that companies ethically report to the IRS. Instead, our arguments hail from the perspective of advocating that we should not allow these entities to abdicate their responsibility to provide for the social good, a good they also depend on. Our recommendations may be seen as practices that will help to readjust corporate practices entrenched in neoliberalism so that they realign with social responsibility.

Finally, we conclude this chapter by recognizing that the student loan debt crisis takes more than a village to solve—it takes a nation. The villages are failing because federal financial aid was never supposed to be primarily a privatized, loan-heavy package without social safety nets. Not even Milton Friedman argued that a privatized, mortgage-like repayment scheme should be the dominant arrangement for individuals repaying financiers of higher education. In fact, Friedman (1955) suggested that, because "Investment in human beings cannot be financed on the same terms or with the same ease as investment in physical capital," loans should be repaid based on income level and, if the income level was too low, repayment should be waived until the individual's pay rises above a minimum floor (p. 102). For various reasons, he also suggested that the only entity that could effectively ensure that society and businesses gain the human capital necessary for the immediate future was the federal government. This argument is counter to Friedman's general disposition that the federal government should be hands-off. Even for the man whom many neoliberals credit with the contemporary free market ideology, higher education was, at its core, a national-level social good.[5] While the Constitution may not determine that education is a right, federal aid policy—dating before HEA of 1965 but clearly solidified with its passage—obviously suggests that the federal government agrees that higher education is a social good that is of national interest.

We think it is the job of national legislators to heed suggestions that bring higher education financial polices back to serve the social and national good and to work toward eliminating debts that actively trap and exploit entire groups of Americans in an endless cycle of devastating debt. The power of the villages lies within applying enough political pressure to force such transitions. Make no mistake: Our suggestions encourage an active political battle between entities that have net wealth and power, on the one hand, and villages of people and small businesses that are indebted, on the other hand. While the wealth and power of large corporations help them to secure favorable policies, those entities can be overcome by the votes and political influences of the villages. Once enough villages collectively decide that the private rewards should again be realigned to the social good, policymakers will have little choice but to adhere to the will of the collective good and to adopt strategies similar to those presented in this chapter. The question we want to raise to the reader in continuing the conversation is: When will the villages begin to collectively decide to demand the rearrangement?

Notes

1 Editors' note: Keep in mind, however, what is behind the federal government, like a puppeteer, in our existing monetary system. Whereas the private lenders' (i.e., banking system's) profit on student loans was (and is) pure profit because banks, in our system, create out of thin air the vast majority of the money they lend to students, the government—ever since it relinquished its authority to

create and monitor our money to the banking system in 1913—must borrow every penny it loans out to students (unless it gets those pennies from us through taxes). The government profits financially on direct student loans only if the interest it charges and collects from students is higher than the interest it must pay its lenders—the bankers pulling the strings of the marionette called Uncle Sam—and even that is only *if* it has anything left after paying for the administrative costs of running the Federal Financial Aid system. In reverting to Direct Student Loans in 2010, the federal government removed the extra middleman between it and student borrowers.

2 Editors' addition: . . . as does the secret, hidden in increasingly plain sight, that behind the federal government stands The Man. The Man acts through our private-interest-driven debt-based money system to enable its net beneficiaries to get their own—which is more and more of everything—one way or another. Though he can see, if he opens his eyes and ears, that he thereby destroys the earth and the conditions for life on it, he will continue to do so as long as we let him, but only that long, even if he might not give up the ghost without a battle.

3 On a personal note, although the rate of return to people at 90% should be applauded, the idea that debtors now are incentivized and rely on a gaming app to repay a debt attached to a function clearly associated toward the social, economic, and technological advancement of our society only shows how far away we have strayed from the original purpose of the federal student aid system and the original intent of the student loan guarantee. It is, in our opinion, sickening.

4 Editors' addition: A fourth and, because it gets to the root of the student debt problem, even more radical proposal is macro-level monetary reform, as discussed in Chapter 15, this volume.

5 Editors' addition: Friedman may have thought similarly about the monetary system, as did many of his contemporaries. He was aware and to some extent supportive of depression-era efforts by fellow economists in Chicago and elsewhere to reform our monetary system (see Allen, 1993, esp. footnote 53). This plan, known as the "Chicago Plan" or "100 percent reserve banking," is one of the bases for macro-level monetary reform being worked on today.

References

Alexander, F. K. (2011). Maintenance of state effort for higher education: Barriers to equal educational opportunity in addressing the rising costs of a college education. *Journal of Education Finance, 36*(4), 442–450.

Alexander, F. K., Harnisch, T., Hurley, D., & Moran, R. (2010). Maintenance of effort: An evolving federal-state policy approach to ensuring college affordability. *Journal of Education Finance, 36*(1), 76–87.

Allen, W. R. (1993, October). Irving Fisher and the 100 percent reserve proposal. *Journal of Law and Economics, 36*(2), 703–717.

Audit Analytics. (2014, April 1). *Overseas earnings of Russell 100 tops $2 trillion in 2013*. Retrieved from www.auditanalytics.com/blog/overseas-earnings-of-russell-1000-tops-2-trillion-in-2013/

Ball, S. (2012). *Global Education Inc.: New policy networks and the neo-liberal imaginary*. New York: Routledge.

Baum, S., & Ma, J. (2014a). *Trends in higher education series: Trends in college pricing*. Washington, DC: The College Board. Retrieved from http://trends.college board.org/sites/default/files/college-pricing-2013-full-report-140108.pdf

Baum, S., & Ma, J. (2014b). Trends in higher education: Trends in student aid. *The College Board*. Retrieved from http://trends.collegeboard.org/student-aid

Berger, S. C., & Gleisner, F. (2014). Emergence of financial intermediaries in electronic markets: The case of online P2P lending. *Business Research, 2*(1), 39–65.

Best, J., & Best, E. (2014). *The student loan mess: How good intentions created a trillion-dollar problem.* Berkeley, CA: University of California Press.

Bills, D. D. (2004). *The sociology of education and work.* Malden, MA: Blackwell Publishing.

Brewer, T. J., & Myers, P. S. (2015). How neoliberalism subverts equality and perpetuates poverty in our nation's schools. In S. N. Haymes, M. V. D. Haymes, & R. Miller (Eds.), *The Routledge handbook of poverty in the United States* (pp. 190–198). New York: Routledge.

Buchheit, P. (2013, September 24). Add it up: The average American family pays $6,000 a year in subsidies to big business. *Moyers & Company.* Retrieved from http://billmoyers.com/2013/09/24/average-american-family-pays-6k-a-year-in-subsidies-to-big-business/

Burdman, P. (2005). The student debt dilemma: Debt aversion as a barrier to college access. *Project on Student Debt.* Retrieved from http://projectonstudentdebt.org/files/pub/DebtDilemma.pdf

Clemente, F., & Auerbach, M. (2015). The Walmart web: How the world's biggest corporation secretly uses tax havens to dodge taxes. *Americans for Tax Fairness.* Retrieved from www.americansfortaxfairness.org/files/TheWalmartWeb-June-2015-FINAL.pdf

Congressional Budget Office. (2015). *CBO's March 2015 baseline projections for the student loan program.* Retrieved from www.cbo.gov/sites/default/files/cbofiles/attachments/44198-2015-03-StudentLoan.pdf

DeHaven, T. (2012, July 25). Corporate welfare in the federal budget. *CATO Institute.* Retrieved from http://object.cato.org/sites/cato.org/files/pubs/pdf/PA703.pdf

Desilver, D. (2014). By many measures, more borrowers struggle with loan-payments. *Pew Research Center.* Retrieved from www.pewresearch.org/fact-tank/2014/05/15/by-many-measures-more-borrowers-struggling-with-student-loan-payments/

Desouza, K. C., & Bhagwatwar, A. (2014). Technology-enabled participatory platforms for civic engagement: The case of U.S. cities. *Journal of Urban Technology, 21*(4), 25–50.

Doyle, W. R. (2013). A new partnership: Reshaping the federal and state commitment to need-based aid. *The Committee for Economic Development.*

Dugan, A., & Kafka, S. (2014). Student debt linked to worse health and less wealth. *Gallup.* Retrieved from www.gallup.com/poll/174317/student-debt-linked-worse-health-less-wealth.aspx

Dynarski, S., & Scott-Clayton, J. (2013). Financial aid policy: Lessons from research. *The Future of Children, 23*(1), 67–91.

FinAid. (2017). Calculator. Retrieved from www.finaid.org/calculators/scripts/loan-payments.cgi

Friedman, M. (1955). The role of government in public education. In R. A. Solo (Ed.), *Economics and the public interest* (pp. 123–144). New Brunswick, NJ: University of Rutgers Press.

Friedman, M. (1962). *Capitalism and freedom.* Chicago: The University of Chicago Press.

Fry, R. (2014). Young adults, student debt and economic well-being. *Pew Research Center.* Retrieved from www.pewsocialtrends.org/2014/05/14/young-adults-student-debt-and-economic-well-being/

Giroux, H. A. (2002). Neoliberalism, coprate culture and the promise of higher education: The university as a democratic public sphere. *Harvard Eduational Review*, 72(4), 425–463.

Giroux, H. A. (2004). *The terror of neoliberalism: Authoritarianism and the eclipse of democracy.* Aurora, Ontario: Garamond Press.

Givling. (2017). *Homepage.* Retrieved from https://givling.com/givling/

Gladieux, L. E. (1995). Federal student aid policy: A history and an assessment. *Financing Postsecondary Education: The Federal Role.* Retrieved from https://www2.ed.gov/offices/OPE/PPI/FinPostSecEd/gladieux.html

Gladieux, L. E., & Hauptman, A. M. (1995). *The college aid quandary.* Washington, DC: The Brookings Institution.

Hancock, K. E. (2009). A certainty of hopelessness: Debt, depression, and the discharge of student loans under the bankruptcy code. *Law & Psychology Review*, 33, 151–166.

Harris, S. E. (1953). Economics of higher education. *American Economic Review*, 43(3), 314–343.

Harris, S. E. (1962). *Higher education: Resources and finances.* New York: McGraw Hill.

Harris, S. E. (1967, May 22–25). *Economics of higher education.* Paper presented at the Third College Scholarship Service Colloquium on Financial Aid.

Harvey, D. (2005). *A brief history of neoliberalism.* Oxford, UK: Oxford University Press.

Hemer, J. (2011). A snapshot on crowdfunding. *Fraunhofer Institute for Systems and Innovation Research.* Retrieved from www.isi.fraunhofer.de/isi-wAssets/docs/p/de/arbpap_unternehmen_region/ap_r2_2011.pdf

Holt, R., & Greenwood, D. (2012). Negative trickle down and the financial crisis of 2008. *Journal of Economic Issues*, 46(2), 363–370.

Horsley, S. (2010, August 9). Obama goes on the road to talk higher education. *NPR.* Retrieved from http://www.npr.org/templates/story/story.php?storyId=129090159

Hovey, H. A. (1999). *State spending for higher education in the next decade: The battle to sustain current support.* San Jose, CA: National Center for Public Policy and Higher Education.

Howe, J. (2006). The rise of crowdsourcing. *Wired Magazine*, 14(6), 1–4. Retrieved from https://www.wired.com/2006/06/crowds/

Howe, J. (2008). *Crowdsourcing: Why the power of the crowd is driving the future of business.* New York: Penguin Random House.

Hungerford, T. (2012). *Taxes and the economy: An economic analysis of the top tax rate since 1945.* Washington, DC: Center on Budget and Policy Priorities.

Janci, J. (2015, March 9). Online trivia game company wants to help students pay off college loan debt. *USA Today.* Retrieved from http://college.usatoday.com/2015/03/09/online-trivia-game-company-wants-to-help-students-pay-off-college-loan-debt/

Keppel, F. (1987). The Higher Education Acts contrasted, 1965–1986: Has federal policy come of age? *Harvard Educational Review*, 57(1), 49–67.

Ketoja, L., & Pajunen, O. (2014). *Equity-based crowdfunding in Finland.* Published Bachelor's thesis, Turku University. Retrieved from www.theseus.fi/bitstream/handle/10024/82525/Thesis%20Final%20Version%203%20Fixed.pdf?sequence=1

Kleemann, F., Vob, G., & Rieder, K. (2008). Un(der)paid innovators: The commercial utilization of consumer work through crowdsourcing. *Science, Technology, and Innovation Studies*, 4(1), 5–26.

Klugman, S. F. (1944). Cooperative versus individual efficiency in problem-solving. *Journal of Educational Psychology*, 35(2), 1939–2176.

Knight, H. C. (1921). *A comparison of the reliability of group and individual judgments.* Published master's thesis, Columbia University.

Kropf, E., & Rodgers, J. (2009). *Collaboration in cataloguing: Islamic manuscripts at Michigan.* Retrieved from www.lib.umich.edu/special-collections-library/collaboration-cataloging-islamic-manuscripts-michigan

Labaree, D. F. (1988). *The making of an American high school: The credentials market & the Central High School of Philadelphia, 1838–1939.* New Haven, CT: Yale University Press.

Labaree, D. F. (1997). Public goods, private goods: The American struggle over educational goals. *American Educational Research Journal, 34*(1), 39–81.

Labaree, D. F. (2007). *Education, markets, and the public good: The selected words of David F. Labaree.* New York: Routledge.

Lambert, T., & Schwienbacher, A. (2010). *An empirical analysis of crowdfunding.* Retrieved from http://papers.ssrn.com/sol3/papers.cfm?abstract_id=1578175

Lipman, P. (2011). *The new political economy of urban education: Neoliberalism, race, and the right to the city.* New York: Routledge.

Markey, F. V. (1934). Variations in judgment. *Journal of Applied Psychology, 18*(2), 297–303.

McIntyre, R. S., Gardner, M., & Phillips, R. (2014). The sorry state of corporate taxes: What Fortune 500 firms pay (or don't pay) in the U.S. and what they pay abroad—2008 to 2012. *The Institute on Taxation and Economic Policy.* Retrieved from www.ctj.org/corporatetaxdodgers/sorrystateofcorptaxes.pdf

McMahon, W. (2009). *Higher learning, greater good: The private and social benefits of higher education.* Baltimore: Johns Hopkins University Press.

Mergel, I., & Desouza, K. C. (2013). Implementing open innovation in the public sector: The case of Challenge.gov. *Public Administration Review, 73*(6), 882–890.

Pardo, R. I., & Lacey, M. R. (2009). The real student-loan scandal: Undue hardship discharge litigation. *American Bankruptcy Law Journal, 83,* 179–235. Retrieved from https://www.bankruptcy-divorce.com/Bankruptcy-Student-Loan/Undue%20Hardship%20Discharge%20Litigation%20Undue%20Hardship%20Discharge%20Litigation.pdf

Piglt. (2017). *Homepage.* Retrieved from www.piglt.com/

Piketty, T. (2014). *Capital in the twenty-first century.* Cambridge, MA: The Belknap Press of Harvard University Press.

Quirk, W. J. (2013, September 5). Federal student-loan sharks. *The American Scholar.* Retrieved from https://theamericanscholar.org/federal-student-loan-sharks/#.VNAll2h4oUN

Robson, C. (2012). *Using mobile technology and social networking to crowdsource citizen science.* Published dissertation. Retrieved from www.eecs.berkeley.edu/Pubs/TechRpts/2012/EECS-2012-195.pdf

Rochelle, B., & Kitroeff, N. (2015, June 22). Courts rule that disabled woman living below the poverty line must repay student loans. *Bloomberg Business.* Retrieved from www.bloomberg.com/news/articles/2015–06–22/courts-rule-that-disabled-woman-living-below-the-poverty-line-must-repay-student-loans

Rolling Jubilee. (2015). *Purchase summary: Rolling Jubilee fund.* Retrieved from http://rollingjubilee.org/assets/docs/debt_buy_summary_06.pdf

Rolling Jubilee. (2017). *Transparency.* Retrieved from http://rollingjubilee.org/transparency/

Schramm, M., & Stoetzer, E. (2015, May 19). Bernie Sanders issues bill to make 4-year colleges tuition-free. *USA Today.* Retrieved from http://college.usatoday.com/2015/05/19/bernie-sanders-issues-bill-to-make-4-year-colleges-tuition-free/

Shaffer, J. (1999). *Historical dictionary of the cooperative movement.* Lanham, MD: Scarecrow Press.

Siegel, L. (2015, June 6). Why I defaulted on my student loans. *New York Times.* Retrieved from www.nytimes.com/2015/06/07/opinion/sunday/why-i-defaulted-on-my-student-loans.html?_r=0

Slaughter, S., & Rhoades, G. (2004). *Academic capitalism and the new economy: Markets, state, and higher education.* Baltimore: Johns Hopkins University Press.

Stiglitz, J. (2013). *The price of inequality: How today's divided society endangers our future.* New York: W.W. Horton & Company.

Stone, C., Van Horn, C., & Zukin, C. (2012). *Chasing the American dream: Recent college graduates and the great recession.* New Brunswick, NJ: Rutgers University, John J. Heldrich Center for Workforce Development. Retrieved from www.heldrich.rutgers.edu/sites/default/files/products/uploads/Chasing_American_Dream_Report.pdf

Surowiecki, J. (2005). *The wisdom of crowds.* New York: Anchor.

Tasini. (2011, May 24). Two trillion in corporate welfare: Start here. *Daily KOS.* Retrieved from www.dailykos.com/story/2011/05/24/978756/-Two-Trillion-In-Corporate-Welfare-Start-Here#

U.S. Government Accountability Office (GAO). (2014). *Older Americans: Inability to repay student loans may affect financial security of a small percentage of retirees.* Retrieved from www.gao.gov/assets/670/665709.pdf

Vershbow, B. (2013). NYPL labs: Hacking the library. *Journal of Library Administration, 53*(1), 79–96.

Vogel, M. (2015). Crowdfunding human capital contracts. *Cardozo Law Review, 36*(4), 1577–1609. Retrived from http://cardozolawreview.com/content/36-4/VOGEL.36.4.pdf

Weissmann, J. (2015, June 8). The *New York Times* should apologize for the awful op-ed it just ran on student loans. *Slate.* Retrieved from www.slate.com/blogs/moneybox/2015/06/08/lee_siegel_new_york_times_op_ed_is_this_the_worst_op_ed_ever_written_about.html

Wilkinson, R., & Pickett, K. (2010). *The spirit level: Why greater equality makes societies stronger.* New York: Bloomsbury Press.

Williams, B. (2004). *Debt for sale: A social history of the credit trap.* Philadelphia: University of Pennsylvania Press.

Wright, G., & Gallegos, S. (2014, September 24). Despite lower rates, more than 650,000 defaulted on federal student loans: For-profit colleges account for nearly half of all defaults. *The Institute of College Access & Success.* Retrieved from www.ticas.org/files/pub//CDR_2014_NR.pdf

Yi, A. (2014). Reforming the student debt market: Income-related repayment plans or risk based loans? *Virginia Journal of Social Policy & the Law, 21*(3), 511–546.

Zerobound. (2017). *Homepage.* Retrieved from www.zerobound.com/

15 Monetary Transformation and Public Education

Lucille L. T. Eckrich

Introduction

It should be clear that our monetary system and the commerce it serves do not have to be as they presently are (see Chapter 4, this volume); they just are this way. Looking back, one can understand how they came to be. At first gradually and, due to its systemic flaws, increasing exponentially, modern money tapped into and was fueled by latent potential, human and otherwise, that was there for the "taking and trading" in the last millennium as long as the potential lasted (Eckrich, 1998; Heinberg, 2003; Jacobs, 1992); and modern money served, at least eventually, although then only initially and not equitably, the interests of the people and societies through whom it gained dominance. In other words, "modern money mechanics" (Gonczy, 1992) was not some sinister plot. Rather it was, or was viewed by an increasing majority to be, in the interest of all as it came to be practiced, legalized, normalized, and institutionalized, even if the long-range vision (Aristotle, 1813; Langholm, 1992) or keen analysis (Del Mar, 1895, 1896; Douglas, Fisher, Graham, Hamilton, King, & Whittlesey, 1939; Fisher, 1935; Gesell, 1916/1958; Soddy, 1931, 1934) of monetary observers detected otherwise. The latter recognized that, unbeknownst to the normative majority, modern money is unsustainable and increasingly serves the net interests of the wealthiest at the expense of everyone else and the public purse.

But understanding why monetary matters remain this way is harder, especially going forward, because the flaw in our monetary relations is hidden in increasingly plain sight. This gives me and other monetary transformers hope that thoughtful people on all sides of the aisle—tea party member and Bernie Sanders supporter, conservative and socialist, middle class and underclass, management and labor, first world and third world, white collar and blue collar, European and African, native American and Asian, northern and southern, schooled and unschooled, educated and uneducated, consumer and producer, industrialist and environmentalist, scientist and artist, bureaucrat and technocrat, Christian and Muslim, Hindu and Buddhist, Jew and Confucian, religious and nonreligious, gay and straight, pro-life and pro-choice, indigenous and cosmopolitan, Republican and Democrat,

Libertarian and Green, to name only a few of the many aisles that connect us—can come to understand and critically coalesce around monetary transformation, which, as one of many possible paths to the future, is arguably the only route worth working and fighting for (I hope nonviolently) because it identifies and supersedes the *systemic* source of modernity's problems.

While superseding modern money won't on its own solve modern problems of hunger, thirst, inequity, poverty, war, racism, sexism, environmental degradation, species extinction, human and drug trafficking, money laundering, global warming, the school-to-prison-pipeline, deficit spending, and student debt, again to name only a few, it creates the conditions of the possibility of our doing so through subsequent mindful and ethical human decision-making so we can *all* move on to flourishing, collectively and individually. Such conditions currently do not exist because all human decision-making in the modern era is, sooner or later, subordinate and subservient to the exponential growth imperative built into our exchange relations through modern money. Thus, without monetary transformation, all our nonetheless needed and well-intending attempts to address any of these problems are Sisyphean tasks that, combined with modernity's press for ever-increasing productivity, keep us very busy and our eyes off the prize.

For this reason, this chapter advocates monetary reform in order to solve the student debt crisis. I begin by describing the two kinds—or levels—of monetary reform being worked on today and their implications for funding public education. After explaining why I advocate macro-level reform first, foremost, and necessarily, I lay out a strategy for its pursuit, one that works on educational and political fronts at national, international, local, and regional levels.

Macro-Level Monetary Reform and Transformation

Macro-level monetary reform is necessary in order to supersede our private-interest-driven debt-based monetary system and end its increasingly devastating ecological and dehumanizing effects. Such reform will also allow for new revenue streams for whichever public goods the people whose name the money bears democratically decide to fund, which in many societies will likely include public education at all levels preschool through adult. Unless "the end of the nation-state" (Guéhenno, 1995) happens, the province for macro monetary reform is the federal/national/central government of any and every sovereign nation on earth. As long as a nation's constitution establishes the creation and regulation of its money to be the prerogative, domain, power, and responsibility of its national/federal/central government, as the U.S. Constitution (Section 8 of Article 1) arguably does, monetary reform is a congressional or parliamentary matter of its national/federal/central government. In this case, citizens must elect representatives and senators or parliamentarians who introduce and pass the kind of monetary reform we need, as detailed below. If a nation's constitution is unclear on money matters, the route is the same; however, the constitutionality of any monetary reform act passed may be challenged, in which case its implementation may be delayed while it is adjudicated through the Supreme Court. If a constitution is silent or ambiguous on money matters, that nation's legislators may be free to act according to the will of the people or whomever they are beholden to unless that nation clarifies or amends its constitution. So, no matter which of these situations a nation is in, macro-level monetary transformation requires drafting, introducing, co-sponsoring, lobbying for, and passing national monetary reform legislation, even if, in some places, it may also entail constitutional amendment. While some activists may not put much stock in legislative campaigns (Strike Debt, 2014, p. 211), in the final analysis, even when direct action and mass mobilization are necessary or deemed more effective than citizen lobbying, a new law—the right new law—will sooner or later be necessary unless we give up on democracy and the rule of law entirely. I, for one, cannot.

So, what monetary reform legislation do we need? Fortunately, significant work on this is already well underway in many countries, including but not limited to the United States, all of which has precedence in depression-era proposals (Douglas et al., 1939; Fisher, 1935; Soddy, 1931, 1934) that reform efforts today draw on and build upon. In the wake of Iceland's devastating financial collapse in 2008, its Prime Minister commissioned two studies of monetary reform in order to come up with "a better monetary system for Iceland" (Sigurjónsson, 2015; Thoroddsen & Sigurjónsson, 2016). The resulting reports advocate the "sovereign money proposal" first articulated by Huber and Robertson (2000) in *Creating New Money: A Monetary Reform for the Information Age*. Such a proposal is also being worked on in England, as laid out by Jackson and Dyson (2013) in *Modernising Money: Why Our Monetary System is Broken and How It Can Be Fixed*, which is also cited in the Iceland reports. Dyson founded England's Positive Money (PM) campaign that is helping to draft legislation for England (PM, 2013) and doing extensive educational organizing work in preparation for its introduction in parliament.

In addition to Huber's (2017) *Sovereign Money: Beyond Reserve Banking*, the most cutting-edge monetary reform work to date is going on in the Netherlands and Switzerland, the former as a member of the European Union (EU), including its Economic and Monetary Union (i.e., the Eurozone), and the latter as a non-member. In the Netherlands, the "Ons Geld" (Our Money) citizens' initiative successfully petitioned their parliament in March 2016 to embark upon a study "to investigate and elaborate in greater detail the option to have money creation returned to public hands" (Wortmann, 2016, p. 2). This work is now well underway. In Switzerland, employing a unique direct-democracy instrument in the Swiss Constitution called Volksinitiative (Peoples' Initiative), Swiss citizens successfully collected, within the required 18-month period of time, well over the 100,000 valid signatures necessary to put a proposal for changing a specific provision of the Swiss Constitution up for a national vote. This particular initiative, called "Vollgeld" (full money), was achieved in December 2015 and will be voted on in a national referendum in 2017 or 2018. It proposes extending the Swiss Federation's existing exclusive right to create coins and notes to bank deposits as well, ending commercial banks' power to create money through lending. If passed, the Swiss National Bank's primary role and responsibility will be managing the money supply relative to the productive economy, while decisions concerning how all new money is introduced debt-free into the economy will reside with the government, and decisions regarding checking, saving, and loan accounts in banks will reside with those who use and offer these banking services. Such macro-level monetary reform efforts are also under discussion in Japan (Yamaguchi, n.d.) and in 24 countries so far (including the four named above) whose citizens are connecting in an international movement for monetary reform.[1]

While there remains much educational, organizing, coalition-building, and lobbying work to do in the United States, technically monetary reform efforts are as advanced here as anywhere. Monetary reform legislation is already written and was first introduced as H.R. 2990 on September 21, 2011, by Representatives Dennis Kucinich (D-OH) and John Conyers (D-MI) during the 112th Congress. Called the National Emergency Employment Defense Act (the NEED Act), this bill addresses many of the objectives of the Occupy movement and may be further strengthened when reintroduced. When passed, this macro-level monetary reform legislation not only will enable the creation of direly needed public infrastructure, valuable jobs, and public goods like education and health care, but will fundamentally change the U.S. monetary system through the following three mechanisms. My summary is based on those of Zarlenga (2011, 2014) who founded the American Monetary Institute (AMI), which was instrumental in the research behind the NEED Act (Zarlenga, 2002).

First, the NEED Act (or whatever its successor legislation is titled) disentangles the Federal Reserve System (a set of private banks that together comprise our central bank) and reincorporates the money-creation and -monitoring parts into the U.S. Treasury where all new money will be created as money (not by banks as interest-bearing debt lent into circulation, as currently happens) and spent into circulation to promote the general welfare and public good, its supply monitored overtime by the governmental monetary authority to be neither inflationary or deflationary.

Second, through its accounting rule changes, the NEED Act halts banks' privilege to create money by ending the fractional reserve system (which is the legalized mechanism that allows banks currently to create what we use as money every time they make a loan) in a gentle and elegant way. All past monetized bank credit is converted into U.S. government money, as are treasury securities as they come due, and banks are held accountable for this conversion. Banks then act as intermediaries, accepting checking and savings or time deposits, and loaning the latter out to borrowers—doing what people think banks now do—but doing so with already existing money and in the same manner as any other commercial entity does its business: by charging a fee for goods or services the price of which revolves around their cost of producing them.

Finally, through the NEED Act, the U.S. government creates (originates) all new U.S. money in accord with democratic budgetary processes of Congress and *spends* it into circulation as needed (probably in large measure as digital dollars) to build postmodern public infrastructure, including for public education, healthcare, and $3 trillion for work that the American Society of Civil Engineers (ASCE) estimates is needed over the next five years for infrastructure repair and development (like fixing bridges, roads, bike paths, clean water, sewage, levees, high speed public transportation, public utilities and facilities, recycling, conservation, etc.). The jobs created through doing all this, and other democratically determined investment in the public interest over time, will re-invigorate regional and local economies without new debt and improve the lives of families and communities as well as their tax-base.

In short, the NEED Act nationalizes the money system, not the banking system. Banking is not a proper function of government, but only government can and must be responsible to provide and secure a nation's money supply. Inflation is avoided because real material or cultural wealth is created in the process and the total quantity of money can be known and monitored in real time. Research and development of superior pollution-free, environmentally sustainable, and humanizing, rather than dehumanizing, technologies is facilitated. At long last, we the people and our elected officials will no longer be subservient to and working for the banks to whom a prior generation of insufficiently educated or conscientious lawmakers ceded our government's money power and responsibility.

Meso-Level Monetary Reform

While macro monetary reform in the public interest is necessary, the earliest and, until recently, most numerous of today's monetary reformers focused their efforts at meso-level reforms. While they share a macro-level critique, their response has focused on grassroots social change and democratic exchange relations by creating alternative or complementary currencies or a community exchange system at local and regional levels. My own entry into the realm of monetary reform for the 21st Century began at this level through reading Margrit Kennedy's (1995) *Interest and Inflation Free Money*, which I learned about and read shortly before meeting this German author at the 2004 "Local Currencies in the 21st Century" conference. This international conference was sponsored by the then 24-year-old E. F. Schumacher Society, which has since evolved, in partnership with the London-based New Economics Foundation (NEF, founded 1986), into two organizations, Schumacher Center for a New Economics (SCNE), an education- and practice-oriented group focused regionally in New England, and the New Economics Institute (NEI), a more continental action-oriented group that went on to sponsor the 2012 "Strategies for a New Economy Conference," which I also attended, and that subsequently merged with another activist organization to form the New Economy Coalition, which focuses to this day on connecting and amplifying "new economy" organizing across the United States and Canada. While these are just a few of the many organizations around the world today seeking economic justice and environmental sustainability, surfing even just their websites (retrievable by name) reveals that a movement for economic transformation is growing.

A significant component of this movement is alternative or complementary currencies at local and regional levels. These community-created currencies "complement" or supplement the national currency in the locale where each circulates among all who choose to use it. It serves to stimulate that economy by connecting otherwise unemployed human resources with unmet human needs. Such currencies act, as all money should, as a transaction lubricant and tangibly improve the quality of life, especially in communities where significant numbers of people are unemployed or underemployed and/or lack sufficient supplies of the national currency. They also teach participants about balanced exchange relations through mutually supportive enterprise and get them thinking about the nature of money. I think those that manage to become "tax-foundation" currencies (Eckrich, 2004; Greco, 2001, p. 69) or a "community exchange system" (CES, 2017) most fully embody and, thus, best teach about the nature of money *sui generis*.

Although I've gone no farther than theorizing them, I've conceived two arguably feasible and legal (Solomon, 1996) tax-foundation complementary currencies that would be spent into circulation through public school districts in a county (Eckrich, 2007) or a state (Eckrich, 2016), circulate parallel to the U.S. dollar within that county or state as partial payment for locally produced goods and services, and be receivable back as partial payment for property and/or income taxes a year later. If such a county- or state-wide complementary currency is successful, the county or state could eventually denominate a portion of its contribution to public school pension funds in that currency, as it could be used for locally provided elder care as already happens in the Netherlands and Japan.[2] Given Illinois' dismal finances and underfunded pensions, it is no small matter that civil servants here had to join the public pension fund system in lieu of federal social security when taking the job. Unless macro-level monetary reform comes first, the statewide complementary currency I propose (Eckrich, 2016) may be what Illinois citizens and politicians need to resolve the budgetary and constitutional crises the state is facing (see Chapter 3, this volume). It will also enable Illinois to demonstrate "the case for a system of local currencies" (Solomon, 1996) and to become a leader for monetary reform for the nation as a whole.

Another education-related complementary currency was theorized for Brazil by Belgian monetary reformer Bernard Lietaer (2006) and widely publicized by Kennedy (2012, pp. 70–74) with whom he collaborated for years. Though never implemented, and ironic in that it was to be funded from a windfall from the privatization of the Brazilian telecommunication system, which did take place to the benefit of national and multinational companies (Boechat, 2015; Casanova, 2016), the proposal is novel in its own right and worth considering. Called "Sabers," this education currency would support primary and secondary education directly, and public higher education indirectly. Its objective "is to increase the learning capacity as well as strengthen the social coherence of Brazilian society, by enabling a learning multiplier effect without risking inflationary pressures in the economy as a whole" (Lietaer, 2006, p. 19). Based on informed projections by public universities of their future enrollment capacity, including through online distance learning, a certain amount of Sabers would be distributed yearly by the government through primary schools in economically weak communities to students who use them to pay for tutoring from older students who, after providing those services, can in turn use them to pay for tutoring they need from even older students. This could occur through several more rounds before being earned by students ready for tertiary education who would use the Sabers for tuition at public universities, which would redeem them 2:1 for national currency from the government. Through this each-one-teach-one model, younger students learn from older students who learn better through teaching their juniors who eventually become tutors themselves and earn the means to pay for higher education that they could not otherwise afford. Sabers would be dated and officially redeemable in a particular academic year, although, if unused, they could be exchanged for Sabers redeemable the next academic year with a 20% penalty in order both to encourage their circulation by giving an incentive not to hoard them beyond their deadline and to ensure the number of university students is not erratic (Lietaer, 2006, p. 23).

More can be read about complementary currencies—variously referred to as community, alternative, complementary, local, regional, or parallel currencies and reportedly growing globally from two in 1984 to thousands by 2010—on the websites of SCNE and NEF and many other organizations.[3] While their development confirms the inadequacy of our existing monetary system, their existence today may also have the consequence of propping up that system, and the damage it does, for yet another day. That, in my view, is a serious charge with dire consequences. Fortunately, I also think it can and will be remedied when (1) those involved in local and regional currencies come to understand that superseding the unnecessary, unethical, and unsustainable flaw at the heart of their national and our now international private-interest-driven debt-based monetary system is a necessary, even if perhaps not sufficient, condition of the new economy they seek, and (2) those involved in transforming a national currency acknowledge that regionally and/or locally created currencies are not inconsistent with, nor necessarily preempted by, macro-level transformation as long as those currencies are issued and managed by democratic units of regional or local government for use in their locales alongside the national currency. While Joseph Huber, Monetative members, and I, among others, exemplify the latter, I am confident that there will be increasing numbers of the former because, shortly before she passed away in 2013, Margrit Kennedy, an architect and urban planner by training and Professor of Ecological Building Technologies, responded to my critique of her omission of macro-level monetary reform in her 2012 book *Occupy Money: Creating an Economy Where Everybody Wins*. She wrote "you are absolutely right about your critique" (personal communication, November 6, 2013) and sent me the link to one of her last recorded lectures where she fills in her prior omission.[4]

In light of the growing consensus on the necessity of macro-level monetary reform, the remainder of this chapter lays out a strategy for achieving it. If the Chicago Cubs and their fans can win after 108 years of trying, we the people should be able to reform our monetary system in the same number of years. That leaves us until 2021 to get macro-level monetary reform accomplished.

Strategy for Achieving Macro-Level Monetary Reform

A combination of educational, networking and coalition building, and political work and activism is needed to achieve monetary reform in the United States through passing the NEED Act or its successor legislation. Doing so will enable us to eliminate student debt once and for all. While in reality these avenues of work must go hand-in-hand, especially the first two, for simplicity sake I detail them one by one.

Education for Monetary Reform and Transformation

Education about money and the monetary system we have and the one we need and how to get it is necessary in order to achieve monetary reform democratically and nonviolently. Once enough citizens understand the way the monetary system is today and how it can be superseded for the common good, we will be able to muster the collective political power to bring about the latter.

Before laying out a strategy for this educational work, it is instructive to look back and see how Americans came to be so ignorant about money, because this wasn't always the case. In the 1800s if not before, money matters were publicly discussed and often addressed in the platforms of the multiple political parties that comprised politics back then (Hawkins, 2015; Lause, 1991, 2001, 2016; Zarlenga, 2002). Even in my town of Bloomington, IL, there was a chapter of the Independent Greenback Party in the 1870s–1880s; and in nearby Chicago the struggle for the eight-hour work day was being waged through direct action (Roediger & Foner, 1989). But as the massification of secondary schooling started around the turn of the century, one major curricular decision was made to stupefy rather than educate pupils. In 1892 the National Education Association, which itself had started in 1857 but gained traction only in 1884, formed "the Committee of Ten," an ad hoc curriculum committee of six college or university professors, five of them presidents, and four administrators of prominent secondary schools, one of whom had just become the fourth Commissioner of Education of the United States (Krug, 1964). Its task was to consider uniform requirements for college admission so as to delineate the purpose and courses of study for the growing number of high schools. Each committee member other than the chair (the then-president of Harvard) led a conference on December 28–30, 1892, in a different locale to discuss one part of the curriculum with ten additional university or school men who were experts in that field. The conference on history, civil government, and political economy met in Madison, Wisconsin. One of its members was Woodrow Wilson, then a 36-year-old professor of history who argued that "scientific history, involving criticism and examination of evidence, had no place in the schools, for it tended to confuse young pupils. Scientific history, he declared, was college work and not school work" (Krug, 1964, p. 54). While that proposition fortunately didn't survive, another resolution Wilson moved passed unanimously: It "excluded formal instruction in political economy from school programs" (Krug, 1964, p. 54). This explains why public high schools in the United States raised generations of students who know and think nothing about money and monetary systems. That this resolution was proposed by someone who not only went on to become president of Princeton University and then president of the United States but who signed the Federal Reserve Act into law is indicative of the well-paved road to internalized oppression (Freire, 2000) and "schooling in capitalist America" (Bowles & Gintis, 1976) that the vast majority of Americans have trod for more than a century now.

So, how do we educate the public on monetary critique and reform? One way is for high school and college teachers of social studies, history, sociology, economics, anthropology, business and accounting, political science, and foundations of education to teach about it while and after studying it themselves. Even though monetary reformers have come from other fields too (e.g., chemistry, architecture, engineering, agriculture, physics, theatre, law, public administration, medicine, and ministry) because all work butts against our monetary system, the subjects listed above are all ones in which human exchange relations and power relations are central phenomena, and, thus, monetary matters belong in their curriculum. We need to make up for lost time in public schools by uncovering and reclaiming the lost history and science of money and bringing them up to date, and engage high school and college students in doing so. The reference lists and endnotes in this and my earlier chapter provide a sound launching pad for such study. A unit about our monetary system within our ecosystem will enable connections to be made throughout the rest of the course. Graduate programs in these disciplines should develop an entire class devoted to monetary critique and reform *vis-à-vis* their field, and use this systems framework as a lens through which students and faculty might understand their entire program.

To nurture the educated and critically-minded populace we need, education on monetary critique and reform must move beyond formal school settings into churches, neighborhood organizations, union halls, civics associations, professional societies, book clubs, and social groups like fraternities, sororities, and other co-curricular organizations. An increasing number of video, PowerPoint, and presentation resources exist online through the myriad monetary reform and new economy websites, so newcomers to monetary reform need not recreate the wheel when getting ready to teach others. For instance, the "Ons Geld" monetary reform group in the Netherlands currently has videos from the U.K. and U.S. monetary reform groups on its own website,[5] not because it can't produce or hasn't produced its own—it can and has many—but because they are good ones that "Ons Geld" goes on to discuss in Dutch. While it may feel daunting to teach others about the counter-intuitive money that modern banking has saddled and rides us with, remember that—as the Saber proposal brilliantly reflects—the best way to really learn something is to have to teach it to others.

In terms of the medium, the arts are invaluable for communicating the monetary message for both educational and political purposes. For example, "[i]n the Netherlands, a popular theatre show inspired by monetary reformers raised monetary awareness. In cooperation with the Dutch NGO "Ons Geld" the actors managed to put the subject on the national agenda" via a citizens' initiative, "supported by 120,000 Dutch citizens," that moved the Dutch parliament to embark upon "closer inquiries into the workings of the current monetary system and its alternatives" (Wortmann, 2016, pp. 2, 1).[6] In the United States, Howard Switzer, an architect and a founding member of the Green Party (GP) of Tennessee and delegate to the national GP, wrote and performs a blue grass song called "Gotta Get a New Kind of Money!" now available on YouTube.[7] Word is, a hip-hop version is being produced as well. While popular culture can easily be misused to skew a message and distract the populace, such as seems to be happening with the Broadway and off-Broadway musical "Hamilton," artists wholly devoted to their crafts tend to dig deep to the source when they create a work of art, so engaging genuine artists in learning about monetary issues will surely bear good fruit.

Finally, it is important that monetary reformers continue to study, research, and educate themselves and each other on monetary matters past, present, and future, at home and abroad, including to improve both monetary reform legislation before it is (re)introduced and the plans for its implementation over the subsequent 10 to 15 year transition or "migration" (Wortmann, 2016, p. 6) to a transformed or new monetary system. Even if we have gotten many crucial factors right, it does not mean there is nothing we have yet to learn, correct, or improve upon. Becoming doctrinaire about monetary reform is a death sentence to it. Staying critically open while keeping our eyes clearly on the prize of systems change through systems thinking is crucial if we are to educate rather than indoctrinate. The latter is never sound ground for building a movement for socio-economic change because it is off-putting and discourages collaboration and may even lead groups down a dead-end.

That said, powers that be today also see reformers' writing on the wall and the current system's inherent flaws, and some are trying to revamp the public-private partnership[8] of modern money in ways that recreate or further entrench it in their private interest at public expense (Ricks, 2016). Since Citizens United, and with recent global trade agreements, they have more means than ever on their side. Public-private partnership, along with internationalization (in English, mind you), is the neoliberal language and ideology increasingly common among well-intending but shortsighted and hard-pressed leaders of colleges, universities, and public schools—especially those "of choice"—across the United States today. Monetary reformers in the public interest, who go radically to the root or source of modernity's systemic problem in order to achieve properly grounded exchange relations and post-modern commerce, must both stay united and work to bring increasing numbers of both the oppressed majority and the powers that be to our side and through the funnel of monetary reform to a sustainable and just future. We must enact that traditional American folk song, which goes back to the first abolition era, as we abolish or supersede modern money and sing in unity:

> We shall not, we shall not be moved
> We shall not, we shall not be moved
> Just like a tree that's standing by the water
> We shall not be moved

As the Rev. Dr. Charles Albert Tindley, Pete Seeger, and the Rev. Dr. Martin Luther King sang in action before us and as the Rev. Dr. Delman Coates leads us in song and action today, "We shall overcome. We shall overcome. Deep in our hearts we do believe, we shall overcome someday."[9]

Networking, Organizing, and Coalition-Building for Monetary Reform and Transformation

Building a movement for systemic change requires building bridges to every constituency that shares some common goals, values, or interests with monetary reform. While doing so must not lead to compromise on fundamental features of the reform, it should seek common ground and shared territory in the quest for achieving that reform. We must "move the moveable middle" and realize that:

> Keeping the public divided along racial, religious, ideological, and partisan lines does nothing but serve the interests of the money power by distracting the American people from the underlying causes of social and economic despair. Monetary reform provides a critical unifying metanarrative for those concerned about addressing injustice and expanding American prosperity beyond the financial elite.
>
> (Coates, 2016)

As the second and third paragraphs of this chapter suggest, there are myriad constituencies with which monetary reformers share common ground. Of course, and fortunately, monetary reform groups in the United States and worldwide are already doing much outreach and coalition-building, and concerned citizens from all walks of life find their way daily—whether through word-of-mouth, the World Wide Web, films and other media, or books like this—to monetary reform because of its inherent logic and moral imperative. Both mainstream associations and groups on the margins must be on our networking radar screen. Once their members become informed, there must be room for varied degrees of individual and organizational involvement in the movement for monetary reform and for the political economic, social, and environmental transformation to which monetary reform can and will lead as long as we continue to do the educational and political work to take it there.

While there is definitely a need for more half- and full-time organizers and activists for macro-level monetary reform—and the material means to support them, whether in national and/or complementary currencies from both large and small donors and/or through in-kind donations like housing, office space, technical support, food, and healthcare—we also need myriad constituencies at local, regional, and national levels to learn about and then vote whether to endorse monetary reform legislation and/or citizens' initiatives in pursuit of such legislation. Like the Chicago Teachers Union (CTU) and the Green Party have already done, hundreds and then thousands of informed organizational constituencies need to fill in their own identity before the stem of "for Monetary Reform" and vote collectively—at local, regional, and national levels—to sign on to macro-level monetary reform.[10] Associations of teachers, educational administrators, farmers, environmentalists, electricians, artists, NBA players, librarians, economists, Marxists, Catholics, native peoples, nurses, doctors, lawyers, civil servants, veterans, fastfood workers, civil engineers, sanitation workers, architects, critical race theorists, and so on . . . *all* for monetary reform. Signatories may start at any level—local, regional, state, or national—of trade unions, professional associations, religious organizations, civic groups, and countless other nationwide bodies and then encourage other chapters or levels of their organization to sign on too, doing the organizational and educational work it takes to make that happen and sending their petitions to their elected officials and movement organizers. With such a groundswell of political support, which itself need not take much time away from the important agendas of those organizations, they will be playing a crucial role in passing legislation that can and will create the political economic conditions that will support their achievement of their own specific goals, values, and interests.

Lastly, branding and marketing monetary reform in ways that are wellinformed, credibly grounded, and culturally catchy will make our organizing work and coalition-building easier and more effective. Other countries' monetary reform movements are ahead of the United States' in this regard, but creative and media savvy monetary reformers, hopefully including young people who got their start with the currently marginalized Occupy Movement, the now vibrant and steadfast Black Lives Matter Movement, or myriad social entrepreneurship initiatives will help to remedy this. One-liners and elevator speeches—"money for all not money for some"—are needed that catch people's attention, with a few clear talking points to follow-up with for those who can listen longer. Short presentations and full-blown workshops and study groups must follow close behind and be easy enough to follow, learn from, and build upon in an each-one-teach-one manner. Thoughtfully and strategically permeating local, regional, and national media in print, on air, and online, including via blogs and other social media, with comments and questions posted or called in, letters to the editor, and articles of our own is a crucial part of our educational and organizing work. But it should not consume all our time and energy such that we don't get to the direct action we need to bring about monetary reform and political economic transformation for the public good.

Political Work and Activism for Monetary Reform and Transformation

Finally, although much else may be learned and gained in the process, the point of our networking, organizing, and coalescing is to bring about monetary reform and transformation through inclusive democratic and non-violent but direct means. Direct action means lobbying both personally and collectively and, as necessary, escalating our political pressure through solidarity marches, mass lobbying events, disciplined protests, and strategic civil disobedience. Since time is of the essence, given the exponential growth imperative built into our current economic system, direct action must comprise the bulk of our political work. But because successful lobbying depends in part on whom we are lobbying, our political work should include some attention to which people and parties we elect to represent us.

The 2016 U.S. elections should be a sobering yet encouraging wake-up call to the fact that the majority of U.S. citizens are not represented through our two-party moneyed politics and their media sidekicks (Frank, 2016) and are in search of representation. Thus, while monetary reform constituencies must work with due haste to move whomever we've got in office at present to co-sponsor and pass genuine monetary reform, we must also look to existing or new third and fourth parties to take up the mantle of monetary reform and then vote them into office. We can and should find courage and lessons for doing so from our own history (Lause, 2001), from the international movement for monetary reform, and from party politics in general elsewhere in the world. At the very least, we must insist that parties who do what it takes to get their candidates on the ballot get a place at the debate table and fair coverage by the media. Who among us gave the Commission on Presidential Debates and the mainstream media and pollsters the authority to exclude and marginalize third- and fourth-party voices in our so-called democracy? But more than getting all parties heard can be expected of and by us.

Once enough of us coalesce around monetary reform as the best if not only funnel to a just and sustainable future, listening to and, as warranted, supporting parties other than the dominant two can only be beneficial, at least indirectly if not also directly, for that cause and all the others we care about. Indirectly, it puts pressure on the dominant parties and their candidates up for (re)election to answer to or take up monetary reform. If that works, great; the third party that had monetary reform on its platform will have served a great historical purpose. To the extent that it doesn't work, the third party that best understands and advocates monetary reform in the public interest will, with our support, grow in popularity and, eventually, gain more and more representatives in office, representatives who will co-sponsor and pass monetary reform. Thus, listening to and even voting for a monetary reform party, such as we already have in the Green Party, never warrants the charge of "spoiler" or "wasted votes," as liberals and too many progressives uncritically claim. In my view, at least once its primary season was over, the 2016 U.S. presidential campaign was a missed opportunity for progressives, conservatives, and critically reflective liberals to overcome their media-induced, self-centered, or short-sighted fears and look at, and encourage others and the media to look at, the third- and fourth-party candidates and their platforms. Though we're doing it the hard way, I hope we've learned this lesson and start now to do otherwise for the upcoming election cycles.

Finally, come what may, the struggle for monetary reform in the public interest is unlikely to be won merely through letter-writing and petitions to our legislators, although for sure we need those methods in mass and will celebrate if they suffice. But this struggle has already taken and will continue to require serious and abiding effort, well-informed conviction, and even sacrifice on the part of an increasing number of people until we become a critical mass able to spread like wildfire throughout this land. The potential for reactionary violence within our ranks but even more so in reaction to us is grave but not inevitable nor insurmountable. Our organized and ethical discipline along with ongoing education and mindfulness will be crucial as we engage in higher profile direct action that seems inevitable in a serious social movement for systemic change. How many marches and protests, not to mention how much civil disobedience, will be needed to secure monetary reform and enduring political economic transformation for the common good is unknown except in retrospect. This "new abolitionism" (Coates, 2016) or new "civil resistance movement" (Coleridge, 2016) will draw strength, wisdom, and inspiration from the abolition and civil rights movements that came before us as we stand on their shoulders and make good on their sacrifice while giving our children and theirs firm, diverse, and plentiful shoulders to stand upon as they flourish.

Notes

1   The Netherlands' "Ons Geld" is online @ http://onsgeld.nu/. Switzerland's Vollgeld Initiative in English is online @ www.vollgeld-initiative.ch/english/; the tripartite MoMo movement behind the Swiss initiative is online in their three

national languages @ www.vollgeld.ch/index.php. The international movement for monetary reform is online at http://internationalmoneyreform.org/.

2 Read about Troeven in the Netherlands @ www.qoin.com/, and about Fureai Kippu ('Ticket for a Caring Relationship') currencies in Japan in Hayash (2012).

3 See http://complementarycurrency.org/, a network through which, as of February 2017, 310 complementary currencies (CC) from around the world have registered, since it began in October 2004; www.lietaer.com/2010/09/what-are-complementary-currencies/, which reports that there are now thousands of CC world-wide up from two in 1984, but see Hayash (2012) for research on CCs in Japan that started in the 1970s; http://monneta.org/, a not-for-profit educational organization founded in 2003 by Kennedy devoted to overcoming economic illiteracy on monetary matters, especially but not only through CCs; www.qoin.com/, a CC group in the Netherlands that started numerous successful CCs there and provides technical support for their development elsewhere; http://iflas.blogspot.co.uk/, the Institute for Leadership and Sustainability at the University of Cumbria which offers a MOOC on Money and Society (http://iflas.blogspot.co.uk/2014/12/money-and-society-mooc.html); and https://ijccr.net/, website of the *International Journal of Community Currency Research* which began in 1997 and was subsumed into the Research Association on Monetary Innovation and Community and Complementary Currency Systems (https://ramics.org/) when it formed in 2015. Two of the earliest CCs in the U.S. were Ithaca Hours (www.ithacahours.com/) started by Paul Glover in 1991, and Time Dollars (http://timebanks.org/) started by Dr. Edgar S. Cahn in 1995. Unlike most CCs, the latter function parallel to (i.e., are not exchangeable for) U.S. dollars. They are still going strong perhaps because, based on a concept in tax law called "imputed income," they have been ruled in two courts to be tax-exempt due to "the non-contractual nature of the exchanges; the charitable purposes advanced; and the focus of the program on rebuilding family, neighborhood, and community" (http://timebanks.org/faq/). A more recent CC in the U.S. is Berkshares (www.berkshares.org/), started in rural MA in 2006 by SCNE. See https://transitionnetwork.org/ for information on myriad "Transition Towns" across the world many of which have started local currencies as part of their efforts. Even mainstream CNN has noticed CCs; see Ellis (2012) which reviews Berkshares, Ithaca Hours, and nine other CCs in U.S. cities including Philadelphia, Portland, Seattle, Washington, D.C, Brooklyn, New Orleans, and three other smaller cities in that many states. Corporate loyalty programs, such as frequent flyer miles, are also forms of CCs. That they are now ubiquitous may suggest that CCs serve to maintain more than threaten the existing private-interest-driven debt-based monetary regime.

4 This German lecture is called "Ist der Euro noch zu retten? Ein Vergleich zwischen Chiemgauer und Euro"—and was presented by Prof. Margrit Kennedy on May 4, 2013, for the 10th anniversary of one of the earliest and successful local currencies in Germany, the Chiemgauer, which was started by secondary school students inspired in part by Kennedy's work. It is available online @ https://www.youtube.com/watch?v=oXOeKaGXQRk. For specific reference to macro-level monetary reform, see the third lesson (Lösung 3) at about minute #11.27.

5 See https://onsgeld.nu/blog/99/verslag-ami-conferentie-door-edgar-wortmann. If that link is no longer current, go to the Ons Geld homepage @ http://onsgeld.nu/ and surf around this very well constructed website.

6 See De Verlieders (2015-2017), www.de-verleiders.nl/doordebankgenomen/

7 See Switzer (2016), https://www.youtube.com/watch?v=aYx6RUHfva4

8 Such neoliberal public-private partnership is typified and well represented today by the World Economic Forum, online @ https://www.weforum.org/.

9 The history of this song can be easily found online. The work of the Rev. Dr. Delman Coates and others at the Black Church Center for Justice & Equality is online at www.theblackchurch.org

10 A copy of the Chicago Teachers Union's January 9, 2012, "Resolution to Support the National Employment Emergency Defense (NEED) Act, H.R. 2990" is available upon request. See http://greensformonetaryreform.org/ for information on the Green Party Platform's endorsement of it.

References

Aristotle. (1813). *Ethics* (J. Gillies, trans., 3rd ed.). London: T. Cadell and W. Davies. Retrieved from https://www.hathitrust.org/

Boechat, L. (2015, August 12). Mobile telephone expansion in Brazil. *TechInBrazil*. Retrieved from http://techinbrazil.com/mobile-telephone-expansion-in-brazil

Bowles, S., & Gintis, H. (1976). *Schooling in capitalist America: Educational reform and the contradictions of economic life.* New York: Basic Books.

Casanova, L. (2016, June 13). What is the future of telecommunications in Latin America? *World Economic Forum*. Retrieved from https://www.weforum.org/agenda/2016/06/has-telecom-privatization-in-latin-america-been-a-success/

Coates, D. (2016, October 1). *The new abolitionism: Money reform and the struggle for civil rights.* Paper presented at the 12th annual conference of the American Monetary Institute, Chicago, IL. Retrieved from https://www.youtube.com/watch?v=n_bhClx-mPw

Coleridge, G. (2016, October 1). *The power elite's 10 strategies opposing monetary reform.* Paper presented at the 12th annual conference of the American Monetary Institute, Chicago, IL. Retrieved from https://www.afsc.org/story/power-elite%E2%80%99s-10-strategies-opposing-monetary-reform

Community Exchange System (CES). (2017). What is the CES? Retrieved from https://www.community-exchange.org

Del Mar, A. (1895). *History of monetary systems.* London, UK: Effingham Wilson, Royal Exchange.

Del Mar, A. (1896). *The science of money* (2nd ed.). New York: Burt Franklin.

De Verlieders (The Seducers). (2015-2017). *Door de bank genomen (Being taken by the banks).* Amsterdam, The Netherlands: BOS Theatre Productions.

Douglas, P. H., Fisher, I., Graham, F. D., Hamilton, E. J., King, W. I., & Whittlesey, C. R. (1939). *A program for monetary reform.* Unpublished paper widely circulated among economists at the time. Retrieved from http://sensiblemoney.ie/data/documents/A-Program-for-Monetary-Reform-.pdf

Eckrich, L. L. T. (1998). *Value in economics, ethics, and education.* Unpublished doctoral dissertation, State University of New York, Buffalo.

Eckrich, L. L. T. (2004, Summer). The inefficiency of the "Cult of Efficiency": Implications for public schooling and education. *Values and Ethics in Educational Administration, 2*(4), 1–8. Retrieved from http://ucealee.squarespace.com/archived-issues/

Eckrich, L. L. T. (2007, April). *Money, distribution, and public schooling: What Freire's "banking" metaphor of education really means.* Paper presented at the annual meeting of the American Educational Research Association, Chicago, IL.

Eckrich, L. L. T. (2016, February). *Proposal for ILEARNs, a tax-foundation complementary currency for the state of Illinois to be spent into circulation through the public schools.* Normal, IL: Author.

Ellis, B. (2012, January 27). Funny money? 11 local currencies. *CNN Money*. Retrieved from http://money.cnn.com/galleries/2012/pf/1201/gallery.community-currencies/index.html

Fisher, I. (1935). *100% money: Designed to keep checking banks 100% liquid; to prevent inflation and deflation; largely to cure or prevent depressions; and to wipe out much of the national debt.* New York: Adelphi.

Frank, T. (2016, November). Swat team: The media's extermination of Bernie Sanders—and real reform. *Harper's Magazine, 333*(1998), 26–35. Retrieved from http://harpers.org/archive/2016/11/swat-team-2/

Freire, P. (2000). *Pedagogy of the oppressed* (M. B. Ramos, Trans., 30th Anniversary ed.). New York: Continuum. (Originally published in English in 1970)

Gesell, S. (1958). *The natural economic order.* London: Peter Owen. (Original published 1916)

Gonczy, A. M. L. (1992). *Modern money mechanics: A workbook on bank reserves and deposit expansion.* Chicago: Federal Reserve Bank of Chicago.

Greco, T. H. (2001). *Money: Understanding and creating alternatives to legal tender.* White River Junction, VT: Chelsea Green.

Guéhenno, J-M. (1995). *The end of the nation-state.* Minneapolis: University of Minnesota Press.

Hawkins, H. (2015, September 12). *The need for and approach to monetary reform.* Paper presented at the 11th annual conference of the American Monetary Institute, Chicago, IL. Retrieved from https://www.youtube.com/watch?v=K6FpIxrV_v0

Hayash, M. (2012). Japan's Fureai Kippu time-banking in elderly care: Origins, development, challenges and impact. *International Journal of Community Currency Research, 16*(A), 30–44. Retrieved from http://dx.doi.org/10.15133/j.ijccr.2012.003

Heinberg, R. (2003). *The party's over: Oil, war and the fate of industrial societies.* Gabriola Island, BC: New Society Publishers.

Huber, J. (2017). *Sovereign money: Beyond reserve banking.* London, UK: Palgrave Macmillan.

Huber, J., & Robertson, J. (2000). *Creating new money: A monetary reform for the information age.* London, UK: New Economics Foundation.

Jackson, A., & Dyson, B. (2013). *Modernising money: Why our monetary system is broken and how it can be fixed.* London, UK: Positive Money.

Jacobs, J. (1992). *Systems of survival: A dialogue on the moral foundations of commerce and politics.* New York: Random House.

Kennedy, M. (1995). *Interest and inflation free money: Creating an exchange medium that works for everybody and protects the earth* (new revised & expanded ed.). Okemos, MI: Seva International. Retrieved from http://userpage.fu-berlin.de/~roehrigw/Welcome.html#english

Kennedy, M. (2012). *Occupy money: Creating an economy where everybody wins.* Gabriola Island, BC: New Society Publishers.

Krug, E. A. (1969). *The shaping of the American High School 1880-1920.* Madison, WI: University of Wisconsin Press.

Langholm, O. (1992). *Economics in the medieval schools: Wealth, exchange, value, money and usury according to the Paris theological tradition, 1200–1350.* Leiden, The Netherlands: E. J. Brill.

Lause, M. A. (1991). *Some degree of power: From hired hand to union craftsman in the preindustrial American printing trades, 1778–1815.* Fayetteville, AR: University of Arkansas Press.

Lause, M. A. (2001). *The Civil War's last campaign: James B. Weaver, the Greenback-Labor Party & the politics of race & section.* Lanham, MD: University Press of America.

Lause, M. A. (2016). *Free spirits: Spiritualism, republicanism, and radicalism in the Civil War era.* Urbana, IL: University of Illinois Press.

Lietaer, B. (2006). A proposal for a Brazilian education complementary currency. *International Journal of Community Currency Research, 10,* 18–23. Retrieved from http://dx.doi.org/10.15133/j.ijccr.2006.004

National Emergency Employment Defense (NEED) Act of 2011, H.R. 2990, 112th Cong. (2011). Retrieved from www.house.gov/

Positive Money (PM). (2013, April 12). *Bank of England (Creation of Currency) Bill: A proposal from Positive Money (not tabled in Parliament).* Retrieved from http://positivemoney.org/publications/draft-legislation/

Ricks, M. (2016). *The money problem: Rethinking financial regulation.* Chicago: University of Chicago Press.

Roediger, D. R., & Foner, P. S. (1989). *Our own time: A history of American labor and the working day.* New York: Greenwood Press.

Sigurjónsson, F. (2015, March). *Monetary reform: A better monetary system for Iceland.* Reykjavik, Iceland: Author, commissioned by the Prime Minister of Iceland. Retrieved from https://www.forsaetisraduneyti.is/media/Skyrslur/monetary-reform.pdf

Soddy, F. (1931). *Money versus man: A statement of the world problem from the standpoint of the new economics.* London, UK: Elkin Mathews & Marrot.

Soddy, F. (1934). *The role of money: What it should be, contrasted with what it has become.* London, UK: Routledge. Retrieved from https://archive.org/details/roleofmoney032861mbp

Solomon, L. D. (1996). *Rethinking our centralized monetary system: The case for a system of local currencies.* Westport, CT: Praeger.

Strike Debt. (2014). *The debt resisters' operations manual.* Oakland, CA: PM Press.

Switzer, H. (2016). *Gotta get a new kind of money.* Song performed at the 12th annual conference of the American Monetary Institute, Chicago, IL. Retrieved from https://www.youtube.com/watch?v=aYx6RUHfva4

Thoroddsen, S., & Sigurjónsson, S. B. (2016, September). *Money issuance: Alternative money systems. A report commissioned by the Icelandic Prime Minister's Office, KPMG.* Retrieved from http://internationalmoneyreform.org/blog/2016/09/kpmg-iceland-report-sovereign-money/

Wortmann, E. (2016, September 18). *A proposal for radical monetary reform.* Paper presented at the 12th annual conference of the American Monetary Institute, Chicago, IL, 9/30/2016. Retrieved from https://onsgeld.nu/onsgeld/2016/wortmann_radical_monetary_reform.pdf

Yamaguchi, K. (n.d.). *Public money forum in Japan.* Retrieved from www.muratopia.org/Yamaguchi/MoneyForum.html

Zarlenga, S. (2002). *The lost science of money: The mythology of money—the story of power.* Valatie, NY: American Monetary Institute.

Zarlenga, S. (2011). *One page summary of what HR 2990 will do.* Valatie, NY: American Monetary Institute. Retrieved from www.monetary.org/wp-content/uploads/2013/01/HR-2990.pdf

Zarlenga, S. (2014). *Presenting the AMI monetary reform manual.* Valatie, NY: American Monetary Institute. (2010 and 2016 editions) Retrieved from www.monetary.org/

16 Reflections on the Future

Setting the Agenda for a Post-Neoliberal U.S. Higher Education

Nicholas D. Hartlep, Brandon O. Hensley, and Lucille L. T. Eckrich

Introduction

Co-editing and co-authoring *The Neoliberal Agenda and the Student Debt Crisis in U.S. Higher Education* was a fatiguing and frustrating process. Fatiguing insofar as synthesizing emergent and extant research in order to generate a multi-vocal inquiry that critiques neoliberalism requires both time and energy. Frustrating insofar as many existing and supposedly alternative models themselves use neoliberal language and big "E" Economic schemas, further normalizing the neoliberal "habitus" (Bourdieu, 1980) of prevailing higher education practices. Reports and studies sounding alarm bells on the mounting student loan debt continue to be released on what feels like a weekly basis, but the proverbial panacea remains elusive, if not quixotic.

Similar to Miguel de Cervantes' characters Don Quixote and Sancho Panza, scholars critical of neoliberalism have been searching for ways to mitigate the student debt crisis through their research and policy, only to find they are "tilting at windmills." For us, the Quixote metaphor means that proposed courses of action will fall short if the "journey" begins with neoliberal trappings. Below we critique the dominant neoliberal *lingua franca* that ironically ensnares much of "critical" scholarship regarding neoliberalism generally and the student debt crisis in particular. Nonetheless, this project yielded applied, theoretical, and praxis-oriented knowledge. In this concluding chapter, we offer our critical reflections on the potential of moving away from debt-based higher education and set an agenda for advancing "post-neoliberal" policy and practice.

First, we reflect on several of the applied research findings that are shared in this book. We highlight key possibilities that surfaced and consider whether they effectively resist and overcome neoliberalism. Second, we reflect on the theoretical research findings that have been shared in this collective project through autoethnography. These personal accounts reveal the lived experience of student debt that grounds our theoretical understanding and praxis. Third, we address praxis-oriented findings from Chapters 4 and 15 on monetary critique and reform that serve to bookend this project. We acknowledge that the historical economic analysis and reform work described in these two chapters will require paradigm shifts and institutional change—two daunting tasks for U.S. higher education, not to mention ourselves and our society, because neoliberal orientations dominate all three. We believe the best way to predict the future is to make it. Thus, we conclude the chapter and book by setting out an agenda for a debt-free future—not only for U.S. higher education but for our society and humanity at large—and the role of praxis therein.

In the landscape of counter-neoliberal scholarship on student debt, *The Neoliberal Agenda and the Student Debt Crisis in U.S. Higher Education* is distinctive in part because it highlights personal narratives. Contributors in Part II share autoethnographic experiences with readers. These personal stories provide qualitative depth and insight that cannot be gained from quantitative accounting and "big data" alone. A second unique aspect of the book compared to others investigating the student debt problem is that it situates the crisis in the larger context of monetary critique and reform. We understand student loan debt as a symptom of a systemic flaw that neoliberalism masks. That flaw is that the sovereign authority only through which money exists was usurped by and/or ceded to private interests in the modern era. This is how modern money came to be what it is today—debt in the service of private interest—instead of a sovereign means of exchange to facilitate a people's commerce and the public good.

In short, we co-edited this book on student debt because we were dismayed that the work we thought was needed to connect the dots didn't exist; thus, we created it. This included the necessity of hearing from those who are indebted themselves and situating their stories in the political economic context that gave rise to those realities. We are hopeful that an agenda can be established that makes its central task dismantling the neoliberal capitalist regime that currently dictates how post-secondary education (and much else) is financed. From our perspective, the roadmap we propose in this volume is new and, if enacted, will help college students in the United States experience post-neoliberal higher education: where education is a public right and a personal responsibility, not a private commodity for sale.

Applied Research Findings

In Chapter 2, Linda Coco investigates the emergence of a "user-pay" approach to funding higher education for individuals, describing how the existing Bankruptcy Code protects educational lenders—making them into a form of "super-creditor" in the process of an individual case. Coco discusses the 2005 amendments to the U.S. Bankruptcy Code, the means-test and disposable-income test, and educational loan monthly payment obligations. Additionally, she links the structure of the means-test and disposable income to neoliberalism and proposes an educational loan modification mediation program that could be implemented in bankruptcy courts to ameliorate the growing student loan debt bubble.

Nicholas Hartlep and Diane Dean, in Chapter 13, explore how student loan borrowing at "Work Colleges" compares to student loan borrowing at comparable institutions. They posit that Work Colleges operate in alternative ways compared to neoliberal colleges and universities. By using recent data from the Integrated Postsecondary Education Data System (IPEDS), they examine the percentage of students who borrow, the average amount students borrow a year, and the level of student debt that graduates of Work Colleges leave with compared to peers who graduate from other comparable institutions. Acknowledging that Work Colleges vary in their approaches, Hartlep and Dean find that Work Colleges graduate their students with significantly lower amounts of student loan debt than their neoliberal counterparts.

Hartlep and Dean's systematic inquiry—questioning whether Work Colleges educate their students in ways that don't require high amounts of student loan borrowing—involves a practical question: "Can Work Colleges serve as an alternative model for other existing public and private neoliberal colleges and universities?" Currently there are seven distinct Work Colleges, with at least one more school working on joining their rank. Whereas it is possible for existing and newly formed colleges/universities to become recognized as Work Colleges, it's improbable because this model may not be scalable for larger universities. Most Work Colleges are small and rural institutions. Nonetheless, exceptions—such as large, urban Work Colleges—may form when university administrators are visionary in their concern for students' prospects for a future free from debt. For example, Paul Quinn College (PQC), an urban Historically Black College (HBCU) led by president Michael Sorrell, has embraced this model. PQC is a private, faith-based, four-year liberal arts college that was founded on April 4, 1872, by a group of African Methodist Episcopal Church preachers in Austin, Texas. The fact that *PBS NewsHour* recently did a feature story on PQC (*PBS*, 2016) may indeed signal mainstream interest in the Work College model and its applicability for other colleges and universities, especially if and as our towns, cities, and society "transition" (Hopkins, 2014) to a post-neoliberal, post-peak-oil, sustainable post-modern era.

In Chapter 14, Daniel Collier, T. Jameson Brewer, P. S. Myers, and Allison Witt explore the viability of crowdsourcing and crowdfunding as a means to assist with student loan debt. They examine a crowdfunding model using data from an active online community, the results of which indicate that—although large amounts of money could be raised—after 15 years the amount of money raised would not rival the amount of combined debt that the group owes. Their conclusions arise from the sobering inability of crowdfunding to make deep impacts on total student loan debt, and they discuss national-level efforts that policymakers can engage in to solve this issue. Collier and his colleagues lament that, as the crowdfund group grows, which is needed to generate more funds, so does the aggregate balance. They demonstrate how inadequate and finally ineffective the crowdfunding model is in helping the broad population of those struggling with student loan debt.

Related to attempting to gain relief by pooling debt as well as payments is the practice of employers offering student loan (re)payment benefits to their employees (Lanza, 2016). These employers provide their workers with funds to (re)pay employees' existing student debt. This may become as common as a 401(k); only time will tell. What this employer-offered benefit illustrates is how little economic power indebted students have compared to the major companies who are able to offer this exclusive resource to their employees. Such a financial benefit also flows disproportionately upward to benefit employees who already hold higher-paying jobs and thus are already more able to repay their debts.

Finally, the "free two-year college option" (F2CO), a recent proposal for public funding of higher education that James Palmer and Melissa Pitcock scrutinize in Chapter 12, represents a potentially popular initiative for funding higher education and reducing the need to acquire large sums of student debt. Even if it achieves too little, at least as long as it takes our existing monetary system for granted, the F2CO proposal still strikes at the heart of the neoliberal approach for funding higher education because it proposes to fund itself by limiting public monies for higher education to students at public colleges and universities (Goldrick-Rab & Kendall, 2014). This would terminate the neoliberal subsidy that has gone to private institutions ever since public funding for higher education in the United States began.

Theoretical Research Findings

Part II shares seven personal stories of individuals who find themselves part of the neoliberal debt crisis. While personal narratives are delegitimized by some scholars who value generalization, we agree with Art Bochner (1994), a pioneer of personal narrative research, who argues that stories can themselves be theoretical because storying lived experience can help oneself and others to make sense of the world around them, and their relationships with the people and systems they encounter. The stories here are told by chapter authors whose perspectives "bring light to the issue—not heat," as the late Peabody award-winning journalist Gwen Ifill would say. The accounts featured in this section are critical for undermining neoliberal ideology. It is vital to recognize that neoliberal ideology naturalizes the myth of the American Dream and blames individuals when they do not succeed. The narratives shared in this book augment readers' comprehension of the depths of the student loan debt disaster, those affected by it, and the culprit to rally against—namely, our private-interest-driven debt-based monetary system and its neoliberal ideology. The stories in Part II illustrate why and how neoliberalism doesn't "work" for everyone.

Amy Swain, in Chapter 5, traces her personal pathway through higher education and the unforeseen barriers presented by neoliberalism in the academy. Swain is mired in a student loan debt of $250,000, with no foreseeable way out. She explores the decline in the number of tenure-track positions within the academy, as well as the financial hardships that come with adjunct professor work. As Swain details in her story, changes have to be made when life collides with debt: repaying debt becomes the biggest priority, at least until one has nothing left to lose but one's soul.

In Chapter 8, Brian Horn utilizes autoethnography to situate his personal experience with graduate education and student debt within a larger national and ideological context. Gone are the days of increased college enrollment—from the 1940s to the 1960s—due to direct legislative action. Horn argues that, since the late 1970s, neoliberal policies regarding higher education have resulted in the United States becoming less democratic, less innovative, and weaker economically. Having been raised in a working-class neighborhood by a college-educated single-parent, Horn worked and paid his own way through a public university to become an elementary school teacher. But the confluence of systems of labor and housing in a context of economic downturn and medical bills for his son born with congenital heart problems conspired to make paying off the cost of his graduate degrees from two Research 1 institutions (the first private, the second public) thus far impossible for Horn despite his now tenured status at a public Research 2 institution.

Antonio Ellis shares his story in Chapter 9 of being a person with a communicative disorder who is forced to speak with student debt collectors over the telephone. Ellis reveals that in their zeal to collect debt repayments, neoliberal student loan companies provide few communication options for indebted students with communication disorders. This practice increases the likelihood that members of this population will default on their loans. He shares his unique struggles repaying his student debt, which exceeds $100,000, as an adjunct professor who stutters. Ellis's narrative and analytical lenses are informed by attention to the intersectionality of age, disability, and race in his lived experience.

In addition to stories told by adjunct, tenure-track, and tenured faculty, our book includes the voice of a former student, Melissa Del Rio, who completed her Associate's degree but has not yet attained a Bachelor's degree. Del Rio questions, in Chapter 11, whether it will ever be "worth it" to do so. In the current debt-based landscape of U.S. higher education, it is hard to admonish such questioning. Who can blame someone who doesn't want to go $35,000 into debt (or more) to buy into schooling as a commodity when there are no guarantees that the product (degrees or credentials) obtained will result in social and class mobility through secure, gainful employment—hallmarks of the so-called American Dream? Must the path to achieving the American Dream be paved in debt? What painful personal struggles accompany student debt (whether in modest or exorbitant amounts)? As editors of this book, we can imagine Zora Neale Hurston shouting from the rooftop: "If you're silent about your pain, they'll kill you and say you enjoyed it." In documenting their personal and financial suffering, these brave "critical storytellers" (Hartlep & Eckrich, 2013; Hartlep & Hensley, 2015) raise urgent questions that prompt each of us to begin imagining and working toward a post-neoliberal future.

Findings From Praxis

As Paulo Freire (2000) reveals in *Pedagogy of the Oppressed*, praxis (theory-informed practice) is at the interstices of theory and practice. Located within and between the applied and theoretical findings noted above are those of praxis found in this book. According to Freire (2000), praxis is "reflection and action upon the world in order to *transform* it" (p. 51, italics added). A transformative monetary reform in the public interest (and most definitely *not* one that further entrenches private moneyed interests in a so-called "public-private partnership" as advocated by Ricks, 2016) is needed that can uproot neoliberal capitalism and supersede it with eco- and people-friendly, non-usurious exchange relations. Then, and only then, will the seven Part II authors who offered critical autoethnographies of their debt peonage, along with the millions of other present and averted student debtors, be able to produce good for themselves and for the meso-, macro-, and mundo-level exchange communities in which they are part.

In addition to historical and applied research and "stories-as-theories" (Bochner, 1994), there are praxis-oriented contributions in this volume that bridge the higher education community with pioneering, historically grounded, theoretical horizons for how informed and engaged people can understand the monetary system we operate under and advocate for its transformation. In Chapter 4, Lucille Eckrich articulates the nature of money and the monetary system that naturally follows from it. Her distillation of the science of money, based on an understanding of its empirical and analytical history, is contrasted through the chapter with the money system we have, how we came to have it, and how student debt derives from its inherent logic. Eckrich notes how transforming the existing monetary system into a publicly grounded one can remedy the student debt problem.

In Chapter 15, Eckrich focuses on monetary reform efforts happening today and their implications for funding public higher education. Macro-level monetary reform at the national level and in the public interest is necessary to supersede private-interest-driven debt-based money and dehumanization. It also would allow for the creation of new revenue streams for PK–20 education. Local and/or regional complementary currencies already exist in many places, and forms have been theorized, even if not yet implemented, to fund public education at PK–12 and higher education levels, and they too would increase revenue for education. Though Eckrich believes macro-level monetary transformation and complementary currencies at meso-levels are compatible and, thus, advocates for both, she urges that macro-level reform be sought first and necessarily. Thus, she lays out a strategy for its pursuit, one that works on both educational and political fronts at national, international, local, and regional levels. Once we attain such monetary transformation, human commerce will look and feel very familiar yet be fundamentally different—and finally post-neoliberal—because that which we know to be negative in neoliberal commerce will have been negated. Existing student debt can then be paid off and need never escalate again.

Of course, bringing about paradigmatic change is a formidable challenge, but not insurmountable, even if the election of Donald Trump as the

U.S. President makes it harder. But we believe that the work of combating the tyranny of neoliberal financing of higher education and helping all who suffer under ballooning student loan debt will not, should not, and cannot wait. The question that readers should ask is, "What (more) can we do?" Three additional relevant reforms—what Freire (2000) might call "untested feasibilities" (p. 102)—are the participatory economics known as "parecon" (Albert, 2003; Albert & Hahnel, 1991), "undercommoning" (2016) at universities, and "The People's Budget" (Blair, 2016) at a Congressional level. Of these three, we believe a national prioritization modeled after "The People's Budget" carries the most promise for the substantive, systemic change required to change the course of U.S. higher education away from neoliberal domination. Building on all the chapters in this book, we suggest the following agenda for moving post-neoliberalism work forward.

Setting the Agenda

We organized this book around a topic—student loan debt—that no previously published text connected explicitly with neoliberalism. Initially, we planned to document alternatives to the neoliberal model of higher education financing. But, even in the face of the scathing critiques and staggering student debt statistics we cite in the volume, very little of the existing research is non-neoliberal. That is, much of the research on the student debt problem is ironically undergirded by neoliberal moorings and assumptions. As we immersed ourselves in the student debt literature, it became clear that our book inaugurates student loan debt as a "neoliberal" crisis in U.S. higher education. This crisis did not come to be because a certain dollar amount of debt was reached and/or because student debt has surpassed credit card debt and is looming as the next asset bubble (Cooper, 2016a). Rather, college debt has been a problem since the 1970s and 1980s, coinciding with the birth of neoliberalism in the United States (Harvey, 2005) and the 1972 creation of recently privatized Sallie Mae. Lawrence Gladieux's (1989) edited *Radical Reform or Incremental Change? Student Loan Policy Alternatives for the Federal Government* identified the escalating numbers of students becoming entrapped in debt already during the 1970s. In that book he wrote, "No federal policy ever decreed that students and families should rely increasingly on debt to finance college costs in the 1980s. The reliance on debt grew, beginning in the late 1970s, from a confluence of legislative amendments and market conditions" (Gladieux, 1989, p. 1) that arise, we argue, from the inherent logic or force that drives capitalism itself—namely private-interest-driven debt-based money. Only recently have scholars such as Best and Best (2014), Collinge (2009), and Johannsen (2016) argued that there is a student debt crisis, and that it is a neoliberal scam or at least resultant from a flaw inherent in neoliberalism itself. And Giroux (2014) has exposed the destructive consequences neoliberalism is having on higher education more broadly.

We, the editors, agree with Giroux that the ideologues of this movement—blinded by their reliance on a banking-model of education (Freire, 2000) and a *mythos* of the "free market"—have waged a sophisticated war on students and faculty. The war, a "scourge" on higher learning, a form of epistemicide, kills the potential for civic education, cultural inclusion, and pursuit of knowledge for its inherent good (Giroux, 2010). Glossy marketing rhetoric helps to euphemize the painful realities of subtle neoliberal warfare by positing that education is a product that must be purchased, and despite a high "sticker price," is worth pursuing. Students may graduate with degrees, credentials, and even jobs in hand, but they are not assured they will secure *gainful* employment in the dual labor market.[1] The specter of underemployment is all the more perilous for every successive graduating class when they commence with staggering amounts of debt, virtually ensuring that decisions to raise families, buy homes, and actualize other vestiges of the American Dream will be more impossible, more quixotic.

The neoliberal war on higher education renders students and graduates with unmanageable mountains of student debt as collateral damage (Giroux, 2014). As has already been noted, student debt is different from other forms of debt because it is not dischargeable, even in bankruptcy or death. According to the National Employment Law Center (2014), "Today, there are nearly two million fewer jobs in mid- and higher-wage industries than there were before the recession took hold, while there are 1.85 million more jobs in lower-wage industries" (p. 2). We also mentioned earlier that scholarly efforts to connect the student debt crisis to a critique of neoliberalism have been inchoate because doing so reaches into a realm still viewed through the lenses of late-capitalism and the dogma of neoliberal hegemony. Too few progressives, radicals, Marxists, socialists, environmentalists, social justice advocates, etc. have been willing to question their own economic presuppositions, which Brexit and the election of Trump expose as self-defeating and short-sighted (Norton, 2016) when it comes to moving toward a post-neoliberal economy.

Critical Thinking and Historical Reflection

The first (and perpetual) item on our agenda moving forward consists of critical thinking and historical reflection. In terms of learning from the past in order to "lead from the future as it emerges" (Scharmer, 2009), we ask readers, "How much longer can a pattern of each successive graduating class being more indebted than the one that preceded it continue?" The average debt load of graduates of the class of 2016 was $37,173 (Picchi, 2016). What will the debt load for the class of 2020 be? What is really going on here? The student loan debt crisis is a $1.4 trillion problem worth solving to be sure, but how much money is $1.4 trillion really?

To place this amount of student loan debt ($1.4 trillion) into a national economic context, the 2011 U.S. federal deficit was $1.4 trillion. Contextualized in visual form, the height of a stack of $1,000,000,000,000 (one trillion) $1 dollar bills measures 67,866 miles, more than a quarter of the way from the earth to the moon. Although this volume has provided new insights into the neoliberal crisis of student debt in U.S. higher education, the real work has only just begun. Many questions remain unasked and unanswered, and much organizing, networking, and coalition-building work must be done for political economic transformation to occur.

Since neoliberal ideology is self-insulating, it conceals unfortunate truths on the damage inflicted upon student debtors, its victims. In spite of these indebted "casualties," the neoliberal higher education agenda in the United States is a well-kept secret. Neoliberal arguments that the market will fix everything and that the country needs a businessman in the White House hold sway and further obscure brutal realities. For instance, there is a widespread misunderstanding that tuition continues to rise primarily due to "cost disease." Writing about cost disease in his book *Revolution in Higher Education: How a Small Band of Innovators Will Make College Accessible and Affordable*, DeMillo (2015) says the following:

> Tuition rises because variable costs rise, subsidies decline, and universities expand their missions to include new programs and activities (or cling to previously subsidized activities when the subsidies disappear). Most of the cost of running a university is tied up in labor costs, and most of the labor costs are due to faculty salaries. This one factor alone accounts for about half of all tuition increases.
>
> (pp. 143–144)

Describing cost disease, Bowen (2012) remarks,

> The basic idea is simple: in labor-intensive industries such as the performing arts and education, there is less opportunity than in other sectors to increase productivity by, for example, substituting capital for labor. Yet, over time, markets dictate that wages for comparably qualified individuals have to increase at roughly the same rate in all industries. As a result, unit labor costs must be expected to rise relatively faster in the performing arts and education than in the economy overall.
>
> (p. 4)

But, as Barnshaw and Dunietz (2015) write in "Busting the Myths," a report published in *Academe*, "Private endowment erosion and declining state appropriations, *not faculty salaries*, have been principally responsible for the rise in average net price tuition" (p. 7, italics added). Consequently, cost disease, an economic concept deployed by neoliberal proponents, is not accurate or at least only part of the story.

Neoliberal orthodoxy is responsible for getting us into this mess. And what got us in cannot get us out. We need to look outside the box and beyond the *status quo* for new answers to old and new questions. We propose a national prioritization modeled after "The People's Budget."

A New Vision of "People Over Profit" and "Prosperity, Not Austerity"

"The People's Budget" empowers our nation's PK–20 students by providing robust early learning opportunities, quality public education for all students, and debt-free college. Blair's (2016) review of the plan notes that "spending proposals adopted over FY 2017–2026 in The People's Budget include refinancing student loans and making college more affordable ($412 billion) and adopting the president's proposed Preschool for All ($66 billion) and End Family Homelessness ($11 billion) initiatives" (p. 9).

When we discovered "The People's Budget" plan, initially launched in April of 2011 for fiscal year 2012 by the Congressional Progressive Caucus (CPC), we saw an opportunity for a post-neoliberal turn, a re-imagining of U.S. higher education financing.[2] U.S. House Representatives Raul M. Grijalva (D-AZ) and Keith Maurice Ellison (D-MN) are currently the co-chairs of the CPC. Regardless of whether the post-neoliberal turn happens through radical expediency or "incremental change" (Gladieux, 1989), a collective flipping of the priorities observed in Chomsky's (1999) *Profit Over People: Neoliberalism and Global Order* is required: Instead of the neoliberal assumption that banks and other institutions (including universities) are necessarily "too big to fail," a post-neoliberal imagination asserts, as a central tenet, that current, former, and future students are "too important to fail" if the United States is to remain peaceful, forward-thinking and verdant, in its own eyes and in the eyes of other nations in the global community. Unlike the $16-trillion bailout of major U.S. banks during the 2008 Great Recession (Collins, 2015; Greenstein, 2011), an agenda based on "The People's Budget" constitutes a U-turn from a neoliberal future (to "people over profit" and "prosperity not austerity").

President Donald J. Trump may have an influential impact on individuals who have student debt. Trump may alter the repayment plan terms in ways that are regressive for indebted collegians. This is an important consideration, given the pattern of increased enrollment in these plans. According to Tom Anderson (2016), "The percentage of federal student loan borrowers enrolled in income-based plans has quadrupled over the past four years from 5 percent in 2012 to nearly 20 percent in 2016" (para. 4). Preston Cooper (2016b) states that Trump's revised plan would cap payments at 12.5% (compared to the current 10% under Obama) of one's income, and remaining balances would be forgiven in 15 years (five years sooner than under Obama, which is already five years less than the 25-year cap originally set when income based payment plans were first instituted; Delisle, 2016). According to Cooper (2016b), Trump's plan would increase the amount of money the federal government is already predicted to lose on the student loan program "and do so in a highly regressive way":

Individuals with large student loan balances generally have higher incomes, as they have accumulated those debts through earning lucrative graduate degrees. As currently written, the plan would be a major boon to the lawyers, doctors and businesspeople of tomorrow. Those who need the most help generally have low student loan balances, and would not benefit from the reform.

(para. 4)

Trump's vision for U.S. higher education will be worse than the *status quo*, in that it will be neoliberalism 2.0. Just recall when then-presidential candidate Trump said in a speech in Nevada, "I love the poorly educated."[3] Who among us was he calling out? Who among us will answer, and what will we say?

The Need for a New Lexicon

We concur with Massey (2015) who writes, "The vocabulary we use, to talk about the economy in particular, has been crucial to the establishment of neoliberal hegemony" (p. 4). Neoliberal higher education relies on and naturalizes a *lingua franca* that is *homo economicus* and financialized (Hill & Kumar, 2009). In *After Neoliberalism? The Kilburn Manifesto*, Hall, Massey, and Rustin (2015) document how neoliberalism normalizes a capitalist lexicon that is dehumanizing. For instance, consider the following neoliberal higher education terms:

- Productivity
- Efficiency
- Financial Aid
- Leveraging Synergies
- Outsourcing
- Chief Academic Officer
- Austerity
- Consumer
- Customer Liaison
- Growth
- Strategic Planning
- Capacity
- Return on Investment
- Human Capital
- Accountability
- Affordability
- Cost and Risk Sharing
- Knowledge Economy
- Responsibility Centered Management
- University Profit Centers

- Estimated Family Contribution
- Income-Based Repayment
- Globalization
- Internationalization

Under the neoliberal finance model of higher education, the college student is a consumer no matter where s/he hails from or attends college (Fish, 2009; Mettler, 2014; Slaughter & Rhoades, 2004). In 2010, when Federal Financial Aid Policy moved back to direct lending by the federal government, to cut out the middleman after 45 years of federally guaranteed student loans from the private sector at market rates, the private lending market extended its reach to international students interested and able to pay for a degree from a U.S. college or university. As Massey (2013) states:

> The message underlying this use of the term customer for so many different kinds of human activity is that in all [or] almost all our daily activities we are operating as consumers in a market—and this truth has been brought in not by chance but through managerial instruction and the thoroughgoing renaming of institutional practices.
>
> (para. 2)

But, as we noted above, the dual labor market is growing for those who have less than a four-year college education; but it's not growing for those with advanced college degrees. Ironically, education is sold to students as being needed, particularly four-year and advanced degrees, for economic security. Web tools like the U.S. Department of Education's College Scorecard[4] assist in the purchasing of higher education and legitimize neoliberal language, which furthers its ideology.

There is a need for a new lexicon, but creating one from scratch is difficult (Majhanovich, 2013). As postmodern feminist author Kathy Acker (1994) observes in *Empire of the Senseless*, attempting to deconstruct hegemony with its own vocabulary is as difficult as cleaning the air on one side of a screen door. Acker (1994) writes:

> [I]t seemed possible to destroy language through language: to destroy language that normalizes and controls by cutting that language. Nonsense would attack the empire-making (empirical) empire of language, the prisons of meaning. But this nonsense, since it depended on sense, simply pointed back to the normalizing institutions. What is the language of the 'unconscious'? . . . Its primary language must be taboo, all that is forbidden. Thus, an attack on the institutions of language via language would demand the use of a language or languages which aren't acceptable, which are forbidden. Language, on one level, constitutes a set of codes and social and historical agreements. Nonsense

doesn't per se break down the codes; speaking precisely that which the codes forbid breaks the codes.

(p. 134)

White supremacy is the DNA of neoliberalism, and it forbids speaking truth to power. In his *Race and the Origins of American Neoliberalism*, Randolph Hohle (2015) states:

> The language of neoliberalism was the result of the white response to the black struggle for civic inclusion. The language of neoliberalism is organized around the white-private/black-public binary. White-private defined the market and economic policy that benefited businesses as white and superior.
>
> (p. 18)

Hohle goes on to write, "Whites resented spending *their* tax dollars on blacks. The preferred method of maintaining white power became exercising white control over state budgets. Austerity freed whites from the economic burden of establishing racial equality" (p. 25). These ideological and political economic relations have older origins, of course. The most elite institutions—Ivy League institutions—of U.S. higher education were built by extracting surplus value from slaves (Wilder, 2013). For instance, Harvard University was built in part by slave labor and its endowments have amassed great wealth upon this exploitation. The same is true for Yale University, Dartmouth University, and others among the most prestigious of U.S. universities.[5] The slave economy was the forerunner to the modern day neoliberal economy and elite university.

White supremacist language is exclusionary, divisive, and exclusive. The same is true about the neoliberal lexicon and logic. As a result, post-neoliberal language must be equitable and egalitarian. The residue of exclusionary leaders is rampant on the campuses of U.S. colleges and universities. Halls and buildings memorialize (mostly male) white supremacists. Reclaiming what white supremacy has robbed humanity of is what a post-neoliberal language will seek.

Concluding Thoughts

We close this project by asking readers to join us on this journey, to speak out, stand up, and question neoliberal doctrine in the myriad spaces it appears, from the lexicon to the lawmakers to the institutions that reinforce its dominance. Neoliberalism is not a tilting windmill—it is a very real monster that has already devastated the lives of many. Saunders (2007) documents how neoliberalism has a negative impact on higher education and students. The major way is that it has altered the reason people attend college in the first place. In times past, individuals attended college to learn for learning's sake and to pursue a calling. The motivation was intrinsic and intertwined with the idea of becoming a more informed, well rounded person through the liberal arts. However, neoliberalism has altered motivations toward the extrinsic, or the economic. According to Saunders (2007), "Neoliberalism sees education as extrinsically good as it enables the student (customer) to purchase a product that will increase his or her human capital and thus allow the student to secure a better job, as defined by salary and wealth" (p. 5). But even if the key to a securing a stable-paying job is a college degree, and becoming indebted is thought to pay off in the end, the stress that accompanies student loan debt is heavy and has even ended in student suicide (Johannsen, 2012).

Thomas Kuhn (1970) writes that "paradigm shifts" are not instantaneous. Paradigm shifts are central to the transformation and evolution of interdisciplinary fields, social institutions, government, law, and public opinion and policy. Paradigmatic change is demanding of institutions, individuals, and groups. Why? Because institutions are run by human beings and people are fallible; even supposed "experts" can accept the *argumentum ad populum* fallacy (un)intentionally. In our experience, imagining a public higher education devoid of neoliberal debt is as difficult as unringing a bell. Because econo-positivist models of "scientific" inquiry are considered the gold standard, unringing the dominant research "bell" is operose. This is where we believe our applied, theoretical, and praxis research findings cultivate discussions and awaken readers to dormant possibilities for breaking the taken-for-granted ubiquity of debt-based money, including student loan debt.

The chapters in this book critique neoliberalism in substantive ways and challenge readers to (re)examine the contested ideals of civic engagement, education as a fundamental human right and responsibility, and public higher education as a necessity in a participatory democratic citizenry. Moreover, the voices featured in this volume lay out existing flaws, consider new directions and reasoning, and offer interventions for addressing the $1.4 trillion and growing student loan debt crisis.

The monster is real. The bell has rung. How will we respond, together, to realize a future unbound by the dogma of neoliberalism?

What Can Readers Do?

- Share this book with friends, family, and colleagues.
- Speak up through traditional and social media; contact local government officials about the student debt crisis.
- Become involved in monetary reform in your local community.
- Join the American Monetary Institute (AMI). More information can be found here: www.monetary.org (https://perma.cc/KF7F-JGA8)

Where Can Readers Find More Resources on Student Loan Debt?

- Mapping Student Debt
  - http://mappingstudentdebt.org (https://perma.cc/ZM7W-KW7S)
- The Institute for College Access & Success
  - www.ticas.org (https://perma.cc/968E-4GWK)
- Strike Debt
  - http://strikedebt.org (https://perma.cc/K2JN-U9JC)
- BFAMFAPHD
  - http://bfamfaphd.com (https://perma.cc/VBL2–9DUH)
- The Debt Collective
  - https://debtcollective.org (https://perma.cc/388P-UTXE)
- Rolling Jubilee
  - http://rollingjubilee.org (https://perma.cc/ZDF9–64SF)
- The Artist as Debtor
  - http://artanddebt.org (https://perma.cc/PR9L-DC7C)
- Undercommoning
  - http://undercommoning.org (https://perma.cc/XT56-DS9L)
- *After Neoliberalism? The Kilburn Manifesto*
  - https://www.lwbooks.co.uk/sites/default/files/free-book/after_neoliberalism_complete_0.pdf (https://perma.cc/9RCJ-ZP65)
- Ph.D. Debt Survey (via "The Professor Is In")
  - https://docs.google.com/spreadsheets/d/1IImqRbOrbWmZuy0xRgq3wh4RjmmuHWYBgZ3WbjBkW2g/edit#gid=17 (https://perma.cc/9J3U-TSLC)
- Student Loan Justice
  - www.studentloanjustice.org (https://perma.cc/8PVS-2GKL)

Notes

1 By dual labor we mean, "Jobs fall into either the primary or the secondary sector. Jobs in the primary sector are 'good jobs' characterized by high wages, job security, substantial responsibility, and ladders where internal promotion is possible. Jobs in the secondary sector are characterized by low wages and casual

attachments between workers and firms and are menial. Workers in the secondary sector envy those in the primary sector, who have both better jobs and higher wages" (Bulow & Summers, 1986, p. 380).

2 The people's budget: Budget of the congressional progressive caucus fiscal year 2012. Retrieved from https://grijalva.house.gov/uploads/The%20CPC%20FY20 12%20Budget.pdf

3 Trump in Nevada: 'I love the poorly educated.' Retrieved from https://www.youtube.com/watch?v=Vpdt7omPoa0 (https://perma.cc/T76C-HPTE)

4 College Scorecard. Retrieved from https://collegescorecard.ed.gov

5 On Harvard's connections with slavery see www.harvardandslavery.com and http://www.harvard.edu/slavery; for Yale's see www.yaleslavery.org; for Dartmouth's see https://dartmouthslaveryproject.wordpress.com.

References

Acker, K. (1994). *Empire of the senseless*. New York: Grove Press.

Albert, M. (2003). *Parecon: Life after capitalism*. New York: Verso.

Albert, M., & Hahnel, R. (1991). *Looking forward: Participatory economics for the twenty first century*. Cambridge, MA: South End Press.

Anderson, T. (2016, November 10). How you could save under Trump's student loan repayment plan. *CNBC*. Retrieved from www.cnbc.com/2016/11/10/how-you-could-save-under-trumps-student-loan-repayment-plan.html

Barnshaw, J., & Dunietz, S. (2015, March/April). Busting the myths: The annual report on the economic status of the profession, 2014–15. *Academe, 101*(2), 4–19. Retrieved from https://www.aaup.org/sites/default/files/files/2015salarysurvey/zreport.pdf

Best, J., & Best, E. (2014). *The student loan mess: How good intentions created a trillion-dollar problem*. Berkeley, CA: University of California Press.

Blair, H. (2016, March 15). 'The people's budget': Analysis of the congressional progressive Caucus budget for fiscal year 2017. Washington, DC: Economic Policy Institute. Retrieved from https://cpc-grijalva.house.gov/uploads/EPI%20 People's%20Budget%20Analysis%202.pdf

Bochner, A. P. (1994). Perspectives on inquiry II: Theories and stories. In M. L. Knapp & G. R. Miller (Eds.), *Handbook of interpersonal communication* (2nd ed., pp. 21–41). Thousand Oaks, CA: Sage.

Bourdieu, P. (1980). *The logic of practice*. Stanford, CA: Stanford University Press.

Bowen, W. G. (2012, October). *The 'cost disease' in higher education: Is technology the answer?* Retrieved from www.ithaka.org/sites/default/files/files/ITHAKA-TheCostDiseaseinHigherEducation.pdf

Bulow, J. I., & Summers, L. H. (1986). A theory of dual labor markets with application to industrial policy, discrimination, and Keynesian unemployment. *Journal of Labor Economics, 4*(3), 376–414. Retrieved from https://faculty-gsb.stanford.edu/bulow/articles/A%20%20theory%20of%20dual%20Labor%20Markets.pdf

Chomsky, N. (1999). *Profit over people: Neoliberalism and global order*. New York: Seven Stories Press.

Collinge, A. M. (2009). *The student loan scam: The most oppressive debt in U.S. history—and how we can fight back*. Boston: Beacon.

Collins, M. (2015, July 14). The big bank bailout. *Forbes*. Retrieved from www.forbes.com/sites/mikecollins/2015/07/14/the-big-bank-bailout/#34e228c23723

Cooper, P. (2016a, August 30). Never let a student loan "crisis" go to waste. *Forbes*. Retrieved from www.forbes.com/sites/prestoncooper2/2016/08/30/never-let-a-student-loan-crisis-go-to-waste/#7176a25d43eb

Cooper, P. (2016b, November 10). Improving Trump's student loan plan. *Forbes*. Retrieved from www.forbes.com/sites/prestoncooper2/2016/11/10/president-trump-must-revise-his-student-loan-plan/#7cbbcacc1183

Delisle, J. (2016, September 22). The coming Public Service Loan Forgiveness bonanza. *Evidence Speaks Reports*, 2(2), 1–8. Retrieved from https://www.brookings.edu/wp-content/uploads/2016/09/es_20160922_delisle_evidence_speaks1.pdf

DeMillo, R. A. (2015). *Revolution in higher education: How a small band of innovators will make college accessible and affordable.* Cambridge, MA: MIT Press.

Fish, S. (2009, March 8). Neoliberalism and higher education. *New York Times*. Retrieved from http://opinionator.blogs.nytimes.com/2009/03/08/neoliberalism-and-higher-education/?_r=0

Freire, P. (2000). *Pedagogy of the oppressed.* New York: Continuum. (Original work published 1970)

Giroux, H. A. (2010). Bare pedagogy and the scourge of neoliberalism: Rethinking higher education as a democratic public sphere. *The Educational Forum*, 74, 184–196. Retrieved from http://dx.doi.org/10.1080/00131725.2010.483897

Giroux, H. A. (2014). *Neoliberalism's war on higher education.* Chicago: Haymarket Books.

Gladieux, L. E. (Ed.). (1989). *Radical reform or incremental change? Student loan policy alternatives for the federal government.* New York: College Board.

Goldrick-Rab, S., & Kendall, N. (2014). *F2CO: Redefining college affordability: Securing America's future with a free two-year college option.* Retrieved from https://www.luminafoundation.org/files/publications/ideas_summit/Redefining_College_Affordability.pdf

Greenstein, T. (2011, September 20). The Fed's $16 trillion bailouts under-reported. *Forbes*. Retrieved from www.forbes.com/sites/traceygreenstein/2011/09/20/the-feds-16-trillion-bailouts-under-reported/#3651d9456877

Hall, S., Massey, D., & Rustin, M. (Eds.). (2015). *After neoliberalism? The Kilburn manifesto.* London, UK: Lawrence & Wishart Publishing. Retrieved from https://www.lwbooks.co.uk/soundings/kilburn-manifesto

Hartlep, N. D., & Eckrich, L. L. T. (2013). Ivory tower graduates in the red: The role of debt in higher education. *Workplace*, 22, 82–97. Retrieved from https://works.bepress.com/nicholas_hartlep/19/

Hartlep, N. D., & Hensley, B. O. (Eds.). (2015). *Critical storytelling in uncritical times.* Rotterdam, The Netherlands: Sense Publishing.

Harvey, D. (2005). *A brief history of neoliberalism.* New York: Oxford University Press.

Hill, D., & Kumar, R. (Eds.). (2009). *Global neoliberalism and education and its consequences.* New York: Routledge.

Hohle, R. (2015). *Race and the origins of American neoliberalism.* New York: Routledge.

Hopkins, R. (2014). *The transition handbook: From oil dependency to local resiliency.* Cambridge, UK: UIT Cambridge. (First published in 2008 in U.S. by Chelsea Green)

Johannsen, C. (2012, September 1). The ones we've lost: The student loan debt suicides. *Huffington Post*. Retrieved from www.huffingtonpost.com/c-cryn-johannsen/student-loan-debt-suicides_b_1638972.html

Johannsen, C. (2016). *Solving the student loan crisis: Dreams, diplomas, & a lifetime of debt*. Los Angeles: New Insights Press.

Kuhn, T. S. (1970). *The structure of scientific revolutions* (2nd ed.). Chicago: University of Chicago Press.

Lanza, A. (2016, March 9). More employers offer student loan repayment benefits. *U.S. News & World Report*. Retrieved from www.usnews.com/education/blogs/student-loan-ranger/articles/2016-03-09/more-employers-offer-student-loan-repayment-benefits

Majhanovich, S. (2013). How the English language contributes to sustaining the neoliberal agenda: Another take on the strange non-demise of neoliberalism. In S. Majhanovich & M. A. Geo-JaJa (Eds.), *Economics, aid and education: Implications for development* (pp. 79–96). Rotterdam, The Netherlands: Sense Publishers.

Massey, D. (2013, June 11). Neoliberalism has hijacked our vocabulary. *The Guardian*. Retrieved from https://www.theguardian.com/commentisfree/2013/jun/11/neoliberalism-hijacked-vocabulary

Massey, D. (2015). Vocabularies of the economy. In S. Hall, D. Massey & M. Rustin (Eds.), *After neoliberalism? The Kilburn manifesto* (pp. 3–17). London, UK: Lawrence & Wishart Publishing.

Mettler, S. (2014). *Degrees of inequality: How the politics of higher education sabotaged the American dream*. New York: Basic Books.

National Employment Law Center. (2014, April). The low-wage recovery: Industry employment and wages four years into the recovery. Retrieved from www.nelp.org/content/uploads/2015/03/Low-Wage-Recovery-Industry-Employment-Wages-2014-Report.pdf

Norton, B. (2016, July 1). How neoliberalism fuels the racist xenophobia behind Brexit and Donald Trump. *Salon*. Retrieved from www.salon.com/2016/07/01/how_neoliberalism_fuels_the_racist_xenophobia_behind_brexit_and_donald_trump/

PBS NewsHour. (2016, September 12). One college turns its football field into a farm and sees its students transform. *Public Broadcasting Service*. Retrieved from www.pbs.org/newshour/bb/one-college-turns-football-field-farm-sees-students-transform/

Picchi, A. (2016, May 4). Congrats, class of 2016: You're the most indebted yet. *CBS News*. Retrieved from www.cbsnews.com/news/congrats-class-of-2016-youre-the-most-indebted-yet/

Ricks, M. (2016). *The money problem: Rethinking financial regulation*. Chicago: University of Chicago Press.

Saunders, D. (2007). The impact of neoliberalism on college students. *Journal of College & Character*, 8(5), 1–9. Retrieved from www.tandfonline.com/doi/pdf/10.2202/1940-1639.1620

Scharmer, C. O. (2009). *Theory U: Leading from the future at it emerges*. San Francisco: Berrett-Koehler.

Slaughter, S., & Rhoades, G. (2004). *Academic capitalism and the new economy: Markets, state, and higher education*. Baltimore: Johns Hopkins University Press.

Undercommoning. (2016). Retrieved from http://undercommoning.org

Wilder, C. S. (2013). *Ebony & ivy: Race, slavery, and the troubled history of America's universities*. New York: Bloomsbury.

Name Index

Subject Index

CPSIA information can be obtained
at www.ICGtesting.com
Printed in the USA
LVOW10*2104080418

572738LV00003B/11/P